Essays on American Humor

T0163561

Blair Through the Ages

Essays on American Humor

Blair Through the Ages

Walter Blair

Selected and edited by
Hamlin Hill

The University of Wisconsin Press

The University of Wisconsin Press
114 North Murray Street
Madison, Wisconsin 53715

3 Henrietta Street
London WC2E 8LU, England

5   4   3   2   1

Printed in the United States of America

Library of Congress Cataloging-in-Publication Data
Blair, Walter, 1900–1992.
    Essays on American humor : Blair through the ages / Walter Blair ;
selected and edited by Hamlin Hill.
    306 p.   cm.
    Includes bibliographical references and index.
    ISBN 0-299-13620-5   ISBN 0-299-13624-8
    1. American wit and humor — History and criticism.
    2. Twain, Mark, 1835–1910 — Criticism and interpretation.
    I. Hill, Hamlin Lewis, 1931–   . II. Title.
    PS430.B497   1993
    817.009 — dc20   92-35534

Contents

Part 4 Practice What You Teach: A Short Story

Illustrations by Walter Blair

Essays on American Humor

Introduction

This selection of the essays of Walter Blair is remarkable for a number of reasons, not the least of which is that they span more than six decades of research and scholarship in the field of American humor. The earliest selection is Blair's tongue-in-cheek introduction to a 1928 edition of the poetry of Julia A. Moore and the most recent is a 1989 introduction to a volume on Davy Crockett's two-hundredth anniversary. In between are studies which shaped the development of American humor as a discipline.

I

Born in Spokane, Washington, in 1900, Blair moved to Chicago to do graduate work in the English Department at the University of Chicago in the late 1920s. As he recalled in 1974, when he accepted the Hubbell Award from the American Literature Section of the Modern Language Association of America for his distinguished contributions to American letters,

> Anyone for whom 1927 is ancient history will find it hard to believe the low esteem in which American writings were held at that time. When a graduate student told a specialist in *English* literature that he was specializing in *American* literature he had to brace himself for a standard put-down: "*Is* there any?" . . .
>
> Unsophisticated and frivolous, I elected to write a dissertation on a subject even less respected than American literature — our humor.

In fact, Blair had entered an unmapped field of study and was himself to become its primary cartographer.

As he pointed out in his introduction to a revised edition of *Tall-Tale America* in 1986 (it had already gone through twenty-six printings in its first edition and 140,000 copies in an Armed Services Edition during World War II), "the years 1930–44 were great ones for the rediscovery, reassessment, and reprinting of vernacular stories of the past. . . . Franklin Meine pioneered in the movement by publishing *Tall Tales of the Southwest* in 1930, as did Constance Rourke with her *American Humor* a year later." Blair himself entered the field with his collection of Julia A. Moore's unintentionally humorous poetry in 1928 (that introduction is reprinted here) and his 1933 resurrection of the forgotten folk hero Mike Fink.

Franklin J. Meine shared the title page with Blair on *Mike Fink, King of Mississippi Keelboatmen* (Henry Holt, 1933), but Meine did most of the researching and Blair most of the writing. The book inaugurated a stream of volumes in which Blair used the informal, vernacular language of the common man — rather than the stilted jargon of the pedant — to popularize "native American humor" on a grand scale. This volume, along with his *Horse Sense in American Humor* (University of Chicago Press, 1942), *Tall Tale America* (Coward McCann, 1944), *Davy Crockett: Frontier Hero* (Coward McCann, 1955), and *The Mirth of a Nation* (with Raven McDavid, University of Minnesota Press, 1983), was a narrative whose casual tone, easy colloquial voice, and occasional deadpan humor made delightful reading and, more important, hinted at Blair's abiding interest in the role of vernacular speech — "A Man's Voice, Speaking," he called it in an essay reprinted here — in the long tradition of American humor.

Mike Fink wove a tall-tale biography of a then unknown frontier "hero" whose exploits fascinated early-nineteenth-century readers. Based on contemporaneous accounts, *Mike Fink* nevertheless "dramatized" its subject, his language, and his adventures. A sample:

> A few years after the death of Mike Fink, a gangling young man of sixteen was working on the farm of James Taylor, at the mouth of Anderson Creek, on the Ohio River. A tall young man he was, with long legs, long arms, a long skinny neck and a homely face. Dressed in his rough linsey clothes and his coonskin cap, he plowed the fields, and, in addition, like Fink, something of a boatman, he operated the ferryboat across the Ohio. His name was Abraham Lincoln.

Contrast this passage with one recounting the same information in Blair and Meine's anthology of original sources of the Fink saga, *Half Horse, Half Alligator: The Growth of the Mike Fink Legend* (University of Chicago Press, 1956), aimed at a higher falutin' audience of academics:

> In 1825, sixteen-year-old Abe Lincoln was living near the mouth of Anderson Creek on the Ohio River. He was a farm hand and the operator of a ferryboat which crossed the river.

The contrast, demarcating the boundaries of scholarly style and informal prose, shows dramatically that Blair was adroit at recognizing his audience and its expectations and catering to their preferences.

Horse Sense in American Humor, even though it was published by a university press, also said its piece in an informal prose that imitated spoken language. Blair explained, "For almost two centuries the best way to make an idea tasty to most of the people of this country has been to serve it up with a sauce of native-grown humor and horse sense. Because they have loved to laugh and because they have thought horse sense was the best kind of truth, Americans everywhere have welcomed an idea served up with such a sauce." He traced that anti-intellectual brand of folk humor from Benjamin Franklin through a pantheon of nineteenth-century weavers of homespun to twentieth-century inheritors of the tradition such as Will Rogers and Ogden Nash.

Tall Tale America followed two years later and was even more rambunctious. In it, Blair focused on the horse laugh rather than horse sense — the frontier rowdies of folk legend rather than wise rural philosophers. Pawky wisdom disappeared as subject matter in favor of wild hoaxes, epic bragging, and the nervous energy of Captain Stormalong, Daniel Boone, Davy Crockett, Paul Bunyan, Pecos Bill, and a dozen more characters who rose to folk hero status in our popular culture. And the book's tone was as down-to-earth and vigorous at its subject. Blair began by noting,

> When it comes to raising up heroes, there's nothing under the sun that's as helpful as hardships. This is because the way a man gets to be a hero is by overcoming hardships.
>
> Well, from the beginning, we Americans have had a better stock of snarling, snorting, rock-ribbed hardships than any other country in the world. And that's one good reason why we've had so many star-spangled heroes like Old Stormalong and Davy Crockett and Paul Bunyan and others that made our high, wide and handsome history.

The chauvinism — during the middle of the Second World War — is obvious and was clearly effective in terms of sales and popularity: the book was included, in 1963, as one which properly belonged in the White House Library.

Blair confessed, in a new Afterword to an edition of *Tall Tale America* in 1986, that "I'd written my mock history with a specific audience in mind — young readers. . . . The publisher decided that it would appeal not only to juvenile readers but also to adults, and he so advertised it and marketed it."

The next work in the popular vein, *Davy Crockett — Frontier Hero* (Coward McCann, 1955), was also aimed at a younger audience, but it followed the formula of basing a breezy and casual biography solidly upon authentic sources and the best of scholarship and primary records. It contrasted the historically accurate Crockett with the mythic hero that legend had built up after Davy's death.

A final volume marked by the informal tenor was Blair's anthology, compiled with the help of his Chicago colleague Raven I. McDavid, titled *The Mirth of a Nation*. Admitting that many of the nineteenth-century American humorists were "outstanding — but unread," Blair confessed that "for years, America's most respected critics badmouthed much of the humor that this book collects. Many unbookish readers loved it — a suspicious circumstance. Such humor often deals in earthy language with common folk," which the two collaborators "translated" into readable, modern English. The selections ranged from the dialect of New England and the frontier to the deliberate misspellers of the second half of the nineteenth century.

II

While Blair was telling popular narratives of our country's comic history to the middlebrows, he was at the same time establishing his reputation as the foremost critic and analyst of that humor. His *Native American Humor* (American Book Company, 1937) was a collection of the same comic pieces that later got translated for *The Mirth of a Nation*, but *Native American Humor* contained a pioneering introduction and bibliography of almost two hundred pages. Blair traced the beginnings of our indigenous humor to colonial jestbooks, newspapers, and almanacs. He pointed out that beginning in the early decades of the nineteenth century the two schools of Down East humor in New England and the humor of the Old Southwest along the frontier began to polarize, with different techniques, characters, and intentions. He labeled two post–Civil War mutants of those two early schools in the Literary Comedians and the Local Colorists. He traced the lineages of these four schools to Mark Twain and showed with scholarly precision how Twain was the amalgam of these four schools. *Native American Humor* was so significant to the study of American humor that it has remained in print, reissued by Chandler Publishing Company and Harper and Row, for fifty-five years.

Just as *Native American Humor* was the academic counterpart to *The Mirth of a Nation*, so Blair's other popular books had their serious and academic doubles. *Mike Fink* was the informal variant of *Half Horse, Half Alligator* and the Davy Crockett book followed several serious examinations of Crockett in erudite academic journals.

Following the chapter on Mark Twain in *Native American Humor* and major scholarly articles on that same subject (several reprinted here), Blair published his remarkable study *Mark Twain and Huck Finn* with the University of California Press in 1960. In it, Blair displayed a virtuoso genius in most of the esoteric areas of literary scholarship. His study traced the rehearsals of *Huck* in earlier studies, followed Twain's biography through the years when Huck was nascent in Mark Twain's imagination, and explored social and political and economic events of the late 1870s and early 1880s which influenced the novel. He found new sources, explained how and why the book changed its focuses, and detailed the composition of the vagrant manuscript through its seven years aborning. It was, literally, the biography of a book, and America's finest book at that. And working on Mark Twain when Blair began the preliminary research for the book was as innovative as working on other aspects of American humor. Blair mused to an interviewer from the *Chicago Tribune* in early 1991, "Twain wasn't recognized as respectable when I started on him. . . . He was a low humorist."

Mark Twain and Huck Finn was itself followed by Blair's edition of previously unpublished Mark Twain material about Huck and Tom, *Mark Twain's Hannibal, Huck and Tom* (University of California Press, 1969, reissued in paperback in 1989 as *Huck Finn and Tom Sawyer among the Indians*). Significant manuscripts, mostly fragmentary, with Huck and Tom as central characters and other documents dealing with Hannibal made up this impressive collection, providing scholars with a wealth of new information about the boys and their environment.

In 1978, Oxford University Press published *America's Humor from Poor Richard to Doonesbury*, upon which I collaborated, although Blair wrote the majority of the chapters. In Walter's own words, "our aim, stated modestly, has been to trace American humor — high-falutin and low-falutin; rustic, frontier and urban; white, black, blue and parti-colored — from colonial times to the present." Among several threads which we tried to trace through American humor were the comic contrasts between an *alazon* and an *eiron* character, between radical and conservative brands of humor, and between bookish and folksy humor. Blair composed chapters showing the indebtedness of American comic types and situations to earlier, European humor, though we both insisted that there was a magical blend that separated strictly American humor from its various forebears. And even at 560 pages, we left out a great deal of humor which we would have preferred to include.

Finally, in 1988, the project upon which Blair had been working officially for a quarter of a century saw light: the Iowa/California edition of *Huckleberry Finn* appeared from the University of California Press. Coedited with Victor Fischer, the volume was a massive, four-pound, 925-page compendium of authoritative text, scholarly apparatus, and documentation galore. It contained, as Walter phrased it felicitously, "everything in it that we thought anybody above the grade of an idiot would want."

In addition to a spectacular shelf of both scholarly and popular books about Mark Twain and American humor, Blair produced equally spectacular scholarly articles for academic journals — the substance of this collection. The scholarship was massive, the footnotes bountiful. His encyclopedic knowledge was formidable. Students who studied under him discovered that he was prodigal with three-by-five cards with exactly the information they needed — sometimes much more than they needed!

These articles were sometimes the preliminary studies for book-length works, transmuted with fewer notes and documentation and a less scholarly style. That transformation or streamlining made them suitable for a general audience but also provides the justification for making them available now in their original form to students and specialists in the field of American humor.

III

Blair completed his Ph.D. at the University of Chicago in 1931 and, except for a year at the University of Minnesota, made his way up through the professorial ranks there. In spite of his colleagues' low esteem for American humor, they elevated him to the chairmanship of the English Department from 1951 to 1960, and they permitted him to teach famous courses in American humor and Mark Twain. His students began to produce their own dissertations in the field of American humor and to spread — slightly, but only slightly, like apostles — the study of American humor to other colleges and universities. Leon T. Dickinson, John C. Gerber, William M. Gibson, and James E. Miller, Jr., studied under Blair and then carried the good news to Missouri, Iowa, New York, and Nebraska. And hordes of others sat in Walter's classes with a mixture of awe, terror, and bemusement.

Blair taught the basics of critical analysis, close reading, and meticulous research. (He edited one of the basic American literature survey anthologies and one of the best introductions to the study of literature, *Better Reading*, in 1945.) His own research branched into Romantic American authors, too, in his scholarly articles "Color, Light, and Shadow in Hawthorne's Fiction," "Emerson's Literary Method," and "Poe's Conception of Incident and Tone in the Tale." He reviewed the studies of American humor and humorists prominently in the journal *American Literature.*

The studies of other scholars in the field of American humor began to proliferate after Meine, Rourke, Blair, and Bernard DeVoto (in *Mark Twain's America*) staked out the territory. Perhaps in part because of the Depression in the thirties, "proletarian" characters became fashionable in the works of Steinbeck, Erskine Caldwell, James M. Cain, and others. That made the study of vulgar, raucous, and illiterate bumpkins more acceptable, too. It was with those nihilistic, irrepressible frontiersmen, the humorists of the Old Southwest, that our native comedy edged its way into the academic establishment. Faulkner, Steinbeck, Sherwood Anderson, and Ring Lardner all acknowledged in various ways their indebtedness to Old Southwestern humor or to Mark Twain's utilization of it.

When T. S. Eliot gave his imprimatur to *Huck Finn* in 1949, it was, to borrow from James Thurber, "the day the dam broke." Books and articles on Mark Twain, almost all of them dependent on Blair in one way or another, flooded the academic marketplace. Blair's other three "schools," Down East humor, Literary Comedian humor, and Local Color humor, are moving more slowly into the spotlight.

In 1962, the Sut Society was formed with Blair on its board of advisors. It produced four annuals, *The Lovingood Papers*, which rescued fugitive stories by George Washington Harris. In the early 1960s, Blair was in the forefront of the complex plans to inaugurate the massive enterprise of producing scholarly critical texts of the works of Mark Twain and the previously unpublished texts housed at the University of California, Berkeley, and other repositories around the United States. He was the last survivor of the original editorial board of the *Works of Mark Twain.*

In the early 1970s the study of American humor was flourishing so beautifully that the scholarly journal *Studies in American Humor* appeared with Blair as an original member of the editorial board. The American Humor Studies Association was founded with annual sessions at the meetings of the Modern Language Association of America. Blair became the first honorary life member of the association. A special issue of *Studies in American Humor* was devoted to him in 1975, and he was the first recipient of the Charlie Chaplin Award that same year. And every study of almost any aspect of American humor acknowledges Blair in its footnotes or bibliography.

His classes taught those of us fortunate enough to study under him that, although American humor was becoming a serious business, the art of teaching it consisted in large part in the informality and lighthearted dialogue which might even withstand large doses of sly, deadpan, and usually outrageous humor—frequently in the form of illustrations on the blackboard to punctuate his lectures. For any question we might have, there was a book or two and those index cards and his unique technicolor mode of critical commentary, with a rainbow spectrum of ballpoint pens that had no particular color code to their use.

Outside the classroom, his friends and colleagues can attest to Blair's eminence at telling a story in exactly the manner that Mark Twain prescribed in his essay "How to Tell a Story"—with a slow drawl and an unhurried manner, deliciously deadpan, a look of quizzical surprise that someone could possibly laugh at the narrative, and a punchline that was almost irrelevant. The closest that we can get to Walter's own humor is the final selection in this anthology, his comic short story "The Ugliest Man in the World" from the *American Mercury*, and the selection of drawings which illustrate this book. Showing Walter himself in the guise of characters from American humor, this is a very small sample of the cartoons that glorified his Christmas cards for many, many years.

IV

I have divided the material in this book into five sections. The first reprints three essays in which Blair traces broad areas and schools of American humor: the durability of Southern humor, the success of nineteenth-century Literary Comedians, and the enduring concern among humorists with the oral or mock-oral tradition of spoken rather than written humor. These three "surveys" of fields and areas of our humor precede the section dealing with individual humorists from the nineteenth and twentieth centuries, specializing in the Old Southwestern tradition. Fink and Crockett (and an antecedent in Baron Munchausen) share billing with Thomas Bangs Thorpe and George Washington Harris.

Third is a collection of essays on Mark Twain, ranging from his early career as a comic journalist through *The Adventures of Tom Sawyer* to *Adventures of Huckleberry Finn*. Readers who assume that scholarship is dull will find an amazing piece of detective work in "When Was *Huckleberry Finn* Written?" It is a story of painstaking analysis that Sherlock Holmes would admire, and that the discovery of the first half of the *Huck Finn* manuscript in 1991 alters only slightly.

Next comes the single fictional work in this collection, Walter's own "The Ugliest Man in the World." And the concluding section contains a selected bibliography of works that followed in the "Blair tradition" either as additions to his own scholarship or occasionally as disputations with his argument. Since there are standard bibliographies of literary scholarship, I have included here only material relevant to Blair's own contributions to the study of American humor.

What I hope appears in this collection is, first, studies that almost literally discovered a discipline and proceeded to chart its outlines, metes, and bounds. This is, indeed, a volume of discoveries, and it would be nice to hope that younger generations of students might also come away with the sense of a scholar with an insatiable curiosity about humor and folklore, a massive interest in the mechanics of humor, and a scrupulous and meticulous attention to detail and substantiation. If some of Blair's own droll humor happens to bubble through, that will be a wonderful fringe benefit.

In May 1991, in addition to the honors he had received earlier, Walter Blair was awarded the first Distinguished Mark Twain Scholar Award from the Mark Twain Circle. He blazed trails and laid foundations upon which generations of his students and other scholars have built. Here is a generous sample of the basis for the admiration, esteem, and awe in which we hold him.

Several years ago, Walter Blair drew what he called the last of his Christmas self-caricatures; it is reproduced below. Walter Blair died quietly on June 29, 1992, while this book was in press.

Hamlin Hill
College Station, Texas

Part One
The Big Picture

Traditions in Southern Humor

The South produced its best humor between 1830 and 1867 — the writings of such men as Davy Crockett, Augustus Baldwin Longstreet, C. F. M. Noland, William Tappan Thompson, Madison Tensas, Johnson Jones Hooper, T. B. Thorpe, Joseph M. Field, John S. Robb, Joseph G. Baldwin, H. E. Taliaferro, and George Washington Harris.[1] These authors established a standard and set many patterns followed in Southern humor down to the present day. The traditions which shaped this Southern humor and, to some extent, later Southern humor, derived from two sources — from folklore and from literature.

It was a folk concept which determined what was the best comic material and what the nature of many jokes, anecdotes, sketches, and tales was to be. This will not seem strange to anyone who has listened to the radio or who has watched movies and television, the most popular purveyors of comedy today. Such a one knows that humor is most fully appreciated by most people when it follows well-worn pathways. People laugh most heartily when comedians take advantage of an audience's awareness that certain kinds of characters and actions are ordinarily funny. Judy Canova's or Dorothy Shay's hillbilly songs, Jack Benny's hillbilly sketches, and Al Capp's Dogpatch comic strips need not be (though they sometimes are) very funny. They will arouse laughter, whether they are very funny or not, because jokes about the naïveté, the illiteracy, and the uncouthness of hillbillies are traditionally mirth-provoking.

Antebellum audiences, like modern audiences, knew that Southerners of certain classes and districts have been traditionally laughable. Not only oral lore but also books and articles by British and American travelers, dating back to the time of William Byrd, had established the tradition of comic barbarians on the frontier. In writing *Georgia Scenes* in the 1830s, Augustus Baldwin Longstreet, one of the great pioneers in Southern humor,

American Quarterly 5(1953): 132–42.

Walter Blair receiving the Charlie Chaplin Award of the American
Humor Studies Association

built upon the premise that Georgians were illiterate, profane, and rambunctious.[2] Humorous writers about the folk of Arkansas and Tennessee
knew of a widely held concept summarized by a Tennessee editor in 1835:
"The southern and eastern people took up a notion at the beginning that
we were all bear-killers and catamount-catchers, and as we have taken no
extraordinary pains to convince them to the contrary, we are occasionally
twitted about our backwoods condition."[3] As Professor Mody C. Boatright remarks,

> the portrait of the frontiersman was by the end of the first quarter
> of the nineteenth century about complete. The frontiersman was unfit
> to live in organized society. He had no respect for law or rank. Rather
> than obey his officers, he expected them to obey him. He was lazy
> and shiftless and talkative, energetic and taciturn. . . . In his playful
> moments he bit off the noses and gouged out the eyes of his friends.[4]

Details about the squalor, the shiftlessness, and the amorality of back-woodsmen were set forth in many passages in Southern humor. A fair number have been discussed by Shields McIlwaine in his chapter "Southern Comic Portraits of Crackers, Woolhats, and Dirt-Eaters" in *The Southern Poor White* (Norman: University of Oklahoma Press, 1939), pp. 40–74. For details about ferocity, see the story of the bloody rough and tumble struggle between Bill Stallings and Bob Duncan in Longstreet's "The Fight." Casualties: one ear, a piece of cheek, a third of a nose, a finger, and "many a bleeding wound and ugly bruise." The sketch typifies many "funny" accounts of frontier rumpuses in which no holds were barred.

The tradition of the backwoods barbarian largely accounts for the neglect of quality folk and the concentration of humorists upon squatters, mountain folk, yeomen, and poor whites living in newly settled districts. A funny character named Randolph Pendleton Byrd living on Westover Plantation in tidewater Virginia was unthinkable. Outstanding comic characters, instead, included Davy Crockett of the Tennessee canebrakes, Jim Doggett of the Forks of Cypress in Tennessee, Simon Suggs of Tallapoosa County in Alabama, Jos. Jones of Pineville, Georgia, and Sut Lovingood of the Smokies in Tennessee.

Ingrained class attitudes determined whether these figures would be depicted with sympathy or with satire. The frontiersmen themselves, as Professor Boatright has noticed, satirized the furriners' concept of the frontiersmen. Were they held to be outlandish? Very well, they would exaggerate their barbarity into ridiculous tall tales. Or they might boast about having the very qualities which their critics deplored. Often, for instance, they boasted of their illiteracy. Indeed, they held that it qualified them to figure out what to do without having their thinking muddied by book larnin'. Thus Crockett boasted that he had had only one hundred and four days of schooling and claimed that his very lack of education helped him make sound rulings when he was a squire:

> My judgments were never appealed from, and if they had been they would have stuck like wax, as I gave my decisions on the principles of common justice and honesty between man and man, and relied on natural born sense, and not on law learning to guide me; for I had never read a page in a law book in all my life.[6]

Davy's attitude persists in some parts of the South (and many parts of the North, too, for that matter). It accounts for hillbilly-band-and-red-gallus campaigns, and for the cultivated poor grammar of even educated politicians. It accounts for the late Huey Long's boast: "I am an ignorant man. . . . I have not had even a high school education. But the thing that takes me far in politics is that I do not have to color what comes into my mind and into my heart. I say it . . . without veneer. I do not have the learning to do otherwise."[6]

But humorists of certain classes and of prouder sections of the South purported to take the concept of the barbaric backwoodsman seriously, and satirized the frontiersman rather than the concept of the frontiersman. Davy Crockett's enemies did this.[7] Lawyer Johnson Jones Hooper reported a remark of Simon Suggs which was in the Crockett tradition:

> Well, mother-wit kin beat book-larnin' at *any* game! . . . human natur' and the human family is *my* books, and I've never seen many but what I could hold my own with. . . . As old Jed'diah used to say, book-larnin' spiles a man ef he's got mother-wit, and ef he ain't got that, it don't do him no good — [8]

Hooper, however, thought that Simon was wrong, and that his ironic biography of the shifty rascal proved it. Joseph Glover Baldwin indicated his social alignments when he dedicated his elegantly written book of humorous essays to "The Old Folks at Home. My Friends of the Valley of the Shenandoah." In all seriousness, in depicting flush time Alabama and Mississippi, he set forth that

> Society was wholly unorganized: . . . the law was well-nigh powerless — and religion scarcely was heard of except as furnishing the oaths and technics of profanity. . . . The pursuits of industry were neglected, vice and coarse debauchery filled up the vacant hours. . . . The groceries [i.e., saloons] were in full blast . . . no village having less than a half-dozen all busy all the time: gaming and horse-racing were polite and well patronized amusements.[9]

Thus, like the other humorists, Baldwin was influenced by the traditional view of frontier folk and also by the traditional attitude of his class.

The folk brought tradition of a second sort into the humor: As has been indicated by various writers, the oral tales which the menfolk exchanged while strolling around the graveyard after church, on trips to the market, across country, or on riverboats, by firesides — almost anywhere men gathered and talked — were many. Since many such yarns were comic, it was not surprising that a large share of the humor used as its substance the stuff of current oral tales.[10] The half-horse-half-alligator boasts of comic frontier bullies at times incongruously echoed the vaunts of Greek epic heroes and the mead-hall boasts of Anglo-Saxons.[11] The Big Bear of Arkansas, as Professor Dorson has noticed, had as a distant ancestor Beowulf's Grendel, and Scandinavian legendry offered parallels to Davy Crockett and the tall tales about him.[12] As one might expect, the lore of the Kelts persisted in the humor of Scotch-Irish settlers in the South; and Mike Fink,

Simon Suggs, and Sut Lovingood became figures in folk sagas not unlike those about Til Eulenspiegel and Robin Hood.

Constance Rourke, Bernard DeVoto and others have commented upon the varied mythical elements which were transferred from oral lore into Southern humor. The landscapes in many stories were full of wonderful geological formations not found in real landscapes, and the soil was likely to be either so fertile or so sterile as to endanger the lives of those who tried to live upon it — the climate in some of the stories was fantastically better or worse than most people had ever known. The flora and fauna were at times monstrous, at times grotesque. And the men and women were often more gigantic, more heroic, more wise or more foolish than any outside of the poetic imaginings which occur in folklore. Thus folk traditions often contributed extraordinary materials to the humor.

Not only folk traditions but literary traditions as well shaped the humor. Since some of these literary traditions have been discussed at length, they need only to be mentioned. A number of authors — particularly those who cultivated elegance — followed eighteenth-century traditions. The idea of the "eccentric" or the "original," important in much of the humor, was a neoclassical conception. The elegant, genteel humorists such as Longstreet, Baldwin, and (at times) Hooper were strongly influenced by the eighteenth-century essay.

The changing literature of the nineteenth century also had its impact. Southern humor developed in accordance with nineteenth-century British critical theories about humor which placed wit and satire upon a lower level than characterization and geniality.[13] The fiction of Scott and others which represented the ways of life of humble people of definite localities and which imitated vernacular speech was an important shaping force.

The influence of another British literary genre probably has not been sufficiently stressed. This was the sporting story and the informal article on sports and sportsmen which became widely marketable journalistic commodities in the decades just before Southern humor began to crystallize.

It is well known that an extraordinary periodical, *Spirit of the Times*, published in New York between 1831 and 1861, was the most important literary influence upon Southern humor.[14] William T. Porter, the editor, spoke justifiably of the "generous feeling of emulation" of this stable of authors which "sprung up in the south and southwest," so that, he continued, "a large number of those who distinguished themselves in this novel and original walk of literature" were shaped by the magazine.[15]

But what — it seems worth while to ask — molded the humor of that influential magazine, *Spirit of the Times?* The subtitle of Porter's periodical has often been commented upon as a striking combination. It was a "Chronicle of the Turf, Agriculture, Field Sports, Literature, and the Stage."

Humor, not specifically mentioned, came to be an important part of the "literary" ingredient in this collection of diverse materials.

The nearest verbal parallel I have found to the subtitle of Porter's *Spirit* occurs in two popular British books, the first of which preceded the *Spirit* by several years—Pierce Egan, *Anecdotes, Original and Selected, of the Turf, the Chase, the Ring, and the Stage* (1827) and *Pierce Egan's Book of Sports and Mirror of Life: Embracing the Turf, the Chase, the Ring, and the Stage* (1832). The resemblance is not an accident. It results from the fact that in England as in America, there was in this period a fairly well-defined group, a "sporting crowd," as it was called, which had certain interests—in horse racing, in hunting, and in the theater.[16] Egan, nicknamed "Glorious Pierce," was "the first writer to make a name for himself as a sporting journalist"[17] writing on sportsmen and sports—what Victorians called "the fast life."[18] Egan, whose *Life in London* (1821) featured two characters whose names are still remembered, especially at Christmas time—Tom and Jerry—and became a craze of the 1820s, was also a founder of a sporting journal. This journal, *Pierce Egan's Life in London and Sporting Guide* (1824–27) was eventually merged with another sporting magazine, *Bell's Life in London* (1822–86).

Porter regarded the *Spirit*, so he said, as essentially "a sporting Journal"[19] which was to cater to American sportsmen just as *Bell's Life* catered to British sportsmen. One is not surprised to find that the obituary of Porter written by an associate editor praised Porter for two rather incongruous but nevertheless related achievements: bringing out a new class of writers of "fresh, crisp, vigorous . . . graphic . . . American Sporting Literature"; and stimulating "the improvement of the breed of horses in the United States."[20] The leading sportsmen's magazine was bound to appeal to Southerners particularly since, outside of metropolitan New York, the South was the section of the country most enthusiastic about the turf and the chase.[21]

The readers of the *Spirit* explicitly urged Porter to "make the 'Spirit of the Times' to the American sporting world what 'Bell's Life in London' is to the English," and Porter boasted that "throughout England 'The Spirit' is known as the 'Bell's Life' of the New World."[22] Contributors to both British and American sporting journals were as a rule amateurs who used pseudonyms and were coy about revealing their identity. As Robert Smith Surtees put it:

> a sporting work differs materially from one of general literature. . . .
> With the former amateur contributions are generally the best; with
> the latter an amateur is not considered worth his salt. Perhaps this
> may arise from the fact that if they are worth anything your con-
> tributors, applying for payment, will very soon cease being amateurs.

But with sporting, condensation is so desirable and sportsmen generally so much above want that the trifle their productions would yield would be hardly worth their acceptance.[23]

Porter, in his preface to a collection of stories from the *Spirit*, indicated that the contributors were amateurs, that they ordinarily remained anonymous, and that most were "highly educated gentlemen . . . endowed with . . . a knowledge of men and the world."[24] There was in addition to these common facts about contributors, a resemblance between the materials in the American magazine and those in the English magazines. In the early years of the *Spirit*, although publications of many sorts were drawn upon, much of the "literature" was excerpted from English books and magazines dealing with sports — quite often from *Bell's Life*, the *London Old Sporting Magazine*, and the *London New Sporting Magazine*. The passages reprinted developed many topics which were to be typical of original American contributions to Porter's magazine. The extracts told of hunts, of races, of sporting events of various kinds, of the travelers' adventures, and of incidents in the playhouse. Most were journalistic accounts, curtly summarizing happenings or explaining the ways of sportsmen in the manner of news stories or feature articles. Some, however, were dramatized: they offered descriptions of settings, directly quoted dialogue, characterized the people involved. Some examples of such passages were: "Jack Jorrocks in the North" represented from the *London Sporting Magazine* (*Spirit of the Times*, March 12, 1836); "The Decapitated Fighting Cock" from *Pierce Egan's Book of Sports* (*Spirit*, May 21, 1836); "The Foot Race" from the *London Sportsman* (*Spirit*, July 27, 1839); and "The Last of the Links" from the *London Sporting Review* (*Spirit*, August 10, 1839).

American contributions at the start resembled the typical journalistic reports or explanatory summaries culled from British sources; and indeed throughout his career as editor, Porter continued to publish "sporting epistles." But as time passed, American correspondents wrote, in increasing numbers, anecdotes developed more expansively, more concretely, and more dramatically. And eventually the American contributions greatly outnumbered reprints from foreign sources.

Some individual writers for the *Spirit* showed a similar trend in their own work. C. F. M. Noland of Arkansas, for instance, began as a correspondent writing businesslike reports on race meetings and other sporting events. But, although he continued to write such reports, in time he turned with increasing frequence to the writing of character sketches, monologues, and dialogues in the vernacular, wherein he developed anecdotes with color, drama, and vivid action in them.[25] George Washington Harris began as a *Spirit* correspondent with "Sporting Epistles from East Tennessee" in the issues of February 11, June 17, and September 2, 1843, and "Quarter Racing in Tennessee" in the April 15, 1843, issue. The third "sporting epistle" described a dance, and his next piece, which showed his real vein as a humorist, was "The Knob Dance — A Tennessee Frolic." With another writer, "The Man in the Swamp," Porter planned at one time to publish a sporting book to deal with "Bear and Panther fights, Quarter racing, Card playing . . . etc., etc."[26] And though Johnson J. Hooper made his debut as a humorist with "Taking the Census" in the summer of 1843, his next extended composition was a lengthy story in the nature of a sporting report, "Our Hunt Last Week," published in the *East Alabaman*, December 2, 1843, and republished in the *Spirit*, which preceded by a year the first piece about Simon Suggs. Hooper's relationship to the tradition of sporting literature is further indicated by his writing of a book with characteristic title and subject matter, *Dog and Gun; a Few Loose Chapters on Shooting. Among Which Will be Found Some Anecdotes and Incidents* (1856). The book, incidentally, drew heavily upon both British and American sporting journalism.[27]

The author who, perhaps, wrote most consistently in the tradition of sporting journalism during the antebellum period was T. B. Thorpe, who began to correspond for Porter's magazine in 1839 and continued for some years. His first book, *The Mysteries of the Backwoods* (1846), indicated his preoccupation with "Characters, Scenery and *Rural Sports*" in the Southwest; and the subtitle of his second, *The Hive of the Bee Hunter*, showed he was dealing with "Peculiar American Characters, Scenery, and [again] *Rural Sports*." The bulk of the pages of Thorpe's second book, typically, dealt with such topics as piscatory archery, wild turkey hunting, the water craft of the backwoods, buffalo hunting, alligator killing, a grizzly bear hunt, hunting and fishing on Concordia Lake, Indian fighting, the American wildcat, and Tom Owen, the Bee-Hunter.

Outstanding portions of the book, however, developed topics from folklore rather than of woodlore. "A Piano in 'Arkansaw'" was an amusing instance of backwoods naïveté. "The Disgraced Scalp-Lock" was a tale about Mike Fink, rip-roaring legendary hero of oral tales told by and about Mississippi keelboatmen. And Thorpe's finest effort was "The Big Bear of Arkansas," typical in both form and content of the oral tale at its best. For "The Big Bear of Arkansas" was a mock oral tale, purportedly told by a backwoodsman in a steamboat gathering. It started by contrasting the backwoodsman with his more civilized brethren. And the tale he told pictured a fabulous realm where the soil, which ran down to the center of the earth, was so rich that beets grew to the size of cedar stumps and potato hills to the size of Indian mounds, where corn grew out of the ground so fast that its percussion killed a hog. The realm's insects included mosquitoes so big and so fierce that they drove strangers out of the locality;

its wild turkeys weighed forty pounds or more. Its bear were huge: one of them "loomed like a black mist" and "walked through a fence like a falling tree would through a cobweb." Its human inhabitants, understandably, were supermen capable of coping with such flora and fauna.

The fact that these particular sketches by Thorpe were superior may be of some significance. Porter, in comparing "the communications in the English Sporting Magazine with those which were contributed to American publications," took for granted that Britons and Americans worked with the same genre, but held that Americans had better materials:

> In England, which for more than a century has boasted the most respectable Sporting Magazines, the appropriate themes are somewhat exhausted. The Great Race meetings are necessarily monotonous. To give spirit and the interest of adventure to their sketches, the greater number of sporting writers lay the scenes of their articles in foreign lands. British India and our own country are most often selected. . . . It is to the exhaustless supply of a frontier settler, incidents of travel over prairies and among mountains hitherto unknown to the white man, the singular variety of manners in different States, springing from their difference of origin, of climate and product, peculiarities of scenery unhackneyed by a thousand tourists, to this is to be attributed the greater freshness of American sketches.[28]

Doubtless, Southern humor did differ from its British antecedents partly because of differences in locale. What is perhaps more important, however, it differed because of the influence of the folk tradition — the tradition of the barbaric backcountryman and the traditions of oral narrative.

The tradition that plain folk were crude and barbaric pushed writing about such folk in the direction of realism or even, at times, naturalism.[29] To show the backwoodsman's barbarism, authors had to include vivid and shocking details, details which conveyed the squalor, the shiftlessness, the energy, and the brutality of plain folk to the reader. To show the backcountrymen's crudity, authors had to quote language not only more illiterate but also more profane or even more obscene than that ordinarily heard in drawing rooms of the quality. Authors might tender an apology that had been used in fiction for years — that their stories were truthful transcripts of life; they might console their neighbors by rejoicing that, thank the Lord, all the happenings they recounted characterized the past rather than the present; they might argue for artistic appropriateness. (Longstreet did all three.) Whether such apologies were made and accepted or not, crude details and coarse language were called for in humor depicting barbarians such as traditionally dwelt in the backcountry.

The other kind of folk influence, that of the oral story, had its impact

The Old Southwest

upon the Southern style of writing and the Southern way of telling a story. To an extent unparalleled, I believe, in English literature or earlier American literature, it encouraged the use of dialogue and even description and narrative couched in the vernacular. It gave narratives an easygoing tempo of the sort Douglas Southall Freeman deplored when he wrote: "Some men who loved tall tales made the most of clocks that ticked slowly."[30] Southern humor sometimes seems unduly longwinded today, perhaps, because many of us, unlike earlier readers, do not have our ears attuned to it by the remembered sound of many luxuriously elaborated fireside yarns.

Finally, the influence of the oral tale may be accountable for certain extraordinary combinations one finds in Southern humor. With the realism needful to depict backwoods barbarians there is combined the fantasy of strange landscapes, of a grotesque bestiary, of superhuman or subhuman figures drawn from oral lore. The soaring poetry of folk imaginings is combined with the earthy vulgarity of vernacular speech and of low characters. Such combinations, to be found in Southern humor at its best, give it much of its delightful quality.

The Popularity of Nineteenth-Century American Humorists

Just how popular were the writers of American humor in the years of the last century during which they were most active (c. 1830–c. 1896)? The question seems worth considering for at least three reasons. An answer will reveal just how true is the impression, fostered by hostile critics of the period, that the great reading public existed on a diet of nothing much except the sugary fare offered by ladies' books and popular romances. Further, an answer will, perhaps, help one understand why *Innocents Abroad* found thirty-one thousand buyers within six months of its appearance and thus launched Mark Twain's remarkable career. And finally, if — as historians have recently held — American humorists were important as predecessors of the realists, data on this subject of popularity will indicate to some extent how these heralds managed to make themselves heard. For these reasons, I have attempted to discover and record some of the facts which show how the nineteenth-century literary comedians recruited an audience.

I

Several factors, apparently, were important in giving American humor the prominence which it achieved. An early and lasting stimulus to a wide interest in native comic creations, it is probable, was the stage presentation by many actors of humorous American characters. When *The Contrast* was performed in 1787, the stage Yankee, Jonathan, stumbled into the theater for the first time, spouting slang, parading his rustic foibles. The play was a pronounced success,[1] and as a natural result of its popularity, dozens of other dramas portraying similarly vulgar characters followed.[2] Not only the Yankee but also other figures important in the new humor of America were portrayed. Ralph Stackpole, frontiersman in *Nick of the Woods*, was a successful stage figure. Davy Crockett, comedian of

American Literature 3(1931): 175–94.

the canebrakes, Colonel Nimrod Wildfire, and other frontiersmen pleased audiences in New York and the provinces. Minstrel troupes offered boisterous blackface jokers who used typical American humor, including some of the jests of Artemus Ward. One play, *Eli among the Cowboys*, pictured Eli Perkins captured by plainsmen during a lecture tour in Wyoming.[3] At least two newspaper paragraphers, J. Amroy Knox and Charles H. Hoyt, became playwrights whose dramas were successful. Thus, throughout the period, humor of the salty native type found its way to the stage.

Actors made reputations as portrayers of Yankees or kindred types. Ludlow, dressed in the picturesque costume of a Western boatman, roared out the words of "The Hunters of Kentucky" while rough audiences in showhouses along the Ohio and Mississippi applauded with "a prolonged whoop, or howl. . . ."[4] J. H. Hackett was Nimrod Wildfire, Jonathan Ploughboy, and Solon Shingle. Yankee Hill won fame in England as well as America by portraying Yankee types. Joseph Jefferson was applauded as he played the role of Asa Trenchard. Chanfrau triumphed as Mose, the tough fireboy, and John T. Raymond as Mark Twain's Colonel Mulberry Sellers in *The Gilded Age*.[5] Some actors, in addition to playing character parts, offered monologues—Dr. W. Valentine, Sol Smith, Sol Smith Russell, and Yankee Hill. These monologues, composed by the actors or perhaps in some cases by humorists,[6] augmented the flood of humorous books, in which monologues were often an important feature.[7] And when J. H. Hackett went to the *New York Leader* as a journalist, writing lines similar to those which he spoke on the stage, he gave printed humor an impetus his stage career had made possible.

II

Thus to the theater audiences of the period the new humor became familiar. An even vaster audience, the group interested in politics, found much material in native comic writings to interest it. As Joel Chandler Harris said:

> First and last, humor has played a very large part in our political campaigns; in fact, it may be said that it has played almost as large a part as principle—which is the name that politicians gave to their theories. It is a fact that . . . the happy allusion, the humorous anecdote . . . will change the whole prospects of a political struggle.[8]

A large part of the humor between 1830 and the end of the century dealt with political themes. Major Jack Downing, from the start of his literary career, and the imitators of Jack Downing as well, constantly commented shrewdly upon political struggles. Davy Crockett, with whom

Downing carried on some correspondence, was apparently exploited as a political figure; and his writings were necessarily tied up with current contests.[9] The story of Simon Suggs was written in the guise of a campaign biography, and *Major Jones's Travels* and Bagby's *Letters of Mozis Addums* contain political comments. W. P. Trent notes the preoccupation of humorists with politics:

> Lowell being put to one side, there are at least five political humorists of importance belonging to the eventful years 1830–70 . . . Seba Smith, Charles Augustus Davis (1795–1867), Robert Henry Newell (1836–1901), the "Orpheus C. Kerr" whose letters gave Lincoln needed relaxation . . . , Charles Henry Smith ("Bill Arp," born in 1826), and David R. Locke [Petroleum V. Nasby]. To these one is almost tempted to add Richard Grant White, whose *New Gospel of Peace* . . . [was] a clever and very popular parody of the style of the historical books of the Old Testament.[10]

To the list also may be added Artemus Ward, whose political writings were, if not numerous, telling.

During the years when several of these political humorists were active, one of America's outstanding political figures did much to focus attention on contemporary humorous works. Lincoln, as Professor Pattee has pointed out, "stood in the limelight of the Presidency, transacting the nation's business with anecdotes from the frontier circuits, meeting hostile critics with shrewd border philosophy, and reading aloud with unction, while battles were raging or election returns were in doubt, from 'Artemus Ward,' or 'Petroleum Vesuvius Nasby,' or *The Flush Times of Alabama and Mississippi*—favorites of his because they too were genuine, excerpts not from books but from life itself."[11]

Furthermore, there were few important comic journals which did not battle valiantly in the field of politics. The pages of *John Donkey* (1848), *Vanity Fair* (1859–63), *Puck* (1877–1907), and *Judge* (1888–) were full of political cartoons and satires. Newspaper comic men constantly carried on political conflicts in the period after the war as before the war: David Ross Locke, George W. Peck, Marcus M. "Brick" Pomeroy of the *LaCrosse Democrat*, James M. Bailey, Robert J. Burdette, and Eli Perkins. It was not a mere accident that one of the most vicious fictional attacks upon industrial control in politics was made by a humorist, Mark Twain, in *The Gilded Age*. The tradition of the use of political material for humorous purposes was extended through the whole period down to the jestings of Mr. Dooley and Will Rogers about statesmen and demagogues. The nation always has been interested in frank and amusing comments upon political events.

III

The newspapers were active in carrying this humorous material into every part of the nation. Not long after 1830, every paper that could discover a comic writer on its staff was encouraging him to provide amusement for its readers. A few comments indicate how the practice of publishing humor grew. In 1847, *Yankee Doodle* said:

> After the perusal of our exchanges we could not but conclude that the demand for wit has increased of late to an alarming extent throughout the press of the country, and that as usual the supply has been equal to the demand. The whole editorial corps must have deadly designs upon the community which they propose to accomplish by making it "laugh itself to death" collectively.[12]

In 1866, the *North American Review* remarked, with mock concern:

> Our own Boston Daily Advertiser—a bulwark of resistance against needless and unauthorized innovations, a host in itself to withstand temptations of levity and trifling—has yielded so far to this demand [for humorous columns in the newspaper] that, though not yet a professedly comic paper, it has introduced a series of general paragraphs of a nature light and humorous enough to make the old issues turn in their very files for amazement. Far and wide, daily, weekly, and monthly publications issue from the press to face us with at least one feature smiling.[13]

Six years later, a historian of American journalism said:

> Our four or five thousand daily and weekly publications have columns of 'Nuts to Crack,' 'Sunbeams,' 'Sparks from the Telegraph,' 'Freshest Gleanings,' 'Odds and Ends,' 'News Sprinklings,' 'Flashes of Fun,' 'Random Readings,' 'Mere Mentions,' 'Humor of the Day,' 'Quaint Sayings,' 'Current Notes,' 'Things in General,' 'Brevities,' 'Witticisms,' 'Notes of the Day,' 'Jottings,' 'All Sorts,' 'Editor's Drawer,' 'Sparks,' 'Fun and Folly,' 'Fact and Fiction,' 'Twinklings.'
>
> These are the daily dishes set before our sovereigns. They are the comic departments of the regular Press. We need not count the names of our wits and humorists on the ends of our fingers. . . . We are a nation full of such characters, perhaps a little thin here and there, but always in abundance and in good humor. . . . Our wit . . . goes into all the papers.[14]

And a year later, in 1873, Edmund Clarence Stedman, one of the old school, a little frightened and somewhat disgusted, was writing to a friend: "The whole country, owing to the *contagion* of our American exchange system, is flooded, deluged, swamped, beneath a muddy tide of slang, vulgarity, inartistic bathos, impertinence and buffoonery that is not wit." He blamed John Hay and Bret Harte and particularly cited Josh Billings and "The Danbury News Man" as responsible with them for what he called "the present *horrible* degeneracy in public taste."[15]

In 1880, when Edgar W. Nye, the last great figure of the old school, began his career, the paper which did not have a humorous column was exceptional. The *Asheville Journal, Boston Post, Oil City Derrick, Philadelphia Bulletin, Oshkosh Banner, San Francisco Post, Ouray Solid Muldoon,* and thousands of othes purveyed humorous writings which were read in villages and hamlets as well as cities.[16]

These numerous papers did not stop with the publication of the jests of their own humorists; in addition, they published material picked up from other publications. This practice was widespread, as the *Boneville Trumpet* (Bridgeport, Connecticut) pointed out at the top of a column headed "Our Grab Gag":

> everybody is informed that GOAKS found in this column never cost this establishment a cent; the Editor having adopted the *grab-game* (at present so popular with the majority of authors and editors of literary papers), not being able to pay the prices demanded for such by patentees themselves.[17]

Giving credit sometimes, often withholding it,[18] newspapers and periodicals all over the country passed along the best humorous sketches, anecdotes, poems, and paragraphs discovered in exchanges. And since laws allowed exchange copies to be sent without postage, and since newspapers were eager to borrow good material, exchange lists were long; each newspaper sprinkled its pages with quotations from papers of every part of the United States. I was able, with little effort, to compile a list of eighty papers which were quoted in at least two publications in 1880.[19]

An author with a faculty for writing skits which caught the attention of editors who, scissors in hand, eagerly scanned exchanges was soon known throughout the nation. As early as 1833, at least twenty-nine and probably far more newspapers clipped and printed Seba Smith's Jack Downing letters in cities as distant from Portland, Maine, as Cincinnati, Louisville, Philadelphia, and Washington, D.C.[20] As years passed the "contagion of our American exchange system," as Stedman called it, spread even wider. B. P. Shillaber could proudly say in his preface to *Life and Sayings of Mrs. Partington* (New York: J. C. Derby, 1854): "Mrs. Partington . . . needs no introduction. In all parts of our land, and over the sea, her name is familiar as a household word." Eli Perkins boasted that a satirical letter of

1888 was "copied into thousands of newspapers, and . . . read by 10,000,000 people within a week," and that "it brought back bushels of letters *pro* and *con* to the writer, and among them letters from so great a man as James G. Blaine and the two presidential candidates, Cleveland and Harrison."[21]

The newspaper blessed with a witty paragrapher or amusing humorist could win national prominence. In the years before the War of the States, George D. Prentice's paragraphs, habitually copied everywhere, made the *Louisville Journal* known in every section,[22] and when Charles G. Halpine became a humorist connected with the *New York Leader*, "the circulation of the paper increased enormously, and it became a political power."[23] The humorist as well as the newspaper gained national prominence. In 1879, Burdette's sketch "The Brakeman at Church" was published in a paper in the little town of Burlington, Iowa. "Its popularity was immediate, and after its publication in the newspaper letter, it was republished . . . as a pamphlet, and was distributed by tens of thousands. It was copied by every newspaper of more than the slightest importance in the country . . . and few of the reading public of that generation but had an intimate knowledge of the 'Brakeman at Church.'"[24] After a few such hits, according to the city editor of the paper, the *Burlington Hawk-Eye* "came to be read not only within the limits of Burlington and Iowa as in the past, but had its circle of readers in practically every state in the Union."[25] While Burdette, soon known as "The Hawk-Eye Man," thus became famous, Bailey, "The Danbury News Man," built up a circulation of forty thousand for the paper employing him, though it was published in a little town in Connecticut.[26] Other newspapers prospered. In the words of H. C. Lukens:

> The *Danbury News* and *Detroit Free Press* became household gods that usurped the thrones of Farmers' Almanacs, and toppled them from their ivy-thatched 'high eminence' . . . . After 1876 much was heard of such special family visitors, like the *Oil City Derrick*, on which Robert Wesley Creswell . . . won his editorial, humorous spurs; of the *Burlington* (Iowa) *Hawkeye*, Robert J. Burdette's auriferous fun mine; of the Yonkers *Gazette*; Cincinnati *Breakfast Table*, long the profitable mirthy quarry of E. P. Brown; of *Peck's Sun*, a Milwaukee luminary of the *Virginia City Enterprise*, identified with "Dan De Quille" (pseudonym of W. W. Wright) and Nevada's ripples of silvered merit. . . .[27]

IV

Perhaps there was much logic in the belief of Frederick Hudson that one important reason why comic journals had very hard sledding lay in the fact that Americans were supplied with humor by newspapers. Yet in addition to newspapers, periodicals which published humorous materials, in spite of hardships and failures, joined other forces in lifting humor to popularity. Treating the magazines of the years between 1825 and 1850, Mr. Frank Luther Mott notes: "Humor is far more prominent in American periodical literature than it had ever been before; all except the most serious now have their 'Fun Jottings' or 'Joke Corner,' or something analogous."[28] Lewis Gaylord Clark, the editor of the *Knickerbocker*, printed the work of Fred S. Cozzens, Charles Godfrey Leland, "Phoenix," and many another humorous writer in a comic department which, by 1853, occupied a third of the magazine.[29] The *Southern Literary Messenger* printed the work of Joseph Glover Baldwin and George W. Bagby. *Harper's Magazine*, after 1851, in its Editor's Drawer, and *Scribner's Monthly*, after its start in 1870, used typical contemporary humor. Henry Wheeler Shaw, creator of Josh Billings, wrote humor of the type that had made him famous over the signature of Uncle Esek in the *Century*.

The most important periodicals, however, from the standpoint of humorists who profited by popularity, were the comic journals. To be sure many of these died at a tender age, after driving editors to despair, and there was some naturalness in the ending of Newell's burlesque novel *The Cloven Foot* (1870), which showed a comic journal editor attempting to hang himself. Nevertheless, whether they survived long or not, comic periodicals were so numerous that Newell, in the novel mentioned, could tell with some accuracy of an undertaker displaying a graveyard full of "projectors of American *Punches*." A list of such publications,[30] though still far from complete, shows that at least 116 such periodicals appeared between 1800 and 1900.

Most of them lived only a short time — the *Wasp*, published in New York, two years (1802–3); the *Red Book*, Baltimore, two years (1819–21); the *Galaxy of Comicalities*, Philadelphia, from October 2, 1833, to July 5, 1834; the *Picayune*, New York, eleven years (1847–58); the *City Budget*, New York, a year or less (1853–54); the *Knapsack*, Philadelphia, October 24 to November 4, 1865; *Texas Siftings*, Austin, Texas, probably no more than fifteen years (1882–97?) in spite of its popularity; the *Fat Contributor's Saturday Night*, Cincinnati, about eleven years (1872–82) — these were fairly typical. "It's a funny thing, certainly," said *Yankee Doodle*, "that a Humorous Newspaper has concluded its second volume in the United States."[31]

But despite the high mortality rate, which, after all, was hardly higher than that of other American periodicals, humorous publications appeared during every part of the century, and there is some evidence that a number achieved rather remarkable popularity. *Yankee Doodle*, for example, published two *Pictorial Yankee Doodles* in 1847 for free distribution to subscribers, and of each of these 100,000 were printed.[32] *John Donkey*, Philadelphia (Jan. 1, 1848–July 15, 1848), though it lived less than a year, had at one time a circulation of 12,000.[33] This compared fairly well with the most popular magazines of the day, *Graham's* (40,000) and *Godey's* (150,000); it surpasses the *Southern Literary Messenger*, whose subscribers numbered 5,500 in its prosperous days under Poe, the *Knickerbocker* (5,000), and dozens of others.[34] The *Picayune* had at one time a circulation of 35,000,[35] although the number fell to 6,500 in 1853.[36] At the same time, the *Reveille* (1853–54?) was issuing 2,800 copies of each number,[37] and the *Pick* (1853–54?) was boasting that it sold 24,000 copies of its first number, 27,000 of its second, and 30,000 of its third.[38] Less than a year after its start, the editor of the *Pick* was proclaiming: "We started with $5 and we have made a property that we would not sell tomorrow for $50,000."[39] And it is probable that, in the period before the war, the *Carpet-Bag*, Boston (1851–53), and *Vanity Fair*, New York (December 31, 1859–July 4, 1863), on which definite figures are not available, surpassed most of these.

Though fewer figures are recorded, those which can be discovered indicate that in the years after the war, comic publications reached even greater numbers. *Peck's Sun*, in 1882, had a circulation of 20,000 and was "rapidly increasing."[40] Opie Read's *Arkansas Traveler* (1883) reached a circulation of 60,000.[41] In 1887, *Texas Siftings* had a circulation which had "long exceeded 100,000 copies each issue," and a popularity which was international.[42] *Puck* (March 1877–September 1918), *Judge* (1881–), and *Life* (1883–) were probably even more popular. In the words of J. L. Ford "It is impossible to estimate the importance of these comic journals in the development and encouragement of American humor. They were read and widely quoted, and they popularized humor to such an extent that many other periodicals found it advisable to maintain departments consisting entirely of original humorous matter."[43]

V

The writings of humorists were published in books as well as magazines, and again there is evidence of mounting popularity which prepared the way for Mark Twain and his contemporaries. *Georgia Scenes* (1835) had by 1894 passed through twelve editions, and a writer in 1874 held it had had a larger circulation than any other Southern book.[44] According to the publisher, when Shillaber's *Life and Sayings of Mrs. Partington* appeared in 1854, at least 50,000 copies, including a first edition of 20,000 were sold.[45] Frances M. Whitcher's *Widow Bedott Papers*, after increasing the circulation of the magazine in which they first appeared, in 1855 sold "something over 100,000 copies."[46] By 1855, *Major Jones's Courtship*, first issued in 1844, had run through thirteen editions in the United States.[47] And before Ward had achieved the pinnacle of his popularity, when his first book came off the presses in 1862, "40,000 copies were sold outright, an enormous edition for the time."[48] Huntley's *Spoopendyke*, now completely forgotten, appeared in 1881, and "over 300,000 copies of the work were manufactured and disposed of within three months after its first appearance." Later several revised and enlarged editions were printed.[49] Then, in 1888, Belford, Clarke & Company, in an edition of Nye's *Baled Hay*, proudly told of the following remarkable sales of the books by Peck:

How Private George W. Peck Put Down the Rebellion	40th thousand
Peck's Bad Boy and His Pa	750th thousand
Peck's Bad Boy and His Pa, No. 2	200th thousand
Peck's Sunshine	125th thousand
Peck's Fun	125th thousand
Peck's Boss Book	50th thousand

Doubtless some allowance should be made for a publisher's enthusiasm here, but since, by now, train butchers were purveying paper editions while bookstores all over the country offered other editions, and since Peck was undoubtedly tremendously popular, the optimistic figures should not be discounted a great deal. Burdette, Bailey, and Nye were probably about as popular.

By the time this announcement was made, humorists were compiling and selling annually almanacs which, like their books, had remarkable sales. Of course, almanacs were not new things; Franklin and others had published them in colonial times; *The Crockett Almanacs* (1835–53?) had had a large sale several years after the death of Davy Crockett, and before 1842, Robert H. Elton "had gained some little notoriety for his comic almanacks . . . made up of reproductions of Cruikshank's and Seymour's designs, interspersed with humorous sketches."[50] In the seventies, eighties, and nineties, the tradition of the comic almanac was revived. In 1870, when Josh Billings published his first *Farmer's Alminax*, it sold 90,000 copies; the following year 127,000 copies appeared, and in 1872, some 100,000 were sold. The publication ran through ten years, during each of which more than 50,000 copies were sold.[51] Carl Pretzel of Chicago published an almanac which had "a large and ready sale" during the late seventies and early eighties,[52] and *The Danbury News Man's Almanac* (1873), was "as successful as his volumes of sketches."[53]

In addition to the works of the humorists which they themselves published, there were humorous anthologies. As early as 1845, Porter's famous *Big Bear of Arkansas* collection appeared, to be followed by another collection by the same author. Sam Slick's two anthologies, each in three volumes, were issued in both England and America. In the sixties, three volumes of *Yankee Drolleries* were compiled by George Augustus Sala. Toward the end of the century, when Eli Perkins and Mark Twain joined the ranks of anthologists, the number increased. *American Humorists,* edited by the Rev. H. R. Haweis in 1883, had a large sale, though one of many such books. At least 32 collections or new editions of collections appeared during the years 1884–90,[54] and at least 28 appeared between 1890 and 1894.[55] All of these publications stimulated interest and indicated the popularity of the humor of American writers.

VI

The literary comedians did not, however, have to depend entirely upon printed works as a medium for spreading their fame. Like motion picture actors and actresses of today, who make "appearances in person" before enthusiastic audiences, humorists went into every part of the land and appeared on lecture platforms.

Started in 1825 as a part of the lyceum system, the popular lecture, which before the war had "spread throughout the country from Boston to Detroit and Maine to Florida" and which after the war was exploited by such enterprising leaders as John H. Williams, James B. Pond, and James Redpath, proved a boon to many humorists.[56] In 1870, an Englishman said:

> America is a lecture-hall on a very extensive scale. The rostrum extends in a straight line from Boston, through New York and Phila- delphia, to Washington. There are raised seats on the first tier in the Alleghenies, and gallery accommodations on the top of the Rocky Mountains. . . . The voice of the lecturer is never silent in the United States.[57]

The Englishman, E. P. Hingston, was well acquainted with the American situation, for he had managed many of the appearances on the platform of the first important humorist of America to acquire money and fame by giving comic lectures, Artemus Ward. Ward started his career in the field in 1861, taking a hint from Barnum, who had overcome scruples of country folk visiting the theater in his museum by calling it "The Moral Lecture-Room," and advertising his speech as a "Moral Lecture."[58] Start- ing modestly by appearing in a few New England towns, the lecturer trav- eled over widening territory.[59] In 1861 he visited New York, Paterson, Cor- ning, Elmira, and other towns and cities. Thereafter "dates followed in thick order," dates arranged with "bureaus and local committees" for appearances at fixed pay. In 1862 he appeared not only on Eastern platforms but also in halls in Cleveland, Milwaukee, and Memphis. The following year, on the bustling frontier of the Far West, he entertained the miners and settlers of California, Texas, Utah, and Nevada. In 1864, he appeared during a period of two months in nightly lectures in New York, had a period of two crowded weeks in Boston, and visited other cities in the United States and in Canada. After another successful season in 1865, he went, in 1866, to England, where he had a notable success which not only augmented his fortunes but also caused Americans to look more proudly upon native humorists. And through the years, there was a rather steady increase both in receipts and in the number attending his lectures.

Other lecturers followed Ward into a field which offered returns of from fifty dollars to three hundred dollars for each appearance. Josh Billings began to appear on the platform in 1863, and thereafter, for at least twenty successive seasons, he

> read the lecture in every town on this continent that has 20,000 people, and in hundreds that have not got 1,000 in them; read it in every town in Texas and California, and in all the Canadian towns, and then down South, from Baltimore to Palatka, Florida, and still across to Memphis, and then into New Orleans, reading each season from fifty to over a hundred nights.[60]

In 1866, Locke (Nasby) began a career as a lecturer which lasted at least five years.[61] Meanwhile A. Minor Griswold had started, in 1865, activity as a lecturer which continued through eighteen years,[62] and which carried him as far as the Puget Sound.[63] Other humorists who had successful lecturing careers included Richard Malcolm Johnston,[64] George W. Peck, J. M. Bailey, Eli Perkins, Bill Arp, Benjamin P. Shillaber (Mrs. Partington),[65] William L. Visscher,[66] Major Burbank,[67] Dr. George W. Bagby,[68] Phillips Thompson,[69] Rufus Griswold,[70] Eugene Field,[71] and others.

Among the others were Mark Twain, whose very popular early works were preceded and followed by almost equally popular lectures, and Robert J. Burdette. Burdette was exceedingly successful from the beginning of his career in 1876 until the end of the century. In addition to presenting "The Rise and Fall of the Moustache," his greatest success, nearly five thousand times, he gave the following comic lectures frequently: "Home," "The Pilgrimage of the Funny Man," "Advice to a Young Man," "Wild Gourds," "Woman with the Broom," "Dimity Government," "Sawing Wood," "Twice Told Tales," "Handles," and "Rainbow Chasers"; and he appeared in every corner of the nation.[72]

Thus the humor of the stage and the humor of politics brought popularity to the American jesters of the nineteenth century, and numerous publications — newspapers, magazines, comic journals, books, almanacs — and lectures as well helped carry the native humor to a growing number of people.

VII

How, near the end of the century, various forces helped a humorist to fame is illustrated in the story of the growth of the popularity of Bill Nye (1850–96). In 1882, a fortunate coupling of humor with politics helped Nye gain attention when, upon being appointed postmaster of Laramie, he wrote a letter to the postmaster general "extending his thanks" and proclaiming: "I look upon the appointment as a great triumph of eternal truth over error and wrong . . . one of the epochs . . . in the Nation's onward march toward political purity and perfection." The amusing letter was widely copied; it was commented upon in distant England by the *London Daily News*. A similar letter in which Nye humorously told the President of his resignation in 1883 was also copied,[73] almost as widely as Nye humorously asserted — "from Japan to South Africa, and from Beersheba to a given point."[74] Later open letters of advice to Cleveland when he entered the White House and political touches in many comic anecdotes and essays continued his appeal to an audience interested in politics.

Newspapers, periodicals, and comic journals augmented Nye's fame. As early as 1876, a squib in the *Laramie Sentinel* was quoted in the *St. Paul Pioneer Press*, and soon after, when he became a contributor to the *Denver Tribune*, he was quoted by "papers in Omaha and Salt Lake, *The Detroit Press*, *Texas Siftings*, *Peck's Sun*, and many others." Then, in 1881, the *Boomerang* was started, a daily paper with a local circulation of 250, and, in addition, the *Weekly Boomerang*, wherein a whole page of Nye's humor was included. The weekly, like the *Hawk-Eye* and the *Danbury News*, served as a humorous periodical, and although the daily steadily lost money, the weekly, selling in "all parts of the Union," made a good profit; when Nye left the paper, it "soon found its level as a small-town daily."[75]

Before he left Laramie, however, the small town's humorist had been discovered by exhanges. By 1882, said Will M. Clemens, he was "widely quoted . . . perhaps more extensively copied than any other humorist of the day."[76] In 1890, Landon said: "Every newspaper in the English language is now filled with his writings,"[77] slightly exaggerating, one fears, but little more enthusiastic than Mark Twain, who said in 1888, "His contributions to the press have given him a reputation commensurate with the country."[78]

But by 1890, Nye had become associated with papers which had wider fame than his Laramie publication. In 1885, he had made arrangements for weekly letters with the *Boston Globe*, and in 1887, he had become associated with the *New York World*, then eagerly hiring contributors who would boom the paper's large circulation. Prior to 1887, some of the writer's works were sold to a list of newspapers, though they were not syndicated until after 1891, when the American Press Association sent out his writings to "one of the leading newspapers in practically all of the leading cities."[79] By 1893, English papers had begun to purchase the letters, and the *London Sketch* of October 1, 1893, said:

> Mr. Nye has become a power in the land; the President himself is not more caricatured. His sayings are quoted everywhere. There is hardly a town with a Sunday paper that does not print his latest column.

At the time of Nye's death in 1896, "about 70 leading newspapers" were using the weekly syndicated article, and later the head of the Press Association, Orlando Smith, asserted that "the success of the Association had been largely built upon the Nye articles and . . . Bill Nye was the most widely read and highly paid writer in the United States."[80]

Magazines as well as newspapers used Nye's writings — the *Century*, the *Cosmopolitan*, the *Ladies' Home Journal*, *Once a Week*, *Good Roads*, the *Ingleside*, the *Northwestern Miller*, and the comic periodical *Puck*. In 1891, he published an *Almanac*.

Furthermore, Nye's lectures in the years between 1883 and 1895 acquainted thousands of people with his comic personality.[81] Adopting the gloomy method of delivery affected by Ward and most humorous lecturers, on the platform always he assumed a "solemnity of look and sepulchral voice when he was saying something he knew would be humorous. At such times he had a queer sort of cross-eyed glint leftward."[82] He began his career by appearing alone. Later, however, during his most successful seasons (1888–90), he appeared with James Whitcomb Riley, who had had some experience in the work before this.[83] With little Riley serving as a foil for the tall nonsensical Nye, the two entertained thousands in scores of cities and hamlets and reaped large returns for the Pond Lyceum Bureau. Capacity crowds greeted them everywhere, and in Wyoming the legislature adjourned to welcome Nye. Then, after a breakup with Riley, Nye, under the management of H. B. Thearle or the Redpath Lyceum Bureau, and accompanied at different times by W. L. Visscher, Alfred P. Burbank, William Hawley Smith, and Bert Poole, continued lecture work, at least one trip carrying him to California.

In 1891, Nye invaded successfully still another field which had been prepared for humorous works — the field of the drama. His play, *The Cadi*, full of his typical humor, had a run of 125 nights in the Union Square Theater.

The story of Nye's activities as a journalist, as a lecturer, and as a playwright indicates that, like many an earlier and many a contemporary humorist, he built up a remarkably large following. Details concerning the publication of Nye's books seem to offer additional evidence. In 1882, Will Clemens noted that Nye's first book "had a tremendous sale,"[84] and apparently other volumes were equally successful. *Boomerang*, *Forty Liars*, and *Baled Hay*, Nye's first three books, according to a conservative estimate of Nye's son, probably sold at least 100,000 copies apiece,[85] and five other works, judging on the basis of the number of editions and Nye's position, must have been equally successful. *Nye's History of the United States* went through eight editions during the first year, and after the plates were sold as late as 1905 to Thompson and Thomas, the company, according to one of the partners, sold 250,000 copies in thirteen years.[86] Nye's son estimates that at least 500,000 copies of the history were sold, and *Remarks* was a close second.[87]

All of these books, with the exception of the history, were sold not only in bookstores but also, in paper-covered editions, at newsstands and on trains. The following table, perhaps incomplete, shows the number of editions (including paper-covered) — probably large editions — through which important works passed during Nye's lifetime:

Bill Nye and Boomerang (1881) 10
Forty Liars and Other Lies (1882) 10
Baled Hay (1884) 10
Blossom Rock (pirated) (1885) 1
Remarks (1887) 7
Chestnuts (1887) 8
Cordwood (pirated) (1887) 1
Thinks (also called Sparks) (1888) 6
Railway Guide (1888) 6
History of the United States (1894) 10

These figures offer interesting evidence that the last of the old school of American humorists, after becoming active in a time when other comedians had cultivated a large public for humorous works, achieved extraordinary popularity. And Nye's career was more typically that of a humorist of the century than, at first glance, one would be inclined to suspect.

Thus when Nye, his predecessors, and his contemporaries practiced and preached simplicity and homeliness of language in a day of grandiloquence, realism in thought and in fiction in a day of pseudoromantic writing, the practical men (including a genius, Mark Twain) who somehow stumbled into writing were assured of a large and attentive audience. And the history of American literature testifies that at the end of the century salutary results had already begun to appear.

"A Man's Voice, Speaking"

A Continuum in American Humor

After spending nearly four years in various sections of the country, Frances Trollope reported in *Domestic Manners of the Americans* (1832) that she had found gaiety nowhere. Saturnine natives begrudged pennies they had to pay to see comedies; humorous publications failed; she looked in vain for "keenly cutting satire" which amputated bad taste and dullness. But updating her book in 1839, the lady inserted a footnote warning that her accusations "must never be repeated": America at last had produced writings that "prove, much beyond . . . contradiction, that humour, rich and original, does exist in the United States, and . . . when such a treat is given them, the people know how to enjoy it."[1]

Mrs. Trollope forecast a pattern: time and again American humor would be declared nonexistent or defunct, only to hop from its deathbed and discredit mourners. E. C. Stedman in 1873 announced the funeral; James T. Thurber did the same in 1962 and Melvin Maddocks in 1970.[2] Looking back, one sees that often viewers-with-alarm simply failed to recognize our humor in some new guise. In 1832 it had an unfamiliar look because it was being Americanized; in 1873 a Funny Man school was emerging; in 1962 and 1970 black humor was muscling in.

But a remarkable fact is that through demises and rebirths one form not only endured but thrived: the comic narrative modeled upon the oral tale. This hardy continuum which survived changes for more than a century and a half merits detailed consideration.

Scholars have cited abundant evidence that the manner and matter of oral stories were seminal to much of the best American humor from its beginning to the Civil War; they have particularly stressed the impact upon antebellum humorists of the Old Southwest. Their emphasis obscures the fact that elsewhere — in New England, the South, and the Far West —

Veins of Humor, ed. Harry Levin. Cambridge: Harvard University Press, 1972.

much oral humor was reincarnated in print.[3] Too, postwar humorists through 1900 were active in every region producing comedy derived from oral storytelling — Mrs. Stowe, Sam Lawson's Yankee yarns; Joel Chandler Harris, the Uncle Remus fables; Mark Twain, Mississippi River and Far Western tales — to name a few among scores.

Oral origins and influences were clearest when a humorist pictured a storyteller spinning his yarn and his audience reacting, and enclosed within his framework a directly quoted traditional anecdote or one resembling it in substance and form (T. B. Thorpe's "The Big Bear of Arkansas," 1841; *Sam Lawson's Fireside Stories*, 1871). Indebtedness was only a bit less clear when the author transcribed allegedly oral tales, but omitted the framework (W. T. Thompson's "A Coon Hunt; or, A Fency Country," 1851; Mark Twain's *Adventures of Huckleberry Finn*, 1884).[4] Although both the "framework story" and the "mock oral tale" underwent changes, as described above they won warm affection or critical praise — often both — of Americans from 1900 to the present. Even a highly selective survey suggests their remarkable persistence.

As the century turned, Edward Noyes Westcott's *David Harum* (1898, 1900) was amassing sales of half a million copies (rough equivalent today: one and a third million) in twenty months. It sold briskly for decades — about a million and a quarter copies by 1965 — thanks largely to many tales in rustic dialect told by horse-sensible David and his sister. Central New York was the setting; but the decade 1900–1910 was a great one for Far Western oral tales — or facsimiles — in frameworks. Owen Wister's *The Virginian* (1902), reprinted fifteen times in nine months, was not only a bestseller (a million seven hundred thirty-six thousand copies by 1965) but also the source of a play performed for decades, three cinematic versions, and an interminable television series. The most amusing parts were based upon oral stories, and three crucial chapters detailed a tall-tale-telling contest between the villain and the hero. Between 1897 and 1913, Alfred Henry Lewis published six popular volumes of discursive tales told in dialect by one "Old Cattleman" about Arizona. And between 1903 and 1905 Andy Adams published three novels that served as a framework for yarns — twenty-nine in all — spun by cowboys resting after their labors. Adams followed these with *Cattle-Brands* (1906), subtitled "A Collection of Western Camp-fire Stories" — boxed narratives enclosing tales in which " the sound of the voice and the turns of everyday speech . . . racy and full of localisms," are heard. Adams still is admired and reprinted as both an artist and the most authentic portrayer of Texas cowmen.[5]

Texas was long the home of O. Henry, who won fame during the same decade and continued to be popular and respected as a master of the short story until 1930 or so. During three years in prison, he launched his career by retelling stories told by fellow prisoners; and until his death in 1910, he utilized oral anecdotes. One group of stories still admired are framed reminiscences of wandering confidence man Jeff Peters, most of them included in *The Gentle Grafter* (1908).[6] Similar stories, many of them tall tales, about and by other characters were included in books which sold several million copies, and the esteem in which he was held was indicated by the establishment of the O. Henry Memorial Award Prizes in 1919.

Authors of the 1920s tended to neglect framework stories; but they produced mock oral tales which were popular and critical successes — Don Marquis' Old Soak and biblical stories; Roark Bradford's Negro dialect legends about "ol' man Adam and his chillun" (which inspired a Pulitzer Prize play); Ring Lardner's highly praised short stories in Midwestern dialect. The form migrated to urban settings in some of Lardner's cynical dramatic monologues, John V. A. Weaver's free verse narratives "in American," and Anita Loos's *Gentlemen Prefer Blondes*.

The same decade produced the best vernacular retelling of tall tales about Paul Bunyan — that by Esther Shephard. This heralded rediscovery, in the 1930s, of several similar heroes and the publication of stories, mostly in dialect, about them — John Henry, Mike Fink, Davy Crockett, and Febold Feboldson. The 1930s also produced Stephen Vincent Benet's esteemed tales about Paul Revere, Dan'l Webster, the Fool-Killer, the Cape Cod Sea Serpent, and others he called "our own folk-gods and giants and figures of earth"; most appeared in America's most popular magazines. Dorothy Parker wrote dramatic monologues of big blondes and brunettes with big problems. H. L. Davis' Pulitzer Prize *Honey in the Horn* spaced many tall tales through a meandering narrative about pioneer Oregon. Thornton Wilder's *Heaven's My Destination*, a monologue by that legendary figure the traveling salesman, exploited the author's skill with dialect — a skill used best in the 1938 Pulitzer Prize play, *Our Town*, by the Stage Manager, an old-fashioned Yankee sage.

During the 1940s Jesse Stuart's *Taps for Private Tussie* — a story, humorous for the most part, told by a teenage Kentucky farm boy — was cheered by critics and sold a million copies. William Saroyan's *Adventures of Wesley Jackson* had a similar, somewhat older, vernacular narrator. Beginning in World War II years, Jesse B. Simple spoke for blacks in monologues recorded by Langston Hughes; these continued into the 1960s.

The 1950s brought J. D. Salinger's greatly admired *The Catcher in the Rye*, which has attracted five million buyers; H. L. Davis' *Winds of the Morning*, a book club selection sprinkled with vernacular anecdotes; several novels in the same mode by Mark Harris or (their title pages claimed) by illiterates whose grammar and punctuation Harris edited; Eudora Welty's admirable *The Ponder Heart*, honored with the Howells Medal for Fiction; and Vance Randolph's five volumes of homespun Ozark anecdotes. Mac Hyman's *No Time for Sergeants* (1954), was a book club choice, a bestseller for two years (two million four hundred thousand copies), and the source of a Broadway hit, a motion picture, and a durable television series. The 1940s, in addition, were the decade which brought forth Robert Louis Taylor's *The Travels of Jaimie McPheeters*, which many reviewers recognized as a book in the mode of *Huckleberry Finn*.

The success of this book (best-seller, Pulitzer Prize) encouraged Taylor to follow it during the 1960s with two other novels with teenage narrators. During the same decade, William Price Fox's *Southern Fried* stories followed the tradition; Thomas Berger's *Little Big Man*, with an elaborate framework, and Charles Portis' mock oral *True Grit*, Westerns, were bestsellers. Racier successes used vernacular narrators in substantial comic stretches—Robert Gover, *The $100 Misunderstanding* (Kitten's monologues) and Gore Vidal, *Myra Breckenridge* (Buck Loner's tape recordings). The 1970s continued the trend in more sanitary narratives: David Wagoner's Andrew Jackson Holcomb, Jr., in *Where Is My Wandering Boy Tonight?* (1970) told the story of his maturing in Wyoming; in 1970 Eudora Welty's *Losing Battles*, nominated for a National Book Award, consisted largely of stories told by Granny Vaughn's multitudinous descendants at a Mississippi family reunion. As recently as the summer of 1971, David Freeman's *U. S. Grant in the City* mounted to comic pinnacles in a Bowery bum's sagebrush tall tales; and in Jose Brown's *Addie Pray* an adolescent orphan girl told a picaresque story which became a book club selection.

This listing omits much fiction the inclusion of which might be questioned because its narrators, though they use the vernacular, may be too educated or too hard-boiled to be accepted without an argument (Pal Joey, Lardner's and Edward Streeter's letter writers, Augie March, Todd Andrews, Alexander Portnoy, private operators whose amanuenses were Hammett, A. A. Fair, Mickey Spillane, and others). But it must not conclude without mentioning books which unquestionably belong high on the list—books by the most admired of all American writers extensively using framework narratives and mock oral tales, William Faulkner. His works employing these forms span four decades and include notably (though far from exhaustively) *The Sound and the Fury* (Jason's segment), *As I Lay Dying* (which may be called a series of mock oral narratives), the Snopes trilogy, and the bestselling *The Reivers*.

Thus, though eighty-eight years ago many would have agreed with Henry Watterson that humor of the sort represented by all these works had survived only because it effectively pictured a bygone race of country folk,[7] it has continued to flourish not only for nostalgic evocations but for narratives with very different aims. Why, one may well ask, did it continue to thrive long after America had lost its frontiers and become urbanized?

Scotsman Andrew Lang in 1889 remarked that Americans, contrasted with Britons, eternally swapped stories. These stories he called "the subsoil of American literary humour, a rich soil in which the plant . . . grows with vigour and puts forth fruit and flowers."[8] If these truly are the soil, today it is far from depleted. The railway smoking cars and steamboat social halls which Lang mentioned as scenes for swappings are no longer much frequented. But bars, his third setting, flourish, and potential storytellers converge on restaurants for coffee breaks, four-martini lunches, and expense account dinners. In nightclubs, amateur raconteurs at tables are regaled by professionals on platforms such as Myron Cohen, Sam Levinson, Bill Cosby, David Steinberg, Joan Rivers, and Phyllis Diller. Introduced by masters of ceremony who lace monologues with anecdotes, these entertainers and others such as Alexander King and Selma Diamond spin yarns for millions of listeners to radio or viewers of television. Even those recurrent guests on conversation shows who are not thought of as storytellers thrive by "ad-libbing" humorous anecdotes. The professionals' oral narratives are immortalized on records or in briskly selling books. One outstanding performer, Jean Shepherd, has supported his claim: "I'm a storyteller; a story-teller can work any medium."[9] For a decade and a half Shepherd has spun leisurely yarns on a New York radio station; he published many in magazines and collected several in *In God We Trust: All Others Pay Cash* (1967); and in 1971 he appeared in a subsidized educational television series, "Jean Shepherd's America."

Sixty years ago, pondering reasons why "the vernacular [is] the natural vehicle for the most persistent and most popular variety of American humor," Joel Chandler Harris suggested that the comic oral lore it embodies "is based upon [the people's] unique experience; it is part of their personality; it belongs to their history; and it seems, in some ways, to be an assurance of independence and strength, of sanity and wisdom, of honesty and simplicity."[10] He perhaps had in mind the fact that since Americans often distrust smart alecks, wits, or book-read men, a narrator may disqualify himself by using highfalutin language while another wins trust by using vernacular phrasings. So canny politicians often deliberately mutilate their grammar, and when Edgar Guest and Rod McKuen write idiomatically they even overcome widespread prejudices against poetry. Moreover, the vernacular is useful for comic effects because: (1) It exploits a conviction that Americans long found hilarious — that there is no necessary relationship between a man's formal learning and his knowledge or even his wisdom. (2) It nurtures indirect statements, and these are better than direct ones for satire; a throwaway comment can be funny when a frontal attack cannot.

Harris quite probably had in mind the appeal of the substance of humor based upon what he called "the pungent and racy anecdote, smelling of the soil" and capturing a vital "memory or tradition." In the discussion cited above he spoke also of the way "the dramatic manner" of an oral rendition gave "an added perfection" which, unhappily, the writer misses. "It's the despair of the writing man who has known the best storytellers," wrote J. Frank Dobie in 1961, "that he cannot translate the oral savor into print." The lament was recurrent. In 1834, eulogizing John Wesley Jarvis, whose oral stories had a prodigious impact on early American humor, William Dunlap found himself incapable of reproducing them "dressed in cold black and white." Lincoln's hearers made similar complaints. Mark Twain felt that some of this best anecdotes, based upon "outrageously funny" yarns told by pocket miner Jim Gillis, became "mild and pale" when he put them on paper; and reporters often despaired of capturing in print the charm of Twain's platform presentations.[11]

Today's raconteurs offer proof that such disparities still exist. Myron Cohen and Harry Hershfield have been praised by peers and by nightclub, radio, and television audiences as superb tellers of stories. But when, respectively in *Laughing Out Loud* (1958) and *Laugh Louder Live Longer* (1959), they parade their favorite anecdotes, only a few retellings compare in excellence with oral tellings. Equally inferior to skilled oral recitals are printed versions of anecdotes in twenty-five other volumes compiling them during the last thirty-six years (many of the stories included have been newly unleashed by modern tolerance of sexual frankness and now await classification in motif indexes by folklorists who enjoy performing heroic drudgeries).[12] A revealing fact is that three such collections are generally more amusing: H. Allen Smith, in *Buskin'* (1968) and *Rude Jokes* (1970), and Leo Rosten, in *The Joys of Yiddish* (1968), rather consistently manage to impart to their printed narrations the appeals such tales have in oral tellings. Possibly they succeeded because they prepared for their chore by cultivating considerable skill as creative writers. The moral — one that Harris, Twain, and others articulated — is that effectively translating oral lore into written humor requires craftsmanship and care.[13] I suggest that the very nature of oral storytelling caused both skill and assid!uity to come into play and that this was greatly to the advantage of the style, the structuring, and the characterization in written humor.

How the style is shaped is indicated by many who have heard stories told well, who remark upon the witchery of their rendition, and who discuss reasons for it. Jarvis' auditors, for instance, suggested that he was a

master because "some of his humour was . . . manual" and because he was
an expert mimic of dialects, gestures, and facial expressions, and neither
the postures nor the mimicry was communicable in print. Something of
a caricature, James H. Delargy's sketch in 1945 of an Irish storyteller in
action indicates other uncommunicable elements: "His . . . limbs are
trembling, as, immersed in his story . . . he puts his very soul into the telling . . . he uses a great deal of gesticulation, and by the movement of
his body, hands, and head, tries to convey hate and anger, fear and humour, like an actor in a play. He raises his voice at certain passages, and
at other times it becomes almost a whisper." An obvious inference, as
Vivian Mercier suggests, is that this raconteur was giving a skilled dramatic
performance.[14]

John Ball, in "Style in the Folk Tale," offers an impressive list of playacting ingredients which elude print — "intonation, voice rhythm, continuity, speaking rate, pitch, voice intensity, pauses, facial expressions, gestures,
pantomime or re-enactment . . . voice imitation (even of the opposite sex
or of animals), methods of reacting to audience response — in fact the
whole delicate and complex process of participating with the audience in
the story-telling situation." Richard M. Dorson adds items to this catalogue — chanted phrases, onomatopoeia, eye contact with the audience, and
the use of props — "all adding up to a small theatrical performance." Dorson notices that Vance Randolph, realizing that some oral tales depend
upon pauses, and that literally transcribed texts take no account of these,
at times feels compelled to edit tales that he has recorded.[15] To compensate
not only for lost pauses but also for other lost playacting devices, skilled
writers of humor based upon oral storytelling constantly employ a great
many expedients.

Some of course are used to give a vernacular sound to the quoted
story. The late Frank O'Connor, reading for radio audiences, was "horrified to see how . . . generations of skilful stylists from Chekhov to Kath-
erine Mansfield and James Joyce had so fashioned the short story that it
no longer rang with the tone of a man's voice, speaking." To restore the
ring he omitted passages or even "departed altogether from the script,"
eliminating "carefully arranged scenes and balanced sentences."[16] Mark
Twain took additional measures. He knew that "the best and most telling
speech is not the actual impromptu one, but the counterfeit of it, [one that]
will seem impromptu," also that "written things have to be limbered up,
broken up, colloquialized, and turned into the common forms of unpremeditated talk" and that "a touch of indifferent grammar flung in here and
there, apparently at random, has a good effect." At best a writer did what
William Dean Howells did — combined "clearness, compression, verbal exactness" with "seemingly unconscious felicity of phrasing."[17]

Paradoxically, the effort becomes too evident when the writing is either too far from the vernacular style or too close to it. Messrs. Bellow, Roth, Barth, and Vonnegut in first person narratives as a rule do not catch the quality of talk because they use too many Latinate words, because they characterize too complexly, and because they scorn simple chronology. At an opposite extreme is George Washington Harris (1814–69). This Tennessee humorist, even his severest critic concedes, is one of America's great writers. But modern readers bog down in a passage like the following one in which Harris' Sut Lovingood pictures a frightened mare which has been mounted by a Yankee with a huge clock tied to his back:

> "'Yu git up, yu pesky critter,' sed he, a-makin his heels meet, an' crack onder her belly. Well she did 'git up,' rite then and thar, an' staid up long enuf tu lite twenty foot further away, in a broad trimblin squat, her tail a-tween her thighs, an' her years a dancin a-pas' each uther, like scissors a-cuttin. The jolt ove the litin sot the clock to strikin. Bang-zee-bang-zee whang-zee. She listened pow'ful 'tentive tu the three fus' licks, an' they seem'd to go thru an' thru her as quick es quicksilver wud git thru a sifter. She waited fur no more, but jis' gin her hole soul up tu the wun job ove runnin frum onder that infunel Yankee, an' his hive ove bumble bees, ratil snakes, an' other orful hurtin things, es she tuck hit tu be. . . . An she jis' tried tu run outen her sorril hide."

Compare a passage about another frantic horse by Mark Twain's Simon Wheeler in the Jumping Frog story:

> "Thish-yer Smiley had a mare — the boys called her the fifteen-minute nag, but that was only in fun, you know, because of course she was faster than that — and he used to win money on that horse, for all she was so slow and always had the asthma, or the distemper, or the consumption, or something of that kind. They used to give her two or three hundred yards' start, and then pass her under way, but always at the fag end of the race she'd get excited and desperate like, and come cavorting and straddling up, and scattering her legs around limber, sometimes in the air, and sometimes out to one side among the fences, and kicking up m-o-r-e dust and raising m-o-r-e racket with her coughing and sneezing and blowing her nose — and *always* fetch up at the stand just about a neck ahead, as near as you could cipher it down."

A third horse cavorts in Faulkner's vernacular "Spotted Horses" after a Texas dealer corners three or four of the pranksome creatures:

Then he jumped into them, and then we couldn't see nothing for a while because of the dust. It was a big cloud of it, and them blare-eyed, spotted things swoaring outen it twenty foot to a jump, in forty directions without counting up. Then the dust settled and there they was, that Texas man and the horse. He had its head twisted clean around like an owl's head. Its legs was braced and it was trembling like a new bride and groaning like a saw mill, and him holding its head wrung clean around on its neck so it was snuffing sky. "Look it over," he says, with . . . his neck swole up like a spreading adder's. . . . Then it was all dust again, and we couldn't see nothing but spotted hide and mane, and that ere Texas man's boot-heels like a couple of walnuts on two strings, and after a while that two-gallon hat come sailing out like a fat old hen crossing a fence.[18]

Harris' attempt to render dialect unselectively (with some cacography thrown in) renders his passage more obviously artful and less spontaneous — in appearance — than the other two: the contrast suggests that this great humorist would profit by some modernization. But the passages share stylistic traits — homespun diction, peccable grammar, informal but rhythmical sentences, onomatopoeia (Bang-zee-bang-zee), mispronunciations (pow'ful, m-o-r-e), portmanteau coinage (swoaring), assorted tropes (similes, metaphors, hyperboles, synecdoche), clarity and precision such as Twain lauded in Howells.

But any compression results from omitting descriptions and interpretations: there is no skimping of ludicrous imagery. These passages typically mingle the circumstantial and the precise with the outrageous and the imprecise. Though meticulous about dates, dimensions, and techniques, the storyteller unashamedly introduces men and animals that are impossible monsters. Often vernacular passages mingle the vulgar with the poetic. Typically, the narrator of "The Big Bear of Arkansas" is squatting to defecate at the very instant when he has a highly poetic vision of a supernatural beast, and seconds later he loses his pants. An unhurried savoring of details, like that of yarnspinners entertaining loafers in bars, by firesides, or on shaded porches, characterizes quoted stories.

Three plot patterns that thrive in oral storytelling recur in written retellings: one meanders scandalously, one details a conflict in which a weak character defeats a strong opponent, and one soars to a comic climax. Mark Twain notes in "How to Tell a Story" that, whereas "a witty story" rushes to a point, "the humorous story may be spun out at great length . . . wander around as much as it pleases, and arrive nowhere in particular." Stephen Leacock also contrasted an anecdote in which "there is no fun . . . until the end is reached" and one "amusing all through." Max Eastman felt these differentiations were between the technique of practical jokes and that of "poetic humor," which involves "the playful enjoyment of a mess, the messier it is, within the limits of patience, the better": so many humorous stories make "slow progress, or no progress at all, or progress backwards."[19] This picaresque meandering is recurrent in our humor: witness *Huckleberry Finn* and *Little Big Man.*

Some humorists follow what Axel Olrik called "Epic Laws of Folk Narrative" in 1909: no subplots, two chief characters in conflict, a peak tableau. Another folklorist, Max Lüthi, in "Parallel Themes in Folk Narrative in Art and Literature" (1967), notices that a common conflict of this sort ends with "the defeat of the great by the small, the mighty by the apparently powerless." Pondering these generalizations, Dorson remarks, brings to mind "the triumphs of Brer Rabbit over the bear and the fox, . . . of Davy Crockett over b'ars, panthers, and armies," and "the perilous odyssey of Huck Finn."[20] The list can be greatly extended. Our humor throngs with tricksters: crafty Yankee peddlers and gamblers of antebellum years; confidence men such as the duke and the dauphin in the 1880s, O. Henry's Jeff Peters in the 1900s, and Addie Pray's Long Boy in 1971; Stuart's Tussies of 1943 and Hyman's Will Stockdale of 1954, who outwit government agencies. Again, there are boasters who are defeated and deflated by quiet opponents — little Davy, for example, in *Life on the Mississippi,* who makes the rampaging Child of Calamity and Bob the self-styled Corpse-Maker "own up that they are sneaks and cowards." A character's vernacular speech, in fact, may suggest that he is an underdog, especially if he is having trouble with more assured or more sophisticated folk.

A third recurrent pattern was described by Norris Yates, in *William T. Porter and The Spirit of the Times,* which provides a fine history of the magazine that published the best pre–Civil War vernacular stories. In many stories in that magazine, the *Spirit of the Times,* says Norris, "Event is piled on event and detail on detail, each taller than the last, until the apex, the tallest incident of all, is reached." This climactic ordering was used in tales which Yates particularly admires, including the most widely praised and reprinted comic narrative the *Spirit* ever published, "The Big Bear of Arkansas."[21] It was used again and again by Mark Twain. In *The Innocents Abroad,* he utilized it in practically all of the most famous passages such as the one about the bedeviling of the guide, the one about Da Vinci's "Last Supper," and Twain's cogitations by the Tomb of Adam. Again in *Roughing It,* he used it to picture the fright-prone jackass rabbit and the omnivorous camel; Bemis' buffalo story; the yarn about the Mexican plug. It provided the overall organization for "Old Times on the Mississippi" and for his best framework story, "Jim Baker's Blue-Jay Yarn." Owen Wister had Trampas and the Virginian use the climactic tall tale form in their confrontation, and of course the same form is the standard one still for lying contests. When a liar tells a series of stories that fill a whole book, naturally they pile up higher and higher. As the man who has recorded Jack Crabb's yarns in *Little Big Man*, Ralph Fielding Snell, remarks: that one man experienced a third of Jack's adventures is "unlikely," half "incredible," the whole lot "mythomaniac."

At best the style and the structuring of the quoted story create not merely the vernacular character but a particularized narrator. When you recite a story to an audience, said Twain, "you absorb the character and presently become the man himself." Elsewhere Twain speaks of so writing a story as to let the imagined character "tell his story *himself* and let me act merely as his amanuensis." Twain seems to have sensed a subtle difference between the written and the oral procedures, but unfortunately he never managed to formulate it, and regardless, the procedures clearly were analogous. That this is true is indicated in Twain's praise of a performance by James Whitcomb Riley, "about the funniest thing I have ever listened to," during which Riley tells a story in such a way as to simulate perfectly the character of a simple, innocent, sincere old farmer who perfectly reveals himself by the telling. In this performance, as in many written works, the most important disclosures are unconscious ones. The delightful revelation of "The Old Soldier's Story," completely unbeknownst to the old man, is that he is constitutionally incapable of telling a funny story well.[22] Twain cherished Robert Browning's dramatic monologues because they too provided illuminations of monologuists — "a splendor of stars and suns" that filled "the whole field with flame" — and believed that by simulative interpretations he could "read Browning so Browning himself can understand."[23] Huck Finn, like the English poet's dramatis personae, acquainted readers with a rather complex character by uttering a monologue.

Unconscious revelations by means of monologues have continued to appeal to Americans: witness those of Lardner's narrators in "Haircut," "The Love Nest," and other stories; of Dorothy Parker's battered womenfolk; of Jason Compson in Part Three of *The Sound and the Fury*; and of Holden Caulfield, who tells perceptive readers much more than he himself knows about his mental state.

George Brush, monologuist in *Heaven's My Destination*, left even discerning critics unsure whether he was a saint or a fool: by surrounding his narrative with a framework, Thornton Wilder might have made clear his creator's conviction, expressed elsewhere, that he was both. Thus, by describing a storyteller and his background, an author may clarify and enlarge his characterization of the raconteur. Thorpe's Jim Doggett gains vividness because he is shown swaggering confidently as he enters the steamboat cabin, then putting his feet on the stove, "his eyes . . . as sparkling as diamonds, and good-natured to simplicity." Twain's Simon Wheeler is helpfully shown "dozing comfortably the the barroom stove of the decayed mining camp of Angel's . . . fat and bald-headed, and [with] an expression of winning gentleness and simplicity upon his tranquil countenance." It is useful to know that as Simon told his story "he never smiled, he never frowned, he never changed his voice from the gentle-flowing key to which he tuned his initial sentence." H. L. Davis generalizes to the advantage of the reader about old Flem Simmons: "he could take the measliest little episode . . . and string it out and wool it around and supple it and driddle it along for hours as joyful and preoccupied as an old squaw tanning a stolen buckskin. . . . He had to start with the way the weather had looked when he woke up and what he thought about it, what fuel he had started the fire with . . . and the most infernal rigmarole of particulars. . . . [He] told a story that began with his getting his boots wet so he had to grease them with tallow before he could put them on. . . . It wasn't very easy on the ears."[24]

Writers of framed tales, as Richard Boyd Hauck suggests, often are enabled to focus attention upon the psychology of a storyteller who is more complex, indeed more ambiguous, than casual readers realize.[25] As revealed by Twain's comments as well as his blue jay yarn, Jim Baker is an opinionated, deranged, and overcomplicated misanthrope. Faulkner was able to sense under the horseplay of Sut Lovingood a character whom he ranked with Don Quixote, Falstaff, and other great fictional creations because "he had no illusions about himself, did the best he could; at certain times he was a coward and knew it and wasn't ashamed; he never blamed his misfortunes on anyone and never cursed God for them."[26] Faulkner himself in "Bear Hunt" and the Snopes trilogy gave his best storyteller, V. K. Ratliff, wisdom, compassion, and irony that deepened meanings of yarns entrusted to his telling.

Revelations in the framework of what happens to the storyteller and to his audience can add a second plot of sorts to the one in the quoted narrative. As early as 1829 in "Otter-Bag" John Neal has an auditor, warmed with flip, find a tale enchanting at first, then become increasingly bored until finally he hurries away to avoid a retelling. Much the same thing happens in 1865 when Simon Wheeler blockades his auditor in a corner and forces him to listen to a frog story that the man finds so long and tedious that, at the first chance, he too escapes. Flem Simmons, it eventuates, is stringing out his "infernal rigmarole" to keep his two auditors from squabbling. This framework tale therefore is one of hundreds involving a hoax. Such a subplot still is attractive in *Little Big Man*, where Jack Crabb dies leaving his pedantic editor uncertain whether Jack is a forgotten hero or

a prodigious liar. Or the plot of the framework may initiate and terminate a climactic development that mounts toward a peak in the enclosed
story ("The Big Bear of Arkansas"). The framework plot may be contra-
puntal, antithetical, or both to that of the quoted story ("Baker's Blue-Jay
Yarn" and parts of the Snopes trilogy).

The framework language usually contrasts with the vernacular of the
quoted story to stress comic aspects: Homer Wilbur's sesquipedalian words
and Latin quotations incongruously introduce Hosea's Yankee doggerel;
Ralph Fielding Snell's prissy "Foreword" and "Editor's Epilogue" bracket
a narrative in the informal style of Jack Crabb. Interruptions of a vernacular account by more pretentious stretches serve the same end: a "gentle-
manly" English huntsman intrudes upon Jim Doggett's narrative; letters
in fustian are inserted every now and then in Jaimie McPheeters' story.

Clearly humor rooted in oral storytelling traditions persists partly because it can be modified to serve many purposes. Brief looks at two novels
in which it plays very different but quite important roles — one by William
Faulkner and one by Eudora Welty — will support this claim.

Although Faulkner's affection for oral humor and for published humor
based upon it, and his indebtedness to them, have been well documented,[27]
critics seemingly have not considered reasons why he embedded vernacular narratives in *Light in August* (1932) at two important points. At the
end of chapter 15, then at the very end of the book (chapter 21), he abruptly
relinquished a style often empurpled by rhetoric and had vulgar storytellers take over.

The earlier anecdote, about the meeting of Uncle Doc and Mrs. Hines
with Joe Christmas following his capture, is told by clerks, loafers, and
farmers around family tables and in shadowed yards. It thus becomes a
community's commentary on an important event, and as such it shows
the community's deep prejudices, which are critically relevant.[28] The contemptuous picturing of Hines is achieved in part by verbs which show the
old man hollering, hobbling, screeching, slobbering, shaking and flopping,
in part by homely similes that liken him to a hypnotist's victim and a
runaway from a crazy house. His wife too is caricatured — as squat and
dowdy — looking like a toy balloon on which Katzenjammer kids have
painted a funny face; so when this weird female completely shuts up the
bombastic little gaffer, plants him in a chair, and forces him to stay put,
the humiliating deflation contributes a great deal to Faulkner's sustained
assault upon the man's fanaticism.

A furniture dealer who has helped hitchhiking Lena Grove and Byron
Bunch on their journey tells the second story to his ardent young wife as
they lie abed between couplings. The pair's earthy quips about their relish
of sex starkly contrast with the man's story about Byron's timid try at se-

ducing Lena, her disdainful but unperturbed refusal, and his hangdog return to her side. Set in such an incongruous frame and stressing ludicrous details, the account enforces a comparison between Lena's and Joe's biographies that runs through the novel and adumbrates the central theme. Its placing as the very last chapter gives it a particular emphasis.

In *Losing Battles,* three generations of the descendants of Granny Elvira Jordan Vaughn gather to celebrate her ninetieth birthday at a home in the hill country of northeastern Mississippi. A few events which occur during the two days and a night of the reunion are recounted by the third-person narrator, but practically all the telling of the narrative takes the form of familial talk, endlessly discussing current events and telling leisurely stories about what happened in the past. The lifelike vernacular style characterizes the speakers as individuals and as members of a clan, evokes ways of living, feeling, and thinking, and in the end works verbal magic of a sort that compassionately deals with evil and suffering — even with the loss of battles by major and minor warriors. Overall the tone is comic, and the end result — like that of most rituals — is propitiation. Miss Welty's impressive achievement provides proof (if any is needed) that narratives based upon oral storytelling are alive and well and living in Mississippi. As they are in other parts of the country.

Part Two
Essays on American Humor

A German Connection

Raspe's Baron Munchausen

I

Soon after alert America-watchers in England noticed that some of our countrymen were trying to be funny and, surprisingly, were succeeding, several of the watchers announced that they had spotted the distinctive ingredient in overseas comedy. After scanning discussions by British critics, Clarence Gohdes summarized their consensus: "By the middle of the [nineteenth] century the critical conclusion was pretty generally fixed that the essence of American humor was exaggeration." For decades, commentators on this side of the Atlantic shared the English belief. In 1899 Bret Harte, for instance, said that our "distinct and original humor" was "delightfully extravagant"; in 1918 Professor Will D. Howe remarked that early comic writers "in the main channel of American humour" developed long-lasting devices, "particularly the tricks of gigantic exaggeration and calm-faced mendacity"; and in 1936, Max Eastman noticed that it was "customary to say that American humor is distinguished from British by exaggeration."[1]

By the 1840s common folk were using the word "tall" to describe the talk and the yarns that most obviously made use of magnification. *Knickerbocker Magazine* was announcing that "one of the striking peculiarities of our people is the disposition to talk tall." Colloquial speech called a narrative "that is highly exaggerated or difficult to believe" a "tall tale," and a Sucker from Illinois told a famous raconteur, Jim Doggett in "The Big Bear of Arkansas," that "his stories smelt rather tall."[2]

The popularity of the tall tale as an American genre has been verified by scholars who read acres of pages in books, newspapers, and periodicals, who cornered storytellers and set down their monologues, then listed and counted occurrences and types and motifs. A leading compiler, Ernest W. Baughman, needed more than six hundred large pages for his

Critical Essays on American Humor, ed. Clark and Turner. G. K. Hall, 1984.

Type and Motif-Index of the Folktales of England and North America, which surveyed publications in the two indicated areas until a few years before its issuance, 1966. "The tall tale," he decided, "constitutes the largest segment of our published tales." His list shows that "the tall tale . . . is an overwhelmingly American form (3,710 American variants, 29 English variants)"—a ratio of 128 American tellings of such fanciful windies to every one that Britons told. International listings indicated that other nationalities did no better than the British, if as well.[3]

These facts show why the thesis of this paper merits development: I suggest that an eighteenth-century German author who never visited the United States, and his immediate imitators, were the most important contributors to the plots, motifs, and techniques of American tall tale literature.

Having made this suggestion, I must hurry and do a bit of weaseling. It must be admitted that unassailable proof of this claim will be impossible. A reason will be found in the very nature of the literary corral in which the obstreperous genre, the tall tale, has been stabled—jokelore. For, like germs, viruses, and great ideas, jokelore is all but impossible to confine. As Gershon Legman has said: "jestbooks, . . . which derive mainly from one another . . . are not so much being alimented by folk sources as constituting, themselves, a main source of the jokes in oral transmission. . . . their copying from one another is only one intermediate step in their migrations: from one mouth to another, one book to another, one land to another."[4] Jokelore, in other words, meanders unpredictably and without leaving a clear trail, from age to age, region to region, talk to print, and print to talk, in mysterious ways ad infinitum. The best I can do, therefore, is set down available evidence, admittedly inconclusive, in the hope that my suggestion will prove to be worth entertaining.

Rudolf Erich Raspe (1737–94) appeals to me as a candidate for the kind of recognition I urge because, for one thing, his German education gave him learning quite incongruous for a begetter of yarns told by untutored farm folk who told them by fireplaces or hunters and fishers who told them around campfires. At thirty he became a university professor and museum director. He wrote erudite tomes in several languages about antiquities, geology, mines, mountains, volcanoes, and literary history. A member of Britain's Royal Society by invitation, he contributed scholarly papers and suggested improvements on Benjamin Franklin's glass harmonica so impressive that Ben invited him to visit Philadelphia. His contribution to art history so impressed Horace Walpole, himself an art historian, that Walpole financed its publication.

For another thing, Raspe himself was a most appropriate predecessor of some great American comic characters — Sam Slick, Thimblerig, Simon Suggs, Petroleum V. Nasby, Col. Sellers, the Gentle Grafter, Egbert Souse and other perpetrators of confidence games. He got his professorship and his curatorship by enlarging upon his qualifications. He puffed up his reputation by browbeating intellectual disputants. Trusted to catalogue and protect a museum's treasures, he pilfered a number, pawned them, tried to bluster himself out of being punished, failed, and absconded to England. There, after a brazen pitch for a Cambridge professorship miscarried, he used his scientific expertise to talk himself into a job as an assayer. In the mines, he again tried some skulduggery — the salting of a Scottish claim — and once more when detected managed to elude punishment.

Pressed for money (as he usually was) in 1785, Raspe hurriedly wrote a one-shilling 42-page booklet about a comic German blowhard and somehow got a London publisher to issue it. *Baron Munchausen's Narrative of His Marvellous Travels and Campaigns in Russia* was a great immediate success. Within a year, impressive sales brought a commission to add materials for a "considerably enlarged" new edition. By 1800, eight "legitimate" English editions, a pirated "sixth" edition, and two editions (1792 and 1796) of a sequel had appeared.

Translated and augmented German editions in 1786 and 1788 — *Wunderbare Reisen zu Wasser und Lande, Feldzüge und Lustige Abentheuer des Freyherrn von Munchhausen* — helped deliver the stories to the European continent. Thereafter, bibliographers have ticked off 138 more editions in English and 237 more in German detailing the baron's yarns, pure or adulterated and without added matter or (more often) with it, plus hundreds in other languages and countries. In addition more adaptations have appeared worldwide than even compilers with lusts for lists have been able to record. The problem was complicated because from the start many publishers of these works were careless or deliberately deceitful about dates and publishers. The first English edition, for instance, came out in 1785 but was assigned to 1786, and the German translations of 1786 and 1788 were said to have been published in London, though in fact they were published in Göttingen. In both England and Germany for some years publishers had a good reason for hiding their true identities: a real German Baron Hieronymus Karl Friedrich von Münchhausen of Bodenwerder, plagued by pilgrims to his estate, was doing his damnedest to sue somebody responsible for the libel bringing unwelcome fame, but he was baffled.[5]

II

It appears that the fictional baron's books about his military and hunting exploits did well in the United States. Early editions were imported from England for the enjoyment of American readers; but less than two years after the first edition came out — in 1787 — our enterprising countrymen, untrammeled by any copyright laws, began to put out their own printings. One of the most successful versions, initiated in 1793, appeared with Americanizations and updatings of its satirical thrusts in 1813, 1832, and 1815. Henry A. Pochman in his *German Culture in America . . . 1600–1900* toted up 39 appearances of Munchausen's *Narrative*, and undoubtedly the impressive number would have been even larger if he had counted reissues. A title page of a printing as long ago as 1835 called that edition the twenty-fourth; and though, to be sure, publishers have been notoriously grandiose when counting copies, as a rule they were more accurate when they counted editions.[6]

But since accurate (or even, in fact, inaccurate) sales figures for editions and adaptations of Munchausen's fabrications are not available, anybody who wonders how popular they were must turn to other indications of their notoriety. Three kinds are useful: (1) usages in common speech of the old liar's name, (2) references to Munchausen that manifest general familiarity over the years, and (3) records of oral and printed retellings of the baron's tall tales.

The terms *Munchausens, Munchausenish,* and *Munchausened* have invaded the vernacular. From the 1830s, on without bothering to explain, popular writers about local champion liars called them *New York Munchausens, Vermont Munchausens, Texas Munchausens,* and the like. Even medical doctors, who do not go in for many literary allusions, have got into the habit of saying that sufferers who exaggerate their agony have *Munchausen's Syndrome.*

More impressive, a reader of popular American publications of various kinds can easily find every now and then casual references – without glosses – to Baron Munchausen that take for granted general familiarity. Examples:

1822–23 When Charles Mathews, a noted British comedian, toured the United States in a one-man show, newspaper reports, the program, and the widely circulated printed text identified Major Longbow, one of the characters he impersonated, as "a modern Munchausen."

1833 A newspaper and then a comic anthology titled a joke "One of Jonathan's Munchausens."

1847 The author of an article, "Tough Stories," in the *Yankee Blade,* remarked that in a little town in Maine "all the villagers" agreed that a local storyteller "left Munchausen 'no whar.'"

1856 In his best-selling *Prue and I,* G. W. Curtis made the ghost of the baron a prominent character.

1864 Robert Carter told in a travel book about his encounter with "a marine Munchausen of the first water [whose] adventures were nearly as wonderful as those of the renowned Baron himself."

1870 A burlesque mining prospectus in the Boston *Commercial* offered stock in "the Munchausen Philosopher's Stone and Gull Creek Consolated Oil Company" which was preparing to work its tract for "quinine, sardines, and the milk of human kindness" under the guidance of Baron Munchausen, the "company director."

1896 A St. Louis book, *Arkansas,* issued as an advertisement for that state, reassured possible migrants: "No, don't be afraid of Arkansas on account of Munchausen reports of ignorance and crime."

1901 The popular humorist John Kendrick Bangs published *Mr. Munchausen, an Account of Some of His Recent Adventures,* with an introduction in which he explained why he became "the medium between the spirit of late Baron Munchausen and the reading public": it was "to render a service to an honest and defenseless man." The fifteen chapters were excellent additions to the tales told in the 1786 booklet.

1913 William Rose Benét published in *Century Magazine* a poem, "The Marvelous Munchausen," nostalgically picturing the baron as he tells three listeners several tales which Benét renders in verse.

1928 Ginn & Company, a leading publisher of textbooks, published an edition of the baron's *Narrative* for grade schools, with an introduction by the editor, Steven T. Byington, which held that "Munchausen's modest seat in the Valhalla of classic literature is undisputed," and that "the education that does not include knowledge" of some of his famous stories is "incomplete." "We all," said Byington, himself a humorist, "bow to the Baron as the patriarch, the perfect model, the fadeless fragrant flower, of liberty from accuracy."

1931 Constance Rourke, in her best-selling history, *American Humor,* told about the time Audubon was called "a new and greater Munchausen" for telling an unbelievable story about a rattlesnake.

1931–43 Jack Pearl (1895–1982), a comedian, playing the role of Baron Munchausen, was a major radio personality. After making a hit by telling whoppers on the Ed Sullivan radio show, Pearl headed national network shows of his own, telling wild tales in German dialect. When his straight man, Cliff Hall, expressed disbelief, he would say, "Vas you dere, Sharlie?"—always winning howls of laughter. The expression became a household phrase. Pearl, as "Baron Munchausen," also appeared in two films, one with Jimmy Durante, the other with not only Durante but also Laurel and Hardy.

1929,   The Limited Editions Club published two editions of *The Travels*
1952   *of Baron Munchausen,* the first with an Introduction by Carl Van
      Doren, who said, "Munchausen is the Euclid of Liars," and the
      second introduced by John Carswell, Raspe's definitive biographer.
1982   When Jack Pearl died on Christmas day, newspapers throughout
      the country played up his death on obituary pages. The Associ-
      ated Press story said that Pearl, after appearing in vaudeville and
      in 18 Broadway shows "made his greatest impression on radio"
      when "he lampooned the widely read adventure tales of Baron
      Munchausen."
1983   In the June issue of *Smithsonian,* James Cox, without elabora-
      tion, quoted an editor's request that he write an article about lies:
      "Just think of Baron Munchausen and Pinocchio's nose."

I list these allusions to Raspe's old liar because they go to prove that his tellings, rather than others, were likely sources of American retellings. Jokelore, as has been said, was widely diffused over time and space, and it is relevant to notice that just possibly Raspe's versions of some were those most likely to be encountered. Raspe himself, however, can serve as a leading witness for the ubiquity of his stories, since the huge amount of reading in many fields that made him a polymath also had acquainted him with oft-repeated windies; he had stored them in his excellent memory and he recalled them when he was writing his booklet. Here, for instance, is one story that the baron tells: During an unusually severe winter — one so cold "that ever since the sun seems to be frost-bitten" — he is journeying across Russia:

> I travelled post day and night, and finding myself engaged in a nar-
> row lane, I bid the postilion give a signal with his horn, that other
> travellers might not meet or stop us in the narrow passage. He blew
> with all his might, but all his endeavors were in vain. He could not
> make the horn speak, which, as he pretended to be a good performer,
> was . . . unaccountable. . . . Soon after we found ourselves in the
> presence of another coach coming the other way. It was very
> troublesome for both parties in this horrid weather, for there was no
> proceeding either way, without taking the carriages to pieces and put-
> ting them together again, past each other. . . . However we reached
> the much-looked-for stage, and . . . all of us hastened to warm and
> refresh ourselves.
> The postilion hung his great coat and horn on a peg and sat
> down near the kitchen fire. . . . I sat down on the other side. . . .
> Suddenly we heard a *Tereng! tereng, teng, teng!* We looked around,
> and now found the reason, why the postilion had not been able to

sound his horn. His tunes were frozen up in the horn, and came out now by thawing, plain enough, and much to the credit of the driver, so that the honest fellow entertained us for some time with a variety of tunes, without putting his mouth to the horn.

This little episode, like others in the *Narrative*, had traveled long and far, and there simply is no telling for sure where Raspe had encountered it. In a study of its multitudinous appearances, Otto Weinreich required 144 pages to trace its reincarnations, none of them, it happens, in America. Plutarch, the ancient Greek biographer (46?–120?), who said he was repeating it as a jest of Antiphanes' instead of inventing it, was the earliest teller identified, but thereafter it was retold by such varied storytellers as Calcagnini, Castiglione, Rabelais, Donne, Butler, Addison, Mandeville, Burger, Jean Paul, Saint-Martin, Balzac, and many others.[7] Such wanderings are typical. As John Carswell says:

> To get at the origins of the stories the Baron tells, we must follow tracks which lead back into the furthest uplands of collective memory, running across one another and finally vanishing into uncertainty, like sheep-runs among the heather. We can chase individual tales through the pages of monkish jest-books and fifteenth-century collections of facetiae, or trace the German traditon of *Lügendichtungen* through its successive phases, until we find that the Bible, or the *Mabinogion,* or the folk literature of almost any country, from the *English* (and Greek) *Six Sillies* to the Serbian *The Biggest Liar in the World* will give us stories the Baron might have told. The fairy fruit which turns to ashes in more sophisticated hands was safe enough with Raspe.

Carswell suggests that, since Raspe drew upon his "common stock," the characterization of Munchausen and Raspe's storytelling skill are his "only original contribution to the tales," and he may be right. However, in all fairness, it should be noted that those indefatigable folklorists mentioned earlier — the readers of many printed works and recorders of oral yarn-spinnings — so far have been unable to find tellings previous to Raspe's of only four of the tales in the first edition of the *Narrative*.

III

Just the same, the listers of types and motifs in huge indexes and in books about folklore pay an impressive tribute to the contributions of Raspe and his hero. In his great six-volume *Motif-Index of Folk-Literature*, for instance, Professor Stith Thompson recognized the most famous teller, worldwide, of tall tales by calling a group "Münchhausen Tales."[8]

Writing in 1946, Professor Harold Thompson thought it "probable that in the past century Americans have owed as much to the Baron Munch-ausen as to any English drawer of the long bow . . . the cosmopolitan source of American fun [and] a welcome immigrant." He noticed that folklorists "from New England to New Mexico" have collected oral versions of tales told by "that suave and poker-faced master of lies." Having read reports and collected tales in New York State, Thompson said "the favorite" may be one that Raspe might have encountered in Julius Caesar's *Commentary on the Gallic War* (45 B.C.).[9] Here is Raspe's version:

> Having one day spent all my shot, I found myself unexpectably in the presence of a stately stag. . . . I charged immediately with powder, and upon it a good handful of cherries, of which I had partly sucked the flesh as far as the hurry would permit. Thus I let fly at at him, and hit him just in the middle of the forehead between the antlers. It stunned him — he staggered — yet he made off. A year or two after I was with a party in the same forest — and beheld a noble stag come out with a fine full-grown cherry tree between his antlers. I recollected my former adventure; looked upon him as my property; and brought him to the ground by one shot, which at once gave me the haunce and cherry-sauce; for the tree was covered with the richest fruit, the like I never had tasted before.

Thompson noticed that only fourteen American variants had been writ-ten about by 1946 and made a prediction — that "doubtless scholars will uncover many more." Sure enough, folklorist Leonard Roberts in 1969 cited an additional variant found in New Jersey, one in Wisconsin, and two each in Indiana, and Michigan, and himself printed "The Peach Tree and the Deer," which he got from an informant in Knox County, Kentucky, who had heard it back in 1920. An old man, the story begins, having feasted on peaches from a tree in a forest, shot a fat deer with a peach stone:

> A few years later he went hunting again in the same woods. This time he . . . looked over beside a big log and there was another peach tree full of good peaches. He cloomb up in it and begin to eat peaches again. The peach tree begin to move. He looked down and to his sur-prise the tree was growing out of a deer's back. He got a switch and started whupping the deer and it bolted around through the woods. Finally it come out to the big road and run up through the church-yard where there was a bunch of chillern playing. He shook the tree and a lot of peaches fell off for the chillern to get. The deer run on and on and went through a big thorn patch. The man looked back and saw the eyes hanging on a thorn winking at him.[10]

In spite of the displacement of the cherry tree and the somewhat grisly fillip at the end, this story's ancestry is quite clear.

Ernest Baughman, whose monumental compilation of American variants of types and motifs has been mentioned, agrees that the story nominated by Thompson was one of the most popular Munchausenized narratives, but he suggests that the tale about the frozen coach horn quoted a few pages back may have been even more popular, especially if some close relations are taken into account. He lists eight versions of the tale in which music congeals and later thaws, then makes what surely are plausible additions in which other "unfreezables freeze"—words, dog barks, train whistles, flames, smoke, fog, air, light beams, and sunbeams—thirty of these in all.

His compilation includes a half a dozen additional descendants of Raspe's whoppers, each with numerous variants (total: 61). "I don't think," he remarked in a recent personal letter, "you can go far wrong in stressing Raspe's importance, especially in the early part of the nineteenth century."[11] The half a dozen do not include variants of the Raspe concoction that I gather he believes is the most popular of all here. This is the one that the late Richard M. Dorson nominated in his book *American Folklore* (Chicago, 1959). Dorson, whose research led him to comment on variants in the United States of at least nine of the "Münchhausen Tales," calls attention to some printed in 1808 as told by liars from New York, Virginia, and Vermont. One of these appeared in *The Farmer's Almanac* for 1809, and was headlined "Amusing." A contributor, addressing the editor, Robert Thomas, speaks of "the wonderful feats and extraordinary stories of *Simonds, old Kidder,* and *Sam Hyde,*" but hopes "to divert some of your evening readers" with a yarn told by a formidable competitor, George Howell, famous in New England as *the Vermont Nimrod:*

> "I was once," said he, "passing down the banks of the Hudson in search of game, and suddenly heard a crackling on the opposite bank. Looking across the river, I saw a stately buck, and instantly drew up and let fly at him. That very moment a huge sturgeon leaped from the river in the direction of my piece.—The ball went through him, and passed on. I flung down my gun—threw off my coat and hat, and swam for the floating fish, which, mounting, I towed to the bank and went to see what more my shot had done for me. I found the ball had passed through the heart of the deer, and struck into a hollow tree beyond; where the honey was running out like a river! I sprung round to find something to stop the hole with, and caught hold of a white rabbit—It squeaked just like a stuck pig; so I thrash'd it away from me in a passion at the disappointment, and it went with such force that it killed three cock partridges and a wood cock."!!!

"This," said Dorson, "is the first recording of America's favorite tall tale, the Wonderful Hunt, also well liked in Europe." Later, in his discussion of Pennsylvania folklore, he wrote:

Again, the best-known of all American tall tales, the Wonderful Hunt, appears in Montgomery County in more fantastic form than ever. Not only does Beltz, the champion hunter, shoot into a tree trunk to split a limb and clamp the toes of seven pigeons, in a standard feat, but he adds the novelty of exciting the pigeons to pull up the tree and fly off; Beltz jumps on the butt, and by waving his hat from side to side guides the pigeons to his home across the Schuylkill River. True, the butt occasionally dipped into the water. Reaching home old Beltz found his trousers full of suckers, adding to his pigeons and winter's wood.[12]

Although Professor Dorson and other folklorists have given these narratives and variants of them the title "The Wonderful Hunt," the fact is that they combine happenings that the baron and his followers often tell about in separate episodes. Professor Baughman, who is sure that "Wonderful Hunt" types and motifs were "borrowed from the Munchausen books," discusses them in remarks about one, "The Lucky Shot." (The numbers are those that have been assigned for classification.)

1890. *The Lucky Shot.* The discharge of the gun kills the heathcock which falls on the sprouts of the tree, killing the bear, etc. [X1124.3]. Compare Munchausen . . . (two ducks, four widgeon, two teal.)
[Note: The accidental discharge of the gun is not a characteristic motif of the English nor of the American forms of the type. In each variant, the weapon is used deliberately, although luckily. There are about seven major subdivisions of the type with considerable overlapping of the subdivisions and of other types, notably 1895. The Man Wading in Water Catches Many Fish in His Boots, 1881. The Man Carried Through Air by Geese, 1900. How the Man Came Out of the Tree Stump, 1894. The Man Shoots a Ramrod Full of Ducks, 1882. The Man Who Fell Out of a Balloon. Buried in the Earth. He Goes for a Spade to Dig Himself Out.][13]

The modification that Baughman mentions—making the shot intentional rather than accidental—is one of several, e.g., the fauna and flora of course are thoroughly localized, and often the domino-like series of happenings are made remarkably elaborate. In general critics agree with Norris W. Yates's comment in his history of America's leading sportsmen's magazine between 1831 and 1858: "A number of hunting stories owed something to Munchausen; for instance, those built around the theme of the 'wonderful hunt' . . . . Variations on the pattern are often ingenious but usually minor."[14]

The above samples, summaries, and commentaries show clearly the nature of the pattern that is repeated time after time in "Wonderful Hunt" stories: Thanks to a sportsman's skill and good luck in a country where fish, fowl, and four-legged critters abound, a sportsman slaughters prodigious quantities of game. It is therefore no trick to figure out why this particular tall tale in its several guises has been so popular for so long in the United States, or why its fame is doomed to fade in the future. For centuries, the North America of promotion tracts and in actuality was truly a hunter's paradise. From colonial times on, our Nimrods and anglers did what their ilk always have done everywhere: they enlarged upon their triumphs. Both the boosters boasting about our salubrious climate and the braggarts celebrating their full bags and creels became common objects of derision, and, as many critics noticed, satirical exaggerations of exaggerations became favorite materials for comedy. And so the baron's tales about hunting and fishing in Russia, where his claim was that game "abounds more than [in] any other part of the world," were ready made for American appropriation and naturalization. But a likely prediction is that — thanks to environmentalists, defenders of endangered species, and sufferers from cholesterolophobia — jokes about the extinction of great quantities of fauna will decline in popularity in the future.

In numbers of the sportsmen's magazine issued between 1846 and 1856, Professor Yates found several Munchausen stories in addition to those I have mentioned. Twice writers (one with a bow to the baron) adapted one about the fellow who "rammed his arm down the throat of a charging wolf, seized it by the tail, and turned it inside out with a jerk," by substituting a panther for the wolf though "the story remains substantially the same." The baron's tale about the bitch which whelped as she ran was improved upon by adding that the precocious pups immediately fetched game. Finally, the baron's hound "that ran its legs off until it was merely a short-legged terrier" inspired a yarn about a pony that ran its hoofs off in pursuit of a buffalo that ran his legs off. Thus, as Yates points out, "these American cousins" have become "backwoods stories in setting, tone, and atmosphere," but still are easily recognized.[15]

Other scholars have recorded American tellings in other media not only of these three Munchausen stories but of additional ones — about a jumper who turned around partway through his jump; about the split dog reassembled with his back legs pointing upward; about the snakebite or sting that caused an inanimate object to swell; about the indefatigable hound that chased birds or game for days, weeks, or even months; about the fellow who made a wolf jump out of its skin by nailing its tail to a tree then beating the poor beast; about the animals that pounced on horses pulling a sleigh, ate their way into the horses' hides, and kept pulling. All these appeared after the *Narrative* and its sequels had been widely distributed in the United States. Add the recurrences in print of these to those about the Wonderful Hunt, and the total is more than a hundred. And beyond a shadow of a doubt, innumerable oral retellings enlarged the total.[16] So widely have Baron Manchausen's tall tales been retold and re-enjoyed again and again from sea to shining sea that anyone who dares to say that they aren't funny must be labeled un-American.

IV

Whether modern Americans (and un-Americans) find the German-made tall tales amusing or not, they have to concede that their popularizer, Herr Raspe, showed remarkable sensibility when he discovered among his wide readings so many plots and motifs that so long would convulse our countrymen. A consideration of his technique provides additional insight concerning taste and artistry unique in the long history of popular jokebooks.

Raspe's contemporary, Horace Walpole, a fine stylist himself, remarked that this emigrant wrote English "much above ill"; and Carswell argues persuasively that "the credit for creating the Baron as a figure belongs to Raspe and to Raspe's English style. . . . the pungency and racy vitality of the Baron's diction that brings him to life" — an achievement "the more remarkable in that it is carried out in a language not the author's own — a *tour de force* accomplished by Conrad and Beckford, but very few others." Carswell cites as proof a fine but quite typical paragraph — one, it happens, for which no source but numerous American retellings have been found — one admirable for its lucid ordering and its economical but apt choice of concrete details:

> "What do you say to this for an example? Daylight and powder were spent one day in a Polish forest. When I was going home, a terrible bear made up to me at great speed, with open mouth, ready to fall upon me, all my pockets were searched in an instant for powder and ball, but in vain — I found nothing but two spare flints: one I flung with all my might into the monster's open jaws, down his throat. It gave him pain, and made him turn about, so that I could level the second at his back door, which, indeed, I did with wonderful success, for it flew in, met the first flint in his stomach, struck fire, and blew up the bear with a terrible explosion. Though I came safe off that time, yet I should not wish to try it again or venture against bears with no other defense."

"There he is," says Carswell, "and as such he has lived, for there is not a word of direct description [of him] in the whole book."[17] True, the completely deadpan and matter-of-fact but efficient style does much to individualize the baron, and true, Munchausen's physical aspects never are indicated. However, both third-person commentaries and his own lengthy monologues further characterize the old prevaricator in ways that the passage does not illustrate.

The publisher's preface and advertisements to early editions, including the 1792 sequel, are third-person frameworks that unfold the baron's family history, compare him with other storytellers, and describe his way of talking — his careful skirting of controversy as he "adroitly turns the conversation so that he may hold the floor," for instance. "A man of great original humor," he has, the tongue-in-cheek publisher announces, a high purpose — "to awaken and shame the common sense of those who have lost sight of it," and to convince those who find his stories "border on the marvellous" that they are true.

So Munchausen bolsters the purported believability of his tales by carefully tracing logical causal relationships. Why does he succeed as a hunter? "Presence of mind and vigorous exertions" bring many triumphs, "chance and good luck [which] correct our mistakes" bring others. Again, "in a case of distress, . . . try any expedient." Using "the very best implements" will help: "I have always been as remarkable for the excellence of horses, dogs, guns, and swords, as for the proper manner of using and managing them." And be alert in watching for a recurrent peril: "There is a kind of fatality in it. The fiercest and most dangerous animals, generally come upon me when defenseless, as if they had a notion or foresight by way of instinct. . . ." These and other insights based upon long experience acquaint readers with Munchausen's ways of thinking.

Though Carswell is right when he notices Raspe's omission of physical descriptions of his storyteller, illustrators nevertheless eventually agreed pretty well about the baron's appearance. Probably this was because one artist's superb picturings that have been printed some sixty times since they came out in 1862 — those of Gustave Doré — have set the fashion. Doré's likenesses as well as those of most subsequent limners are not greatly unlike the description of Raspe in the 1775 German warrant for his arrest for embezzlement — "of middle height, face long rather than round, small eyes, nose somewhat large, beady and pointed, red hair under a short tie wig, wearing a red coat with gold facings." The resemblance (though pretty surely this is a coincidence)[18] is appropriate because, as Carswell perceives, Raspe "may have . . . given away something of himself, the seedy failure, by creating Munchhausen, the fabulous success." Personal tragedy was transmuted into closely related comedy when Raspe supplanted his own overweening arrogance with the baron's patently overblown self-esteem, his own sordid dishonesty with the baron's playful and transparent exaggerations, and his own frustrating, disastrous failures with triumphant, comic successes. Raspe's fantasies, in other words, identify the creation with his creator but with refurbishings that make the old storyteller a sympathetic figure.

Similarly, the American authors of many renditions of our country's (and Raspe's) favorite tall tales empathize with highly individualized, likeable or even loveable fabricators, and the characterizations of the storytellers — the tellers, for a century and a half, of falsehoods, medium tall tales, and very tall tales — vie in interest and in appeal with the monologues unfolding the stories. Let us count a few of the most admired storytellers, listed roughly in the order of their appearances: T. C. Haliburton's Sam Slick, James Kirke Paulding's Nimrod Wildfire, *Crockett Almanack* makers' Davy Crockett, T. B. Thorpe's Jim Doggett, J. R. Lowell's Birdofredum Sawin, Ned Buntline's Jim Bridger, H. E. Taliaferro's Fisher's River storytellers, C. F. Browne's Artemus Ward, G. W. Harris' Sut Lovingood, J. C. Harris' Uncle Remus, A. H. Lewis' Old Cattleman, Owen Wister's Trampas and the Virginian, E. N. Westcott's David Harum, O. Henry's Jeff Peters, Frank Bacon's Lightnin' Bill Jones, Don Marquis' Old Soak, W. C. Fields' Egbert Sousé, Ed Wynn's Fire Chief, H. L. Davis' Flem Simmons, Jack Pearl's Baron Munchausen, William Faulkner's V. K. Ratliff, Thomas Berger's Jack Crabb, and Richard Pryor's Oilwell.[19] Mark Twain created a goodly series of such storytellers and made them memorable as characters: Simon Wheeler, Col. Sellers, Jim and Dick Baker, Corpse Maker and the Pet Child of Calamity, the King and the Duke, Huck Finn, Hank Morgan and the Paladin come to mind; and this list is only a partial one.

Now quite obviously anyone who hailed Raspe as the sole begetter of all these offspring would be perpetrating a stretcher, and I shan't do anything of the sort. But because of Raspe's priority, his creative literary skill, and the long-lasting popularity of his storyteller and that storyteller's tales, I believe that the German author deserves credit, if not for setting off this American chain reaction, at least for helping it along during a great many years.

For another thing, Raspe early found a way to do something quite a few American humorists would do — to surround his deadpan yarnspinner with a very palpable, attentive, and appreciative audience.

The baron's remarks about the chase, the chaser, and the chased do something more than show zest for a pastime; they help evoke an attractive ambience — that of a genial entertainer with a receptive group of like enthusiasts drinking, taking its ease, and appreciatively listening to him. As early as the title page of the first edition, a dedication announces a book-length oral-storytelling session: "Humbly dedicated and recommended to Country Gentlemen; and, if they please, to be repeated as their own, after a hunt, at horse races, in watering-places, and other polite assemblies; round the bottle and fireside." The forewords describing Munchausen's way of talking and praising his skill as a teacher help body forth not only a yarnspinner but also his amused listeners. And on one occasion after the baron retires, a third-person commentator tells about the group's response: "the company much diverted and in good spirits" one by one comment on "the extraordinary entertainment," and "a near relation" of Munchausen tells a smutty story in which the baron figures.

Every few pages, too, the baron's speeches remind readers of what is going on by having him directly address his listeners: "I shall not tire you Gentlemen with the politicks, arts, sciences and history . . . nor trouble you with the various intrigues . . . I shall confine myself . . . to the greater and nobler objects of your attention, to horses and dogs, of which I have always been as fond as you are, to foxes, wolves and bears. . . . You have heard, I dare say, of the hunter's and sportsman's saint and protector, Saint Hubert. . . . But gentlemen, for all that; I was not always successful. . . ."

Writing what Bret Harte called the "distinctly original and novel" American story — "orally transmitted . . . in bar-rooms, the gatherings in the 'country store,' and finally at public meetings," humorists often did what Raspe did to recreate the atmosphere of its telling, including a storyteller and a charmed audience. George Washington Harris for instance introduced a narrative: "By the light of a campfire, after a hunter's supper, enjoyed with a hunter's appetite," and others pictured yarnspinning sessions at political barbecues, on stagecoaches, in steamboat social halls, alongside cowboys' chuck wagons, around dinner tables, and so forth. Like Raspe, humorous writers told of listeners' interruptions: "Where did all this happen?" "Sam, what do you suppose was in that pot?" "Allow me to interrupt you." "Is it possible?" And like Raspe, authors told about listeners' responses: "When the story was ended, our hero sat some minutes with his audience in a grave silence."[20]

Now of course, without ever reading *Munchausen's Narrative* or its sequels, our humorists could have encountered oral or written versions of the baron's tales told by others, and could have learned from others how to have a deadpan liar spin his yarns amusingly, and how to show him diverting a pleased and attentive audience.

But on the other hand, thanks to Raspe, especially during the early part of the nineteenth century but later as well, there is a good chance that a fair number of them made a valuable German connection.

Introduction to *Davy Crockett*
at Two Hundred: New Perspectives on the Man and the Myth

Although many Americans abominate historic dates and believe that only pedantic schoolteachers cherish them, when such dates come along in century and half-century sizes, a large number of Americans not only tolerate them but actually join in celebrations of them. So in 1986 the 200th anniversary of David Crockett's birth and the 150th anniversary of his death were enthusiastically commemorated. As a result, our country's most durable legendary hero enjoyed still another of many resurrections.

His first, it might be asserted, took place during the man's lifetime — in 1816, when he had just started his rise by winning fame as a Tennessee hunter, fighting Indians, and getting elected a militia lieutenant. He'd left his family to explore a new frontier in Alabama. Laid low by malaria, he couldn't write home, his horse came back riderless, and his wife received reports that he'd died and had been buried. When at long last he turned up, Mrs. Crockett understandably was "utterly astonished."

Crockett's second reincarnation would occur twenty years later. Meanwhile, he'd risen from local officeholder to three-term U.S. Congressman and national celebrity. A reason: he was exactly the kind of fellow Americans were going for — a garish eccentric from the section then building power under Andrew Jackson. Speeches and tall tales attributed to him, whether justifiably or not, were cited as his typical frontier talk.

An instance: his name as a hunter even spread among the animals. So the minute a treed raccoon recognized him, it yelled, "Don't shoot! I'm a-comin' down!" And though political opponents spread anecdotes about his horrible gaucheries, he and his backers played up a favorite democratic paradox — that if a man has experience and horse sense, a lack of book learning actually helps him be smart and amusing. So he coined a personal motto perfect for flush times: "Be sure you're right, then go ahead." And his warning to his constituents was terse and clear: "Vote for me or not; but if you don't yawl can go to hell and I'll go to Texas."

Ed. Michael A. Lofaro and Joe Cummings. Knoxville: University of Tennessee Press, 1989.

72

They didn't, he did, and his death fed posthumous fame that promptly took the form of a second comeback. During two decades a play about him, *The Lion of the West*, showed him still boasting, storytelling, and cracking wise. Gossip, books about him (some purportedly his), and minstrel show songs sung countrywide repeatedly told about his exploits.

Most notably, Crockett almanacs, published for every year from 1835 to 1856 in Boston, New York, and other cities, told not only old anecdotes about him but many new ones about travels and adventures of his that took place years after the Alamo fell. Over fifty almanacs were published, and these illustrated pamphlets — the calendars, weather forecasts, feature sections, and comic books, so to speak, of that day — had huge readerships: few homes were without one.

And for them, journalists concocted some of the best and most often repeated tall tales about Davy; e.g., one about his deflecting Halley's comet from a collision course and one about his unfreezing the earth's axis one cold morning by pouring bear oil onto it, thus saving the planet and all its flora and fauna a couple of times.

Between 1871 and 1896, writings of two then very popular sorts brought another Crockett recycling. Six Beadle & Adams dime novels, chiefly about the hero's hunting exploits, fetched legions of childish buyers of all ages. And a melodrama, *Davy Crockett; Or, Be Sure You're Right*, was a vehicle for an admired actor, Frank Mayo, that had more than two thousand performances before Mayo's death ended its run.

Paying minimal attention to biographical facts, this dramatization turned Davy into one of nature's noblemen — one who strikingly resembled Natty Bumppo and who even, like Natty, forsook his dialect at crucial times. In one big scene, for instance, a pack of ravenous wolves tried to break down a cabin door and dine on him and the heroine. Davy vowed he'd hold it closed all night by using "the strong arm of a backwoodsman" for a bar, did so, and only after hours remarked, "this is kind of monotonous."

And when, on a stallion, he rescued the girl from an unloved groom, he hollered, "Whoop, I'm Lochinvar! Who dares to follow?" The script was so much admired that in 1916 it was recycled into a movie starring matinee idol Dustin Farnum.

Between 1954 and 1956, the most awesome of all the Crockett resurrections so far triggered a national craze. A popular new toy — television — brought into American homes a Disney Studio series about Crockett, with its haunting theme song. The program attracted an obsessed viewing audience of parents and their many baby-boom offspring, ripe for exploitation by modern merchandisers.

Everybody had to watch telecasts in which big, handsome Fess Parker, as Davy, played a role sort of based upon the historic frontiersman's biography and the legends about him, gussied up for mid-1950s viewers. As portrayed, Crockett now and then was a humorist, but more often he was so wise, noble, brave, athletic, and ept as a hunter and warrior that he seemed rather too good to be true. More memorable as a comic character was his sidekick, Georgie Russel, played by Buddy Ebsen, later a star clown in "Beverly Hillbillies."

The spinoffs were prodigious. Every Spock-marked kid had to have a coonskin cap, and raccoon-tail prices shot up 1,900 percent. Three thousand other Crockett items amassed huge sales — seven million records of that theme song, for instance; millions of new books and reprints of old ones; an industry with a total gross of $400 million in two and a half years.

In 1960, a little late to partake in Davy's Disneyfied resurrection, John Wayne produced, directed, and starred in *The Alamo*, which recreated Crockett in the Duke's own blowsier (and historically more accurate) image. The movie, the show, and scores of woodcuts, drawings, and paintings had convinced many viewers that they knew for a fact one thing about the battle of the Alamo: that Davy had died heroically during the siege.

But in the 1970s, several reputable scholars reexamined some previously discounted old evidence and uncovered some new evidence with startling results. They decided that — though no less heroically — Davy actually had been killed after the fortress had been taken that fateful morning. When Dan Kilgore, a former president of the Texas State Historical Association, offered strong support for this thesis in *How Did Davy Die?* outraged Crockettophiles fiercely attacked him and suggested that he and others who agreed with him were probably atheists, Communists, or intellectuals, or maybe all three.

The roundhouse swings some Texans took at Kilgore's book suggest how Crockett's latest reincarnation differs from the earlier ones. Each earlier postmortem reincarnation had been appropriate for its period. In the 1830s, '40s, and '50s, a comic demigod was popularized by tall tales that the man himself, his acquaintances, political backers, political opponents, newspaper reporters, and almanac makers told about him. In the 1870s, '80s, and '90s, the updated Davy was a sentimental and sensationalized creation of melodrama and dime novels. In the 1950s and '60s, affectionate heroic portrayals in television series, motion pictures, comic books, cartoon strips, and popular biographies gave the world the idol of the masses, the "King of the Wild Frontier."

As early as 1927, Vernon L. Parrington, in the second volume of his in many ways admirable *Main Currents in American Thought*, had noticed that two representations of Crockett contrasted sharply. One was of "the real man" — a "wastrel," "an assertive, opinionated, likable fellow, ready to fight, drink, shoot or brag, the biggest frog in a very small puddle, first

Davy Crockett Blair and Mike Fink Blair

among the Smart Alecks of the canebrakes." The other was the mythical Davy—"a deliberate fabrication," Parrington believed, resulting from "the exploitation of Davy's canebrakes waggery, the exploitation of his anti-Jackson spleen, and the exploitation of his dramatic death at the Alamo."

In the years that followed, other writers studied contradictory portrayals of Crockett and decided that reasons for disparities were more complex, even, than Parrington had claimed. "The real man," for instance, had been more of a mixture of admirable and not so admirable traits. And the "mythic" Davy was the product not only of "exploitations" but also of imaginative tales spread by different kinds of narrators—fireside yarn-spinners, East Coast almanac makers, newspaper feature writers, and the authors of cinema and television scripts.

Two kinds of reactions to the contrasting representations resulted.

Members of one group championed one kind of picturing and attacked other picturings. James A. Shackford, the author of *Davy Crockett: The Man and the Legend* (1956), the best account so far of the life of the historic Crockett, did his best to say some kind things about the mythical Davy but, in the end, dismissed him in favor of his own documented representation of "the man himself." And during subsequent decades, admirers of "the mythical Davy"—in fact both admirers and some detractors of contrasting versions of "the mythical Davy"—have voiced resentment toward those who differed with them.

A second kind of response has been the one embodied in recent symposiums and books, including *Davy Crockett at Two Hundred.* Typically, its practitioners are eager to sort out historical facts and fanciful legends and, as appreciatively as possible, to explore the significance of both. The first two chapters of Richard Boyd Hauck's *Crockett: A Bio-Bibliography* (1982) are entitled "The Facts" and "The Fictions." *Davy Crockett,* edited by Michael A. Lofaro and published in 1985, reveals its concerns by its subtitle, *The Man, the Legend, the Legacy, 1786–1986.* And a book of the same year much concerned with Crockett, the fat, handsomely illustrated *Alamo Images,* edited by Susan Prendergast Schoelwer with Tom W. Glaser, has as its appropriate subtitle *Changing Perceptions of a Texas Experience.*

Mike Fink in Legend and Story

In both oral and printed narratives, Mike Fink cavorted precariously on a line between history and legend or between folklore and more sophisticated fiction.

Some material classifies pretty safely as history. There is, for instance, the oral testimony of one Claudius Cadot of Scioto County, Ohio (born in 1793), set down on the basis of an interview by James Keyes in his *Pioneers of Scioto County: Being a Short Biographical Sketch of Some of the First Settlers of Scioto County, Ohio* (Portsmouth, 1880), pp. 3–4:

> When the war [of 1812] was ended Claudius went on the river to follow keel boating for the purpose of raising money to buy a piece of land. Keel boating on the river was the only place where a man could go to earn money at all; and the wages paid was very low even there. The first boat he applied to was commanded by the celebrated Mike Fink. The boat belonged to John Finch who was one of a company that run keel boats from Pittsburgh to all the various points in the west. Fink eyed young Claudius very closely, and asked him if he could push. Claudius replied that he could try. So Fink, liking the appearance of the young man, agreed to give him 50 cents a day, that being the wages for a common hand on the Ohio at that time. Claudius soon learned the art of keel boating and stayed with Fink a long time. As he went on to the river to make money, he did not spend it as fast as he got it, which was the usual practice among boatmen at that time. He very soon acquired a considerable pile, all in silver. He got Mike to put it in his trunk for safe keeping. Mike observed to him as he had the biggest pile he ought to carry the key.
>
> It was the usual practice among boatmen at that time when they

Half Horse Half Alligator: Growth of the Mike Fink Legend, ed. Walter Blair and F. J. Meine. Chicago: University of Chicago Press, 1956.

landed at a town to go up into town and get on a spree. Mike Fink was as fond of spreeing and rowdying as any of his hands, and it was always necessary for some one to stay with the boat. Claudius, not choosing to spend his money in that way always remained with the boat, which suited him better than spending his money in drinking and carousing, and was very satisfactory to the captain and the rest of the crew.

Mike Fink was a very noted character in his day. He could scarcely be called a good man, although he had some good traits in his composition. He was one of the most wild and reckless rowdying men of his class. Yet he had respect for a man of different habits, and when a man like Claudius Cadot, whose sole aim was to do his duty and save his money [worked for him], Fink placed greater confidence in him and gave him greater privileges than the rest of his crew. When he paid him at the end of the year he gave him sixty two and a half cents a day, when the bargain was for only fifty cents a day.

Mr. Cadot followed keel boating four years, during which time he saved money enough to purchase a quarter section of land and settle down to the life of a farmer.

This bears evidence of authenticity partly because of its context, partly because of its picture of Mike as an intelligent businessman is somewhat at odds with the popular conception of Fink which was contemporaneous with it. Yet it is possible that even this apparently straightforward reminiscence is touched by the lore about the boatman, since it makes a great deal of Mike's constant roistering — one of the most persistent motifs in tales about him.

A similar reminiscence of eighty-two-year-old Captain John Fink appears to be a compound of history and legend. Also based upon an interview — this one in 1887 — it was published in the Ohio Centennial Edition of Henry Howe's *Historical Collections of Ohio* (Columbus, 1888), 1:321–22:

Capt. John Fink in his youthful days arose bright and early. He was smart, and so he got to Bellaire long before the town; indeed, officiated at its birth. He was born in Pennsylvania in 1805. Mike Fink, the last and most famous of the now extinct race of Ohio and Mississippi river boatmen, was a relative, and he knew Mike — knew him as a boy knows a man. "When I was a lad," he told me, "about ten years of age, our family lived four miles above Wheeling, on the river. Mike laid up his boat near us, though he generally had two boats. This was his last trip, and he went away to the farther West; the country here was getting too civilized, and he was disgusted. This was about 1815.

"In the management of his business Mike was a rigid disciplinarian; woe to the man who shirked. He always had his woman along with him, and would allow no other man to converse with her. She was sometimes a subject for his wonderful skill in marksmanship with the rifle. He would compel her to hold on the top of her head a tin cup filled with whiskey, when he would put a bullet through it. Another of his feats was to make her hold it between her knees, as in a vice, and then shoot."

Here some new facts have the appearance of being part of the informant's recollection — that Mike "generally had two boats" and that he at one time moored his boat near Wheeling. The claim that Mike went "to the farther West" in 1815 seems dubious unless (as is possible) it means that Mike thereafter operated only on rivers west of Wheeling. Also, Mike's sternness as a disciplinarian is in contrast with the usual picture of him.[1] But the rest of the interview is based upon widespread stories about Mike and his women, except for one detail which, according to Victorian standards, had been considered too horrible to record[2] — that he tested his girlfriend's faithfulness by shooting a cup held between her knees.[3]

A purported interview with an old-time boatman, Captain Jo Chunk, published in 1837, classifies as legend. It appeared in a publication not noteworthy for historical accuracy, a *Crockett Almanac.* Chunk was quoted as saying, "There ain't a boatman on the river to this day but what he strives to imitate him [Fink]. . . . Mike was looked upon as a kind of king among the boatmen, and he sailed the prettiest craft there was to be found about these 'ere parts." The information may be correct, but it is also quite in line with tradition. Chunk's further claim that Mike was "the first boatman who dared to navigate a broad horn down the falls of the Ohio" almost certainly is fiction or legend rather than history.[4]

These reminiscences, true and legendary, not only represent the tendency of fantasy to mingle with fact, they also, it happens, give us almost all the information available concerning Fink's skill or activity as a boatman.[5] Mike's fame rests upon other talents. As one historian, quoting Mike's traditional challenge, remarks, Mike has "left the record, not that he could load a keelboat in a certain length of time, or lift a barrel of whiskey with one arm, or that no tumultuous current had ever compelled him to back water, but that he could 'out-run, out-hop, out-jump, throw down, drag out, and lick any man in the county.'"[6] One reason may be that the stories as a rule were recorded by writing fellows who knew little about boating. A more important reason probably is that the most memorable stories dealt with something more significant — Mike as an archetype and as a heroic figure.

Since the development of the backwoodsman and of his kin spirit, the boatman, as a type, has been traced and documented elsewhere,[7] we shall merely sketch it here. The story starts in the early days of the nineteenth century when the Kentuckian or the backwoodsman, as the generic frontiersman was called, became as well known a type as, say, the stingy Scotsman in many anecdotes of today. He was, in general belief, a man who was lawless, ignorant, rough mannered, strong, a heavy drinker, and a ferocious fighter. Story after story so pictured him. Later, when former Indian scouts, ex-Revolutionary soldiers, and fugitives from the law or the plow found that boating offered the roughest adventures and the best tests of a man's toughness, boatmen won fame as a breed of super-Kentuckians. "With the freer ways of the waters," as Constance Rourke suggests, "the boatman perhaps emerged more quickly as master of his scene than the backwoodsman."

When, eventually, western settlers became worried about their reputation, there was, on occasion, a tendency to suggest that the Kentuckians had been maligned because they had been confused by outsiders with the more savage men of the rivers. In 1830, for instance, Mathew Carey wrote:

> the character of the citizens of Kentucky . . . is on the whole estimable. . . . I am well aware that it by no means corresponds with the prejudices of the generality of the citizens of the other states. . . . One circumstance which tends to perpetuate the prejudice is the conduct of the Kentucky boatmen on the Ohio and Mississippi, some of whom appear to pride themselves on the roughness and rudeness of their manners — "half horse, half alligator, &c."[8]

And James H. Perkins, writing on "The Pioneers of Kentucky" in 1846, said:

> The first settlers of Kentucky have had no little injustice done them, in consequence of the existence at a later period of a class of "river men," who became, in the view of many, the representatives of the whole race of pioneers. But nothing could be more unlike the boasting, swearing, fighting, drinking, gouging Mike Finks than Boone, Logan, Harrod, and their comrades, the founders of the commonwealth.[9]

The indication is that there was a succession of type portrayals: first the Kentuckian or backwoodsman emerged; then an attempt was made to transfer his fame, such as it was, to the boatmen. When Mike Fink rose to preeminence among the boatmen, he became the personification of their qualities. As Leland D. Baldwin has remarked:

> Mike Fink was the archetype of the western boatmen. [As we read about him] from the depths of our easy chairs we . . . follow

him in his relaxations of raiding camp meetings, battling with berserk rage against other mighty "gougers," shooting the tin cup from his comrades' heads, and chasing the spangled skirts of New Orleans. Boastful, blasphemous, and brutal, save for rhetorical purposes he acknowledged no code nor deity not of his own making — that is, none beyond the spirits that dwelt within the whisky jug. With this familiar oracle ever waiting at his elbow to be consulted Mike toiled and rollicked and gouged his way through the world. . . .[10]

Baldwin's summary of the stories is excellent. The accounts we have of Mike's victories in single combat, to be sure, are more generalized than we would like. Time and again, we are told that the red feather in his hat — and his boasts — proclaimed him king bully-boy of the rivers. We are told that when he was stimulated by whiskey — and we are instructed that he could drink a gallon a day without staggering — he was able to "clear three ball rooms" and to lick two New Orleans gens d'armes sent to arrest him. But the most extensive stories are those which tell of his defeats. One account of a fight, said to have been published between 1824 and 1826, we have been unable to find: it may be an exception.[11] A few stories, recorded only recently, tell of victories. For the rest — in stories at least — he was humbled by Peter Cartwright, Jack Pierce, the sheriff of Westport, and probably others. (It may be worth noticing that all these tales came late in the development of the legend.) When he and his crew were involved, they came out better, notably in the narratives of Field and Bennett. But in at least one late unprinted story, he and his crew suffered ignominious defeat.[12]

Other stories about Fink during his period as a boatman for the most part tell of his brutal or lawless practical jokes and his marksmanship, often in combination. Early and late, we hear of his unchivalrous treatment of his wenches. We hear often of his shooting off a Negro's heel for the fun of it, and one story tells how he shot off an Indian's scalp lock. We learn of his playfully stealing some of the cargo with which he had been entrusted and of his making a mockery of law courts on several occasions. So he emerges from a whole series of anecdotes and tales as a boatman's boatman — a champion of the unrestrained and unrestrainable roughnecks.

The nature of the stories, and the attitudes which they reveal, cast an interesting light upon the Americans who cherished them. As Daniel C. Hoffman remarks:

In a folk group the areas of shared interest and common sympathy encompass almost the whole of the people's lives. Hence, from their socially accepted stories we can infer a great deal about the ways in which members of a group look at their relationships to each other, to nature, to the supernatural, and to others outside the group. In short, we can generalize from the folk tale about the society which it represents.[13]

In Fink we have, in Constance Rourke's words, "one of those minor deities whom men create in their own image to magnify themselves." In the tales about this savage and lawless brawler, his creators were either tolerant or actually adulatory: "Many of the tales exhibited the broad, blind cruelty of the backwoods; yet many of them insisted that Fink was good."[14] A British critic comments: "He endeared himself as a lawbreaker to men who were hindered by the law in exploiting the lucrative possibilities of the frontier; and he was the more admired for being as distinguished as a drinker as he was as a gunman."[15] And Bernard DeVoto furnishes an excellent summary:

> The boatmen were the sublimate of frontier hardness. And America, incurably artistic, demanded a culture hero. Mike Fink . . . became the symbol. The legend of Mike Fink is the boatman apotheosized. He was the marksman who could not miss, the bully-boy who could not be felled, unmatchable in drink, invincible to wenches. He was a Salt River roarer. . . . To the admiration of the frontier, he shot the protruberant heel from a nigger's foot or the scalplock from an Indian's head. He fought a thousand combats, whose resonance increases through the years till they are hardly separable from Paul Bunyan's. He was superior to the ethics of timid souls and no court restrained him, though, for a favor, he might ride to one in a keelboat pulled by oxen. . . . His purer escapades rippled across the nation. . . . The water fronts of three thousand miles cherished the less printable stories of a frontier Casanova. Casanova, together with Paul Bunyan, merges into Thor, and Mike is a demigod of the rivers even before he dies — the boatman immortally violent, heroic, unconquerable.[16]

The final sentence in the paragraph by DeVoto introduces another way in which the stories were shaped, since it compares Mike with several mythical heroes. As early as 1828, Morgan Neville (partly for literary reasons) had compared the river champion with another assortment of such figures — Hercules, Roland, "the favourite Knight of the Lion Heart," and Rob Roy. Thereafter his name was frequently linked with that of Hercules. J. M. Field in 1844 compared him with Jason and "a river god." In 1933, a British admirer saw him doubling "the character parts of two national heroes — the strong man, Kwasind, and the great boaster, Iagoo . . . like Iagoo he was a great story-teller."[17] Beyond the resemblance to particular heroes, however, there is a resemblance to the typical hero. Although the tales about Fink were never fused into a saga or an epic,[18] one may say of them what Richard M. Dorson has said of the stories of Davy Crockett, that in many ways they "possess the leading motives and conform to the growth structure of all Old World heroic story."[19]

Fink, like Old World heroes, is (to quote Dorson) "a mighty hero whose fame in myth has a tenuous basis in fact." He does not have a "remarkable birth" but he has "precocious strength," which enables him to handle a rifle, to take part in the defense of the Fort Pitt stockade, and to become a ranger at an early age. He utters "vows and boastings" in story after story, and these parallel in many ways the vauntings of ancient heroes.[20] One of his boasts, in an 1838 almanac story, runs: "I've got the handsomest wife, and the fastest horse, and the sharpest shooting iron in all Kentuck." This follows the formula of "pride of the hero in his weapons, his horse, his dog, his woman"—and the personal name Mike has for his gun, "Bang-all," or "Old Bets," also is in the tradition. "From precocious infancy," says Dorson, ". . . the heroic life cycle is apt to follow an established pattern embroidered with fierce hand-to-hand encounters and conquests, ardent wooings, travels in far lands, and superhuman exploits"—and again the parallel is clear.

Finally: "A fundamental requirement of heroic legend is some means of terminating the career of the unconquerable hero in a way that crowns rather than mars his record. Accordingly death, characterized always by a strong sense of fatalism, comes through supernatural decree or artifice, through treachery or overwhelming odds; omens, visions, warnings, and portents inform the champion that his time is up," says Dorson. Fink died an extraordinary assortment of deaths. When he left the rivers to go to the Far West, it was something like a defeat and a departure for Valhalla. Then came a death which, according to the earliest accounts of it, was sordid enough. But as time passed, folk fancy and the fancy of fiction writers changed the story time after time, bringing it closer to the patterns of the heroic story. Field in 1844 had Mike treacherously killed because he pleaded for understanding from a man who was afraid of him. In 1847, Bennett had an old crone, who was a fortuneteller, predict the dire event. In 1847, also, Field, in another account, had a superstitious character, Jabe Knuckles, issue a series of cryptic warnings, while a chain of strange coincidences and vengeful pursuits led to three interrelated deaths, of which Mike's was one; "as if," he said, "fate had but one end reserved for all those who through life had been woven in his checkered history." And many others modified the account in a variety of ways.

Of course there were divergences from the pattern which were unmistakably American. The Old World heroic story was about royalty: these stories were about a king, but a king of keelboatmen. The society of the American stories had as its equivalent for the central hall or gathering place the deck or the cabin of a keelboat or the brothels of New Orleans. And many of the elements were comically represented: the boasts and the vows were consciously comic, and so were the accounts of many of the super-human deeds. Even in its Heroic Age, America was too sophisticated, or perhaps too lacking in the sense of religion, to take all the heroic ingredi-ents without a pinch of salt or a dash of pepper. Yet the tales, relieved though they were by laughter and satire, conformed to many of the tradi-tions of ancient mythology.

In the field of "respectable" American fiction during the years of Mike Fink's waxing fame, the giants were Washington Irving, Nathaniel Haw-thorne, James Fenimore Cooper, and Herman Melville. These may seem to be pretty remote from the relatively "unrespectable" writers who wrote about the legendary boatman, yet they had some relationships. Irving showed how legends such as "Rip Van Winkle" (1819), "The Legend of Sleepy Hollow" (1820), and "The Devil and Tom Walker" (1824) could be adapted to the American scene; and in "A Tour of the Prairies" (1835), *Astoria* (1836), and *Adventures of Captain Bonneville* (1837), he used life in the Far West as his subject matter. Hawthorne, too, between 1830 and 1851, discovered the attractions and the possibilities of native legends. Cooper in his Leatherstocking novels (1823–41) and other writings wrote vastly popular narratives, with a legendary quality, about frontiersmen and Indians. Melville in his picaresque travel romances and his sea stories recorded the comic adventures and wanderings of common sailors; here and elsewhere he frequently referred to the West;[21] and in *Moby-Dick* (1851) he wrote what several discerning critics have seen to be a superbly trans-figured tall tale.

And during the first half of the nineteenth century these great writers as well as lesser ones were much concerned with theorizings about fiction which shaped the forms of the writings about Fink. They were worried, for instance, about finding ways to give their writings a national colora-tion and (astonishing though it now seems) about the possibility of find-ing characters who were distinctly American.[22] In time, they managed to see that, although Americans did not divide into classes like those of the Old World, they did divide into sectional and occupational classes which were somewhat analogous. "We do most seriously deny," wrote the critic W. H. Gardiner belligerently in 1822, "that there is any . . . fatal uniform-ity among us. . . . We boldly insist that in no country on the face of the globe can there be found a greater variety of specific character than is at this moment developed in these United States." He asks rhetorical questions, providing instances: "Is the Connecticut pedlar, who travels over mountain and moor . . . the same animal with the long shaggy boatman 'clear from Kentuck' who wafts him on his way over the Mississippi or the Ohio? . . . Is there no bold peculiarity in the white savage who roams over the remote hunting tracts of the West?"[23] Gardiner was not unique in seeing boatmen as a class to be pictured imaginatively. Ralph Waldo Emerson in "The Poet" (1844) spoke of "our boats" as part of the "incomparable materials" available for American poetry. And in 1860, Walt Whitman in "Our Old Feuillage," talking of the "free range and diversity" within the unified nation, gave this picture among others of similar classes:

> On rivers boatmen safely moor'd at nightfall in their boats under
>   shelters of high banks,
> Some of the younger men dance to the sound of the banjo or fiddle,
>   others sit on the gunwale smoking and talking. . . .

Longfellow in "Evangeline" (1847) made his heroine's lover a rather ethereal boatman and trapper in the Far West.

But most critics and authors tended to feel that members of such groups were unsatisfactory as main characters in novels or poems. Gardiner said of the "varieties of specific character" he had discovered that they were proper for a minor fictional form, "the popular and domestic tale." "But where," he asked, "are your materials for the higher order of fictitious composition? What have you of the heroic and the magnificent?" The trouble, he implied, was that there were no buildings in America with antique associations, and, although the forests were magnificent, "they are connected with no legendary tales of hoary antiquity." Thus like many writers of his day, including Cooper and Hawthorne,[24] he was worried about America's brief past.

These attitudes meant two things about the writings on Fink—that they were likely to be brief and unpretentious rather than long and heroic, and that they would do what could be done to give him at least a touch of antiquity. Essays, tales, and anecdotes—rather than novels or epic poems—were used for most of the incidents in Mike's life. When he got into a longer fiction, such as Bennett's novel of 1848, though his name was in the title, he almost had to be, in accordance with the fashion, a minor character, disappearing from the book for chapters at a time, while a milksop hero and a peaches-and-cream heroine took over the stage. Or if he became the hero of a longer narrative—Field's serial of 1847, for instance—the novelette was destined to remain in its obscure place in a St. Louis newspaper, never to be published as a book. The popular tale was the place for such a lowly character.

Even in writing such tales, however, authors had a try at pushing

Mike back into the past. Beginning five years after his death, three stories and a play all took for their title or subtitle "The Last of the Boatmen," and it was customary for authors to use the phrase in writing about him. Actually he was nothing of the sort. As late as the year 1840, there were four hundred and fifteen arrivals of keelboats (presumably manned by boatmen) at Pittsburgh; and in 1847, some fifty-five keelboats were still plying the Mississippi. Keelboats were operated in numbers as late as 1885.[25] Why, then, this dubbing of Fink as "the last of the boatmen" by men who knew better? The reason probably is that the writers were trying to connect this fairly recent figure with a fairly remote age. "Last" was a favorite word during the era — as in *The Lay of the Last Minstrel* (1806), "The Last Rose of Summer" (1808), *The Last of the Lairds* (1826), *The Last of the Mohicans* (1826), "The Last Leaf" (1831), *The Last of the Foresters* (1856), and, in the form of a juvenile story, *The Last of the Huggermuggers* (1856). Edward Bulwer-Lytton, who knew a good thing when he found it, used the word in *The Last Days of Pompeii* in 1834 and thereafter in the titles of three of his novels.[26] Writers about Mike were doing what they could with the magic word to give the embarrassingly new fellow a little antiquing. The same desire doubtless led writers to compare him on numerous occasions with such ancient heroes as Hercules, Jason, Apollo, Roland, and others. One author had the gall to put words into Mike's mouth that were an elegy for the past — "Where's the fun, the frolicking, the fighting? Gone! gone! The rifle won't make a man a living now — he must turn nigger and work. If forests continue to be used up, I may yet be smothered in a settlement."[27] But most stuck at giving Fink words so incongruous with his reputation.

The narratives which gave him that reputation were shaped by two influences in addition to the theories about portraying such a character in fiction — the nature of their origin and the nature of the genre to which they belonged. The folklore from which many stories derived, as Ruth Benedict has pointed out, is often characterized by the use of authentic details: "Among any people . . . the pictures of their own daily life is incorporated in their tales with accuracy and detail. . . . People's folk tales are in this sense their autobiography and the clearest mirror of their life."[28] Furthermore, many of the stories were humorous. Particularly in a romantic period, humor tends to be antiromantic, emphasizing the incongruity between its characters and its style and the pretentious character and the ornate style of romantic writings. And in tall tales, mundane or even vulgar characters and diction are wonderfully incongruous with the soaringly imaginative scenes and happenings. As Bernard DeVoto has said: "The Fink stories belong to the category of legend — or fable, if you like, or folklore.

And yet . . . they are the vehicle of realism. Wearing the form of . . . humor, realism first enters American fiction; it is with the frontier humor that the realistic depiction of character first becomes a literary force. There had been before it no opposition to the swooning Angelinas, the bearded barons with pasts in piracy or bastardy, of our romance."[29] DeVoto somewhat overstates the case, but the claim that these stories and others like them were important in initiating the development of realism in fiction is a valid one.

The realism in the stories meant that these narratives gave emphasis to an important aspect of the westward movement elsewhere neglected. V. L. Parrington noticed this in relation to the lore about Crockett and Fink (of whom he disapproved):

> The crossing of the Appalachian barrier . . . was an undertaking that had fired the imagination. Romantic in spirit and scope, it was meanly picaresque in a thousand unlovely details. Plain men engaged in it, provident and improvident, hard-working and shiftless; heroes had a share in it, but blackguards and outlaws and broken men — the lees and settlings thrown off from the older communities — had a share as well. The world that provided a stage for the courage of Daniel Boone and the fighting qualities of George Rogers Clark bred also the Davy Crocketts and Mike Finks and Col. William [sic] Suggses, who discovered their opportunities for the development of less admirable qualities; and it engulfed in its depths a host of nameless adventurers who drifted into the wilderness settlements, drank and quarreled and begot children, . . . spread a drab poverty along the frontier.[30]

Parrington is possibly too severe with men such as Fink, and his implication that they scattered poverty as they went westward is subject to some doubt. Some of the rascals doubtless prospered tremendously. And they were important in the movement. When it came to fighting Indians, steering downstream, or battling upstream, and when it came to blazing trails into the wilderness, the roughnecks were as useful as the pious brethren, perhaps even more useful. As a British critic suggests: "it is not irrational to admire those of whom Mike was typical, for their defects were defects of qualities which were to make the frontier habitable for law-abiding but less enterprising citizens. They were reckless, and because they were reckless they were useful."[31]

One other literary aspect of the stories is worth a few words — the handling of dialogue. The theory of the time recognized that the use of dialect was one of the important devices for the depiction of low characters. Reviewing ten recent novels, Jared Sparks in 1825 found a new vogue of which he approved: "The actors . . . have not only a human but also a national, and often a provincial character . . . exemplified in modes of speech."[32] A few years later a Southern critic was telling authors that novelists' "success . . . as delineators of real life . . . is in proportion to the fidelity with which they copy the diction of whatever rank they introduce — of the vulgar, no less than the exalted."[33]

In the varied narratives about Fink, this injunction was quite faithfully followed. Mike had to follow frontier ritual and shout boasts, and writer after writer gave this champion of boasters the most imaginative boast he could concoct. He was reputed to be a witty tall talker, and throughout the stories there runs a fine stream of figurative speech mingled with earthiness — the typical amalgam of this kind of utterance. In an almanac of 1839, for instance, after telling how wonderful he is, he shouts, "and if any man dare doubt it, I'll be in his hair quicker than hell can scorch a feather." Following the idyllic elegy he is given to mouth in Thorpe's story of 1842, he gets back into character by saying, "If the Choctaws or Cherokee or the Massassip don't give us a brush as we pass along, I shall grow as poor as a strawed wolf in a pitfall." In Robb's story of 1847, he suggests, "Jest pint out a muskeeter at a hundred yards and I'll nip off his right hinder eend claw at the second jint afore he kin hum, Oh, don't!" He emerges from the tangled web of coincidences and improbabilities of Field's story in 1847 to say, "that cussed old cow . . . had the orfullest holler hind its shoulders you ever did see, and the old folks being petiklar careful about the crittur, they jest insisted that I should foller it around in wet weather and bale its back out. . . ." In Bennett's melodramatic novel of 1848, he addresses his crew: "Boys, this here's a night. . . . How the wind rolls and trembles about like a dying craw-fish, and sprinkles the water in your faces, my hearties; and all for your own good, too. . . . Why, ef it warn't for sech times like this what in natur would become on ye, my angels? . . . fur ye never git water nearer to ye nor the river. . . ." Even the pious biographer of the Rev. Peter Cartwright in his anecdote of 1850 gives Mike an appropriate speech: "By golly, you're some beans in a barfight. I'd rather set *to* with an old *he* in dog-days."

Passages such as these led Constance Rourke to say of Fink, "His language was one of his glories, matching his power to push a pole. The ear attuned to delicate melodies may hear only the roar. Yet a loosely strung poetry belongs to these apostrophes, and its elements are worth mastering."[34] "As a talker," agrees Mark Van Doren, "he is sublime."[35]

Here the American language began to bring about a revolution in American writing by finding its way into subliterature. Before the end of the century, Mark Twain, reared in a town by the Mississippi, was going to put it into literature to stay. Snatches of talk such as this make the reading of a fair share of these narratives about Mike Fink rewarding even today. Furthermore, these combinations of history and legend, of humor and of fiction—good, mediocre, and downright bad—teach the reader a great deal about our American past.

The Technique of
"The Big Bear of Arkansas"

I

The fine artistry of the fiction of Poe, Hawthorne, and Melville in pre–Civil War days has been analyzed by various critics. They have not, however, noted with comparable care the merits of some of the admirable humorous fiction written by more obscure authors active during the same period. The following comments on T. B. Thorpe's "The Big Bear of Arkansas" (1841),[1] long considered a masterpiece of Southwestern humor,[2] may suggest something about its artistic structure.

This is a story within a story. In other words, it employs a method similar to the one whereby Chaucer, Boccaccio, and many who followed them introduced a narrator and his audience, and then quoted the words of the narrator. Thorpe describes a group on a Mississippi steamboat, and then brings onto the scene Jim Doggett, the yarnspinner, and has Jim tell of his contest with the Big Bear.

A notable thing about Thorpe's handling of this form is the way he sets off various worlds involved in the story by identifying various groups and various scenes with these contrasting worlds. Furthermore, such contrasts become vital to the achievements of the narrative.

The opening paragraphs, which introduce Doggett's audience, depict a crowd which is composed of "men of all creeds and characters"—the rich Southern planter and the poor Yankee pedlar, "the Northern merchant and the Southern jockey—a venerable bishop, and a desperate gambler—the land speculator, and the honest farmer," and so forth. Such violent contrasts are emphasized in all the details about this "heterogeneous" crowd. And when Jim Doggett enters the social hall where this group is gathered, another disparity appears: he stands out from all of them.

Jim's monologue begins at the end of the second paragraph, and Jim,

Southwest Review 28 (1943): 426–35.

like Thorpe, suggests a contrast. "Perhaps," he begins, "gentlemen . . . perhaps you have been in New Orleans often; I never made *the first visit before,* and I don't intend to make another in a crow's life. I am thrown away in that ar place, and useless, that ar a fact. Some of the gentlemen thar called me *green* — well, perhaps I am, *but I arn't so at home;* and if I ain't off my trail much, the heads of them perlite chaps themselves wern't so much the hardest; for according to my notion, they were real *know-nothings,* green as pumpkin-vine — couldn't, in farming, I'll bet, raise a crop of turnips; and as for shooting, they'd miss a barn if the door was swinging. . . ."

Jim recognizes a difference between his audience and himself, and an even greater contrast between himself and the "perlite" New Orleans dudes. He has had trouble, he indicates, even talking to the New Orleans men. When they talk about "game," they do not mean "Arkansaw poker and high-low-jack" but fowl and wild animals, which Jim habitually calls "meat." Moreover, New Orleans game is "chippenbirds and shite-pokes" — "trash" that the people of Arkansas do not bother with. Jim mentions that the smallest bird he will shoot in his home state has to weigh at least forty pounds.

Arkansas, he goes on, is "the creation state, the finishing-up country. . . . Then its airs — just breathe them, and they will make you snort like a horse." A Hoosier mildly suggests that the mosquitos are a flaw. Jim admits that these are enormous, then defends them in a way which underlines the differentiation which he has begun to make between Arkansas and the rest of the world: Natives are as impervious as alligators to the gallinippers, and the only case of injury resulting from them that he knows about was to a Yankee. "But the way they used that fellow up!" exclaims Doggett, "first they punched him until he swelled up and busted; then he sup-per-a-ted, as the doctor called it . . . ; then he took the ager . . . ; and finally he took a steamboat and left the country." This setting apart of Arkansas from the rest of the world is summarized a few paragraphs later, when Jim quotes the remarks Squire Jones made after marrying an Arkansas couple: "Marriage according to law is a civil contract of divine origin; it's common to all countries as well as Arkansas. . . ."

II

Jim, however, is eventually going to tell a story with a setting and with characters even more splendid than those provided by Arkansas. As he attacks the Hoosier's remarks about mosquitos, Doggett mentions details in the scenery of his state in the order of their size. Not only are the mosquitos of the state large; "her varmints are large, her trees are large, her rivers are large." After that mounting scale, he comes to the bears of the creation state, and shortly he is suggesting that they differ not only from bears anywhere else but also from bears of any other time: "I read in history that varmints have their fat season and their lean season. That is not the case in Arkansaw, feeding as they do upon the *spontenacious* productions of the sile, they have one continued fat season the year round." It is when a "foreigner" asks, "Whereabouts are these bears so abundant?" that the storyteller gets to a specific mention of the greatest district in this marvelous country of Arkansas — "Shirt-tail Bend" on the Forks of Cypress — Jim's own place.

Shirt-tail Bend is at first described as "one of the prettiest places on old Mississippi," but a few sentences later such mild terms are dropped, and "the government ain't got another such piece to dispose of." Three months after planting, beets there may be mistaken for cedar stumps and potato hills for Indian mounds. "Planting in Arkansaw," says Jim, "is dangerous." Shirt-tail Bend is fittingly inhabited by Doggett, "the best bar hunter in the district"; his gun, "a perfect epidemic among bar"; his dog Bowie-knife, "acknowledged to be ahead of all other dogs in the universe," and an abundance of gigantic bears.

All this (half of the whole piece) is preparatory to the story of the bear hunt itself. It is at this point that two paragraphs of narrative interrupt Jim's talk. Here the scene is switched from the Forks of Cypress back to the social hall of the steamboat. Here several skeptics dispute with Jim about the existence of such a place as Cypress Forks, "particularly . . . a 'live Sucker' from Illinois, who has the daring to say that our Arkansas friend's stories 'smell rather tall.'" And one of the passengers says that, though he is no sportsman himself, he would like to hear Jim tell about a particular bear hunt.

Responding to the request for a bear story, Jim first mentions two ordinary bear hunts — ordinary, that is, for the Forks of Cypress — and then has an inspiration: "Stranger . . . in bar hunts *I am numerous*, and which particular one . . . I shall tell, puzzles me. There was the old she devil I shot at the Hurricane last fall — then there was the old hog thief that I popped over at the Bloody Crossing, and then — Yes, I have it! I will give you an idea of a hunt, in which the greatest bar was killed that ever lived, *none* excepted. . . ."

This is the Big Bear, who eludes the peerless Jim, his epidemic gun, and his incomparable dog, for two or three long years. As a rule, Jim mentions, a story of a Doggett bear hunt "is told in two sentences — a bar is started, and he is killed." "Once I met with a match though," he continues, "and I will tell you about it; for a common hunt would not be worth relating." In the account which follows, detail after detail shows this varmint eluding and outwitting Jim.

Meanwhile, the size of the bear has been noticed. Jim's first evidence is the claw marks he makes on a sassafras tree — marks which, experience has taught Jim, show "the length of the bar to an inch." This beast's marks are "about eight inches above any in the forest that I knew of. Says I, 'them marks is a hoax, or it indicates the damnest bar that was ever grown.' In fact, stranger, I couldn't believe it was real, and I went on. Again I saw the same marks, at the same height, and *I knew the thing lived.* That conviction came home to my soul like an earthquake."

Some details about hunting the bear, and about Jim's wasting away in flesh because of his frustration, come in before the size of the bear is mentioned again. This time, the creature is "a little larger than a horse." Next the preparations for the final hunt and the start of the hunt are described. During this hunt, when Jim sights the huge beast, he "looms up like a *black mist,* he seems so large." And when Jim shoots, the varmint "*walks through the fence* like a falling tree would through a cobweb." Thus, like beets and potatoes at Cypress Forks, the Big Bear grows at a terrifying rate.

The bear has reached his maximum size but not his maximum power. Earlier, telling how he pined away because the bear eluded him, Jim has mentioned briefly something quite disconcerting: "I would see that bar in everything I did; *he hunted me,* and that, too, like a devil, which I began to think he was." As bullets bounce off of the beast's head, the wonder grows; and when the bear unaccountably disappears in a lake and a she bear replaces him, says the hunter, "It made me more than ever convinced that I was hunting the devil himself."

Such weird thoughts are preparatory for the way, after growing to the size of a black mist, the Big Bear becomes a supernatural being. Doggett's last words about the monster are: "Strangers, I never liked the way I hunted, and *missed him.* There is something curious about it, I could never understand — and I never was satisfied at his giving in so easy at last. Perhaps, he had just heard of my preparations to hunt him the next day, so he just come in, like Capt. Scott's coon, to save his wind to grunt with in dying; but that ain't likely. My private opinion is, that that bar was an *unhuntable bar, and died when his time came."*

Thus the biggest bear in Shirt-tail Bend, which has the biggest bears in Arkansas, a state which itself is greater than any other country — such a bear in the end is slain not by bullets but by an inscrutable fate. And clearly everything in the narrative from the first sentence to this point is preparatory for this climax.

III

Noteworthy is the way the language used by Thorpe helps mark off the worlds of the story from one another. When Thorpe wrote, the language of literature or business differed much more from the vernacular language than it does now, and he effectively used contrasts in diction.

The first sentence in the story goes: "A steamboat on the Mississippi frequently, in making her regular trips, carries between places varying from one to two thousand miles apart; and as these boats advertise to land passengers and freight at 'all intermediate Landings,' the heterogeneous character of the passengers on one of these up-country boats can scarcely be imagined by one who has never seen it with his own eyes." The language of this sentence is factual, unimaginative — almost of the sort used in a steamboat advertisement such as the one quoted. In its structure, it is stilted, literary. The next sentence is similarly factual, even pedantic or literary in words and order; it ends with a figure of speech which is slightly more imaginative but trite and bookish: "Starting from New Orleans in one of these boats, you will find yourself associated with men from every state in the Union, and from every portion of the globe; and a man of observation need not lack for amusement or instruction in such a crowd, if he will but trouble to read the great book of character so favourably opened before him."

Next, about halfway in the first paragraph, as he begins to particularize this "book of character," Thorpe employs more informal diction — words closer to the vernacular — when he speaks of "the wealthy Southern planter, the pedlar of tinware from New England," a jockey, a land speculator, and the like. The list continues with a series of figurative nicknames bestowed in common speech (but not in dictionaries) on men of various states — "Wolverines, Suckers, Hoosiers, Buckeyes, and Corn-crackers, beside a 'plentiful sprinkling' of the half-horse and half-alligator species of men, who are peculiar to 'old Mississippi'. . . ." Thus in the second half of the paragraph, the progress in diction is similar to that in the first half: the change from the factual to the imaginative in the "elegant" prose is paralleled by a movement from the moderately informal diction to the commonplaces of vernacular speech in which the imaginative figures more and more. A few phrases at the end of the paragraph return to the stilted style of the beginning.

Something like the same movement in diction occurs in the second paragraph: there is a trend from stiff, unimaginative literary prose to more informal, more imaginative vernacular language. Here, it may be mentioned, the vernacular commonplaces start a good deal earlier — in a phrase in the first sentence. But throughout the paragraph, vernacular phrases occur more and more frequently until, at the end, there is a solid passage of oral (as opposed to bookish) speech. Moreover, the vernacular language progresses from various phrases which were widely used in the talk of the folk in 1841 to some very original phrases — from "horse," "screamer," "lightning is slow" (all commonplaces in frontier boasts), to such a phrase as "they'd miss a barn if the door was swinging, and that, too, with the best rifle in the country." Not only does the language become more picturesque, more inventive; it also becomes less grammatical, and its rhythms change to approximate those of ordinary talk.

As the story moves on from this point, there are infrequent interruptions in more formal language after various paragraphs in the vernacular; but after a while these (with the exception of two paragraphs) cease, and the vernacular only is used. With the exceptions noted, vulgar speech is employed almost to the end of the tale. At the conclusion, two paragraphs of literary language occur.

The appropriateness of such a handling of diction is indicated when one considers what is happening in the narrative while these changes in the language take place. The diction of the opening paragraphs appropriately sets off the civilized world, represented by elegant speech, from the Arkansas world, represented by Jim's vernacular. The gradations in the language, from the factual and formal to the highly imaginative, occur simultaneously with the shift of the story from commonplace New Orleans to the heterogeneous world of the steamboat then to the uniquely wondrous state of Arkansas.

After Arkansas has been described, and Jim has first mentioned Shirt-tail Bend, two paragraphs of relatively stilted prose offer a contrast to the flow of Doggett's salty chatter. They tell of the skepticism of the social hall group concerning Jim's claims about Cypress Forks. Hence, in something like the way the opening paragraphs of the story help emphasize a contrast between the rest of the world and Arkansas, these paragraphs help set off Shirt-tail Bend and its inhabitants. The final paragraphs of "literary prose," as will be indicated, also serve a purpose for which their style is appropriate. Thus Thorpe uses language, from beginning to end, in ways admirably adapted to help with the movement of his story.

IV

Three points about this narrative, in addition to those which I have noted, occur to me as possibly worth mentioning. The first has to do with a happening which occurs in Jim's yarn immediately after Doggett has fired and the Big Bear has "walked through the fence like a falling tree would through a cobweb." At this thrilling moment, says Jim, "I started after, but was tripped up by my inexpressibles, which either from habit, or the excitement of the moment, were about my heels. . . ."

The spectacle of Jim, at the great moment of his conflict with the supernatural bear, losing his pants is a notable achievement in the way of wild incongruity.[3] For the most splendid of the great bear hunters of the earth, at such a moment, to be tripped up by his "inexpressibles" is a calamity without a shred of dignity or, in some senses, appropriateness. And if, as the context makes possible, this is an act of malignant Fate, even Fate loses its dignity and splendor by using a low comedy expedient. It would be hard to conceive of a more complete descent from imaginative grandeur.

The second point has to do with the characterization of Doggett and its relationship to the narrative as a whole. The uniqueness of Jim's appearance and of his diction ties him up with the unique world of Cypress Forks and helps to contrast that world with the heterogeneous steamboat world. His way of emphasizing words, commented on by Thorpe and indicated by italicization, makes possible the stressing of important details in the story he tells — often details developing the patterns of increasing size which I have been tracing.

Other characteristics — Jim's good nature, his naive superstition, and his great talent for narration — motivate one of the most amusing developments in the narrative. This change may be traced by contrasting Jim's attitude at the beginning and at the end of his yarn.

When he starts, Doggett is jocose, humorous; his eyes sparkle as he flings in comic comments and playfully imagines details which are wildly improbable. For instance, he invents details about Cypress Forks with gusto, showing his expectation that they will arouse raucous laughter. But as he gets on with his story, there are fewer and fewer evidences of his being amused by his narrative. At the end of his yarn, says Thorpe, "our hero sat some moments with his audience in grave silence; I saw there was a mystery to him connected with the bear whose death he had just related, that had evidently made a strong impression on his mind. It was evident that there was some superstitious awe connected with the affair. . . ."

The picture is of a man who tells a beautiful lie — such a beautiful one that he convinces not only his audience but also himself. Fantastic Cypress Forks, which Jim has created out of sheer air, becomes a reality for him. By the soaring of his own eloquence, paradoxically enough, Jim is pulled into a confusion of the real and the imagined.

The final point has to do with Thorpe's conclusion, which, with the return to literary rather than vernacular language, comes down to earth and stays there but which sends Jim back to the world apart from ours that Doggett has been describing. Jim, so Thorpe remarks, is the first to break the silence following his tale: he makes the suggestion, generally adopted, that everybody liquor up before going to bed. Then comes this concluding paragraph:

"Long before day, I was put ashore at my place of destination, and I can only follow with the reader, in imagination, our Arkansas friend, in his adventures at the 'Forks of Cypress' on the Mississippi."

Johnny Appleseed Blair

Harris' Best

"Bill Ainsworth's Quarter Race"

Beginning late in the eighteenth century and for about a hundred years thereafter, quarter races were popular throughout the Old Southwest as sporting events and as subjects for sketches. Since these competitions ranked with cheaper sports such as cockfighting, deer driving, 'possum hunting, partridge netting, and gander pulling, they could be held even when hard times halted more expensive events. And they were run almost everywhere there were two horses (even plow horses), two riders, and two or more sportsmen eager to make a wager.

At the start they were simple affairs: horses and riders were lined up at a post from which they raced a distance of about a quarter of a mile; hence the name, although in time a race for a longer distance was also likely to be called a quarter race. In the early days, because such a contest could not be run on a proper race track, superb horsemanship was necessary. When the race was held in a clearing, the rider not only had to jockey for the lead but also had to steer his steed around boulders, logs, and stump holes. When it was held on unimproved village streets, deep dust or mud might make the going almost as rough; and pedestrians, wagons, and even entrants in simultaneous races hampered speedy movement. Godly citizens often took stern measures against such events. The trustees of Lexington, Kentucky, for instance, in 1798 levied fines "for firing guns and running horses within the bounds of the in-lots"; a few years later the folk of Greensboro, Alabama, literally threatened to shoot sportsmen who raced horses in the streets; and in 1821 the General Assembly of the sovereign state of Kentucky levied a ten-dollar fine for the running of horse races "on the public highways."

The contests were frowned upon by solid townsfolk for another reason — because a crowd that gathered for a quarter race, like any other frontier assemblage, was pretty sure to turn the affair into a social occasion.

The Lovingood Papers 1965. Knoxville: University of Tennessee Press, 1967, pp. 16–20.

Stump speeches, games of chance, shooting matches, foot races, no-holds-barred fights, and dances that were nearly as rambunctious erupted all over the place. Drinking parties too, of course. The remark of the Arkansas pioneer who said that she hadn't a drop of whiskey when she actually had a barrel of it indicated an attitude: "Why, goodness gracious! What do you reckon one barrel of whiskey is to me and my children when we're out of milk?"

Such affairs naturally appealed to the writers interested in color and action, particularly to George Washington Harris, a peerless chronicler of lively Southwestern functions. If a reminiscent passage that Harris wrote in 1846 is to be believed, by the time Sut's creator was fifteen he himself had "ridden a few quarter races" and knew a thing or two about guiding a horse over a dangerous course. Thereafter Harris must have watched many races in the Knobs and on the Knoxville track owned by his brother-in-law, Pryor Nance.

Like several other Southwesterners who later became well known as humorous writers, Harris started his career as a contributor to the *Spirit of the Times* by writing "sporting epistles," four of which were published in 1843. The first epistle of that year, though apparently not the first that Harris wrote, appeared on February 11 and was signed with his current pseudonym, "Mr. Free." It mentioned quarter racing as a sport that was being enjoyed around Knoxville during a time of "scarcity and pressure." A second, in the issue for April 15, was called "Quarter Racing in Tennessee," and recounted a recent race held at the Stock-Creek Paths "in that rare place for sport south of the Holston River, known as 'South America,'" between F. K.'s horse Little Breeches and W. R. B.'s Brown Mary. A third, in the June 17 issue, lamented the cancellation of spring races in Knoxville because of hard times and looked forward to the imminent running for the Peyton Stake in Nashville. The fourth, printed on September 2, mentioned the quarter race on July 4 in Tuck-a-Lucky Cove "between those notorious crowders, Terrapin and Snapping Turtle," "a fast thing, beyond all previous conception, and so extremely close, that the judges decided it a draw race."

Soon after, Harris began writing contributions that no longer pretended to be sporting reports, some in conventional—and rather stuffy—literary English and some in the vernacular. That he planned an even more ambitious venture was indicated by a Tennessee contributor to the *Spirit* for November 15, 1845, who announced that Harris and a contributor who signed himself "The Man in the Swamp" planned to collaborate on a book, *Smokey Mountain Panther*, "illustrative of the manners and customs of East Tennessee—containing an account of Bear and Panther fights, quarter racing, Card playing . . . etc."

The book, and hence the promised account of quarter racing, never appeared; but more than two decades later, in the Knoxville *Press and Messenger* for June 4, 1868, Harris published "Bill Ainsworth's Quarter Race." Here the humorist's creation Sut, who by now had become famous as a political satirist and spinner of yarns, recounts the great race of 1833 between Kate, Hunter's fast Alabama mare, and Ainsworth's even faster horse, Ariel.

This narrative, published late in Harris' career, in fact about a year before his death, in my belief and that of a number of other Sutologists, is the author's best. Edmund Wilson, Harris' most famous detractor, would, I assume, find our liking for this piece incredible. For if Wilson ever read this sketch, he would be hard put to it to find support in it for his description of a Sut who is "avowedly sadistic" and "a peasant squatting in his own filth." It is hard to believe that even Wilson's ineffable delicacy would be offended by the bits about "a mess ove boys stonein a sqirrel, up a tree"; some other boys "chasin out the hogs with dorgs"; Jo and Tom emerging from "jis a fis' fight, with sticks . . . with bloody heads an' no shirts"; or about Sut's difficulty, referred to but never specified, when he caught "a flea, or a bug, off a young lady." These, nevertheless, are the only touches that I can find that might distress even the nicest sensibility. Nor could Wilson cite this piece to justify his astonishing claim that "in the Lovingood stories . . . the fun entirely consists of Sut's spoiling everybody else's fun," since the only prank that the "peasant" mountaineer plays is that of avoiding the telling of a story that he has promised to tell. Can it be that in guessing wherein the humor of Sut's stories lies Wilson missed things rather important to Harris' admirers?

Not, I believe, entirely. Wilson does say in passing that "the language [of Sut] is often imaginative," then hastily darts away from this grudging concession. But the language is one of Harris' chief assets in this piece and elsewhere. One may see the quality of the language here with some clarity by comparing some of Harris' own words with those of Sut since, like Mark Twain, Harris became a far more original, zestful, and exciting stylist when he spoke with the voice of a vernacular character rather than with his own. Here is Harris' voice in a story published on September 17, 1868:

> Those of us who have not yet reached the ferry, so dreaded by many, yet anxiously looked forward to by the footsore and weary ones, who have passed but few cool fountains, or hospitable shelters, along their bleak road, must well remember the good old days of camp meetings, battalion musters, tax gatherings, and shooting matches. Well! there was the house raisings too, and the quiltings, and the corn

shuckins, where the darkey's happy song was heard for the last time. And then the moonlight dance in the yard. . . .

Compare Sut's voice in "Bill Ainsworth's Quarter Race," slightly more than three months earlier:

Ox carts . . . full ove har trunks an' kaigs, an' them full ove cider an' ginger cakes. While fat ole wimmen sot on top, in brass speks, an' frilled cap borders, kep' busy a drappin' fourpence ha'pennys into a black, press'd paper snuff box, with a red face an' cock'd hat, called the juke of Wellington, painted on the lid. While a favorit dater sot on the tail board, keepin off the flies with a green bush, lookin' soft an' sweet. . . . Young men, in their shirt sleeves, with the collar un-button'd, an' a fresh cut hickory club in their han's, slung'd roun', winkin' at the red daters ove the cake wimmen, or listen'd to Claib Nance, sittin' the porch, playin' "Billy in the low groun's," like no other man ever has, or ever will, play that tchune.

Both passages are expressions of nostalgia, an attitude that mellows Harris' writings far more often than casual readers might guess. But while the first passage is abstract and is spotted with clichés in the elegant mode, the second is concrete and easygoing. The details in the first are evocative only for those who have experienced "the good old days"; those in the second convey what was delightful even to the uninitiated. Exactly the right fragments in the scene are recalled to make unforgettable and wistfully appealing the fat old women, their snuffboxes (even — poignantly — the picture of Wellington on the cover), the "soft and sweet" daughters, the young men. Only when he talks of Claib Nance does Sut explicitly voice an attitude which carefully handled brush strokes in the rest of the passage already have conveyed.

A great charm of the entire sketch derives largely from a like choice and rendition of details throughout — a caressing of memories that the author obviously delights to recall. Again after all these years the two horses seem to live and breathe again: Kate, walking "with a limber, sassy step, that look'd like she cud step as fur again, if she wanted to," and Ariel, his muscles moving "onder his glossy grey hide like cats crawlin' onder a carpet." So do card players, women, girls, boys, young men, old men, athletes, the sheriff, the tax collector, the Negro woman by the old spring house, Hunter, Ainsworth, Wash Morgan, and the enraptured crowd which watches the contest. The lingering over details is so thorough and at the same time so delightful as to give a quality of gusto typical of the most ebullient member of a school of almost uniquely zestful authors. A community is re-created, some of its folk not in the least comic, some amusing, but all of them partaking of life and knowing and conveying the joy of simply being alert and alive.

Whether the somewhat complex effect should be called a humorous one may be debatable, but surely the sympathetic reader's enjoyment is closely allied to that of humor. In pictorial art, the nearest thing to Harris' achievement seems to me to be a sixteenth- or seventeenth-century Flemish painting of some lively village festival. In American writing, the nearest thing I know is one of Mark Twain's evocative picturings of life in an antebellum Mississippi river town.

Introduction to *The Sweet Singer of Michigan: The Collected Poems of Julia A. Moore*

Because 1876 marked the hundredth anniversary of American independence, in that year a group of patriotic Philadelphians erected some of the conventionally atrocious buildings used for expositions, jammed them full of sundry displays, and announced the Centennial. The nine million visitors who thronged the grounds were delighted with the sight of machines and their products and with the sound of florid patriotic songs and spread eagle oratory. The point made by most of the perspiring orators was that the United States was a very fine country.

Yet many a citizen would have been pleased to admit, even in that jubilant hour, that America had several things of which to be ashamed. Citizens might not have agreed on details, but the general conclusion of most Americans would have been that something was wrong. People were still talking of "Boss" Tweed and the Fisk-Gould fracas. Jesse James was still at large, and so was Brigham Young; the God-fearing folk of the seventies were inclined to class both heroes together and to suggest, in cracker box conclaves, that each should be hung. There had been a riot in Hamburg. Custer's gallant band had been massacred in a woeful fashion by the Indians, and the noble red men, having escaped to Canada, looked across the border and derisively thumbed their noses at the United States. Another matter for indignant discussion was the championing of an American poet by a group of English literary men, who claimed that he was ill and in need. But the man, as several critics pointed out, was a rank fake. His name was Walt Whitman.

Furthermore, marching clubs, led in torchlit night parades by brass bands, shouted to the world that if Rutherford B. Hayes was elected President the nation would be as badly off as it had been under Grant, or (in case the marchers happened to be Republicans) that Samuel Jones Tilden's election would blot out the results of the Civil War and put the Ku Klux

Chicago: P. Covici, 1928.

Klan into power. Another party, the Greenbackers, was sure that either Hayes or Tilden would send the nation to the dogs. Their leader, Peter Cooper, after making a fortune in iron and glue, had decided to save the poor people by becoming President. Later, Tilden was to be jockeyed out of the Presidency by political hokus pokus.

To add to the general uneasiness, a Prohibition Reform Party had been started, and in Ohio, a number of determined women were entering saloons and embarrassing bartenders and bibbers by praying earnestly with them. The custom, it was feared, might spread.

It was a climactic year of the period Mr. Don C. Seitz has felicitously styled "the Dreadful Decade." The age called for a singer, and a worthy lyricist responded, lifting a voice in praise of the Centennial, the Temperance Movement, Peter Cooper, the Chicago fire, George Washington, the Civil War, and other timely topics. The nation listened to her solemn songs — and doubled up with laughter. In the person of Julia A. Moore, the Dreadful Decade found its poet laureate.

Her rise to fame was sudden. She had been born Julia A. Davis, in Plainfield, Michigan, in 1847. Three other children had followed her, two sisters and a brother. Because her mother was an invalid, Julia had the task of managing the family, a task which became a harder one when, in 1857, the family moved to a hundred-acre farm near Algoma. Still, the young woman had time to attend school, some two miles from the farm, about half the time, and to write songs which she proudly described as "sentimental." The deaths of neighbors, stories she read in her histories and in newspapers, heroic gossip of Civil War deeds, and her own happy memories supplied her with subjects. The year 1876 found her married to a farmer named Moore, living humbly in a plain farm house near Edgerton, about to embark on the task of rearing a family of her own. More significant, from the standpoint of American literary history, was the fact that the year also found her preparing to issue, in honor of the nation's Centennial, a volume of her poems, the first book from the pen of "The Sweet Singer of Michigan."

In due time, the book issued from the press, modestly bound in paper covers, and adorned, more or less, with an engraving of the countenance of the author. The publisher, J. F. Ryder, of Cleveland, Ohio, sent copies to reviewers, accompanied by letters which said:

> Dear Sir — Having been honored by the gifted lady of Michigan, in being entrusted with the publication of her poems, I give myself the pleasure of handing you a copy of the same, with my respectful compliments.
>
> It will prove a health lift to the overtaxed brain; it *may* divert

the despondent from suicide. It should enable the reader to forget the "stringency," and guide the thoughts into pleasanter channels. . . . It *must* be productive of good to humanity.

If you have the good of your fellow creatures at heart, and would contribute your mite towards putting them in the way to finding this little volume, the thanks of a grateful people (including authoress and publisher) would be yours.

If a sufficient success should attend the sale of this work, it would be our purpose to complete the Washington monument.

The critics read, marveled, and wrote reviews which either frankly asserted that the book was a milepost in the history of bad poetry or which ironically praised the work as a masterpiece. One who reads the reviews finds them almost as pleasing as the book itself, for they are typical compositions of a school of rough American humor which began to come to fruition in 1876 when Mark Twain published Tom Sawyer. They made the most of the appearance of the engraving of the author. Bill Nye, starting his newspaper career in Wyoming, wrote:

the Muse was getting in its work . . . even while Julia was a little nut-brown maid trudging along to school with bare feet that looked like the back of a warty toad. In my visions I see her now standing in front of her teacher's desk, soaking the first three joints of her thumb in her rosebud mouth, and trying to work her off toe into a knot-hole in the floor, while outside, the turtle-dove and the masculine Michigan mule softly coo to their mares.

A portrait of the author appears. . . . There are lines of care about the mouth — that is, part way. . . . Lines of care will do anything . . . reasonable, but they can't reach around the North Park without getting fatigued. These lines look . . . as though the author had lost a good deal of sleep trying to compose obituary poems. The brow is slightly drawn, too, as though her corns might be hurting her. Julia wears her hair plain, like Alfred Tennyson and Sitting Bull. It hangs down her back in perfect abandon and wild profusion, shedding bear's oil over the collar of her delaine dress, regardless of expense.

Having disposed of the author's body, they turned to her poems, and wrote with wild enthusiasm. Said the *Rochester Democrat* of the book, "Shakespeare, could he read it, would be glad that he was dead. . . . If Julia A. Moore would kindly deign to shed some of her poetry on our humble grave, we should be but too glad to go out and shoot ourselves tomorrow." The *Chicago Tribune* asserted: "Mrs. Moore's fame . . . will live as it deserves in the memories of men. Joaquin Miller can hardly survive the test of competition." The *Hartford Daily Times* ejaculated: "To meet such steady and unremitting demands on the lachrymal ducts one must be provided, as Sam Weller suspected Job Trotter was, 'with a main, as is allus let on'. . . . We believe in the Sweet Singer of Michigan. To this author, manifestly all things are possible." The *Danbury News* pointed out that "each page" of this book "is a coal of fire on the altar of poesy." The author, said the *Connecticut Post*, had "presented a collection the like of which has never tested the strength of type before . . . well calculated to lift the broken heart, though unmercifully shattered; rare food for the lunatic. . . ." The *Post* critic offered some ingenious hypotheses concerning some of the author's cryptic lines. The *Pittsburg Telegraph* called Mrs. Moore the Great American Poet and tried to insult her by putting her in the same class with Walt Whitman. In the opinion of a writer on the *Worcester Daily Press* the poet was one "who reaches for the sympathy of humanity as a Rhode Islander reaches for a quahaug, clutches the tendrils of the soul as a garden rake clutches a hop vine, and hauls the reader into a closer sympathy than that which exists between a man and his undershirt."

From coast to coast, newspapers printed long reviews in which the comic men used Mrs. Moore's poems as springboards. The humorists were well qualified for their task of publicity. Be it said to their credit that, almost without exception, they saw the joke involved and cheerily passed it on with the solemn manners of a literary Charlie Chaplin. And each quoted many of the choicest lines in the songs. As a result, in 1878, when the author published a few new poems she was able to preface them with seventy-four pages of notices such as the above, which she apparently believed commendatory, and to assert of the book that, "although some of the newspapers speak against it, its sale has steadily progressed. Thanks to the Editors that has spoken in favor of my writings; may they ever be successful. . . . The Editors that has spoken in a scandalous manner, have went beyond reason. . . ."

Thanks, indeed, to these editors the work passed, apparently, through three editions, all of which sold well. *The Sweet Singer of Michigan Salutes the Public*, as it was first styled, or *The Sentimental Song Book*, as it was later known, was one of the poetic "best-sellers" of the time. When, however, in 1878, a new work, called *A Few Words to the Public With New and Original Poems by Julia A. Moore*, fluttered in its paper covers from the presses, the rage was over, and this defense of Mrs. Moore and this new collection of excellent poems apparently did not find the market they deserved. At any rate, she seems to have published no more poetry. The author, like Herman Melville, lapsed into a long period of silence, broken only in her last years when she published *Sunshine and Shadow*, a romance of the Revolution, in 1915. And when Mrs. Moore died at her home near Manton, Michigan, in June 1920, so thoroughly was she forgotten that her death created hardly a stir; even the *World Almanac,* which did not hesitate to record the death of "the world's heaviest woman," had nothing to say of the end of the life of the Sweet Singer of Michigan.

As anyone who gazes through the pages of her work can see with half an eye, Mrs. Moore deserved a better fate. Read without any thought of their historical setting, her songs endure the test of true literature by charming the reader. Considered against the background which made them possible, they present an interesting and vivid picture of a forgotten period in America's past.

One who wishes to know what the common Americans were singing at that time will find excellent hints in the tunes assigned for the musical rendition of many of Mrs. Moore's songs. John Robinson dies quite gracefully to the air of "The Drunkard"; the Page boys march to war and back to the tune of "The Fierce Discharge"; Grand Rapids is celebrated to the music of "Bright Alfaretta"; and the Temperance Reform Clubs carry on their glorious work in accompaniment to the dubious tune "Perhaps." "Three Grains of Corn," "The Major's Only Son," "The Texas Rangers" and many another favorite were embellished by Julia's words. In many a song, the influence of the Irish "Come All Ye" is very evident; this type of music probably inspired two of the Singer's most famous lines:

> Come all good people, far and near,
> Oh, come and see what you can hear.

But the creations serve a still more important purpose: they show what the people of Mrs. Moore's heyday were thinking. References to contemporary events and especially to contemporary attitudes bathe in light the psychology of the seventies.

One notes a patriotism in this post–Civil War period which is astonishing to us of this present jaded after-the-war period. There is a rejoicing in the sufferings of wartime heroes which is almost fiendish; there is a celebration of the Centennial which contrasts strikingly with the recent halfhearted celebration of the Sesquicentennial of the self-same nation, grown a little old and very fat. And the popular heroes of the period seem rather queer. The enthusiasm for cricket players and for George Washington we can understand; but the high-flown praise of Peter Cooper, Lord Byron, and Andrew Jackson daze us a little, especially as we note there is not a word of eulogy for Abraham Lincoln. We are reminded of the shock the nation sustained when it heard of the Ashtabula disaster, of the yellow fever plague in the South, of the Chicago fire, now dimly remembered. When the author takes a few cracks at the styles, we are on firmer ground, and the infrequent love songs make us feel quite at home. For the most part, however, the poems transfer us to a strange land which we can hardly recognize as our own. And of all the songs, the most frequent type of all seems the strangest: we are astounded and amused at the predominance of poems which treat the subject of death as if it were a delightful topic.

Yet of all the poems in the works of Mrs. Moore, these very obituary lyrics are the best mirror of contemporary psychology.

"In the early forties," says Miss Constance Rourke, in *Trumpets of Jubilee*, "the thought of death was breaking through into verse and hymns and common talk — not as mystery or as terror . . . but as drifting ease and escape. The new generation was floating on flowery beds of ease in happy anticipation, or seeking distant far-flung shores . . . as if present burdens were too heavy." Hence it was that Poe's songs and dialogues on tender death, the songs of the marvellously terrible Chivers and of others of the American graveyard school won wide acclaim. Hence it was that Harriet Beecher Stowe, in the forties, wrote with evident self-satisfaction: "As for my health, it gives me little solicitude; although I am bad enough, and daily grow worse. . . . It appears to me that I am not destined for a long life."

By the seventies, this joy in death had blossomed into common expression in delightful obituary poetry which flowered in newspapers large and small throughout the land. In 1870, Mark Twain wrote an article called "Post-Mortem Poetry," applauding the habit of the *Philadelphia Public Ledger* of printing obituary poems with death notices. He said:

> In Philadelphia, the departure of a child is a circumstance which is not more surely followed by a burial than by the accustomed solacing poetry in the *Public Ledger*. . . . There is an element about some poetry which is able to make even physical suffering and death cheerful things to contemplate and consummations to be desired. The element is present in the mortuary poetry of the Philadelphia degree of development.

G. Washington Childs, A. M., it appears, was the Philadelphia exponent of obituary art; when *The Sweet Singer* appeared, the *Hartford Daily Times* accused Childs of stealing inspiration from Mrs. Moore. In 1870, however, Mark Twain was able to quote an excellent obituary poem by M. A. Glaze, on the deaths of Samuel and Catharine Belknip's children, clipped, Clemens swore, from a country newspaper.

So typical was the love of death that when Clemens wrote *Huckleberry Finn*, he presented a picture of a girl who had been enamored of the subject, a daughter of Col. Grangerford. She made very dark pictures with such charming titles as "Shall I Never See Thee More Alas," with tombstones and weeping ladies for characters. And she amused herself by clipping "obituaries and accidents and cases of patient suffering" from the *Presbyterian Observer* and by writing poems of her own on death. Huck gives a specimen called "Ode to Stephen Dowling Bots, Dec'd," who fell into a well:

> They got him out and emptied him;
> Alas it was too late;
> His spirit was gone for to sport aloft
> In the realms of the good and great.

Common report has it that this poem was inspired by Mrs. Moore's poems, and in *Following the Equator* Clemens confessed that *The Sweet Singer* had brought him joy for twenty years. The book, he holds, "has the same deep charm for me that the *Vicar of Wakefield* has, and I find in it the same subtle touch — the touch that makes an intentionally humorous episode pathetic and an intentionally pathetic one funny." But there is no reason to suppose that Mrs. Moore, any more than any other great mortuary songster of her day, was the direct inspiration. In *Following the Equator,* Mark Twain compares to the poetry of Mrs. Moore a hilarious poem of his own, which he quotes. In addition he preserves some of Mrs. Moore's beautiful stanzas.

One finds many reflections of the obituary craze in the humorous writings of the period. If American humor performed any task aside from amusing people — and of course it did, as students of the beginnings of local color know — it was no more persistent and no more helpful in any of its performances than it was in its work of burlesquing the most unhealthy features of the hothouse American literature popular from about 1830 to 1880. The obituary poetry was a wide target for the shafts of the humorists, and a number of excellent parodies were committed.

Some of the poems by Charles Heber Clark (Max Adeler), published in *Out of the Hurly-Burly,* in 1874, for example, are first-rate. Clark told of an obituary writer hired by an editor who gave the following instructions:

Lighten the gloom. Do not mourn over the departed, but rather take a joyous view of death, which, after all, Mr. Slimmer, is, as it were, but the entrance to a better life. . . . Touch the heart-strings of the afflicted with a tender hand, and endeavor, for instance, to divert their minds from contemplation of the horrors of the tomb. . . . And at the same time combine elevated sentiment with such practical information as you can obtain from the advertisement. Throw a glamour of poesy, f'r instance, over the commonplace details of the everyday life of the deceased. People are fond of minute descriptions.

The description, be it noted, might well be applied to Mrs. Moore's songs of death. The obituary poet wrote best on the deaths of children. The death of the sheriff's daughter inspired this lay:

> We have lost our little Hanner in a very painful manner,
>> And we often asked, How can her harsh sufferings be borne?
> When her death was first reported, her aunt got up and snorted
>> With the grief that she supported, for it made her forlorn.
> She was such a little seraph that her father, who is sheriff,
>> Really doesn't seem to care if he ne'er smiles in life again.
> She has gone, we hope, to heaven, at the early age of seven
>> (Funeral starts off at eleven), where she'll nevermore have pain.

The following lament on the death of Willie won national approval, and is still remembered by those who cherish good song:

> Willie had a purple monkey climbing on a yellow stick,
> And when he sucked the paint all off it made him deathly sick;
> And in his latest hours he clasped that monkey in his hand,
> And bade good-bye to earth and went into a better land.
> Oh! no more he'll shoot his sister with his little wooden gun;
> And no more he'll twist the pussy's tail and make her yowl, for fun.
> The pussy's tail now stands out straight; the gun is laid aside;
> The monkey doesn't jump around since little Willie died.

In 1880, Eugene Field wrote "The Little Peach," which is evidently a parody of the same sort of poetry. That the man chiefly remembered as the author of "Little Boy Blue" should create such a biting satire on writing of the class to which his masterpiece belongs seems rather ironical; yet certainly "The Little Peach" is a telling parody:

> A little peach in the orchard grew,—
> A little peach of emerald hue;
> Warmed by the sun and wet with the dew,
>> It grew.
>
> One day, passing the orchard through,
> That little peach dawned on the view
> Of Johnny Jones and his sister Sue —
>> Them two.
>
> Up at that peach a club they threw —
> Down from the stem on which it grew
> Fell that peach of emerald hue.
>> Mon Dieu!

> John took a bite and Sue a chew,
> And then the trouble began to brew,—
> Trouble the doctor couldn't subdue.
>   Too true!
>
> Under the turf where the daisies grew
> They planted John and his sister Sue,
> And their little souls to the angels flew,
>   Boo hoo!

In 1882, Knox and Sweet, in *Sketches from Texas Siftings*, made the parody even broader by writing a touching obituary on a roast turkey, and Bill Nye, in 1884, in *Forty Liars and Others Lies*, took a sardonic fling at the death-of-a-little-child school by writing extravagantly of "The Vacant Chair of a Little Child." One who reads much of Nye's work cannot help discovering that many of his finest passages are brightened by phraseology from current obituaries. These hits at the "literary" obituary stand as interesting indications of the unholy eminence obtained by this form of writing in the period of *The Sweet Singer*.

If Mrs. Moore's poetry indicates the literary subject matter and attitude of the seventies, her "A Few Choice Words to the Public" are no less successful in their revelation of the popular literary philosophy. In Mrs. Moore's distinction between the poetry of the mind and poetry of the heart, we find a popularization of the romantic philosophy so gallantly espoused in England by Wordsworth, Coleridge, and their followers, and in America by the Transcendentalists. It was exactly the sort of an adaptation one would expect from average Americans, who memorized *Poor Richard's Almanac*, who were spurred to revolution by a pamphlet called *Common Sense*, and who always put kindness of intention and natural philosophy above "book l'arning." When Simon Suggs said: "Well, mother-wit kin beat book-larnin' at any game! . . . As old Jed'diah used to say, book-larnin' spiles a man ef he's got mother-wit, and ef he ain't got that it don't do him no good"—he voiced an opinion which, as Mrs. Moore indicates, should have been generally accepted by the common folk of America.

So much for the historical value of Mrs. Moore's works. Great though this value is, the Sweet Singer's poems are not lyrics of the sort which stand only when propped against a historical background. They have charms which lift them, if need be, out of time and space. Their greatest charm, I believe, is their naiveté. No one, evidently, ever suspected Mrs. Moore's poetry of being a hoax; no one ever should. In every line of her poetry and in every sentence of her critical prose, artlessness and ingenuousness are written in clear characters.

This quality of unaffected simplicity makes possible the childlike grammar, the youthful certainty, and the amazingly cheerful attitude for the poet in a world of deaths in smoking cars, demises caused by misguided pieces of roast beef, sad memories of youth that will "nevermore return again," Ashtabula disasters, and Chicago fires. It makes possible the unconscious incongruities which led Samuel McChord Crothers to say, "I have read every poem of the Sweet Singer with delighted surprise."

Only a natural singer could compose the following lines:

> Many a man joined a club
> That never drank a drachm,
> Those noble men were kind and brave
> They do not care _____

and surprise everybody by writing, in place of the two words which every second-rate poet would use to end the stanza, the far more felicitous words, "for slang." Only a genius could sing of "Little Libbie" without a thought of a smile, could praise a cricket club with fitting pathos, could jestingly color the story of a sleigh which upset by the use of gruesome suggestion, could write, in short, so many poems with a continuous sense of grandeur in humble things and great things alike. If these songs were only a little closer to the conventional modes of meter, rhyme, thought, and expression they would not impress us at all. Touched, however, by the magic wand of genius, the novel works of this great poet cause readers to slump down in their chairs, hold their agitated and aching sides, wipe tears from brimming eyes, and fill the air with the sounds of distinctly raucous laughter.

"Kind friends," said Mrs. Moore, in introducing her last great book, "All of you which peruse my work will find a great many things in this book to please you, especially the words I have took the time to say to the public. If all books could be read as I am sure you love to read this one, there might be less ignorance and crime in the world, and I would be well paid for the valuable time I have spent in doing good to mankind." To these words, I am sure, every reader will be glad to add a fervent "Amen." We talk a great deal about "our debt to posterity." It is high time for posterity to pay its debt to Julia A. Moore.

Laughter in Wartime America

Old jokes, of course, never die. They may become worn out, tired, even anemic; but they never pass away.

Such was the sombre reflection of Mark Twain's Connecticut Yankee when, in 1889, after being miraculously transported to King Arthur's Court, he listened to the jokes of the court jester. He wrote:

> It seemed peculiarly sad to sit here, thirteen hundred years before I was born, and listen again to poor, flat, worm-eaten jokes that had given me the dry gripes when I was a boy thirteen hundred years afterward. It about convinced me that there isn't any such thing as a new joke possible. Everybody laughed at these antiquities — but then they always do. . . .

Today the bewhiskered quality of much American humor is publicly recognized each year by a number of our leading professional laughsmiths when they banquet in New York to celebrate the birthday of Joe Miller. *Joe Miller's Jests,* they admit on each such occasion, though it was published away back in 1739, is still a gold mine for them. "We have been doing very well," boasts Comedian "Senator" Ford, "reroasting Joe Miller's chestnuts." And at other times of the year, comedians pay tribute to their patron saint by calling their jests "joe millers."

Since a large share of our jokes are thus perennial, almost every type of humor is available to convulse at least some lovers of laughter in practically every period. Paul Bunyan tall-tale humor, for instance, is being perpetuated today by comic-strip Superman and by radio's Fibber McGee; the strain of crackerbox humor which won fame for Ben Franklin in distant Colonial times is continued by such diverse characters as Orphan Annie and Ogden Nash; and even polished verse like that typical of the Restoration period has modern practitioners in Leonard Bacon and F. P. A.

College English 6 (April 1945) 7:361–67.

But though practically all types of humor continue brazenly to out-live the centuries, each period—in America, at least—is likely to have its favorite humorous motifs, its own particular patterns. These, for one rea-son or another (and the reason often is very hard to learn), will have a strong appeal to the audiences of the day. It may be worth while to ex-amine a few such themes prevalent in our modern wartime humor and to speculate about their significance.

Three types of American humor continuously successful in recent years have been the Humor of the Irresponsibles, the Humor of the Rug-ged Individualists, and the Humor of the Poor Little Men.

A cartoon by Paul Webb published in *Esquire*, in February 1945 ad-mirably represents the first of these types. A huge bear, looking rather peevish, is stalking through the snow up to the front door of a disinte-grating frame house in the Southern mountains. In his arms he carries an old man who is bewhiskered, bepatched, barefoot—and extraordinarily sound asleep. Other bears trail behind, glaring murderously at the slumberous gaffer. From behind a tree peer the old man's sons, all of them unkempt and bedraggled mountaineers. According to the caption, they are saying, "Looks like they ketched Paw a tryin' to hibernate in their winter hide-out ag'in."

Webb's humor, typified by this and a whole series of cartoons, ex-ploits the irresponsible shiftlessness of the mountaineers. Forever, in his pictures, they sleep or rest in their ragged clothes, with a moonshine jug beside them. The comic point of every caption is that they are prodigiously ignorant, dirty, or lazy.

Humor of this type—that of the Irresponsibles—has been presented in a number of forms and locales in recent years. Mountaineer and hill-billy cartoons, oral tales, and fiction have placed such humor against the background of both Kentucky and Tennessee. It is a mainstay of the "Li'l Abner" comic strip. Erskine Caldwell's stories and novels of poor-white sharecroppers have also made use of it, sometimes, at least, humorously. Nor has it been located in the South alone. Sketches in the *New Yorker* and plays—very popular ones—such as *You Can't Take It with You* and *Harvey*, have given it a metropolitan backdrop. John Steinbeck has given it a California setting in *Tortilla Flat* and in his latest novel, *Cannery Row*. Two Russian-born authors recently entertained Americans with it in *Any-thing Can Happen*.

One of the most popular books exploiting such humor in recent years was Jesse Stuart's *Taps for Private Tussie*, a best-selling Book-of-the-Month Club selection in 1943. This earthy novel unfolds the escapades of a fam-ily of Southern poor whites who, following the news of the demise of Pri-vate Tussie, collect ten thousand dollars in government insurance. The group is five in number when they move into the best mansion in town, but when relatives get the news of the family affluence, this number soon increases to approximately four dozen. There are many comic happenings which display the improvidence, the squalor, and the earthy amorality characteristic of these folk, and at the end of the novel the money has all been spent and the house has been completely wrecked.

Wrecking property seems to be one of the favorite pastimes of the Irresponsibles. One recalls the maltreated Ford car, for instance, in *Tobacco Road*. Or consider *Cannery Row*. This is a rather aimless narrative, but what plot continuity it has is concerned with the two parties which the nondescript loafers of the Row plan for their friend, Doc. The first party gets started before Doc returns from a trip, and by the time he returns, all the liquor has been consumed, an expensive phonograph has been broken, and Doc's place is a shambles. The second party is rather similar, but since Doc is on hand to help his hosts drink the liquor, tear up the place, and stage a roughhouse, it is considered a tremendous success.

The formula for such humor is fairly well indicated by these summaries. Whether they inhabit McSorley's Wonderful Saloon or Cannery Row, a sharecropper's hovel or an ancient mansion in Brooklyn, the characters involved in the Humor of the Irresponsibles live their shiftless lives with animal simplicity, enjoying themselves with no thought of law or order, despoiling a saloon, an automobile, or a house every now and then just to show that they don't care a hang whether school keeps or lets out.

The Humor of the Rugged Individualists, which, as will be seen, has affiliations with the first type, often deals with the past and frequently takes the form of childhood reminiscences. The characters are usually members of a relatively respectable class, but a number of them are likely to be kinsprits of the Irresponsibles. They may be relatively respectable, as Irresponsibles go, but they will have the same tendencies — tendencies to be shiftless, unsystematic, amoral. In their midst, however, will be an old-fashioned Rugged Individualist, "sot" in his ways, sure of himself and his standards, and eager to see people conform to them. If such a character lives today, he is considered stuffy or at best old-fashioned. When, however, he is seen in the costumed past, he is quaint and amusing.

Clarence Day's *Life with Father*, extremely popular as a book and phenomenally successful as a long-lived play, is an outstanding example. The Day boys are adolescent Irresponsibles; Mother Day, genteel though she is, with her disregard for truth and money, her amoral connivings to get her gentle way, is a grown-up one. Surrounded by such a group, irascible and stern Father Day fights valiantly, though vainly, to retain his self-respect and the morals of his family.

Other family records — half-fictional, half-autobiographical — of a similar sort include Rosemary Taylor's *Chicken Every Sunday*, which eventually did very well as a play; Kathryn Forbes's *Mamma's Bank Account* (later dramatized as *I Remember Mamma*); and Eva Bruce's *Call Her Rosie.* Sketches in the same vein have dotted the pages of the *New Yorker* and other magazines ever since Day set the pattern.

The pattern serves for humorous creations on every level from the lowest to the highest. On a low level it appears in some sequences of the comic strip "Abbie an' Slats." In such sequences, respectable Aunt Abbie and Daughter Becky Groggins try in vain to reform ignorant, lazy, whisky-drinking, amoral old Bathless Groggins. Another comic strip which uses it is "Bringing Up Father," which shows Maggie and her daughter trying to reform Jiggs.

The pattern is elevated to a somewhat higher level in the play *Chicken Every Sunday*. Here Mrs. Blachman, descendant of an old Southern family, is a housewife who runs a boardinghouse to support her visionary husband and their offspring. The husband's operation of the traction line, the bank, and the laundry in Tucson is woefully inefficient; and the boarders, some of whom he brings home, are a strange crowd of Irresponsibles — a strumpet, an old woman who yodels when drunk, a vulgar old miner, a rich Bostonian dude, and others. In the midst of all the turmoil Mrs. Blachman is lonely but brave-hearted.

On the highest level, quite possibly John P. Marquand's two most humorous books — *The Late George Apley* and *H. M. Pulham, Esq.* — owe their remarkable appeal, in part at least, to their using a very similar pattern. In each, a somewhat stuffy leading character who subscribes to time-hallowed New England standards battles against those who would depart from them. The quaintness of these standards, their inapplicability to changing ways of life, provide laughable situations.

The Humor of the Poor Little Men, however, is probably the most prevalent of all in modern times. Sergeant Baker's "Sad Sack" comic strip, beloved by readers in the Army, shows the inept and dull-minded little private with the big nose baffled by one situation after another in his unmilitary military career — at one time by the bossiness of a sergeant or an officer, at another by the trials of kitchen police, at still another by the medical men, with their medicines and serums. "Casper Milquetoast" is a civilian cartoon series with a similar formula.

The frustrated bungler is also very popular as a radio type. Fibber McGee and Frank Morgan lie valiantly to build up their ego, only to have their lies exposed as such in a spectacular fashion. Jack Benny poses as a paragon, only to have his stinginess, his ineptitude, his stupidity exposed by his girlfriend, his bandleader, his singer, his announcer, or his Negro butler. Bob Hope, another leader in popularity polls, also uses the Poor

Little Man motif consistently. When he does not get laughs by wisecrack-
ing, Hope gets them by employing a simple formula: In Part I he tries to
establish the fact that he is a hero, a brilliant thinker, or a lady-killer. In
Part II — probably after one of his magnificently timed pauses — he is shown
to be a coward, a chump, or an ineffectual flirt. His is the comedy of the
bluffer who is exposed.

When Hope turned author in 1944 to write, in *I Never Left Home*,
of his adventures while entertaining soldiers, a number of humorous passages conformed to the pattern. The title of chapter i conformed to it, for
instance, when it began with "Hope Springs Eternal" and then concluded,
significantly, "For Cover." And the account was only two pages along when
he told of winning the respect of a soldier from Texas, over in Bizerte. "After
that," he continued, "Tex kind of softened up, and there was the usual for-
mality about my autograph. But I finally made him take it."

In the more sophisticated reaches of contemporary humor, continuous frustrations are likely to make the Poor Little Man a mite neurotic —
perhaps even to afflict him with a touch of dementia praecox. Robert
Benchley, both in the movies and in his writings (in the character he portrays, of course), is an example. "He sees himself," points out J. Bryant III,
"not the master of high comedy, but the victim of low tragedy. King Lear
loses a throne; Benchley loses a filling; Romeo breaks his heart; Benchley
breaks his shoelace. They are annihilated; he is humiliated. And to his
humiliations there is no end."

After a time, naturally, such humiliation is likely to make a man edgy,
as Benchley's sketches show. These are full of records of frustrations and
consequent maladjustments. He tells, for example, how his inferiority complex causes him to let a salesman bully him into buying not the three-dollar
shirt he wants but an eighteen-dollar number, how his fear of ridicule
prevents his wearing a white suit or exercising with a rowing machine,
how a phobia inspired by pigeons drives him to a frenzy. And so on, ad
infinitum — all of it, somehow, quite funny.

Benchley, in a preface to a book by S. J. Perelman, called himself and
others workers in "the dementia praecox field." "Perelman," he said, gen-
erously, "did to our weak little efforts at 'crazy stuff' what Benny Good-
man has done to middle-period jazz. He swung it." But Perelman was closely
followed, one supposes, by E. B. White and other *New Yorker* humorists,
who operate in pretty much the same amusing way. Probably the most
popular of all such authors is James Thurber, whose omnibus volume,
Thurber Carnival, was a Book-of-the-Month Club choice in February of
this year.

Such are the three patterns which, it seems to me, are most recurrent
in contemporary American humor. There may be others which I have

missed. There are several notable humorists, of course, who conform to none of them — Mauldin, the Army cartoonist, for example, and the incomparable Ludwig Bemelmans. It seems clear, nevertheless, that the Humor of the Irresponsibles, the Humor of the Rugged Individualists, and the Humor of the Poor Little Men are captivating formulas — that there must be something in each of them which makes it, if properly handled, particularly amusing to Americans today.

It is illuminating to place this humor of the World War II period alongside of humor which flourished in our country during previous wartimes.

In 1836, for instance, when the Texans were battling the Mexicans, a character in some ways comparable to the Irresponsibles of today was a comic hero, soon to be transformed into a serious one by his heroic death at the Alamo. This was Davy Crockett of Tennessee, who had been reared in a ramshackle log cabin, who had eluded education, who was crude, often vulgar, in his ways. Today, with such a background, Davy would be well outfitted to join the Irresponsibles and to while away days and nights with them, lazing around and enjoying himself. But Davy, far from being a Jeeter Lester, was a tall-tale hero; and stories about him told not how little he did but how much he did — told how, when he went to Congress, he ran the country; how, when he went hunting, he killed his cords of bear; how, when a rampaging comet threatened to destroy America, Davy climbed a high mountain and wrestled it to a standstill. In 1836, apparently, stories of such prodigious achievements were laughable patterns for humor.

In the middle forties, when the United States tangled with Mexico, a leading comic character — typical of the times — was Hosea Biglow, created by James Russell Lowell. Hosea, in several ways, was like one of the Rugged Individualists of contemporary humor. Like them, he was determined to have his own way; he had a respectable and time-hallowed code to live by, and he resolutely tried to live by it. However, Hosea was not surrounded by improvident zanies who tried to avoid his guidance and who made his efforts ridiculous. Instead, he was surrounded by like-minded men and women who agreed with his preachments and followed them, since they knew that he had acquired his wisdom in the best possible way — by using good horse sense. He was thus comparable to the peerless Mr. Dooley, destined to preach to a similarly respectful, though amused, public during the Spanish-American War — Mr. Dooley, "the Sage of Archey Road," another purveyor of common-sense philosophical wisdom. In 1846 and 1898, it appears, such characters conformed to the American idea of what was funny.

In the eighteen-sixties, when the North and the South were fighting the Civil War, two humorous figures — one a favorite in each section —

were preeminent. Petroleum V. Nasby, created by David Ross Locke, was the comic idol of the North, while Bill Arp, created by Charles H. Smith, was admired and loved by the South. These characters, in some respects, were not unlike our Sad Sacks, our Bob Hopes, our Robert Benchleys — our Poor Little Men. They, too, suffered from phobias; they, too, were bluffers; they, too, were afflicted with illogic. In other respects, though, these Civil War funny men were like unto the modern Irresponsibles. They were lazy and improvident; they were devoid of morality; and Nasby, at least, could think of no happier career than one which involved endless loafing, accompanied by constant application to a jug of kill-devil whisky.

But as soon as one considers what made for the humorous appeal of Arp and Nasby back there about eighty years ago, one notices that they differed greatly from either group of their modern prototypes. For whereas the characterizations of the Irresponsibles and the Poor Little Men, today, are intended to make them sympathetic and comically representative, the characterizations of Nasby and Arp were intended to make them unsympathetic and unrepresentative. Nasby and Arp, in other words, were the opposites of sympathetic and normal men such as Biglow and Dooley: the Civil War zanies were dimwits, always in the wrong, so that readers were sure that their opinions on any important question would be so wrong as to be hilariously funny. Southerners chuckled at Arp's support of the North, for instance, while Northerners laughed at Nasby's Copperhead sympathies.

At least some creators of today's Irresponsibles underline the fact that they consider their characters wise *because* they are Irresponsibles. Steinbeck, in his preface to *Cannery Row*, notes that his characters are the scum of the earth — fallen women, procurers, rascals — and that they are also "saints and angels and martyrs and holy men." The whole tone of the book is such as to imply that there is a cause-effect relationship between these assertions. Practically, the same concept, it may be recalled, is brought out explicitly in several speeches in *You Can't Take It with You*. There, as in some other humor of the same class, the Irresponsibles are given an opportunity to give tongue lashings to the stuffy folk with moral codes, standards, and ambitions.

Similarly, at least some of the creators of Poor Little Men imply that their characters, instead of being unlike the general run of humanity, are pretty typical. When, for instance, Thurber unfolded his own sincere philosophy not long ago, his description of man sounded extraordinarily like an explanation of the frustrated strivings of Poor Little Men. He wrote:

> In giving up instinct and going in for reasoning, man has aspired
> higher than the attainment of natural goals; he has developed ideas

and notions; he has monkeyed around with concepts. The life to which he naturally adapted he has put behind him; in moving into the alien and complicated sphere of Thought and Imagination he has become the least well-adjusted of all the creatures of the earth, and hence the most bewildered.

Convincing evidence might easily be cited to show that others in addition to Thurber believe that Poor Little Men are laughably representative of mankind.

These facts suggest that a chief difference, perhaps, between old wartime humor and modern wartime humor is that the earlier humor was more clearly in harmony with widely accepted and socially approved standards. Davy Crockett, in his exaggerated way, was shown achieving goals which were, to be sure, fantastic but which, by general agreement, were worthy. Today's humor shows no such achievements by its characters. And laughter not only at Biglow and Dooley but also at Nasby and Arp was possible because Americans could discover congruity or incongruity with widely accepted standards of virtue and truth and with the sure pathway to wisdom. Today, a failure to achieve, shiftlessness, a lack of certainty, even amorality, are portrayed as admirable or at least normal.

To put the matter in another way, the older humor was affirmative; the modern humor is negative. The older humor asserted current values; the modern humor playfully attacks them.

Thus, so far at least, our humor today seems to lag behind current nonhumorous writings. For though they differ — at times bitterly — about many matters, such diverse critics as Van Wyck Brooks, Alfred Kazin, Maxwell Geismar, Bernard DeVoto, Archibald MacLeish, and J. Donald Adams seem to agree, at least, that the trend both in fiction and in poetry has been in recent times — and will be in future — in the the direction of affirmations.

There is a significant point about this trend, however, so far as humor is concerned. The word is in the plural, not the singular — affirmations, not affirmation. For when novelists and poets, these days, speak out, their formulas for a better world vary greatly. They do not have to depend, therefore, as humorists do, upon widespread agreements concerning standards, values, properties. In fact, the serious writers (and they are terribly serious as a rule) realize that their task is to persuade dubious readers to accept their prognoses and their prescriptions.

The only attitude that all these affirmative writers share is thus one of doubt — doubt concerning the validity of old values, old standards. Understandably, this is also the only attitude which is held by the general public: they, too, agree in seeing faults, although they, too, disagree about remedies. The only possible course for modern humorists, therefore, is to shape their comedy so as to exploit incongruities inherent in this one widely shared attitude. Only when, some time in the future, their general audience shares common tenets of belief, such as those of past wartimes, will modern humorists be able, in the words of a current song, to "accentuate the positive" and "latch onto the affirmative." Until such a time we shall doubtless continue to laugh hilariously at the Humor of the Irresponsibles, the Humor of the Rugged Individualists, and the Humor of the Poor Little Men — and to cherish the rather healthy skepticism which they embody.

E. B. White

Introduction to *One Man's Meat*

When the first issue of the *New Yorker* came out in 1925, the cover pictured a dandified gentleman in a top hat superciliously staring through his monocle at a butterfly. This portrait of the legendary Eustace Tilley, which for sentimental reasons has since adorned each anniversary number, was at the start a fitting emblem for a magazine that tried to be polished, jaunty, and witty.

The prospectus promised that this twentieth-century periodical would not be "edited for the old lady in Dubuque" but "avowedly published for a metropolitan audience" in Manhattan and elsewhere. People bought the new magazine, read it, and found it urban, suburban, and urbane. Some subscribers in that disillusioned and perky era considered it a stylish thing to have around the house, and when they had exhausted its contents they snipped its handsome covers and pasted them on metal wastebaskets and serving trays. The *New Yorker*, however, soon showed that whatever else it was or failed to be, it was a rapidly changing magazine. Within ten years, under the editorship of Harold Ross, it had largely forsaken its original pretensions and settled down to the difficult business of achieving excellence and opening its doors to new and unheard of writers and artists.

These facts relate to *One Man's Meat* because its author had a very large share in charting the *New Yorker*'s course, and, as was no more than fair, the magazine had a large share in charting his. Mr. E. (for Elwyn) B. (for Brooks) White contributed to early issues, became a part-time editor in 1926 and a full-time handyman, or contributor-with-desk-space, not long after. Contrary to general belief, he was never an editor and did not have a hand in the selection and editing of manuscripts, but he was, as one colleague called him, "a wheel horse." He did routine reporting and rewrite, rewrote captions for comic drawings (among them James Thurber's works of art, whose great merit he was the first to recognize); at some time he

New York: Harper Torch-books, Harper & Brothers, 1964. pp. vii–xix.

123

contributed to nearly every department. He even painted a cover — it showed a seahorse wearing a nosebag. His first job was to edit the items from magazines and newspapers used to fill out columns, writing taglines which topped the hilarity of their inept or garbled contents, and to this day these "newsbreaks" are still his work. More important, he wrote "Notes and Comment," the opening page of the magazine which sounded its keynote and became one of its most admired features. As Marc Connelly put it, he "brought the steel and music to the magazine."

Mr. White's early life was hardly calculated to lead him straight to a magazine with a dandy on its cover. He was born in Mount Vernon, a suburb of New York, the son of a well-to-do manufacturer whose entire life was his business and his large family of children. Elwyn, the youngest, went to public school and eschewed society, what little there was of it in Mount Vernon. At Cornell University his education was interrupted briefly so that he might serve in World War I. He made average grades (except a few A's in English), explored the surrounding countryside on a motorcycle, wrote some verse, and made, first, the editorial board, later, the chief editorship of the *Cornell Daily Sun.* His editorials for the *Sun,* some faculty members managed to recall years later, showed grace and style. Professor William Strunk, who had a fondness for both of these qualities and for wit as well, helped him learn to write; long after, the student's laudatory comments on his teacher's laconic textbook on composition would bring about its reprinting. After graduation, Mr. White was a journalist in Seattle for about a year, made a trip to Alaska, then returned to the East, where he was destined to remain. Fond of New York City (he would fill a book with praises of its charms in 1949), he settled there and entered advertising. He was making thirty dollars a week in an advertising agency when the *New Yorker* began to issue. His first contributions were bits of light verse and pieces which he called "oddities."

The matter and manner of some of Mr. White's pieces, early and late, show that he felt a kinship with other *New Yorker* contributors — Robert Benchley, Frank Sullivan, James Thurber, Franklin P. Adams, and others — and that he was influenced by their work. At the start, writers for the magazine delighted in shooting barbs at almost any fixed or moving target and were particularly eager to topple the over-solemn pundits in the 1920s who were cocksure about having answers to cosmic problems. Mr. White and his office mate Thurber mocked these deep thinkers with a burlesque called *Is Sex Necessary?* Benchley and Thurber often caricatured themselves as ridiculous figures ill at ease in the complex modern world. Both made much of the way they were baffled and humiliated not only by more lucky fellow men but even by inanimate objects and brute beasts. Of the typical writer of light pieces, that is, of his fictionized self, Thurber wrote,

Eustace Tilley Blair

"Such a writer moves about restlessly wherever he goes, ready to get the hell out at the drop of a pie-pan or the lift of a skirt. His gestures are the ludicrous reflexes of the maladjusted. . . . he hears with acute perception the startling sounds that rabbits make. . . ." Benchley held that he knew what to do when people attacked him, "even if it is only to run," but confessed that inanimate objects — "bits of wood and metal" all "bent on my humiliation and working together . . . have got me licked"; and in several pieces he gave harrowing accounts of animals, even birds, victimizing him.

Mr. White also is capable of self-depreciation: "In the minds of my friends and neighbors who really know what they are about and whose clothes really fit them, much of my activity has the quality of a little girl playing house." He tells of a struggle he carries on "setting pictures straight, squaring rugs up with the room," and foresees that in his lifelong battle against these inanimate objects he "shall fall at last." In "Dog Training" he recalls how one dog after another has overmastered him; in "Clear Days" he shows a fear that his farm clothes would give him the appearance of a scarecrow, so "I should think twice before I dared stand still in a field of new corn." It is not surprising therefore to find him confessing that he knows what it is to have "one of those days when inanimate objects deliberately plot to destroy a man, lying in wait for him cleverly ambushed, and when dumb animals form a clique to disturb the existing order."

Prefacing *My Life and Hard Times,* Thurber says that he knows that his memoirs will not picture his period well because they will be too preoccupied with his own insignificant adventures: "The 'time' of such a writer . . . is hardly worth reading about if the reader wishes to find out what is going on in the world. . . . All that the reader is going to find out is what happened to the writer." The preface to *One Man's Meat* calls it "a collection of essays which I wrote . . . while engaged in trivial, peaceable pursuits, knowing all the time that the world hadn't arranged any true peace or granted anyone the privilege of indulging himself for long in trivialities." Mr. White, then, joins Thurber and Benchley — and one might add others — in playfully putting before the reader a character, purportedly the writer, who is poorly equipped to cope with inanimate objects and animals, let alone his fellow men and the complex problems of the modern world.

Mr. White's manner as well as his matter has qualities of which his good friend Thurber approved. When Thurber defined humor as "a kind of emotional chaos told about calmly and quietly in retrospect," he prescribed a mode of expression which achieved remoteness because the writer was composed, undemonstrative, and removed by time from the events of which he wrote. Paradoxically, the writers for that determinedly modern magazine the *New Yorker* tried, by being calm, quiet, and retrospective, to return to an aloofness not unlike that of old-time essayists. These included the detached "Spectators" and "Observers" of the eighteenth century, and perhaps more to the point, the rather less aloof DeQuinceys and Hazlitts of the nineteenth century. (Mr. Tilley's costume appears to be not an eighteenth- but a nineteenth-century one.) The magazine was old-fashioned in another way: its usage was painstakingly, almost pedantically, correct. The choice of words of most of its authors, furthermore, showed the nicest discrimination.

Lightness of tone and polish have always been standard equipment for *vers de société* such as Mr. White wrote when he broke into the *New Yorker* and later included in *The Lady Is Cold* (1929) and *The Fox of Peapack, and Other Poems* (1939). The same qualities have generally distinguished the author's prose. Even when writing about farming, he has displayed himself as a quiet-voiced man of the town; his usage is impeccable; and despite his air of writing with careless ease, he has weighed his every word and found it wanted.

In various ways, then, Mr. White belongs solidly with other writers for Mr. Ross's magazine. But as an essayist he took pleasure in writing the way he felt like writing at any given moment, and in consequence his work often defied the neat classifications of literary critics and historians. In 1938, "desiring," he said, "to simplify my life," he vacated his city house and his editorial page and with his wife and young son went to live on a Maine coast farm. For about four and a half years, he contributed monthly pieces under the heading *One Man's Meat* to *Harper's Magazine.* These deal with the adventures of a salt-water farmer and are essentially in contrast with typical contributions to a smart metropolitan weekly.

The essays make clear from the start that the author has not assumed a patronizing attitude about country people and that he does not regard his neighbors as hicks. He does not indulge in comic writing of the sort that many citified invaders of the country employ. When he contrasts himself with rural folk he often gives them much the best of it, and from the evidence it would appear that that's the way it struck him. Nor do the essays go to the opposite extreme and do what far too many urban converts to rusticity do — sentimentalize about the glories of Nature and rebuke city dwellers for not giving Nature a chance to improve their characters and uplift their souls. Mr. White has called Frank Moore Colby "one of the most intelligent humorists operating in this country in the early years of the century," and there is evidence that he is fond of Colby's essay "When Nature Lovers Write Books," which wittily excoriates "outdoor snobbishness." Shortly before leaving New York, Mr. White was told by a leering friend, "I trust that you will spare the reading public your little adventures in contentment." He has.

Mr. White has sometimes been called a modern Thoreau, and some critics have found a convenient parallel between his move from New York to North Brookline and Thoreau's from Concord to Walden, forgetting, perhaps, that White was one of thousands of Americans who at that time were gravitating from city to country. The author himself, despite the opening words of "Removal," in which he expressed a desire to simplify his life, has not indicated that he found any such parallel; the essays harp on the complexity that he managed to saddle himself with by acquiring a house and forty acres of land. Mr. White admires and envies Henry David Thoreau, but in 1938 he knew there was not the slightest resemblance between his own condition and that of the cantankerous, dryly humorous, and blissfully unattached author of *Walden*. In the final paragraph of the essay "Walden," he makes it quite clear that while a husband and father may admire simplicity, he will inherit tumult. He perceptively characterizes *Walden* as "a tale of individual simplicity" and commends it as "the best written and the cockiest" of all such tales. Again, "Thoreau," he has said admiringly, "makes one laugh the inaudible, the enduring laugh."

When Mr. White joined Mrs. White in compiling an anthology, *A Subtreasury of American Humor*, published in 1941, he met or renewed acquaintanceships with scores of American humorists both old and new. Whether his own temperament, the new rural surroundings, the influence of Thoreau, that of certain humorists, or (as I think likely) a combination of these was responsible, no one can be sure, but the fact is that his writings have shown interesting likenesses to those of comic writers who for the most part lived and wrote in an earlier America of farms, woodlands, and pawky horse-sense philosophy. So instead of ticketing him with a *New Yorker* label, that veteran biographer and classifier of American authors, Henry Seidel Canby, "placed him . . . unhesitatingly . . . in the main stream of the homely American humorists, which begins in the eighteenth century and, regarded as literature, includes Franklin, as well as wisecrackers like Artemus Ward; and Thoreau and Mark Twain and Don Marquis and Robert Frost."

Reading Mr. White's essays, anyone familiar with the writers mentioned (and with their contemporaries and literary heirs) will be reminded of them rather often. It is true that the modern essayist in his preface to the anthology of humor has characterized the nineteenth-century "cracker-barrel philosopher" with what appears to be some coolness as "sometimes wise, always wise-seeming, and nowadays rather dreary." But his further remarks suggest that while some of these writers in dialect irritate him by their pointless use of cacography, others, who use misspelling sympathetically and as "a necessary tool for working the material," appeal to him. In "Farm Paper," "The Practical Farmer," "Book Learning," and other essays, he shows great respect for the basic practice of many dialect humorists: dependence upon practical experience and horse sense as a guide to wisdom and action. Nowhere will one catch him showing a book-learned city man's contempt for farm and frontier ways of learning and reaching decisions, and from the record it appears that he felt no such contempt. More often than not his thinking has a homespun quality reminiscent of that of the old-timers.

His comic pictures of himself as a poor innocent put upon by inanimate things and arrogant animals, and confused by life's complexities, are not, he has learned, permanent likenesses. On the day when everything is going wrong — separator, lantern, grain sack, weather, lamb, cow, cook, and child — as a result of his experience he realizes that the condition is temporary: "I'm not fooled any more by an ill wind and a light that fails. My memory is too good."

Having achieved such assurance, Mr. White can, and does, believably resemble the humorists of gumption in another way: Aided by native wit and experience, he confidently forms opinions and comes right out with them. Humorous writing, he finds, "plays, like an active child, close to the big hot fire which is Truth. And sometimes the reader feels the heat." Self-mocking and equable though he usually is, Mr. White often conducts heat. He warmly resents sentimentality, unction, pretense, regimentation, parochialism, exploitation (of movie queens and laborers), prejudice, and a number of other blemishes on our body politic. Usually, like earlier native satirists, he makes his attack effective by using a jocular approach: he has equated gaiety with "truth in sheep's clothing." But on occasion, as in the essays "Freedom" and "The Wave of the Future," he is driven to seriousness as unrelenting and unrelieved as Thoreau denouncing slavery or Mark Twain clobbering imperialism. And because of its rarity his unsmiling earnestness is all the more impressive.

Whether his mood is jocular or serious, Mr. White's good sense and his sensitivity make him something in addition to a critic of the contemporary scene. They also make him, like other humorists such as Twain and Dooley, a fine reporter of its significant facets. Despite his lament about "engaging in trivial, peaceable pursuits" during a time of tremendous happenings, in *One Man's Meat* he has superbly recorded the historic period from July 1938 to January 1943 and predicted some of its surviving problems. His salt water farm was not sufficiently remote to prevent his looking out from it, seeing clearly, and setting down precisely crucial developments. The rise of dictatorships, the tendency of some Americans to accept them, the worriment of many about the eroding of individual freedoms, the fateful drift toward World War II, our country's inexorable involvement, the winning of the war and the growing need for World Government all get into the record. A remarkable number of insights still are valid. A single paragraph about a scene at the World's Fair of 1939, for example, formulates a great dilemma which two and a half decades later still baffles humanity:

> So . . . man dreams on. And the dream is still a contradiction and an enigma — the biologist peeping at bacteria through his microscope, the sailor peeping at the strip queen through binoculars. . . . Out in the honky-tonk section, in front of the Amazon show . . . there was an automaton — a giant man in white tie and tails, with enormous rubber hands. At the start of each show . . . a couple of girls would come outside and sit in the robot's lap. The effect was peculiarly lascivious — the extra-size man, exploring with his gigantic rubber hands the breasts of the little girls, the girls with their own small hands (by comparison so small, by comparison so terribly real) restrainingly on his, to check the unthinkable impact of his mechanical passion. Here was the Fair, all fairs, in pantomime; and here the strange mixed dream that made the Fair: the heroic man, bloodless and perfect and enormous, created in his own image, and in his hand (rubber, aseptic) the literal desire, the warm and living breast.

Some aspects of the manner of writing are not unlike those of the older humorists. There are exaggerations of the sort many believe characteristic of our humor: "It was from stewed rhubarb that the gods got their idea for ambrosia." More often there is dry Yankee wit like that of Thoreau and other New England humorists, which is more in keeping with the quiet tone of the *New Yorker;* an instance is the comically inadequate statement following a devastating catalogue of the faults of modern automobiles: "The public's passive acceptance of this strange vehicle is disheartening. . . ." What is perhaps Thoreau's favorite device, paradox, is not missing: "In a free country it is the duty of writers to pay no attention to duty." The homely figure of speech with a bite to it common not only in Thoreau but also in many other American humorous writers is frequent: "Until we quit composting our young men we shall not get far with a program of conservation."

Although Mr. White foreswears the wholesale use of dialect, he has an appreciative ear for the vernacular (see the essay "Maine Speech"), and like some older humorists he often uses it at intervals: "A true poem contains the seed of wonder; but a bad poem, egg-fashion, stinks." "A despot doesn't fear eloquent writers preaching freedom — he fears a drunken poet who may crack a joke that will take hold." Fused though they are with sophisticated prose, the vernacular snatches, like those in old-time humor, are valuable for color and comic emphasis.

The sentence about poems illustrates a device not patented, to be sure, by American humorists but often used by them. Artemus Ward, watching a lobsided grindstone whirling in a wobbly ellipse, called it "wit personified" because, "When you can express an eccentric anti-climax instead of a rounded sentence, then you have something funny." He and his contemporaries would have appreciated Mr. White's "The poet's dream of cattle winding slowly o'er the lea is a pleasant idyll, but the bald fact is that you suddenly find yourself with a heifer who shuns the bull, lavishes kisses on a horse, and eats cardboard." Again: "Our parents were in possession of a vital secret—a secret all but lost to the world: the knowledge that a puppy will live and thrive without ever crossing the threshold of a dwelling house, at least till he's big enough so he doesn't wet the rug."

Often the use of words recalls the praise Mark Twain bestowed upon William Dean Howells. Twain quoted Howells' picturing of Machiavelli as "an idealist immersed in realities who involuntarily transmutes the events under his eye into something like the visionary issues of revery." "Here, in twenty words," says Twain, Howells "catches that airy thought and ties it down to a concrete condition, visible, substantial and all right, like a cabbage." Twain who, in the fashion of most authors, greatly admired achievements resembling his own, had illustrated the procedure in his bit about "the calm confidence of a Christian with four aces." The trick is to relate an abstract quality to a specific manifestation with impaling precision. Just so White, the modern essayist, recalls the striptease beauty who bravely forewent a needed appendectomy so that she might "preserve, in unbroken loveliness, the smooth white groin;" invokes talkative New York parties "when the air was crowded with loud intellectual formations"; or hears a sentimental song broadcast over loudspeakers "bathing heaven and earth in jumbo tenderness." The aptness of the vital words makes them memorable.

One final device, as old as Aesop but much favored by Twain and other American humorists, is illustrated in the *Subtreasury of American Humor* by older humorists Josh Billings and Joel Chandler Harris and the moderns Don Marquis and James Thurber: the anthropomorphic depiction of animals. Mr. White tells of a dog: "'I'm in love,' he would scream. (He could scream just like a hurt child.) 'I'm in love and I'm going crazy.'" He indicates how his dachshund Fred shows his contempt: "When I answer his peremptory scratch at the door and hold the door open for him to walk through, he stops in the middle and lights a cigarette, just to hold me up." He pictures a white hen "chaperoning thirteen little black chicks all over the place, showing them the world's fair with its lagoons and small worms." He notes the way sheep, "after one or two driving storms . . . abandon the pastures altogether, draw up chairs around the fire, and settle down for the winter." Mr. White's books for children, *Stuart Little* (1945) and *Charlotte's Web* (1952), use the same device. A feeling of kinship with animals seems to have characterized hunters and farmers for a long time.

Mr. White thus appears to belong with both the citified and the countrified humorists, who supposedly are deadly enemies. He combines the self-depreciation, the uneasiness in a chaotic world, the book-learning, the worldiness, and the polish of the former with the self-assurance, the gumption, the earthiness, and the *patois* of the latter. Inconvenient though this ambivalence may be for classifiers of authors, it is an asset for this particular essayist.

Mr. White suggested an important value when he remarked that the most popular humorists (he might have added the longest lasting) are those "who create characters and tell tales." He continued, "Advice to young writers who want to get ahead without annoying delays: don't write about Man, write about *a* man." The man whom the essayist at his best 'creates' for us and reveals to us is of course his very self. Unlike the journalist or biographer who can seek out and portray a pleasing and interesing character, unlike the fiction writer who can invent one, the essayist is stuck with the portrayal of his own character. Telling us as he must face-to-face in essay after essay a piecemeal story of what he himself does, sees, thinks, and feels, he is constantly and thoroughly exposed. Unless he appeals to us as a person, he is sunk without a trace.

This worldling and farmer in one and the same skin today has appeals for many readers. We who find ourselves wavering between self-doubt and self-assurance, between respect and disrespect for learning, and between refinement and earthiness recognize a lifelike kindred spirit who amuses us, wins our liking, and prepares us to accept his arguments. The consistency of such a character gives unity to a book made up of assorted short pieces. At the same time the shifts in subject matter and the changing backgrounds from season to season on the farm and from farm to city provide welcome variety. So does the alternation of jocosity, playful seriousness, and complete seriousness — a very valuable technique which Mark Twain recommended and which far too few modern authors of humorous books have learned to follow.

Such are some of the qualities and values of Mr. White's style — one which probably has been more generally praised than that of any other living American writer. Additional elements of that style are of course important. One looms large enough to deserve the emphasis of final mention: a distinct poetic quality hardly surprising in a man who has confessed that he "would rather be a poet than anything."

A wedding of sound and sense that is characteristically poetic led James Thurber to claim that his associate's "silver and crystal sentences

. . . have a ring like nobody else's sentences in the world." The words of the essayist praising country talk apply equally well to his own prose and cite some of its other lyric qualities: it is "alive and accurate, and contains more pictures and images than city talk." In *The Points of My Compass* (1962), Mr. White has said, "As a writing man, or secretary, I have always felt charged with the safekeeping of all unexpected items of worldly or unworldly enchantment, as though I might be held personally responsible if even a small one were lost." One sees him performing this task, so habitually assumed by poets, by capturing the magic of such diverse things as country scenes, a moonlit night, a church service, a Ferris wheel, an El train, a newly dropped lamb, a brooder stove, and a coon hunt. As the author knows well and as many passages by him demonstrate (the paragraph, for instance, about the giant robot and the showgirls), it is not by outright statement but rather by a subtle, even evasive handling of details, images, and symbols that this "extra content" is conveyed.

The Funny Fondled Fairytale Frog

In the summer of 1981, when Britain's royal wedding was the big news, America's humorists briefly made "Cinderella" their favorite fairytale. But once the newlyweds were managing to get into the media only by sassing the queen, gestating a baby, or posing in bikinis, an earlier favorite climbed back to the preeminence it had enjoyed for a number of years. Television script writers, advertisers, comic strip artists, cartoonists, columnists, and sundry higher-browed jokesters again were having fun most often with "The Frog Prince" in comparison with other märchen.

Even during the premarital ballyhoo, one cartoonist merged the competing tales when he pictured Diana strolling hand in hand with Charles and wondering whether England's royal troubles had ended. One glance at her Prince Charming would show they hadn't: he'd turned into a frog. Soon after the nuptials Prince Charles himself helped recall "The Frog Prince" by giving his bride a silver frog sculpture to serve as a figurehead for her car.

During a typical six-week period just before the royal wedding: In a Bob Hope TV skit, Phyllis Diller, cast as a princess, bussed a frog: he became a prince and bussed her back; she turned into a frog. Four syndicated comic strips played with osculations that humanized frogs or frogized humans. Stationery stores sold greeting cards that portrayed bekissed frogs that at once changed into humans or vice versa. A mail order catalogue advertised men's T-shirts with a frog's picture captioned "The Handsome Prince" on them. Three other catalogues offered T-shirts or aprons labeled "You Have to Kiss a Lot of Frogs Before You Find Your Dream Prince." Still another listed an amphibian-topped music box that plays "Some Day Your Prince Will Come" ($13.95 plus postage). An x-rated movie advertisement in newspapers showed a frog leering at a prince and prin-

---

Prospects, 1985.

cess who were necking: the caption tactfully revised the song title to "Some Day My Prince Will Arrive." Ann Landers' widely circulated advice column headed an exchange, "They Want Princes, and Not Toads." A folklore journal prepared for publication a learned article, "Modern Anglo-American Variants of 'The Frog Prince.'"[1]

And getting into the spirit of the thing though a mite vague about cause-effect relationships, a Japanese auto maker advertised with a television film: A frog appeared on the screen; there was a gaudy explosion; he was transformed into a Subaru.

These related phenomena challenge any trend spotter worth his salt to survey them and similar ones and, if possible, to figure out their profound significance.

For centuries frogs have shaped our lives. As folklore proves, in addition to curing toothaches and cancers, they brought warts, wealth, immortality, and death. God used them to plague old Pharaoh. The little creatures gave their lives to help William Harvey trace blood circulation and to educate Luigi Galvani about electricity and generations of students about biology. From Aesop, Aristophanes, and La Fontaine to Mark Twain, Owen Wister, and John Steinbeck, frogs were featured in imaginative literature.

But it wasn't until the last two and a half decades that caressed, caressing, and transformed frogs hopped into innumerable sketches, jokes, stories, poems, comic strips, and cartoons to pay their disrespects to one ancient fairy tale for a mass audience's amusement. The story from which the spin-offs spun was the one that folktale indexes summarize this way: "Type 440.[2] *The Frog Prince.* . . . A maiden promises herself to a frog in a spring. The frog comes to the door, the table, the bed. He turns into a prince." And instead of reverently retelling this märchen, the popular recyclings leave out most of the story, greatly modify part of it, and poke derisive fun at almost every detail in the original narrative.

Playful greeting cards offer recipients special birthday treats if they follow the traditional magic formula: "Kiss the ugly frog and he'll become a handsome prince." Open one card, and the amphibian turns into a mongrel named Prince. Unfold another, and you're told, "The joke's on you, WART LIPS!" In the syndicated comic strip "Wizard of Id," a frog tells an ill-favored crone that a witch hexed him, and "only a kiss from a beautiful woman can turn me back." The hag's smack transforms him into a dog. "You didn't tell me you were a dog!" "We're even!" Oral yarns have incredulous parents discover a young man in bed with a concupiscent daughter. In the Ozarks: "She told her father about the little old toadfrog, and the witch that put a spell on him, and how it all happened. But the old man didn't believe the story, any more than you do."³ In New York City, "You'd be surprised at the difficulty she had, in the morning, convincing her mother."⁴

All too often, frogs simply refuse to cooperate. One in a cartoon is doing his frantic damnedest to hop away from a buxom old woman who lustfully chases him. A comic strip frog, similarly harassed by a harridan, hollers, "Knock it off, you old bat. I *like* being a frog!"

A frog may fail to keep his promise. An *Esquire* drawing portrays a disgusted princess at dawn, scowling at a smirking frog beside her in her bed and saying, "You lied!" One *Penthouse* cartoon shows a nude princess sourly watching a surfeited frog as he redons his pants; another shows an amphibian accomplishing his foul purpose while his disgusted victim complains, "Hey, I thought you were supposed to change to a prince first!"

The spell may be only partly broken. A newspaper cartoon and a *Penthouse* drawing show a semi-prince griping about the low voltage of a princess's recent smack — obvious since the osculation has not defrogified his lower extremities. Even after the caress seems to have worked, his royal highness may retain awkward predisenchantment habits: In *Harper's Magazine*, then *Playboy*, then a newspaper cartoon, and then a comic strip, the prince embarrasses his mate in front of God and everybody by darting out a long tongue and catching a fly.

The Bob Hope blackout summarized earlier combines a couple of foulups that previous jokesters had exploited: A Charles Addams cartoon in the *New Yorker* and a Valentine had had a princess buss an amphibian, then become one herself; and a Muppet show had had frog Kermit kiss a human bride and thereby turn her into a frog.

Even when a disenchantment comes off according to schedule, several spinoffs show, a "they-lived-happily-ever-after ending" may not follow. In a *Ladies' Home Journal* cartoon, an enthroned king glares at his queen and growls, "If you must know, yes! I was happier when I was a frog." A poem in the *New Yorker* has the prince gripe because his human bedmate is unappealingly warm and, unlike a female frog, has "breasts . . . soft and dry as flour." A cartoon shows a troubled princess and her prince, still a frog, keeping an appointment with a marriage counselor. The comic strip "Momma" tacks a new one-liner onto an old favorite: "You know how before you find a prince, you have to kiss a lot of frogs? Well, even after you find a prince, you have to worry about his croaking." The warning has been justified by a newspaper drawing: Two ladies-in-waiting stand beside a prince's robe and crown lying on the shore of a pool and stare at widening circles on the water as one says, "A shame. When he was a frog he was a swell swimmer."

Several cartoonists have made use of such underminings of the old tale and others to comment on current events. A queen tells a dejected king who sits by a genealogical chart tracing his ancestry to an amphibian: "I told you you'd regret getting all involved in this *Roots* business!" A princess asks a visiting frog, "How do I know you're a prince and not just a presidential candidate passing through?" After a female labeled "Iran" kissed Ayatollah Khomeini, he turns into a frog. A winged sprite labeled "Congress" waves a wand above a frog labeled "Social Security"; he shoots out his long tongue and slurps down his would-be disenchanter.

Any guess about the implications of these and similar jokes must take into account the popularity of fairy tales, the way they've been tampered with, and widespread feelings about them.

The many spinoffs from the Cinderella story, "The Frog Prince," and other märchen make one fact quite obvious — that the tales are known and remembered by a huge audience. All the playful indignities that artists and writers perpetrate would fail to get laughs if everyman, everywoman, and everychild did not recognize at once each deviation. And it is noteworthy that the incongruities that have to be seen — between wild imaginings and earthy naturalism — are of a sort that long have tickled Americans. (In old-fashioned tall tales, for instance.)

Poet Anne Sexton gave a likely reason for such familiarity: "They hit you — give you low blows — because you see, you learn them as a kid."[5] The Grimm Brothers' tales kept on hitting her as an adult; her retelling of them in verse was crucial to her survival and her development as an artist. Other authors testifed that fairy tales nourished their creative genius in important ways, among them Rudyard Kipling, G. K. Chesteron, J. R. R. Tolkein, Louis MacNeice, Randall Jarrell, Donald Barthelme, and Eudora Welty.[6] And ever since märchen began to fascinate folklorists, not only writers but also scholars and scientists have venerated them. Beginning with Freud and Jung, psychologists agreed that they were profoundly influential. So did anthropologists and social scientists. Albert Einstein told a mother that the best way to prepare her son to succeed in science was to "read fairy tales, more fairy tales, and even more fairy tales" to him.[7]

Enthusiasts long have protested against tampering with such narratives. Back in 1853, Charles Dickens fiercely attacked a "perverter" of "the literature of our childhood." "It is a matter of grave importance," he said, "that Fairy tales should be respected, . . . as much preserved in their simplicity and purity . . . as if they were actual fact. Whoever alters them is guilty of an act of presumption."[8] More recent admirers of the genre have issued similar warnings. Critic Roger Sale in 1978 summed up their beliefs when he classed such stories with "the great kinds of literature," noticed that "they do what no other literature does," and held that "the ancientness of the tales" and "their persistence in so many different countries . . . make them a literature that latter day people need to treat with great care and respect."[9]

So some advocates of high regard for märchen call pranksome spinoffs "twistings," "misrepresentations," or even "attacks." Max Lüthi, a leading scholar of the tales, predicts that, as they have been in the past, the frivolous distortions will be forgotten: "Astonishingly unyielding, the Grimm märchen always have overcome attacks, parodies, and travesties. They are impregnable and will put down distortions."[10]

This may be. But a change that is worth noticing has taken place. Writers, it is true, long have made jokes about different fairy tales, and about spells, transformations, and other fairy tale conventions. But in the past the audiences who laughed at such tamperings were, with few exceptions, relatively small groups of disillusioned, cynical intellectuals. The vast majority didn't encounter, let alone find amusing, the burlesques. In the past, as folklorist Hermann Bausig says, "the folk belief in magic was much too innate" to permit widespread appreciation of the spinoffs.[11] Nowadays, the public that makes posters, cartoons, jokebooks, newspapers, and TV advertisements pay no longer is immunized by faith. The Lady in Dubuque, excommunicated in 1925 by the *New Yorker*, may not go for irreverent witticisms about motherhood, patriotism, or God, but she evidently giggles at today's blasphemies against fairy tales.

"Blasphemies" may be too strong a word. But the jesters who have put down practically every detail in "The Frog Prince" and other venerable fairy tales thrive upon disbeliefs in things long considered sacred. They, and their audiences, take for granted the skepticism played up not long ago in a cartoon: When that much-admired schlemiel, Ziggy, asked in a bookstore for *How to Beat Inflation*, the clerk told him that it was out of stock but an equivalent substitute was available — *Grimm's Fairy Tales*. Burlesques of a number of these indicate that what Russell Baker calls "a kind of rage — as if people are saying, 'Let's pull the temple down'"[12] is widely shared.

And the preeminence of irreverent "Frog Prince" takeoffs in particular signals burgeoning mass popularity of black — or at least dark grey — humor. During the first decades of the present century, "Red Ridinghood," "Snow White," and "Cinderella" were the fairy tales most often debunked and derided. But in the last three decades, as has been noticed, except when "Cinderella" took over for a few summer weeks, the amphibian bridegroom tale has won and held first place. The rash of naughty cartoons featuring fondled and fondling amphibians in *Esquire, Playboy, Playgirl,* and *Penthouse* suggests why: This story offers parodists particularly good chances to joke about racy aspects of sex. Another victory in a popularity race among folktales supports this hypothesis — the triumph of the frog over a lengthy list of fauna which become bridegrooms of humans in märchen. (The most popular next to the frog is the Beast that Beauty weds; the least practical are the whale and the louse, for opposite reasons.) Psychologist Bruno Bettelheim tells why he believes the frog won:

> Compared with lions or other ferocious beasts, the frog (or the toad) does not arouse fear; it is an animal which is not at all threatening. If it is experienced in a negative way, the feeling is one of disgust, as in "The Frog King". . . . What happens to both frog and girl confirms the appropriateness of disgust when one is not ready for sex. . . . Preconsciously the child connects the tacky, clammy sensations which frogs (or toads) evoke in him with similar feelings he attaches to the sex organs.[13]

Anne Sexton rendered the feeling poetically in her poem "The Frog Prince": "At the feel of the frog / the touch-me-nots explode / like electric slugs / . . . He says: Kiss me. Kiss me."[14]

However, as a leading folklore scholar, Kay F. Stone, has noticed, in "Der Froschkönig," placed at the very start of the Grimm Brothers' famous collection, the frog says nothing of the sort. And the princess does not break the spell by giving the slithery creature a kiss — not at all — but by bashing him against the wall. Professor Stone wonders about the reason for the departure from the original version, and suggests a likely one:

> In our modern parody, the story is first made more romantic than it is in the original, and then it is made more absurd. Such treatments are skeptical not only about magic enchantments, but about "true love" as a long lasting thing — another kind of enchantment? . . . We feel the need as adults to laugh at stories we were probably moved by as children.

The iconoclastic amusement, Stone adds, "seems to be a nervous laughter."[15]

The incongruity in "Frog Prince" spinoffs between disillusionment, skepticism, disgust, and carnality on the one hand, and, on the other hand, innocence, trustfulness, hopefulness, and continence, is a funereal sort increasingly popular with a *general* American audience, a massive group that only recently has found this kind of incongruity appealing.

The Little Man

Part Three
Essays on Mark Twain

Mark Twain, New York Correspondent

During the five months before he started the journey made famous by his account of it in *Innocents Abroad*, Mark Twain managed to elude the close scrutiny of his biographers. Albert Bigelow Paine and others who have ferreted out details in the humorist's history note that he stayed in New York for a time, that he briefly visited his boyhood home in the Middle West, and that he published his first book.[1] But how he lived, what he did, what his thoughts were, they have not known.

All these details, however, recorded in Clemens' own words at the time, have been waiting since 1867 for some reader to come upon them in the browning files of the San Francisco *Alta California*. Here, in a series of travel letters, written at irregular intervals, is the humorist's personal account of his adventures in New York.[2] Because the well-trained journalist who wrote them worked hard at his job as correspondent, trying to go everywhere, to see everything, they vividly recreate the New York of that day.[3] But they are even more interesting as indications of how the Wild Humorist of the Pacific Slope amused himself in New York and how he told of his adventures in a period just before Mrs. Fairbanks and Olivia Langdon shouldered the task of civilizing him, and as practice flights for the travel letters which were shortly to bring world fame. And at least one important happening about which biographers have revealed only vague details shifts from the realm of legend to the realm of fact as he tells in some detail how he went to jail.[4]

I

Aided by his famous flaming temper, the "Special Travelling Correspondent," recently of Virginia City and San Francisco, started his stay in the city by becoming angry at what he called "the overgrown metropolis." His

American Literature 11 (1939): 245–59.

complaints sound peculiarly modern. The bustle and flurry of the congested traffic made him uneasy; the street numbering system unhinged his reason; he was annoyed by the inhuman attitude of people who lived, as he put it, in "a solitude in the midst of a million."

It was hard to get anywhere. "You cannot ride," he said. "I mean you cannot ride unless you are willing to go in a packed omnibus that labors, and plunges, and struggles along at the rate of three miles in four hours and a half. . . . Or, if you can stomach it, you can ride in a horse-car and stand up for three-quarters of an hour, in the midst of a line of men that extends from the front to the rear (seats all crammed, of course,) — or you can take one of the platforms, if you please, but they are so crowded you will have to hang on by your eye-lashes and your toe-nails."[5]

Prices — even to one who had lived in Nevada in boom times — seemed outrageous. Private board and lodging over on East Sixteenth Street cost Clemens between twenty and thirty dollars a week. Butter cost sixty cents a pound, eggs sixty cents a dozen. A shave, administered by a barber who evidently had sharpened his razor on a curbstone, was twenty cents. "Simple, 'straight' whiskey, gin, and such things," he complained, "are fifteen cents; brandy and mixed beverages, twenty-five, (and they don't know how to mix them — besides their whiskey is bound to make a temperance man of a toper in a year or kill him)." Theater tickets were a dollar and a half apiece, and the tradesmen and landlords were the most independent people in the world.[6]

The newspapers of the wicked city were full of murders and trials and sensational divorce cases. Streets were dotted with peddlers who were selling to foolish buyers little painted horses, clowns, and balls suspended from India rubber strings. The sole virtue of such a toy

> was that when expelled from one's hand, it returned again, provided the end of the string was firmly held. Everybody bought this toy and played with it — men, women, and children — everybody neglected graver pursuits, and revelled in the fierce intoxication of this amusement. The happiness it occasioned was universal. The inventor found himself suddenly famous and as suddenly wealthy.[7]

People in New York were always grumbling, in 1867, because upstate voters ruled the city through the state government.

Finally, feminine fashions at the time were, the visitor implied, particularly distressing. The waterfall hairdress had reached a high state of development. After early stages during which it had looked first like a bladder of Scotch snuff, then like a canvas-covered ham, then like a counterfeit turnip on the back of milady's head, it now stuck straight out and looked like a wire muzzle on a greyhound.

Nestling in the midst of this long stretch of head and hair reposes the little battercake of a bonnet, like a jockey-saddle on a race-horse. You will readily perceive that this looks very unique, and pretty, and co-quettish. But the glory of the costume is the robe — the dress. No fur-belows, no flounces, no biases, no gores, no flutter-wheels, no hoops to speak of — nothing but a rich, plain, narrow black dress, terminat-ing just below the knees in long saw teeth, (points downward,) and under it a flaming red skirt enough to put your eyes out, that reaches down only to the ankle-bone, and exposes the restless little feet. Charming, fascinating, seductive, bewitching! To see a lovely girl of seventeen, with her saddle on her head, and her muzzle on behind, and her veil just covering the end of her nose, come tripping along in her hoopless, red-bottomed dress, like a churn on fire, is enough to set a man wild.[8]

When Mark went to the "matinee performance" of the famous Bishop Southgate, he noted that the church had attracted whole platoons of ti-tillating females in loose jackets and in short narrow dresses

terminating well up in long bugle-fringed points over a red under-dress — trimmed with bugles all over, I should rather say — bless me, when the girls filed up the aisles yesterday, rattling their fringes against the pews, you could shut your eyes and imagine you were in a hail-storm. When I see a pretty girl in this charming costume, I want to fall down and worship her. And yet she is bound to look a good deal like a Chinawoman when her back is toward you. This costume would provoke many a smile in San Francisco, where Chinawomen abound.[9]

Clemens, as the last sentence suggests, was still touched somewhat by California provincialism. This was indicated not only by his criticisms but also by frequent puffs for his home state worked into his columns. Coast theatrical folk, he reported more than once, were making good in the East.[10] He dutifully recorded the doings of native sons who had paused in New York or who were living there.[11] One senses a nostalgia for the happy, rip-roaring days at Washoe in his tale of what happened to two fellow visitors from the West, Billy Fall of San Francisco, Marysville, and Carson, and Harry Newton, formerly of Esmeralda. These two gentlemen met on Broad Street one day, got into an argument, then a fist fight, and finally into a gun battle. They wounded nobody "but a telegraph operator, who had nothing to do with the matter, and was both surprised and mor-tified when he received a bullet in his ribs." The large crowd "took no inter-est in bombardments, and went away — and all went first, as near as they could come to it." "To fire pistols at people, or even to carry such furniture about the streets," observed the columnist, "is a grave offence in New York; and both these men are in a very unenviable position at present."[12]

Perhaps to show characteristic irreverence, however, the correspondent blasphemed against California weather compared with that in Manhattan. Sometimes, he admitted, New York weather made him fearfully angry, but on the whole he liked it. It furnished surprises and variety — unlike the eternally fair weather of San Francisco, where a man would put in a great deal of time wistfully waiting for storms which never managed to arrive.[13]

II

The references to California, though, were, as time passed, increasingly infrequent. Eventually, for the most part, Clemens told of meanderings which took him to a miscellaneous assortment of places. One evening he dropped in at the Century Club, and estimated that the average member probably wore a size 11 hat.[14] Draped in flowing robes, purporting to be the king of some country or other, he went to the Bal d'Opera in the new Academy of Music and had a splendid time.[15] Somehow, he wandered into a Nantucket reunion, and enjoyed the antique New England jokes. He spent long evenings listening to tall tales at the Travellers' Club, where (probably because he drawled some of his own yarns for members) he was given visiting privileges for a month.[16] He made shuddering tours of the slums or loafed in hotel lobbies.[17] Week by week, as complaints about New York grew fewer, it became clear that the Westerner had begun to be fascinated by the varied entertainments offered by the great city. These ranged all the way from church services to exceedingly low entertainments.

Several of his columns were reports of visits to churches. Everybody went to church on Sunday, Clemens explained with some bitterness, because there was nothing else to do. A new excise law having made illegal all public drinking on the Sabbath, practically all places of resort and amusement were closed. He pictured himself on a Sunday wandering glumly through the city, unable to find even a bootblack or a newsboy on the quiet deserted streets.[18] To keep from getting lonesome, he joined the throng of all ages at one or more of the popular churches.

Of course, quite early in his stay, he found it interesting to go across the river to hear the noted Henry Ward Beecher. He thought, when he walked into Beecher's church at ten o'clock, that he was arriving early; but he soon found that one might be too late if one waited until after breakfast. Luckily he captured the last available seat, a little stool which he managed to jam into an opening about large enough, he noted, for a spittoon. Perched uncomfortably on this, he stared down over hundreds of heads at the famous religionist. Beecher, who was as "homely as a singed cat when he wasn't doing anything" or when he was smugly surveying his huge audience, surprised Mark by becoming remarkably handsome once he had launched into his oration. His sermon, delivered in a rich and resonant voice, "sparkled with felicitous metaphors and similes (it is his strong suite to use the language of the worldly), and might be called a striking mosaic work, wherein poetry, pathos, humor, satire and eloquent declamation were happily blended upon a ground work of earnest exposition. . . ." And whenever Minister Beecher forsook his pile of sermon notes to go marching up and down the stage, waving his arms or halting now and then to stress a point by stamping three times, Clemens felt that if somebody clapped just once the whole house would rock with applause. Mark had, he admitted, a suffocating desire to slap his palms together.[19]

Of course, Clemens was not satisfied with the sort of entertainment furnished by sermons alone. He belonged—at intervals, at least—to the intelligentsia, and one who belonged to that group when he visited New York could show his taste by attending one of the popular lectures—one, say, by Miss Anna Dickinson.

That would be in the Cooper Institute, where twenty-five hundred people would gather to listen. Peter Cooper himself would bring the speaker on the stage, and Horace Greeley would introduce her. Clemens' keen eyes would note her thick straight hair, cut so short it barely touched her collar behind, her plainly cut cherry-colored dress, her deep-set eyes in a youthful face. Her speech, delivered rapidly, without the aid of notes, would be an eloquent plea "that the number of avenues to an honest livelihood that were open to women be increased." Said the *California*'s correspondent:

> Her vim, her energy, her determined look, her tremendous earnestness, would compel the respect and the attention of an audience, even if she spoke in Chinese—would convince a third of them, too, even though she used arguments that would not stand analysis. She keeps close to her subject, reasons well, and makes every point without fail. Her prose poetry often moves to tears, her satire cuts to the quick. . . . She made a speech worth listening to.[20]

If one lecture was enough to satisfy the visitor (it evidently was enough to satisfy Clemens), he could proceed to view some of the architectural sights of the city. If his taste corresponded with Mark Twain's, the visitor would feel that Fifth Avenue was the noblest street in America. "Nothing," said he, "could be more beautiful, more refined, more elegant, than the brown stone used in facing buildings here; and for light, graceful architecture, nothing could be more charming than the rich, cream-colored Portland stone which has lately come into vogue, and which so fascinates the eye of a stranger, as he saunters up the new end of the magnificent avenue."

Clemens was moved to explosive wrath when he saw an atrocity called Stewart's Palace rising to desecrate this fine street. The millionaire builder, he snorted, unsatisfied with good Portland stone, had thought he had to send to Italy "and get some dismal ornamental tombstones, carved at immense expense by those foreigners, and have them brought over here and piled on high in the midst of that cheerful street, to dampen people's spirits, and set them thinking of the grave, and death, and the hereafter."[21]

The correspondent's aesthetic sensibilities suffered fewer shocks when he went to an art show at the Academy of Design. To be sure, more than half the subjects were the fashionable innocuous sort—"the same old party of kittens skylarking with a cotton ball; . . . the same old detachment of cows wading across a branch at sunset; . . . and the same old stupid wenches marked 'Autumn' and 'Summer,' etc., loafing around in the woods or toting flowers, and all of them out of their shirts, in the same old way. . . ." And to be sure, there was an old master of a sort he was beginning to dislike heartily—a picture in which six bewhiskered faces glared out of Egyptian darkness at a naked babe. Clemens felt that the infant was not shaped or colored like any he had ever seen. "I am glad," he said, "that the old masters are all dead, and I only wish they had died sooner."

Of the three hundred or so pictures, however, thirty or forty, in his opinion, were very beautiful. He liked "all the sea views, and the mountain views, and the quiet woodland scenes, with shadow-tinted lakes in the foreground," and he "just revelled in the storms." The picture he liked most was, according to his description, strikingly like the sort of scene typical of a Walt Disney cartoon:

> In a little nook in a forest, a splendid gray squirrel, brimful of frisky action, had found a basket-covered brandy flask upset, and was sipping the spilled liquor from the ground. His face told that he was delighted. Close by, a corpulent old fox-squirrel was stretched prone upon his back, and the jolly grin on his two front teeth, and the drunken leer of his half closed eye told that he was happy, and that the anxious solicitude in the face of the black squirrel that was bending over him and feeling his pulse was uncalled for by the circumstances of the case.

On the street once more, Clemens took a horrified glance at the Academy of Design. A little reflection convinced him that it looked like "a preposterous stable, invented by some vulgar sporting man who has grown suddenly rich."[22]

III

Lectures and architecture and art shows, stimulating though they were, interested Clemens less than did the theatrical diversions of the city: to these he devoted many words. His sternest criticism was directed at a show place to which most sightseers in New York would be likely to hurry, Barnum's Museum. Though its owner's fame, always great, had recently been enhanced by his running for Congress, and though Twain found every floor crowded, he characterized the whole display as dirty, moth-eaten, and tawdry.

He glanced at a plaster of Paris statue of Venus which stood neglected in a corner, and perceived that little stacks of dust had piled up on her nose and eyebrows. When he heard that a freak was missing, the humorist guessed that she had been moved out to make room for another peanut stand. Everywhere he went in the building, he seemed to bump into a stand or an impudent Negro sweeping up hulls. Thrown together higgledy-piggledy were many attractions which bored him profoundly—bugs impaled on pins, a photograph gallery, an oyster saloon, a shooting gallery, a shop where cheap jewelry was raffled off, and a collection of atrocious waxen images. Outstanding in the waxworks was an effigy of Queen Victoria, "dressed in faded red velvet and glass jewelry," with "a bloated countenance and a drunken leer in her eye."

The freaks—two giants, two dwarfs, and a speckled Negro—were unexciting. So was the collection of animals misnamed the Happy Family because they were all supposed to live blissfully together—"a poor, spiritless old bear—sixteen monkeys—half a dozen sorrowful raccoons—two mangy puppies—two unhappy rabbits—and two meek Tom cats, that have had half the hair snatched out of them by monkeys." A dictatorial monkey had taken charge of the cage, and was making life miserable for all the other animals. Lately he had nipped the tail from one of his brethren. "It almost moves one to tears," reported Clemens, "to see that bobtailed monkey work his stump and try to grab a beam that is a yard away."

The play being presented on the museum stage was *The Christian Martyr*, intended to be downright bloodcurdling. But the climactic scene in the last act, which showed a martyr tossed into a cage with a couple of lions, lost some of its appeal because the ferocious animals were asleep, and no amount of punching the martyr could do, and no amount of cursing under his breath, could make them forget that they preferred fresh beef to martyrs.[23] "Why," asked Clemens, "does not some philanthropist burn the Museum again?" Barnum's was out of date: in his opinion, the theaters offered far more thrills.

Thrills of an old-fashioned sort were available at the most popular cheap theater, the Old Bowery. The audience there was no less diverting than the play, for the house was much patronized by the city's urchins. Even before he saw them at the theater, Clemens had been charmed by this "wild, independent lot" who would "make good desperado stuff to stock a mining camp with." He had recorded their tendency to talk profanely about national affairs or to criticize "old Johnson," the current president, and he had watched them pitch pennies.

At the playhouse, he discovered with delight that the newsboys and bootblacks applauded ranting speeches furiously and scornfully howled down sentimental passages. One of them, hearing a woman ask Clemens to buy her a drink in the bar on the fifth tier, beckoned him aside to say (the parenthetical translations are Twain's):

> "You keep away f'm them women. I've been around here for years, and I know all about 'em. Don't you go no wheres with that curly-headed one, nor t'other one either — they'd go through you for everything you've got. That's their style. You ask any cop (police-man) — they'll tell you. Why, that curly girl's rid in the Black Maria (conveyance for prisoners) oftener'n she's rid in the street cars. And don't touch that liquor in there — don't tell anybody I told you, 'cause they'd highst me out of this, you know — but don't you drink that dern swipes — it's pisen."

And another urchin, with whom the humorist chatted about dramatic art, nominated big-voiced Proctor as the newsboy's favorite. "Oh, geeminy!" he exclaimed. "Why you can hear Proctor f'm here to Central Park when he lays hisself out in Richard Third."[24]

In the costlier theaters a newfangled system which made it possible to reserve seats had been worked up to what Clemens characterized as "a rascally perfection." The system made it possible for the theatergoer to buy a ticket as much as a week ahead or to get a place in the parquette as late as ten o'clock at night. The prices were likely to run as high as a dollar and a half, but most presentations, his enthusiastic comments indicated, were worth that much. In such theaters, for example, one could view some of the Pacific Coast entertainers who were doing well in the big city. The columnist cited with pride the San Francisco minstrels, who had leased a hall right on Broadway, had played to packed houses, and had taken in receipts of a hundred ten thousand dollars in a year. He cited also the "colossal sensation" of Maguire's Japanese Jugglers, also from the Coast. And he mentioned that little Miss Lotta Crabtree of the Gold Coast was in New York, as pretty as ever, suffering a little from huskiness but hoping soon to fulfil an engagement in one of the fine playhouses.[25]

Edwin Booth and the legitimate drama drew immense houses, but Clemens thought the signs of the times indicated that the tragedian would "have to make a change by-and-by and peel some women." Nothing else could capture popular taste, the way things were going during that depraved period in American history.[26]

Things, noted Mark, who was to retain to the end of his life certain puritanical attitudes fostered by his churchly mother, were going pretty far. Sallie Hinkley was playing in what was called "a nude fairy piece." Her assisting chorus was disgusting — "about thirty padded, painted, slab-sided, lantern-jawed old hags . . . so mortal homely that nothing tastes good to them." But large audiences evidently put up with them for the pleasure of seeing Sallie in the last act, when she made a statue of herself and stood aloft, about as naked as she could be.[27]

Even more scandalous, in Clemens' opinion, was *The Black Crook*. This drama, displayed nightly at Niblo's Garden, attracted women with its ingenious scenic effects, but men and boys went to see the seventy beauties "displaying all possible compromises between nakedness and decency." The traveling correspondent was still blushing, he proudly claimed, when he wrote about it. The spectacle, he suggested, might be less immoral if it were less beautiful. "But I warn you," he said, "that when you put beautiful clipper-built girls on the stage in this new fashion, with only just barely enough clothes on to be tantalizing, it is a shrewd invention of the devil."[28]

IV

Harrowing as the spectacles were, however, probably the most vicious spots Clemens described were not the theaters but the nightclub-like place wherein he spent an evening and the Station House wherein (inadvertently) he spent most of a night.

At Harry Hill's Club House, near Broadway, Clemens and his friends, after being admitted by a mashed-nosed guard, climbed stairs to a room wherein men and women whirled in what he called a "giddy waltz." The high moral tone of the place was manifested by signs which read "People Who Are Drunk Must Leave the Premises" and "All Sociable — No Lovers Allowed." The high spot in the entertainment was furnished by a young man in a Highland costume who danced: he ought, said the journalist, "to have danced modestly, because he had nothing in the wide world on but a short coat and stockings. This was apparent every time he whirled around." Clemens reported that he bought one of the girls in the hall some soda water and an orange, but that he refused her request to see her home because he "began to have some suspicions about her."[29]

Mark Twain's report of his stay in the Station House indicated that the whole lamentable affair resulted from a misunderstanding. On their way home one midnight, he and a friend came upon two men fighting:

> We interfered like a couple of idiots, and tried to separate them, and a brace of policemen came up and took us all off to the Station House. We offered the policemen two or three prices to let us go, (policemen generally charge $5 on assault and battery cases, and $25 for murder in the first degree, I believe,) but there were too many witnesses present, and they actually refused.

The prisoners were put into separate cells, and for an hour or so Clemens peered through the bars at the tramps and dilapidated old women sorrowing and swearing in the stone-paved halls. When this became tiresome, about three in the morning, he went to sleep on his stone bench.

At dawn, Clemens was led to a lockup near the courthouse where he and other prisoners, cheerful but sleepy, sat on wooden benches for four hours, awaiting judgment. His assorted companions included an Indiana storekeeper charged with drunkenness; a college boy and a clerk accused of assault and battery; a seedy battered hobo; a taciturn Negro; a bloated old hag; and two flashy girls of sixteen and seventeen arrested for street walking. "I felt sorry for those two poor girls," the correspondent sniffed for his constituency, "and thought it was a pity that the merciful snow had not frozen them into a peaceful rest and forgetfulness of life. . . ."

He found the old hag most ingratiating. She sat in a corner, he said,

> with a wholesome black eye, a drunken leer in the sound one, and nothing in the world on but a dingy calico dress, a shocking shawl, and a pair of slippers. . . . I went over and started a conversation with her. She was very communicative; said she lived in the Five Points, and must have been particularly drunk to have wandered so far from home; said she used to have a husband, but he had drifted off to somewhere, and so she had taken up with another man; she had a child, also — a little boy, but it took all her time to get drunk, and keep drunk, and so he starved, one winter's night — or froze, she didn't know which, because it snowed in "horrible" through the roof, and he hadn't any bedclothes but a window-shutter. "But it was a d——d good thing for him, anyway," said she, "because he'd have had a miserable rough time of it if he'd a lived"; and then she chuckled a little, and asked me for a chew of tobacco and a cigar. I gave her a cigar and borrowed the tobacco for her, and then she winked a wink of wonderful mystery and drew a flask of gin from under her shawl, and said the police thought they were awful smart when they searched her, but she wasn't

born last week. I did not drink with her notwithstanding she invited me. She said she was good for ten days, but she guessed she could stand it, because if she had as many dollars as days she had been in limbo she could buy a gin-mill.

While Clemens sat there, glancing up at new arrivals now and then, his eye happened to wander to a witticism some predecessor had scribbled on the wall. "The trouble," it read, "will begin at eight o'clock!" The last time he had seen that sentence, he recalled, it had appeared in an advertisement for one of his lectures in San Francisco. It had been written by his own hand and published in the *Morning Call*.

The trouble really began at nine, when the prisoners went out one by one to stand before the judge and receive sentences. The judge, after consultation, advised Clemens against contesting this case on the ground of unjust impeachment, and then let him go.

So Twain claimed in 1867.[30] But some decades later, after the ex-traveling correspondent had become rich and famous, William Dean Howells found a bit of table conversation at the Clemens mansion interesting. Somehow the talk drifted to jails and the experience of being locked up in a cell.

"I passed a night in jail once," volunteered Clemens.

Clara Clemens was shocked. "Why, Father," she said, "how in the world did you happen to be in jail?"

He looked at her mildly. "Drunk, I guess," he answered.[31]

On the Structure of *Tom Sawyer*

I

Since, as several critics have suggested, *The Adventures of Tom Sawyer* (1876) attacked earlier juvenile literature in something roughly like the way *Joseph Andrews* attacked *Pamela*,[1] a note on the structure of the novel may well start (though it should not, I think, terminate) with a considera-tion of Clemens' book in its literary contexts. Such a consideration, by indicating the nature of the writings attacked and the way Mark Twain and other American humorists assaulted them, may emphasize certain ar-chitectural peculiarities in the volume and suggest more clearly than crit-ics have done,[2] a unifying narrative thread.

Notable in earlier juvenile fictional works had been their characters, their preachments, and their plots. The children portrayed had been, for the most part, characterized with extraordinary simplicity: they had been good or bad, and that had been an end of it.[3] Horatio Alger's street boy heroes in the sixties, to be sure, had been more inclined toward naughti-ness than flawless Little Eva or even beautifully trained Little Rollo had been.[4] But Alger's Ragged Dick, though he used profanity, patronized the Old Bowery Theatre, smoked, and played jokes on country folk, was "above doing anything mean or dishonorable . . . or imposing upon younger boys. . . . His nature was noble and had saved him from all mean faults."[5] And as a rule, as a critic of the Alger books has recently remarked:

> Our hero was . . . a good boy, honest, abstemious (in fact sometimes unduly disposed to preach to drinkers and smokers), prudent, well-mannered (except perhaps for preaching), and frugal. . . . Nor did any subtleties of character-drawing prevent one from determining who were the good characters and who were the bad ones. They were labeled plainly.[6]

Modern Philology 37 (August 1939) 1:75–88.

The bad children — as lacking in complexity as the good — had been distinguished, perhaps, more by their proclivities toward sin than by their accomplishments. Their crimes had ranged all the way from simply being lazy or playing truant to the most horrible outrages within their infantile powers — lying, stealing, battering the helpless and the weak, swearing, smoking, and even drinking. In short, with few exceptions, a bad child had been as totally depraved (in intention) as the nonelect of Calvinistic theology.[7]

The authors of juvenile tales, employing these angelic or villainous children, had provided sermon-like commentaries and had fashioned lesson-teaching plots. Constantly these writers had "extolled the precocious child, deprecated wholesome pleasure, and delighted in didactic sentimentality,"[8] patting good children on the back, and scolding bad children sternly. Even when he had skipped the sermons, the reader of a typical story had been able to get its point by noticing that the author's dénouement observed the strictest poetic justice. In stories following what seemingly was the earliest pattern — the best known instance of which is the tale of Little Eva — the pallid virtuous child had died at the age proverbially prescribed for the Good, but had promptly gone to Heaven. The Alger boys, somewhat better adapted to the Gilded Age, had survived childhood to become successful businessmen. But the bad boy who had played truant "and was not really sorry for what he had done . . . went from one bad thing to another, and grew up to be a very wicked man, and at last committed a murder"; while naughty Thomas, who loafed all day or played with his kite, had a depressing adulthood:

> Without a shilling his his purse,
> Or cot to call his own,
> Poor Thomas went from bad to worse,
> And hardened as a stone.[9]

During the years before *Tom Sawyer* appeared, such good-bad-child tales, with their preachments and predetermined conclusions, had suggested incongruities between fiction and life useful to many American humorists. Beginning in the forties comic writers had sporadically beguiled readers with amoral portraits of unregenerate boys. Johnson J. Hooper's Simon Suggs had cheated his father at cards in 1845,[10] and in the fifties adolescent Sut Lovingood and young Ike Partington had perpetrated sundry deviltries. Ike, perhaps the most notorious of these juvenile delinquents, in the first volume in which he had appeared, had told lies, scratched letters on a newly japanned tray, broken countless windows, stolen oranges and cakes and doughnuts, hanged a cat, and imitated the hero of *The Black Avenger, or The Pirates of the Spanish Main*.[11] In the seventies Max Adeler's Cooley boy was creating commotions in church, and kindred spirits in the writings of other humorists were behaving, in sketches, as Tom was to behave in a book. Doubtless the incongruity between these youths and those in contemporary books not only augmented their comic appeal but also molded the form of stories about them.

At least as early as the sixties, various authors had begun an even more direct onslaught upon juvenile fictional characters. Henry Ward Beecher, for example, had said in an essay written for a New York paper:

> The real lives of boys are yet to be written. The lives of pious and good boys, which enrich the catalogues of great publishing societies, resemble a real boy's life about as much as a chicken picked and larded, upon a spit, and ready for delicious eating, resembles a free fowl in the fields. With some honorable exceptions, they are impossible boys, with incredible goodness. Their piety is monstrous. A man's experience stuffed into a little boy is simply monstrous. . . . Boys have a period of mischief as much as they have measles or chicken-pox.[12]

In 1869, Thomas Bailey Aldrich had launched his somewhat mild full-length portrait of Tom Bailey with a defiant passage calling attention to the difference between the Model Boy and the human youngster:

> I call my story the story of a bad boy, partly to distinguish myself from those faultless young gentlemen who generally figure in narratives of this kind, and partly because I really was *not* a cherub. I may truthfully say I was an amiable, impulsive lad, blessed with fine digestive powers, and no hypocrite. I didn't want to be an angel . . . and I didn't send my little pocket-money to the natives of the Feejee Islands, but spent it royally on peppermint drops and tiffy candy. In short, I was a real human boy, such as you may meet anywhere in New England, and no more like an impossible boy in a story-book than a sound orange is like one that has been sucked dry.[13]

The story carrying this foreword could swell the circulation of *Our Young Folks* in 1869, and, in book form, could quickly run through eleven editions.[14]

By the middle of the seventies, the Moral Boy had become a dependable butt for humorists. During the year 1873, when *Tom Sawyer* was incubating, James M. Bailey was surmising that the nine-year-old Concord boy whose ability to repeat the multiplication table backwards had been recorded in a news item was the same hateful paragon who had lived next door to Bailey in his childhood — a youth who "always went to bed at eight o'clock . . . brushed his hair back of his ears, and carried a store handkerchief. . . . He was the model boy, the boy our parents used to point to, and speak of . . . while unfitting us for sitting on anything harder than a poultice."[15] The year before *Tom Sawyer* was issued, a Detroit humorist published sketches, "The Good Boy" and "The Bad Boy," satirizing some of the excesses of Sunday School fiction.[16] In the year Clemens' novel appeared, Robert Burdette humorously referred to "well-known 'good boys' who wash their faces every morning, keep their clothes clean, wear white collars, and don't say bad words."[17]

None of these attacks, it is probable, can be thought of as a direct inspiration of Mark Twain's book about boys. They are useful only to show a common conception of the humor of childhood and the nature of children of which he could take advantage. As a matter of fact, Twain himself had been rather early in the field with "The Story of the Good Little Boy Who Did Not Prosper" (1865) and "The Story of the Bad Little Boy Who Didn't Come to Grief" (1870) — both burlesques.[18] Jim, the hero of the former sketch, stole jam without the usual consequences: "all at once a terrible feeling didn't come over him. . . . He ate that jam and said it was bully." He stole apples and survived, purloined the teacher's penknife and shifted the blame to "the moral boy, the good little boy of the village, who always obeyed his mother, and never told an untruth, and was fond of his lessons, and infatuated with Sunday-school." Jim was delighted when the paragon was whipped, because he "hated moral boys. Jim said he was 'down on them milksops.'" Thus "everything turned out differently with him from the way it does to the bad Jameses in the books." In manhood, Jim "got wealthy by all manner of cheating and rascality; and now he is the infernalest wickedest scoundrel in his native village, and is universally respected, and belongs to the legislature."

Jacob Blivens in the 1870 sketch behaved so abnormally — refusing to play hookey, to lie, and to play on Sunday — that other children decided he was "afflicted," though the real trouble was simply that he "read all the Sunday-school books. . . . This was the secret of it." Again there was an attack upon the endings of stories about children. In them, the models "always had a good time, and the bad boys had the broken legs; in his case there was a screw loose somewhere, and it all happened the other way."

II

One who turns to *Tom Sawyer* with the conventional literature and the humorous attacks on that literature by various writers including Twain in mind may see some important achievements of Clemens' novel. These were suggested by a contemporary critic who said:

This literary wag has performed some services which entitle him to the gratitude of his generation. He has run the traditional Sunday-school boy through his literary mangle and turned him out washed and ironed into a proper state of collapse. That whining, canting, early-dying, anaemic creature was held up to mischievous lads as worthy of imitation. He poured his religious hypocrisy over every honest pleasure a boy had. He whined his lachrymous warnings on every playground. He vexed their lives. So when Mark grew old enough, he went gunning for him, and lo, wherever his soul may be, the skin of the strumous young pietist is now neatly tacked up to view on the Sunday-school door of to-day as a warning.[19]

That the attack thus suggested may have been responsible in part for the organization of the narrative becomes clear if the story is restated in the way it would have been handled in the literature attacked. The opening chapter of Clemens' novel reveals a character who, in terms of moralizing juvenile literature, has the indubitable earmarks of a Bad Boy. As the story opens, Tom is stealing. Caught in the act, he avoids punishment by deceiving his aunt. He departs to play hookey, returns to stand slothfully by while a slave boy does his chores for him, then enters the house to deceive his aunt again. His trickery exposed by his half-brother Sid, he dashes out of the door shouting threats of revenge. A few minutes later, he is exchanging vainglorious boasts with a stranger whom he hates simply because the stranger is cleanly and neatly dressed. The action of the chapter concludes with Tom pounding the strange boy into submission (for no righteous reason), then chasing him home. "At last," says the author, "the enemy's mother appeared, and called Tom a bad, vicious vulgar child. . . ." If earlier moral writers had had a chance at Tom, they would have been much more eloquent, for within a few pages he has committed many of the enormities against which they had battled for years.

But as the story continues, Bad Boy Tom continues to sin (as these authors would have put it) in a fashion almost unprecedented in the fiction of the time. Up to the last page of chapter 10, he piles up enough horrible deeds to spur the average Sunday school author to write pages of admonitions. His actions are of a sort to show that he is—in the language of such an author—thievish, guileful, untruthful, vengeful, vainglorious, selfish, frivolous, self-pitying, dirty, lazy, irreverent, superstitious, and cowardly.

What a chance for sermonizing! But Clemens makes nothing of his opportunity: he indicates not the least concern about his hero's mendacity. In fact, his preaching (such as it is) is of a perverse sort. Instead of clucking to show his horror, he writes of Tom's sins with a gusto which earlier authors had reserved for the deeds of Good Boys, and on occasion (as when he tells about the whitewashing trick), he actually commends the youth for his chicanery. A ragged ruffian named Huckleberry Finn who smokes and swears is set up as an ideal figure because

> he did not have to go to school or to church, or call any being master or obey anybody; he could go fishing or swimming when and where he chose, and stay as long as it suited him; noboby forbade him to fight; he could sit up as late as he pleased; . . . he never had to wash, nor put on clean clothes; he could swear wonderfully. In a word, every-thing that goes to make life precious, that boy had. So thought every harassed, hampered, respectable boy in St. Petersburg. (Chap. 6)

On the other hand, the sort of spiteful disdain which had been used to chasten Bad Boys in other books is actually employed here to introduce an indubitable Good Boy. To church on Sunday, says Clemens,

> last of all came the Model Boy, Willie Mufferson, taking as heedful care of his mother as if she were cut glass. He always brought his mother to church, and was the pride of all the matrons. The boys hated him, he was so good. And besides, he had been "thrown up to them" so much. His white handkerchief was hanging out of his pocket behind, as usual on Sundays — accidentally. Tom had no hand-kerchief, and he looked upon boys who had, as snobs.[20]

The ending of the book departs as determinedly from the patterns of juvenile fiction. It staggers the imagination to guess the sort of punish-ment which would have been deigned fitting for such a monster as Tom by fictionists who had felt hanging in adulthood was an appropriate result of youthful truancy. From their standpoint, the author of *Tom Sawyer* must have outraged poetic justice to the point of being hideously immoral. Here were Tom and his companions, who had run away, played truant, and smoked to boot, actually lionized because they returned from Jackson's Island. Here was Tom cheered to the echo because he saved an unjustly accused man, compared with George Washington by Judge Thatcher be-cause he took Becky's punishment, lionized because he saved the girl from the cave.[21] More shocking, here was even the unregenerate Huck dramati-cally saving the life of the Widow Douglas. And to top it all, these boys were allowed at the end to accumulate a fortune of the size exclusively awarded to only the best of the Alger heroes.

   Thus the characterization, the perverse preaching, the unconventional ending of the book, which gave the volume in its day a comic appeal now all but irrecoverable, also, it is possible, did much to mold the form of the narrative. The simplest explanation of the arrangement of happenings in Clemens' book is that it represented a fictional working-out of the author's antipathy to the conventional plot structure of juvenile tales. Here, in other words, is a repetition of the plot so broadly developed in "The Story of the Bad Little Boy Who Didn't Come to Grief"—a more serious handling of a reversed moralizing narrative.

III

One effect of this method of telling a story was, of course, to give youthful readers exactly the sort of a series of happenings likely to please them.[22] Here was the story of a character who, in their opinion, was a real boy, a character who, furthermore, time after time, when he was idolized for his achievements, fulfilled the sort of daydreams which had been their own.[23]

A second effect was perhaps even more important. In attacking in other than a burlesque fashion fictional representations of boys who were unreal, Clemens was faced with the problem of depicting, through characterization and plot, boys who were real.[24] What a real boy was was suggested by the very terms of the attack: he was not simply good or bad but a mixture of virtue and mischievousness. And he could play pranks at the same time he was developing qualities which would make him a normal adult.

This concept allowed elements of incongruity which an author might develop humorously. In this view, youngsters of Tom's age were diverting combinations of ignorance and wisdom, deviltry and morality, childhood and adulthood. These incongruities, of course, were useful to Clemens again and again.[25] But the incongruities of boy nature not only had humorous possibilities; they also had potentialities—far beyond those in good-bad-boy books—for plot structures closely linked with developing characters. As a "real" boy grew up, the common sense theory implied, unlike the consistent actions of the static character in goody-goody books, the nature of his actions would change. Not only would they change from year to year but also from month to month. Less and less, he would behave like an irresponsible and ignorant savage; more and more he would act like a responsible and intelligent adult.

If *Tom Sawyer* is regarded as a working out in fictional form of this notion of a boy's maturing, the book will reveal, I believe, a structure on the whole quite well adapted to its purpose. My suggestion, in other words, is that Clemens' divergence from the older patterns of juvenile fiction and his concept of the normal history of boyhood led him to a way of characterizing and a patterning of action which showed a boy developing toward manhood.

That this was the unifying theme of the story will be indicated, per-haps, by a consideration of the units of narrative, the lines of action, in the novel. There are four of these — the story of Tom and Becky, the story of Tom and Muff Potter, the Jackson's Island episode, and the series of happenings (which might be called the Injun Joe story) leading to the dis-covery of the treasure. Each one of these is initiated by a characteristic and typically boyish action. The love story begins with Tom's childishly fickle desertion of his fiancée, Amy Lawrence; the Potter narrative with the superstitious trip to the graveyard; the Jackson's Island episode with the adolescent revolt of the boy against Aunt Polly, and Tom's youthful ambition to be a pirate; the Injun Joe story with the juvenile search for buried treasure. Three of these narrative strands, however, are climaxed by a characteristic and mature sort of action, a sort of action, moreover, directly opposed to the initial action. Tom chivalrously takes Becky's pun-ishment and faithfully helps her in the cave; he defies boyish superstition and courageously testifies for Muff Potter; he forgets a childish antipathy and shows mature concern for his aunt's uneasiness about him. The Injun Joe story, though it is the least useful of the four so far as showing Tom's maturing is concerned, by showing Huck conquering fear to rescue the widow, has value as a repetition — with variations — of the motif of the book.

That these actions are regarded by the older folk of St. Petersburg as evidences of mature virtue is suggested in each instance by their reactions. Every subplot in the book eventuates in an expression of adult approval. Sometimes this is private, like Aunt Polly's discovery that Tom has come from the island to tell her of his safety, or like Judge Thatcher's enthusias-tic comments upon Tom's chivalry at school. Sometimes it is public, like the adulation lavished on the hero after the trial and after the rescue of Becky, or like the widow's party honoring Huck Finn.

The book contains various episodes extraneous to these lines of action — episodes whose only value in the scheme is variation in the dis-play of the incongruities of boy nature from which the actions arise, but it is notable how much of the novel is concerned with these four threads. Only four of the thirty-five chapters are not in some way concerned with the development of at least one of them.[26] Hence a large share of the book is concerned with actions which show the kind of development suggested.

More important is the fact that, if the novel is regarded as one nar-rative including the alternately treated lines of action and the episodes as well, as the story progresses, wholly boylike actions become more infre-quent while adult actions increase. No such simple and melodramatic a device as a complete reformation is employed: late in the book, Tom is still capable of treasure hunts and fantasies about robber gangs. (Clemens remarked that he "didn't take the chap beyond boyhood.")[27] But actions which are credible late in the story—actions such as Tom's taking Becky's punishment (chap. 20) or testifying for Potter (chap. 23)—would, I think, seem improbable early in the book.[28] One of a few slips Clemens makes strengthens this point: in chapter 24, Tom tells Huck that when he is rich he is "going to buy a new drum, and sure 'nough sword, and a red necktie and a bull pup, and get married." Mr. Edgar Lee Masters finds this jarring. "Can any boy of that age," he asks, "be imagined talking in this way . . . ?"[29] It is jarring in chapter 24, to be sure, but at any point in the first five chapters of the book, say, it would be highly appropriate.[30]

There is perhaps, then, reason for believing that the theme, the main action, and the character portrayal in the novel are one—the developing of Tom's character in a series of crucial situations. Studying the progress of the novel with this in mind, the reader will see, I believe, that though the earlier chapters emphasize Tom's mischievousness, and though a Sunday school fictionist would therefore call him a Bad Boy, there are potentialities in these chapters for his later behavior.[31] To put the matter negatively, his motives are never vicious; to put it positively, he has a good heart. In his aunt's words, he

> warn't *bad*, so to say—only mischeevous. Only just giddy, and harumscarum, you know. He warn't any more responsible than a colt. *He* never meant any harm, and he was the best-hearted boy that ever was. . . . (Chap. 15)

An appeal to his sympathy, he himself indicates in chapter 2, is more efficacious than physical punishment or scolding. "She talks awful," he says of Aunt Polly, "but talk don't hurt—anyways it don't if she don't cry." Inevitably then, when at the end of chapter 10, his aunt weeps over him, "this was worse than a thousand whippings." And a chapter later, tenderhearted Tom is ministering to poor Muff Potter as he languishes in jail.

Significant, too, is Tom's acceptance, in times of stress in the early chapters, of the adult code of the particularly godly folk of idyllic St. Petersburg.[32] His feeling that it would be pleasant to die disappears when he remembers that he does not have " a clean Sunday-school record" (chap. 8), and the howling dog's prophecy of his death brings regret that he has been "playing hookey and doing everything a feller's told *not* to do." "But if I ever get off this time," he promises, "I lay I'll just *waller* in Sunday-schools!" (chap. 10). Surrounded by night on Jackson's Island, he inwardly says his prayers, and a little later, his conscience gnaws as he recalls his sins (chap. 13). He wants to be a soldier, or a plainsman, or a pirate chiefly in order that he may stroll into the drowsy little St. Petersburg church some Sunday morning and bask in the respect of the village (chap. 8). And his impelling desire for a place of honor in the community is a key to his initiating three of the four lines of action;[33] hence the plot strands are closely linked with his character.

Beginning with the final pages of chapter 10, these potentialities for something more mature than inconsiderate childhood begin to develop. Tom is touched by his aunt's appeal to his sympathy; his conscience hurts because of his silence about Potter's innocence; he suffers pangs because he realizes he has sinned in running away; he worries about his aunt's concern for his safety, and so on. And well in the second half of the book, in a series of chapters — 20, 23, 29, 32 — come those crucial situations in which he acts more like a grownup than like an irresponsible boy.

IV

There are some indications that Clemens was aware of the pattern I have suggested. He was aware, undoubtedly, of the divergence from the older fictional models patently burlesqued in his "Bad boy" and "Good boy" travesties. Did he perceive, however, that deliberate divergence from older patterns had led him to create a new structure of his own, nearer to the history of boyhood as he and others conceived it? It is impossible to be sure, but some facts may have a bearing on the problem.

In Clemens' "Conclusion" to *Tom Sawyer* (the italics are his) he wrote: "So endeth this chronicle. It being strictly a history of a *boy*, it must stop here; the story could not go much further without becoming the history of a *man*." When in 1875 he wrote Howells asking him to read the manuscript, Mark Twain asked him particularly to "see if you don't really decide that I am right in closing with him as a boy."[34] And writing to Howells, shortly after the critic had read the manuscript, the humorist said he had decided to discard or not to write what would have been chapter 36, and to add nothing in its place. "Something told me," he said, "that the book was done when I got to that point" — presumably, from the context, the present concluding chapter (35) of the book.[35]

The concluding passage in this chapter tells how Huck Finn, tired of civilization, sneaked away from the widow and started to live again a life free from adult restraints. In chapter 6, it may be recalled, this sort of life had been, in Tom's opinion, most enviable: "everything that goes to make life precious, that boy had." So Tom had thought when all adult curbs had been hateful to him, when grown folk had seemed to be natural enemies, and their ways unnatural ways. But now Tom, bent on dragging Huck back to that civilization, tells the runaway that everybody lives cleanly and according to schedule. "And besides," he urges, "if you'll try this sort of thing just awhile longer you'll come to like it." Craftily, when Huck's chance remark helps Tom "see his opportunity," Tom dangles the bait of the robber gang. But though in chapter 13 Huck in rags was eligible for piratehood and even as late as chapter 33 his savagery has not been mentioned as a bar to his joining the robbers, now, to lure the boy back to the Widow's, Tom insists that Huck the Red-handed will have to live with the good woman and be "respectable" if he is to be allowed to join the gang. Something has happened to Tom. He is talking more like an adult than like an unsocial child. He has, it appears, gone over to the side of the enemy.

Mark Twain's Other Masterpiece

"Jim Baker's Blue-Jay Yarn"

I. "At His Best and Brightest"

Grizzled Jim Baker, the lone dweller in a deserted California mining camp, begins a story about favorite woodland neighbors by summing up his scientific findings during seven years:

> "There's more *to* a blue-jay than any other creature. He has got more moods, and more different kinds of feelings than other creatures; and mind you, whatever a blue-jay feels, he can put into language. And no mere commonplace language, either, but rattling, out-and-out book-talk — and bristling with metaphor, too — just bristling! And as for command of language — why, *you* never see a blue-jay stuck for a word. No man ever did. They just boil out of him! And another thing: I've noticed a good deal, and there's no bird, or cow, or anything that uses as good grammar as a blue-jay. You may say a cat uses good grammar. Well, a cat does — but you let a cat get excited, once; you let a cat get to pulling fur with another cat on a shed, nights, and you'll hear grammar that will give you the lockjaw. Ignorant people think it's the *noise* which fighting cats make that is so aggravating, but it ain't so; it's the sickening grammar they use. Now I've never heard a jay use bad grammar but very seldom; and when they do, they are as ashamed as a human; they shut right down and leave."[1]

Bernard DeVoto thought "Jim Baker's Blue-Jay Yarn," an interlude in *A Tramp Abroad* (1880), typified Mark Twain's humor in part because of the way it combined fantasy and reality. Baker's furred and feathered friends not only talk but achieve levels of diction, metaphors, and even grammar. But Baker, "a creation from the world of reality," DeVoto says, is born not of fantasy but of "the sharp perception of an individual." "Fantasy," he

Studies in American Humor 1 (January 1975) 3:132–47.

concludes, "is thus an instrument of realism and the humor of Mark Twain merges into the fiction that is his highest reach."[2]

Critics of several persuasions saw Baker's yarn as what W. E. Henley called it in an early review of *A Tramp Abroad*. Twain "at his best and brightest, . . . delightful as mere reading [and] of a high degree of merit as literature."[3] DeLancey Ferguson, for example, thought it stood out in a book which "contained phrases and passages that were Mark Twain at his best," and added, "were one asked to choose from all Mark Twain's works the most perfect example of the genuine Western tall tale, patiently and skillfully built up . . . the choice would come down at last" to this story.[4]

A case can be made for the claim that, just as *Huckleberry Finn* is the greatest of Twain's longer comic works, "Blue-Jay Yarn" is the greatest of the shorter ones. Although it does not have the depth, the scope, or the variety of the novel, it is equally characteristic, and judged on its own terms it is in some ways superior: it has fewer flaws and greater unity. Besides, it is delightfully funny. So it is worth a close look.

The story's background partly accounts for its preeminence and helps one define its genre. Storytelling sessions with some masters of the art in the winter of 1864–65 helped the humorist not only discover the substance of the yarn but rediscover the form that was appropriate for it. Later practice and analysis helped him give the written narrative qualities that — quite rightly — he prized. And literary traditions and models also in important ways contributed to its excellence.

II. Calaveras County Bonanza

During the years before he went West in 1861, Sam Clemens constantly heard stories told well. His mother, an "obscure little woman" with an "enchanted tongue," he called "the most eloquent person" he ever met. Ned, his father's slave, told "The Golden Arm" story which Twain retold year after year to lecture audiences. On the Missouri farm where he spent boyhood summers, he enjoyed his uncle's storytelling; at night in the Quarters he heard Uncle Dan'l "telling the immortal tales which Uncle Remus Harris was to . . . charm the world with, by and by." (Dan'l effectively prepared childish listeners for jimdandy nightmares by unloosing a blood-curdling ghost story just before he sent them to bed.) During Sam's Wanderjahren, fellow jour printers and steamboatmen were memorable yarn-spinners.[5]

He grew up when American humorists were trying to catch in print the substance and the manner of oral yarns. At his printer's case in Hannibal and elsewhere he set up their writings; in his leisure hours he read them. At about the time he went West, however, new styles of writing became fashionable. Many comic journalists replaced rustic yarnspinning with wordplay, topsy-turvy sentences, parodies and burlesques.[6] Writing for the Virginia City *Territorial Enterprise* and for San Francisco newspapers, Twain ground out comedy of the sort currently popular.[7] Throughout the rest of his life, he would often — *too* often — write Phunny Phellow humor of diction. But a visit to the California mining country reacquainted him with the stuff and the style of fireside storytelling that shaped many of his best writings.

Clemens, a twenty-nine-year-old San Francisco journalist, peeved officials by publishing feisty exposés. When he found it expedient to absent himself a while, Jim Gillis, pocket miner out in the area where Baker lived, asked him to be a guest. Between December 4, 1864, and February 25, 1865, the budding author stayed with Gillis and his partner, Jim Stoker, in a Jackass Hill cabin or bunked in a nearby Angel's Camp hotel.

The region once had swarmed with goldseekers, but the rich diggings had played out, and now only a few desultory pocket miners dotted fields, hills, and forests. Clemens did a little pocket mining without luck and was kept from doing more by a rainy season which — even for a state where what natives call Unusual Weather flushes houses down hills — was worse than usual. He, his hosts, and soggy neighbors huddled for hours around the cabin fireplace or the hotel barroom stove. His notebook jottings gripe about endless deluges and the "beans and dishwater" monotonously served by the hotel's French restaurateur. He complains that "4 kinds of soup which he furnishes to customers only on great occasions . . . are popularly known among the Boarders as Hellfire, General Debility, Insanity and Sudden Death." The booze must have been as corrosive: in a plaint that has the poignancy of a personal reminiscence, Clemens holds that a shot of the tavern's straight whiskey "will throw a man a double somerset and limber him up like boiled macaroni before he can set his glass down."[8]

All the same, looking back, he would call this area a "serene and reposeful and dreamy and delicious sylvan paradise" where he had "a fascinating and delightful time." He fondly remembered dates with the Eves of this Eden, a miner's pneumatic daughters whom he called "the Chaparral Quails."[9] More important, every few years during more than four decades, he praised the purveyors of the chief entertainment aside from drinking, the mining camp yarnspinners, analyzed their artistry, and at the top of his form imitated them and retold their stories.

There is support for the guess several scholars have made that the mining country visit, because of the impact of those storytelling orgies in Jim Gillis' Jackass Hill cabin and the Angel's Camp caravanserie, brought a turning point in the author's career. The very first sketch he published after he got back to San Francisco had as its best and chief ingredient a vernacular monologue by one of the Angel's Camp crowd.[10] One evening he told anecdotes to a group of fellow reporters so well that they lost all track of time. Within months he decided that he had a "call" to "drop all trifling . . . & strive for a fame" by cultivating his "talent for humorous writing."[11] Soon after this discovery of his vocation, he published one of the tales that he had heard "around the tavern stove"—"the germ," as he put it, "of my coming good fortune," a piece of writing that "became widely known in America, India, China, England—and the reputation it made for me . . . paid me thousands and thousands of dollars. . . ."[12] The story furnished the chief part of the title of Twain's first book, and though he infrequently revised any piece once it had been printed, he carefully—and substantially—revised this one three times. Other retellings of California mining camp yarns came out in 1865, 1867, 1871, 1880, 1884, 1893, and 1907.[13]

The cream of what turned out to be a bumper crop was the "Blue-Jay Yarn" on eleven pages of *A Tramp Abroad*, published in 1880 when the author paused part way through the writing of *Adventures of Huckleberry Finn*.

The "lovable" personality and the skill of the original teller of this story in the Mother Lode country doubtless helped Twain see its merit. This was Jim Gillis, "gray as a rat, earnest, thoughtful, slenderly educated, slouchily dressed and clay-soiled," but "a gallant creature" whose "styles and bearing could make any costume regal . . . a man, and a whole man." "A much more remarkable person than his family and his intimates ever suspected," Jim in the humorist's opinion was a genius—"a born humorist, and a very competent one" who "would have been a star performer if he had been discovered, and had been subjected to a few years training with a pen." Twain identified Jim, who he thought was the best raconteur in the diggings, as the originator of three of his mining camp tales, though one of them almost certainly was told by Jim's partner. The writer's notebook jottings, his characterizations of the tellers, and his vivid picturings in memoirs and in the stories themselves justify the other attributions.

When inspired, Jim stood with his back to the fire, unleashed his imagination, and spun yarns. Each was a gaudy lie created as he went along but soberly told as "history undefiled." Usually he made his "pard" Stoker the incongruous hero, and Stoker sat smoking, listening solemnly but amiably to his "monstrous fabrications." One of the stories that Twain retold celebrated Stoker's prodigious cat, Tom Quartz, a beast that "had never existed," Twain said, "outside of Jim Gillis's imagination." Another was "Jim Gillis's yarn about the blue jays"—"a charming story, a delightful story, and full of happy fancies."[14] When he theorized about oral storytelling and a writer's adaptation of its ways, he found Jim Gillis a useful teacher.

III. A "High, Delicate Art" Adapted

Twain would call the oral story as Gillis told it "high and delicate art," and would find "no merit in ninety-nine out of a hundred [stories] except the merit put into them by the teller's art."[15]

He deliberately tried to use that art in his books. But he repeatedly said that *written* art had to modify the ways of oral storytelling. If an author merely set down the golden words of a fine storyteller, a funny thing happened on the way to the printer: they turned to dross. Clemens prohibited publication of an interview he gave because quoting talk in print is "an attempt to use a boat on land or a wagon on water."[16]

He decided that careful artistry alone could give printed words the sound of free-and-easy speech. "I amend dialect stuff by talking and talking and *talking* it till it sounds right."[17] Measures like those he took to give painstakingly memorized platform monologues the qualities of off-the-cuff utterances helped him write colloquial passages—"a touch of indifferent grammar flung in here and there, apparently at random" but in fact shrewdly deployed: "heaving in . . . a wise tautology"; "sprinkl[ing] in one of those happy turns on something that has previously been said."[18] The chief incongruity in the two-hundred-word opening paragraph of Baker's story—between fulsome praise of book-talk and grammar and abysmal ignorance about both—is made apparent by only four assorted— and strategically placed—grammatical mishaps. And the paragraph illustrates "wise tautology" by reiterating half a dozen times the belief that a jay can express whatever it feels.

Twain lauded Gillis for "build[ing] a story as it goes along, careless of whither it is proceeding, enjoying each fresh fancy as it flashes from the brain." In "How to Tell a Story," he held that the very basis of the American art was "to string incongruities and absurdities together in a wandering and purposeless way."[19] He downgraded jokes with payoff lines, praised stories with "pervasive" humor which, like that of William Dean Howells, "flows softly all around about and over."[20] So his aim was to ape in print the leisurely imagining and inundating humor of Gillis and other experts.

Twain makes "The Blue-Jay Yarn" seem to meander, for one thing, by prefacing it with an apparent unhurried digression of his own, then by having Baker sidle into his monologue at his leisure. The humorist, a continent and an ocean away from the Mother Lode country, strolls into the woods above the Neckar. Soon, remembering German legends that he has been reading about the area, he falls "into a train of dreamy thought about animals which talk, and kobolds, and enchanted folk." Later, lost and alone in the dense silent woods, he fancies that he glimpses some of these creatures in the shadows under the trees.

Suddenly the quiet is shattered by the croak of a raven staring down from a branch at the intruder. A second bird comes along:

> The two sat side by side on the limb and discussed me as freely and offensively as two great naturalists might discuss a new kind of bug. . . . They called in another friend. This was too much. I saw that they had the advantage of me, and so I concluded to get out. . . . They enjoyed my defeat as much as any low white people could have done. They craned their necks and laughed at me (for a raven *can* laugh, just like a man), they squalled insulting remarks after me as long as they could see me. . . . When even a raven shouts after you, "What a hat!" "O, pull down your vest!" and that sort of thing, it hurts you and humiliates you, and there is no getting around it with fine reasoning and pretty arguments.[21]

The confrontation leads Twain to recall the man who could understand birds and animals — Jim Baker. Baker's background and some of his opinions are detailed. Only after this preamble — one that at first glance appears to be very loosely related — does Baker's monologue start with the remarks about the great skill with which jays communicate. In a passage a bit longer than the first, and therefore an apparent overelaboration, Jim next argues that "a jay is just as much a human as you be" by mentioning sundry human traits and ("wisely tautological") repeating the claim several times:

> "You may call a jay a bird. Well, so he is, in a measure — because he's got feathers on him, and don't belong to no church, perhaps; but otherwise he is just as human as you be. And I'll tell you for why. A jay's gifts, and instincts, and feelings, and interests, cover the whole ground. A jay hasn't got any more principle than a Congressman. A jay will lie, a jay will steal, a jay will deceive, a jay will betray; and four times out of five, a jay will go back on his solemnest promise. The sacredness of an obligation is a thing which you can't cram into no blue-jay's head. Now on top of all this, there's another thing: a jay can out-swear any gentleman in the mines. You think a cat can swear. Well, a cat can; but you give a blue-jay a subject that calls for his reserve-powers, and where is your cat? . . . Yes, sir, a jay is everything that a man is. A jay can cry, a jay can laugh, a jay can feel shame, a jay can reason and plan and discuss, a jay likes gossip

and scandal, a jay has got a sense of humor, a jay knows when he is an ass just as well as you do—maybe better. If a jay ain't human, he better take in his sign, that's all.

The impression that Baker is loquacious is heightened by the introduction here of a different type of comedy. These remarks, proving as they do that his birds are human chiefly by arguing that they are depraved in as many ways as human beings are, have the bite of satire. Twain would have said that Jim's equating of humanity with total depravity, in addition to "wandering in an apparently purposeless way," introduces an important component. "It takes a heap of sense to write good nonsense," he told himself in a note shortly before he wrote the blue-jay yarn.[22] As an oldster, he would marvel at the way his humor outlasted that of more than eighty popular contemporaneous humorists, thus living "forever." ("By forever," he explained, "I mean thirty years.") His explanation: "I have always preached."[23] The humorist was repeating a judgment of his best friend, Howells, who said that "what finally appeals to you in Mark Twain . . . is his common sense."[24]

The way the tale that follows is unfolded reinforces the impression that it wanders since—simple though it is—it (in Twain's phrase) seemingly "fools along and enjoys elaboration" for almost thirteen hundred words. It does not, in fact, detour: each of two parts illustrates a claim Baker makes as he starts his monologue.

Part one: Baker describes the comic doings of some jays around a deserted log house near his cabin. One finds a knothole in the roof and decides to fill it with acorns. Though he dumps in huge numbers, since the house is "just one big room," he fails. The bird becomes increasingly frantic, frustrated, outraged; and his more and more eloquent orations prove that "whatever a blue-jay feels, he can put into language."

Part two: Attracted by his commentaries, first one, then more jays gather and discuss the phenomenon. Finally one learns what the trouble is and announces his discovery. Thereupon greater and greater numbers of birds fly in, study the scene, and jeer about the frustrated jay's mistake. The reactions prove that jays are "just as human as you be." When he makes this uncomplicated fable laughable, Twain proves that the effect of a humorous story depends less upon matter than on manner, in a printed story as well as an oral one, if the author of the printed version adapts oral procedures.

IV. Literary Influences

Writings as well as oral storytellers of course shaped the blue-jay yarn. A beast fable, this narrative is in a genre that had amused audiences, literally, for ages. Even before Aesop, its beginnings, like Aesop himself, are hidden in the mists of antiquity, and from those beginnings to the present, the form has flourished. A few outstanding practitioners were Hesiod, Aristophanes, and Socrates in the ancient world; Chaucer and myriads of anonymous celebrators of Reynard the Fox in the Middle Ages, Robert Henryson and William Caxton in the fifteenth century; Francois Rabelais in the sixteenth; Jean de la Fontaine (twelve books; "I use Animals to teach Mankind") and Sir Roger L'Estrange in the seventeenth; Jonathan Swift, John Gay, Gotthold Ephraim Lessing, Bernard Mandeville, Matthew Prior, William Cowper, Johann Wolfgang Goethe, and Benjamin Franklin in the eighteenth; Leo Tolstoi, Ivan Krylov, Rudyard Kipling, Trilussa (C. A. Salustra), Guy Wetmore Carryl, and others in the nineteenth.

Since (as scholars have proved) Clemens read widely, he knew several of his remote predecessors in the anthropomorphic field. About the time he wrote Baker's yarn, his reading had helped him remember or discover three Americans working in the genre in the 1880s. As co-editor of a forthcoming anthology — Mark Twain's Library of Humor (1888) — he was jotting down in Notebooks 15 and 16 lists of possible inclusions. Four times he mentioned George T. Lanigan (1846–86) or his World's Fables, and the anthology would include seven of Lanigan's pieces. Twice he named Ambrose Bierce; one entry recalled fables published in a newspaper as many as thirteen years earlier; and the anthology had seven of Bierce's fables, at the time still uncollected. In Bierce's "The Robin and the Woodpecker," the latter bird admits that he does not know why he pecks holes in a dead tree: "Some naturalists affirm that I hide acorns in these pits; others maintain that I get worms out of them." Alert source hunters will notice the bird's theoretical kinship with Baker's blue jay, which dumped acorns into his knothole for reasons that never were clarified. They also may be interested in the fact that at one time when he talked about his story long after he wrote it, Twain called it "a tale of how the poor and innocent *woodpeckers* tried to fill up a house with acorns."[25]

"Uncle Remus (?) writer of colored yarns," another notebook entry, Clemens made before the yarns had appeared between hardcovers and, evidently, before he had learned that the creator's name was Joel Chandler Harris. Clemens and his co-editors included two of Harris' narratives in their anthology; he read Harris' tales to audiences, corresponded with him, swapped stories, arranged meetings, called him "a fine genius," and even tried to get the shy little man to share lecture platforms. It seems possible that partly because he so admired Harris and, like him, as a boy had heard black storytellers tell animal legends, he did well when he exploited what Harris called "that incongruity of animal expression that is just human enough to be humorous" in the "Blue-Jay Yarn."[26]

Several passages in Jim Baker's story are enriched by comic linkings between bird and animal — for instance the jay's discovery of the hole: "He cocked his head to one side, shut one eye and put the other one to the hole, like a possum looking down a jug"; or the doglike gesture showing the jay's puzzlement: "he took a thinking attitude . . . and scratched the back of his head with his right foot." (A kinship — perhaps something more — is indicated when one compares a passage in "Uncle Remus Initiates the Little Boy," the first Uncle Remus story and one included in Twain's anthology: "Den Brer Rabbit scratch on one year wid his off hine-foot sorter jub'usly. . . .") More incongruities are of the sort Harris mentioned — between bird and humans. After he drops the first acorn into the hole, the jay

> "was just tilting his head back with the heavenliest smile on his face, when all of a sudden he was paralyzed into a listening attitude and that smile faded gradually out of his countenance like breath off'n a razor,[27] and the queerest look of surprise took its place. . . . He cocked his eye at the hole again, and took a long look; raised up and shook his head; stepped around to the other side of the hole, and took another look from that side; shook his head again."

His puzzlement grows; so does his anger:

> "He fetched another acorn, and done his level best to see what become of it, but he couldn't. . . . Then he begun to get mad. He held in for a spell, walking up and down the comb of the roof and shaking his head and muttering to himself; but his feelings got the upper hand of him, presently, and he broke loose and cussed himself black in the face. I never see a bird take on so about a little thing."

Now he decides that he'll be damned if he doesn't fill that hole if it takes a hundred years, and for two hours and a half, he heaves in acorns without stopping:

> "Well at last he could hardly flop his wings, he was so tuckered out. He comes a-drooping down, once more, sweating like an ice-pitcher, drops his acorn in and says, '*Now* I guess I've got the bulge on you by this time!" So he bent down for a look. If you'll believe me, when his head come up again he was just pale with rage. He says, 'I've shoveled acorns enough in there to keep the family thirty years, and if I can see a sign of one of 'em, I wish I may land in a museum with a belly full of sawdust in two minutes!'"

The culmination of his frantic efforts and of his frustration is accompanied by his greatest flight of eloquence:

"He just had strength enough to crawl up on to the comb and lean his back agin the chimbly, and then he collected his impressions and began to free his mind. I see in a second that what I had mistook for profanity in the mines was only just the rudiments, as you may say."

In addition to the animalization or the humanization of birds, the story as Baker tells it amuses because of its comic picturings. Incongruities, as Max Eastman has noticed,[28] are stressed when they are made highly concrete. Twain creates pictures because, as Howells says, "he is the impassioned lover, the helpless slave of the concrete":[29] the jay peering into the knothole, shaking his head, cussing himself black in the face, turning pale with rage, taking a thinking attitude, and leaning his back agin the chimbly attest to this slavery.

There are more humanizations and bodyings forth in the second movement of the story. A jay passing by hears the baffled bird "doing his devotions," stops, learns the reason, and calls in other jays:

"They called in more jays; then more and more, till pretty soon the whole region 'peared to have a blue flush about it. There must have been five thousand of them; and such another jawing and disputing and ripping and cussing, you never heard. Every jay in the whole lot put his eye to the hole and delivered a more chuckle-headed opinion about the mystery than the jay that went there before him. They examined the house all over, too."

The figurative comparison to "a blue flush" helps make this vivid, joining earlier figures to give substance and a comic quality to the proceedings and to justify Baker's aperçu that a jay's language, sharing a conspicuous merit with written as well as oral American humor, just bristles with figures of speech. In the final paragraphs, after the old jay solves the mystery and announces his findings, his fellow jays become "a blue cloud," manifest vividly additional human traits, and prove their sense of humor is superior to an owl's:

"They all came a-swooping down like a blue cloud, and as each fellow lit on the door and took a glance, the whole absurdity of the contract that the first jay had tackled hit him home and he fell over backwards suffocating with laughter, and the next jay took his place and done the same.

"Well, sir, they roosted around here on the house-top and the trees for an hour, and guffawed over that thing like human beings. It ain't no use to tell me a blue-jay hasn't got a sense of humor, because I know better. And memory too. They brought jays here from all over the United States to look down that hole, every summer for three years. Other birds too. And they could all see the point, except an owl that come from Nova Scotia to visit the Yo Semite, and he took this thing in on his way back. He said he couldn't see anything funny in it. But then, he was a good deal disappointed about Yo Semite, too."

DeVoto felt that the last sentences "mar the effect of a passage in pure humor" because "they strain toward a joke, escaping from the clear medium of the tale itself into burlesque." Those who have heard an audience respond to the recitation of the sentences by a master — a Hal Holbrook, say — may disagree. Blemish or not, the sentences (as DeVoto adds) are typical of Mark Twain. And their mingling of horseplay with delicate fancifulness is typical of both printed and oral American tall tale humor.

V. "The Principle of Life"

An exchange between Clemens and Joel Chandler Harris indicates that the humorist might well claim that this discussion so far has failed to deal with the chief aim of this story. Clemens had complimented Harris on his picturing of Uncle Remus as he told Negro folktales to a boy on an antebellum Georgia plantation. Harris, as modest as he was shy, protested that the folktales were far more important than characterization: "my relations toward Uncle Remus are similar to those that exist between an almanac maker and a calendar." Nonsense, Clemens answered, "the principle of life" was in the frameworks. The enclosed tales were

> only alligator pears — one merely eats them for the sake of the salad dressing. Uncle Remus is most deftly drawn, and is a lovable and delightful creation; he, and the little boy, and their relations with each other, are high and fine literature, and worthy to live for their own sakes; and certainly the stories are not to be credited with *them*.[30]

Granted that Clemens overstated, he was sincere in praising an achievement that he admired and tried to duplicate: the using of a framework to make up for attritions — over and above those previously discussed — that an oral story suffers when it is reduced to print.

When Clemens refused to let that interviewer publish an accurate transcript of an interview he had granted, he explained that he did so because

> an immense something has disappeared from it. That is its soul . . . everything that gave that body warmth, grace, friendliness and charm and commended it to your affections — or, at least, to your tolerance — is gone and nothing is left but a pallid, stiff and repulsive cadaver.
> Such is "talk" almost invariably, as you see it lying in state in

an "interview." The interviewer seldom tried to tell one *how* a thing was said; he merely puts in the naked remark and stops there. When one writes for print his methods are very different. . . . He loads, and often overloads, almost every utterance of his characters with explanations and interpretations. . . . Now, in your interview . . . you have not a word of explanation; what my manner was at several points is not indicated. Therefore, no reader can possibly know where I was in earnest and when I was joking, or whether I was joking altogether or in earnest altogether. Such a report of a conversation has no value.[31]

A fiction writer, this implies, has the obligation of so representing his listener and his storyteller as to relate them to the story. Somehow, by showing the pair in action and reaction, an artist must clarify such matters as why the one hearkens to a long-winded monologue and why the other gives it the substance and form he does. Somehow, too, the writer must simulate what Twain called "the spontaneity of a personal relation, which contains the very essence of interest."

The "Mark Twain" who listens to the jay story, and enjoys it and repeats it in toto, is characterized by the long first-person account of his ramblings in the Black Forest and his recollection of a faraway friend. He is a relatively complex and ingratiating person—a fact that is made clear when one compares him with the "Mark Twains" who were auditors for a couple of other mining camp storytellings. One of these "Mark Twains," gifted with as little humor, say, as a Canadian owl, is steered by a practical joker into the clutches of a monologist who mercilessly corners him and bores him to death with what he feels are irrelevant maunderings, but which are actually hilarious, before he gratefully escapes. He gives his account because he is outraged. The other "Mark Twain" has his curiosity raised to a fever heat by jocose miners. He therefore listens eagerly to a long-winded chatterbox who barely mentions his subject but spins out (very funny) irrelevancies till whiskey overcomes him, he falls asleep, and his listener at long last learns that he has been hoaxed.[32] By contrast the Black Forest "Mark Twain" has humor and understanding. He relished the "deep and mellow twilight" and the silence of the pine wood; he has enjoyed the German Märchen; he imagines that he glimpses "small flitting shapes here and there down the columned aisles of the forest." When the ravens jaw at him, he can relish their insults and joke about the way "the thing became more and more embarrassing." His amused and amusing account of his adventures has shown why he can hear Jim Baker's monologue with delight, remember it, and at a much later date lovingly repeat it verbatim. He has prepared the reader for his mock-solemn claims that animals talk to each other, that Jim is the one man he has known who can understand them, and whimsical proof: "I knew he could . . . because he told me so himself."

Jim, like his auditor, benefits when compared with his counterparts in the two Mother Lode stories mentioned above. Both of the other story-tellers are nonstop babblers simply because they are cursed with total re-call and are allergic to relevance. Besides, one of them is "tranquilly, serenely, symmetrically drunk—not a hiccup to mar his voice, not a cloud upon his brain thick enough to obscure his memory." By contrast, Jim is lo-quacious because he has an appreciative audience; he has endless leisure; and his way of living has given him his awestruck reverence for birds which most normal people find completely unlovable.

The biography of this "middle-aged, simple-hearted miner" shows how he discovered that jays can talk and he can understand them. He has been pushed by solitude into a strange companionship that he fondly recalls and celebrates at length. He "had lived in a lonely corner of California, among the woods and mountains, a good many years, and has studied the ways of his only neighbors, the beasts and the birds." Finally—to put it more bluntly than his compassionate portrayer does—this hermit has become a mite touched in the head. Seemingly random sentences give per-tinent evidence: "Seven years ago, the last man in the region but me moved away. There stands his house—been empty ever since. . . ." And a bit later: "Well one Sunday morning I was sitting out here in front of my cabin with my cat, taking the sun, and looking at the blue hills, and listening to the leaves rustling so lonely in the trees. . . ." The statistics, and the pathetic fallacy of "lonely" leaves, are doubly poignant because they are unobtru-sive. Equally unstressed is the casual relationship between the recluse's his-tory and (1) a misanthropy that equates the birds' prodigious orneriness with human-ness, and (2) admiration for creatures that eloquently curse a thwarting world and that band together to jeer damfoolishness. Not sur-prisingly, he fantasizes about these kin-birds, and as DeVoto says, "His pa-tient, explanatory mind actually works before our eyes and no one can doubt him."[33]

Awareness of one of the humorist's favorite devices may help the reader to notice a final touch in his portrayal of Baker. For years, Twain had been making use of counterpoint—repetitions with meaningful modulations: While writing *A Tramp Abroad*, he cited one use of the device and its ef-fect. He would, he said, place cheek-by-jowl "a perfectly serious descrip-tion of 5 very bloody student duels which I witnessed in Heidelberg" and a broadly burlesqued account of a pretentious but completely harmless French duel. "The contrast," he predicted, "will be silent but eloquent com-ment."[34] Another echoing with variations comes in "Blue-Jay Yarn" when the account of the jeering at "Mark Twain" by raucous ravens is followed by Baker's account of the jeering at the befooled blue jay by other jays. But note the contrast: Whereas the victim richly elaborates on "Twain's" droll humiliation and abject retreat, Baker says not a word about the mental state, the retorts, or the behavior of his embarrassed protagonist. This chief character, in fact, at this point vanishes from the story. The "silent but eloquent comment" that this contrast suggests is: So completely has Jim Baker identified with a woodland neighbor who, like him, has been defeated and, unlike him, has beautifully and directly voiced his feelings, that he skips any report on the jay's humiliation.

A way of talking, telling a story, thinking and fantasizing that is delightful and funny thus is made probable by a characterization of Jim Baker which is complex enough to encompass a heartwarming touch of pathos.[35]

The French Revolution and
Huckleberry Finn

I

I

The late Bernard DeVoto once called the study of Samuel L. Clemens' sources "tiresome, repugnant, and quite meaningless."[1] His reading of many of this author's letters and manuscripts convinced him that

> Mark Twain was at his best . . . writing most memorably, when he was dealing with either historical events he saw or participated in or the phantasies associated with them. . . . And he is clumsiest and least convincing when he is trying to make something up to fit the needs of a book, especially the needs of fiction.[2]

Long before, Brander Matthews had been shocked when a former associate of Twain had told him, "Mark Twain has a very good memory; and that's where he gets his very best stories." But, on coming to know Clemens well, Matthews had perforce agreed that he excelled "when he had a solid fact to deal with, an actual episode of his own boyhood or the experience of a friend of his youth." Twain had encouraged this belief by remarking that "everything in *Tom Sawyer* and *Huckleberry Finn* was taken straight from life."[3] Many other students of Twain before and since DeVoto have come to similar conclusions.

Yet DeVoto noticed that a fine chapter in *The Gilded Age* and two memorable episodes in *Huckleberry Finn* derived not from memory but from sketches by pre–Civil War humorists,[4] and I have done the same for a major character and an episode in *Tom Sawyer*.[5] Twain himself told of several instances of what he called his "unconscious plagiarism" and agreed with a victim of such borrowing, Oliver Wendell Holmes, that it was inevitable.[6] For instance, he wrote Howells in 1875:

Modern Philology 55 (August 1957) 1:21–35.

> I have just been delighting my soul for two weeks over a bran new and ingenious way of beginning a novel — and behold, all at once it flashes upon me that Charley Warner originated the idea 3 years ago and told me about it! . . . I would not wonder if I am the worst literary thief in the world, without knowing it.[7]

And in an unpublished portion of a letter of 1876, he indicates that he often consciously transplanted ideas from stories by others into new contexts of his own.[8] These contradictions of accepted beliefs about Clemens' way of writing justify a study of some possible sources of his masterpiece.

It was not by chance that a sizable body of Twain's reading during the years 1876–83, when he wrote *Adventures of Huckleberry Finn*,[9] was in a period of history. "I like history, biography, travels, curious facts and strange happenings, and science," Clemens wrote in 1874. "And I detest novels, poetry and theology."[10] Since he instinctively followed Emerson's injunction to "damn consistency," he managed to make important exceptions to his antipathies and to read not only histories and biographies but also legendary lore and fiction dealing with a period which fascinated him — that of the French Revolution and the decades immediately following it.

Exactly when he began reading about what he once called "his subject" cannot be determined. His memory was that he first read Carlyle's *The French Revolution* in 1871.[11] By 1877, he reported in a letter that he had also read S. Baring-Gould's *In exitu Israel*, Charles D. Yonge's two-volume *Life of Marie Antoinette*, "a small history of France in French," an unidentified story by Mme de Genlis, Taine's *Ancient Regime*, Dumas's *The Taking of the Bastille*, and an unspecified book on "the march of the rioters on Versailles."[12] In Paris in 1879, he "visited the scenes of that grim period," guided by Carlyle, Dickens' *Tale of Two Cities*, *Le Moniteur*, Michelet, Dumas, "and others."[13]

His two favorites were Carlyle's history and Dickens' novel. He read the former, says Paine, "every year or so,"[14] and in 1877 described it as "wonderful . . . one of the greatest creations that ever flowed from a pen."[15] In Book 2, chapter 14, of Dickens' novel, a frightened boy watches three body snatchers at work in a graveyard at midnight — a scene closely resembling one in *Tom Sawyer* (1876). This may be evidence — though, of course, it is not conclusive — that Twain had read it before 1879. Thereafter, evidently, he read it often: a friend quotes him as saying, "I have always been a great admirer of Dickens and his 'Tale of Two Cities' I read at least every two years. . . . I have finished it for the 'steenth time. . . ."[16] An 1885 notebook entry mentioned as an unamusing character, a relatively rare thing in Dickens, "the body-snatcher — Tale of 2 Cities."[17]

These favorites and other books on the French Revolution seem extremely remote from the adventures of Huck and Jim on a raft on the Mississippi or ashore in the 1840s. But there is evidence that, like other authors, Twain echoed — and transfigured — even such remote materials in his writings.

II

Portions of Twain's novel containing the most obvious literary echoes are chapters 2–3, about Tom's robber gang, and the last eight chapters, about Tom's and Huck's helping Jim escape from the Phelpses. These passages, burlesquing literature dealing, respectively, with the etiquette of robbers and the careers of prisoners, set forth many clichés of such writings. Tom, who at times sounds like a student trying to impress a professor by citing as many sources as possible, mentions in the two passages "pirate-books and robber books," *Don Quixote*, *The Arabian Nights*, Baron Trenck, Casanova, Benvenuto Cellini, Henri IV, and two novels by Dumas. As Professor Olin Harris Moore has shown, two or more of these books refer to prisoners' improvising a rope for use in escaping, improvising tools, manufacturing ink, writing messages, and taming rats or other unpromising cell mates.[18]

Throughout these burlesque passages it is usually impossible to establish unique indebtedness. Tom does refer to a specific source (not heretofore identified) when, in chapter 37, he urges Jim to raise a flower in the hovel which is his prison. When Jim doubts that it would be worth the trouble, Tom says: "Don't you believe it. We'll fetch you a little one, and you plant it in the corner over there, and raise it. And don't call it mullen, call it Pitchiola — that's its right name when it's in prison. And you want to water it with your tears." The reference is to X. B. Saintine, *Picciola*, which tells in exhausting detail how the Count of Charney raised such a plant and gave it such a name when imprisoned.[19]

Neither Carlyle, whom Tom might have read, nor Dickens, whose book was published after Tom's adventures took place,[20] is cited by Tom, but Twain may have had both in mind as "authorities" on robber gangs. Carlyle told of the taking of solemn oaths such as the boys took (1.5.2; 2.1.6, 11), Dickens of a cross of blood being used to mark a victim of revenge (3.9).[21] It is fairly likely that Twain had in mind Carlyle (3.5.3) or memorable incidents in Dickens' novel when he had one of Tom's band suggest that "it would be a good idea to kill the *families* of boys that told the secrets." Commonplaces of prisoner literature — the improvising of pens and ink and writing on cloth and on cell walls — are mentioned by Dickens (3.10; 2.6, 21).[22] And both books — and others — tell of prisoners changing clothes in order to escape (Carlyle 2.4.3; Dickens 3.13).[23]

However, though none had to derive exclusively from these sources, other passages in the account of Jim's escape are rather closer to Carlyle or Dickens. Carlyle, for example, tells how Commandant Gouvion, "watching at the Tuileries," where Louis XVI and Marie Antoinette were confined, became suspicious: "He . . . is paying some similitude of love-court to a certain false Chambermaid of the Palace, who betrays much to him: the *Nécessaire*, the clothes, the packing of jewels,— could he understand it when betrayed." Carlyle tells how, when the escape is planned, she warns him (2.4.3). Tom generalizes about this incident when in chapter 39 he says that the time has come for "nonnamous letters"—

> "Warnings to the people that something is up. Sometimes it's done one way and sometimes another. But there's always someone spying around that gives notice to the governor of the castle. When Louis XVI. was going to light out of the Tooleries a servant-girl done it. It's a very good way, and so is the nonnamous letters. We'll use them both."

It is necessary, Tom explains, to warn Jim's keepers because "they're so confiding and mullet-headed they don't take notice of nothing at all." Their attitude resembles that of Carlyle's glassy-eyed Gouvion, who, even after the maid's warning, fails to discover the escape until "some Patriot Deputy, warned by a billet" (possibly the source of Tom's nonnamous letter), hurries to the Tuileries and starts an investigation (2.4.4). Again, Twain may have in mind Carlyle's account — and that of Michelet — of Louis XVI's escape, which emphasize mistake after mistake in the bungled affair,[24] when he has Tom boast about his superior performance:

> "Boys, we done it elegant!—'deed we did. I wish *we'd* 'a' had the handling of Louis XVI., there wouldn't 'a' been no 'Son of Saint Louis, ascend to heaven!' wrote down in *his* biography; no, sir, we'd 'a' whooped him over the *border*—that's what we'd 'a' done with *him*—and done it just as slick as nothing at all, too." (Chap. 40)

The words which Tom quotes occur at the climax of Carlyle's dramatic account of the execution (3.2.8),[25] as well as in other less impressive accounts.

A story written by Dr. Manette (Dickens 3.10) is close to a suggestion made by Tom: Manette is picked up by two noblemen, who take him to minister to two victims of violence. "The things that you see here," one captor tells him, "are not spoken of." After the doctor has ministered to the patients, the nobleman gives him "a rouleau of gold." Tom, wounded while helping Jim escape, shouts as Huck starts for a doctor, "Well, if you're bound to go, I'll tell you the way. . . . Shut the door and blindfold the doctor tight and fast, and make him swear to be silent as the grave, and put a purse full of gold in his hand. . . . It's the way they all do" (chap. 40).

The number of books Twain burlesques in his opening and final chapters is remarkable. Unfortunately, though, the passages reiterate — too often, many feel — the point that Tom, by following bookish authorities, needlessly complicates playing robber or freeing Jim. When, for example, Tom insists that both a servant girl and "nonnamous letters" be used, letters have to be written, and Huck has to go to the trouble of smouching a dress, donning it, then shoving a letter under a door. Frequently, Twain has Tom exaggerate grim details, as when he insists that Jim's plant be watered with tears, although the count in the source simply uses water.[26] Twain often replaces highfalutin language with the vernacular: A passage in Dickens (3.10) runs, "I, Alexander Manette, unfortunate physician, and afterwards resident in Paris, write this melancholy paper in my doleful cell in the Bastille. . . . Some pitying hand may find it . . . when I and my sorrows are dust." Compare Tom's inscriptions, composed for Jim to scribble on the wall, "Here a captive heart busted," and "Here a poor prisoner, forsook by the world and friends, fretted his sorrowful life."[27] Usually, the seriousness with which Tom carries on his foolery adds to the humor: "Tom's voice trembled whilst reading [the inscriptions], and he most broke down." And always there is an incongruity between Tom's historic — sometimes tragic — models and Tom's insignificant and far from tragic actions in imitating them.

III

Much of the burlesque material, as DeVoto has pointed out,[28] is "excellent in its own kind." But since it wears its jokes thin by repetition, a study of Twain's use of sources here shows little about his versatile skill in adaptation. One learns much more about Twain's artistry by comparing passages in other — and superior — parts of *Huckleberry Finn* with analogous ones in Dickens and Carlyle.

Though Twain in 1885 was to call Dickens' Jerry Cruncher unamusing, in 1884 in *Huckleberry Finn*, he included a scene reminiscent of two passages involving him. Jerry (2.1) awakens one morning to find his wife upon her knees and forces her to admit that she is praying. "You're at it agin, are you?" he demands:

> "Saying your prayers! You're a nice woman! . . . Here! your mother's a nice woman, young Jerry, going a praying agin your father's prosperity. . . . You've got a religious mother, you have, my boy; going and flopping herself down, and praying . . . B-u-u-ust me! . . .

if I ain't, what with piety and one blowed thing and another, been choused this last week into as bad luck as ever a poor devil of a honest tradesman met with! . . . Ah! yes! You're religious, too. . . ."

Mr. Cruncher's temper was not at all improved when he came in to breakfast. He resented Mrs. Cruncher's saying grace with particular animosity.

Cruncher later makes similar remarks (2.14). The aggrieved attitude and the outrage are incongruous with the admirable activity provoking them—the practice of religion by a pious woman. Similarly, Pap Finn is abused and outraged because Huck has gone and put on fine clothes, has got himself educated, and may do something even worse—get religion (chap. 5):

He kept a-looking me all over. By and by he says:

"Starchy clothes—very. You think you're a good deal of a big-bug, *don't* you? . . . You've put on considerable many frills. . . . You're educated, too, they say—can read and write. . . . I'll learn people to put on airs over his own father. . . . You lemme catch you fooling around that school again, you hear? . . . Say, lemme hear you read."

I took up a book and begun something about General Washington and the wars. When I'd read about half a minute he fetched the book a whack with his hand and knocked it across the house.

"It's so. You can do it . . . you stop putting on frills. I won't have it. . . . First you know you'll get religion, too. I never see such a son. . . . *Ain't* you the sweet-scented dandy, though? A bed; and bedclothes; and a look'n'glass; and a piece of carpet on the floor—and your own father got to sleep with hogs in the tanyard. I never see such a son."

The adaptations here are functional: Since Huck has no tendency toward religiousness, Twain has Pap emphasize more justifiable accusations and subordinate the claim that getting religion may be Huck's next downward step. What Pap says serves admirably to characterize him on his first appearance and to motivate his future actions. Huck's cleanliness is shown to be an irritant to a man who is shortly to mess up a guestroom until his hosts "have to take soundings before they can navigate it." Huck's education is shown to be an affront to a man whose outrage will mount to frenzy when he meets an educated Negro. And his furious resentment of the inferior station into which bad luck has shoved him soon will motivate his showing "who is Huck Finn's boss" by taking Huck over to a hovel on the Illinois shore from which the boy is to start his wanderings.

Two other passages in *A Tale of Two Cities* may be relevant to a par-

ticularly amusing passage, Huck and Jim's argument about the French language. "Mr. Charles Darnay," says Dickens of a noble French emigrant,
"was established in England as a higher teacher of the French language.
. . . Princes that had been, and kings that were to be, were not yet of the
Teacher class, and no ruined nobility had dropped out of Tellson's [Bank]
ledgers, to turn cooks and carpenters." After Huck has told Jim about the
rumor that the French dauphin has come to America, the compassionate
slave suggests (chap. 14) that "the po' little chap" will be "pooty lonesome"
in a country where there are no kings: "he cain't git no situation. What
he gwyne to do?" "Well," says Huck, "I don't know. Some of them gets
on the police,[29] and some of them learns people how to talk French."

This remark, clearly reminiscent of Dickens' novel, initiates a discussion between Huck and Jim in which Jim's stand may have been suggested
by the strange attitude of the heroine's duenna in the same book (3.7)
toward the French language:

> Although Miss Pross, through her long association with a French
> family, might have known as much of their language as of her own,
> if she had had a mind, she had no mind in that direction; consequently,
> she knew no more of that "nonsense" (as she was pleased to call it)
> than Mr. Cruncher did.

On one occasion (3.14), she tells a French woman that she never has thought
she would want "to understand her nonsensical language." Twain's Jim is
puzzled when Huck tells him of the eccentric Frenchman's habit of saying,
"Polly-voo-franzy," when he means, "Do you talk French?" Jim says, "Well,
den, why couldn't he say it?" "Why," says Huck, "he *is* a-saying it. That's
a Frenchman's way of saying it." "Well," says Jim, "it's a blame ridicklous
way, en I doan' want to hear no mo' 'bout it. Dey ain't no sense to it." There
follows a hilarious argument, ending with a clincher by Jim:

> "Is a Frenchman a man?"
> "Yes."
> "Well, den! Dad blame it, why doan' he *talk* like a man? You an-
> swer me *dat*."
> I see it warn't no use wasting words — you can't learn a nigger
> to argue. So I quit.

Patriotic Miss Pross is contemptuous of French because she is "a subject of His Most Gracious Majesty King George the Third" and the un-
British ways of foreigners arouse her suspicions. Jim, a slave, has no thought
of such matters: he is simply ignorant — and logical. Huck, strong in his
belief that he is superior to a Negro in every way — a belief which is later

to be changed — fails to see Jim's logic. The passage therefore both represents the two characters and reveals a relationship which is to undergo a change important in the novel.

IV

Huck and Jim's talk in chapter 14 about the dauphin is initiated by a brief lecture: "I told about Louis Sixteen . . . and about his little boy the dolphin, that would 'a' been a king, but they took him and shut him up in jail, and some say he died there. . . . But some says he got out and got away, and come to America." Three chapters later, when two rascals join Huck and Jim, one introduces himself as a duke and asks to be treated accordingly. The other, to get even better treatment, says that he is "the pore disappeared Dauphin, Looy the Seventeen, son of Looy the Sixteen and Marry Antonette . . . in blue jeans and misery, the wanderin', exiled, trampled-on, and sufferin' rightful King of France."

The alleged dauphin belongs to the folklore rather than the history of the period after the French Revolution.[30] Huck has learned of the real dauphin and the legend about him from one of the books taken from the *Walter Scott:* quite possibly Twain went back and inserted the whole episode so that Huck might do this.[31] Though the book is not identifiable, some of Twain's reading about the lost dauphin probably is. Horace W. Fuller, *Imposters and Adventurers: Noted French Trials* (Boston, 1882), with "S. L. Clemens, June, 1882" in his hand on the flyleaf, was in Twain's library when he died.[32] A long chapter (100–142), called "The False Dauphins," tells the stories of "seven imposters [who] have claimed the name and the rights of the unhappy Louis XVII."

Four of these men, scoundrels as outrageous as any who ever misled a trustful public, are particularly interesting. The first, Jean Marie Heragault, like Twain's pretender, combined his "manoeuvers with swindling." The second, "the Duke of Normandy," visited New York, traveled through the South and along the Amazon. He claimed in his memoirs (1831; revised in 1843 and 1848): "I travelled through these uninhabited wilds, nourishing myself with fruits and turtle eggs, which I found everywhere along the banks of the river; sleeping at night upon [sic] the trees. . . ." The third, Eleazer the Iroquois, though born in the United States to an Indian mother, claimed that when struck on the head by a stone when a boy, he recalled more kingly facts about his past. These were verified in 1841, when M. le Prince de Joinville, meeting him on the Mississippi, recognized him as the dauphin. Both Heragault and Eleazer lived beyond the period of Twain's book.

The fourth, Mathurin Bruneau, since he once had an American passport, may have visited this country. Bruneau rehearsed for his big role by pretending to be an assortment of noblemen and gentlemen. One anecdote tells how

> he presented himself at a little inn near Saumur. There a peasant perceived in him a certain resemblance to the son of a widow Phelippeau, from whom she had received no news for many years, and who was supposed to have died in Spain. Bruneau caught the ball on the bound; hastily acquired information in regards to the family, and at once presented himself to the poor mother as her returned son. Received with joy by the widow he sustained for some time this deception, and then disappeared. (105)

This false dauphin's adventure is like one involving Twain's rascals. On the river, the king one morning gives a lift to "a nice innocent-looking young country jake," who mistakes him for one of two brothers of Peter Wilks, recently deceased. After the king quickly learns all about the Wilks family, he and the duke, with Huck acting as their servant, present themselves to the daughters as Peter's two brothers and for some time dupe the family (chaps. 24–28).

Then comes a twist: two rival claimants arrive, offer proofs of their identity, and suggest a test involving the disinterment of Wilks's body (chap. 29). This part of the episode may have come from Fuller's account of a trial of "the Duke of Normandy," which tells how a second claimant to the kingship interrupted the proceedings (131–32). It seems likely, however, that another chapter in Fuller's book, "The False Martin Guerre"— one of four about imposters who profited by passing themselves off as lost relatives — suggested it. Guerre, who has passed himself off as a lost husband, has, like the king and the duke, disposed of most of the opposition when an interruption of his trial occurs:

> At this moment, when . . . the judges of Toulouse were about to give the accused the benefit of the doubt, there arrived . . . a new Martin Guerre . . . he recognized the house where he was born, his neighbors, his relatives, his friends, as the other had done before him. . . . The new-comer arrived just at the right time to drag the judges back into uncertainty, if one may believe that they had finally satisfied themselves upon the proofs. (21)

In addition to providing details of plot, Fuller may have influenced the characterization of Twain's rascals and their victims. Constantly, Fuller comments upon the sheer audacity of the false dauphins and the childlike trustfulness of their victims. His summary (142) goes: "That such charlatans have found dupes, that they have been accorded such importance, and that they have been carried before judges rather than dragged to horse-ponds, the present generation finds it difficult to believe."[33] Like Fuller, Huck emphasizes the rash assurance of his rogues and what Fuller (100) calls the "imperturbable" credulity of their gulls. Like Fuller's false dauphins, the king and the duke — and frequently Huck himself — are brazen in their impersonations. Like Fuller' imposters, they easily win credulous or even violently partisan backers. Thus Twain, whose book frequently stresses brash deception and foolish credulity, takes without change from Fuller details in accordance with his view of humanity. But Twain's manipulations of his materials are more revealing than his borrowings. He makes an obvious change: so that both the king and the duke may play roles, he creates a situation involving two brothers. More important, instead of using skeletal summarized narrative as Fuller does, he creates characters — the Wilks family, the townspeople (including the unforgettable undertaker of chap. 22) — and he concretely represents actions in a way appropriate for a novel as contrasted with a bald "factual" record.

Both of Twain's imposters know enough history to notice that if, as Huck says, the latter's age is "about seventy or upwards," he is too old; for at the time of the novel, the dauphin, had he lived, would have been between fifty and sixty. "You! At your age! No!" says the duke (chap. 19). The king explains that "trouble . . . has brung these gray hairs and premature balditude." The king gives no evidence of knowing other details about his alleged past, but the duke shows that he has picked up from some source an interesting bit of information. Carlyle sets forth that after his removal from the throne Louis XVI was given the rank of "Citizen Louis Capet." Thereafter, Carlyle emphasizes the king's lowered estate by calling him "Louis Capet" (3.2.6, 7). The duke twice (chaps. 21, 26) uses a similar but even more derogatory term: he calls the dauphin merely "Capet." The attack is perhaps rather subtle for anyone who has not read Carlyle or some other historian or novelist who is fairly detailed,[34] and the dauphin fails to object; but the dauphin is in part repaid for constantly insulting the duke by calling him not Bridgewater but Bilgewater.

V

As recent critics have indicated, the themes developed by *Huckleberry Finn* are important elements in its richness. Not surprisingly, therefore, some of the most interesting relationships are between sources involving not only happenings but also attitudes and their counterparts in the book. Deeply interested in moral issues, despite his dislike for "theology," Twain studied his subject with lessons it might teach in mind. His course of reading gave him new ideas or bolstered old ones about humanity.

"The Reign of Terror," he wrote in a notebook in 1879, "shows that, without distinction or rank, the people were savages. Marquises, dukes, lawyers, blacksmiths, they each figure in due proportion to their crafts."[35] Having thus learned that men of all ranks are beasts, according to their opportunities, Twain in *Huckleberry Finn* manages to condemn the full range of classes, from kings to commoners.

Kings get their comeuppance in chapter 14. Kings, Huck informs Jim, "don't do nothing! . . . They just set around . . . except, maybe, when there's a war. But other times they just lazy around; or go hawking — just hawking and sp——." The attitude is shared by several of Twain's writers. Carlyle, for instance, twice levels this criticism. "Who is it," he asks, "that the King (Able-man, named also *Roi, Rex*, or *Director*) now guides? His own huntsmen and prickers: when there is no hunt, it is well said, *'Le Roi ne fera rien'* (To-day his Majesty will do *nothing*)" (7.7.2). Again: "Were not the king so languid! . . . Unhappy king, *he* has but one resolution: not to have a civil war. For the rest, he still hunts . . . still dozes, and digests; is clay in the hands of the potter" (1.7.2). Huck's highly vernacular comment — so different from Carlyle's mannered passages — makes his kings figures in a comic picture. An anticlimactic sentence helps, too, and Carlyle has no perceivable tendency, as the plebeian Huck does, to follow "hawking," mechanically, with two other words.

But Twain felt that he moved beyond Carlyle in his attitude. When he first read Carlyle, he wrote Howells, he had been a moderate revolutionist, "a Girondin"; but after several readings, "changed, little by little, by life and environment (and Taine and Saint-Simon). . . . I am a Sansculotte! And not a pale, characterless Sansculotte, but a Marat. Carlyle teaches no such gospel; so the change is in me — in my vision of the evidence."[36] Though he does not define his terms, his remarks then and later suggest that, for him, a Sansculotte is one who fiercely and recklessly battles to destroy nobility and royalty. With the exception of Yonge's biography of Marie-Antoinette most of the books which Twain read about the French Revolution would have inclined him toward the attitude he mentions. His letter of 1877 characterizes as "a very able novel" Sabine Baring-Gould's *In exitu Israel*, "the purpose of which," he says, "is to show the effect of some of the most odious of the privileges of the French nobles under *l'ancien regeme* [sic] & of the Catholic Church by the Assembly in '92." The chapters in Taine which, in the same letter, he says have been useful were probably among those which Edmund Wilson has called "admirable social-documentary chapters" showing "the intolerable position of the peasants."[37] Dickens, Baring-Gould, Dumas, Carlyle, and Michelet all melodramatically picture the heartless cruelty of nobility and royalty which forced revolt.

In chapter 23, "The Orneriness of Kings," when Jim voices astonishment at the low morals of the king and the duke, Huck refuses to be surprised because, says he, "all kings is mostly rapscallions":

> "You read about them once — you'll see. Look at Henry the Eight: this'n's a Sunday-school Superintendent to *him*. And look at Charles Second, and Louis Fifteen, and James Second, and Edward Second, and Richard Third, and forty more; besides all them Saxon heptarchies that used to rip around so in old times and raise Cain. . . . I don't say that ourn is lambs, because they ain't, when you come right down to the cold facts; but they ain't nothing to *that* old ram, anyway. All I say is, kings is kings, and you got to make allowances. Take them all around, they're a mighty ornery lot. It's the way they're raised."
>
> "But" [says Jim], "dis one do *smell* so like de nation, Huck."
>
> "Well, they all do, Jim. *We* can't help the way a king smells; history don't tell no way."
>
> "Now de duke, he's a tolerable likely man in some ways."
>
> "Yes, a duke's different. But not very different. This one's a middling hard lot for a duke. When he's drunk there ain't no nearsighted man could tell him from a king."

This passage, largely because of its humor, is much more devastating than Clemens' frequent direct attacks upon the hereditary classes.[38] The disgust of Huck and Jim, both lowly — and both relatively tolerant — with the king and the duke and Huck's nonchalant suggestion that these rapscallions are relatively admirable specimens are impressive.

Twain's study of the ways of those below the privileged classes during the Revolution led him to a conclusion quite the opposite of that drawn by Michelet. The French historian found in the period documentation for his mystical belief that "the very people, the whole people," were responsible for "the humane and benevolent period of our Revolution."[39] In the letter of 1877 previously cited, Clemens reports that his reading, by contrast, has led him to "hate all shades & forms of republican government . . . with an intensified hatred." He cites Carlyle, Dumas, and Taine as his most valuable instructors. Of this trio, Carlyle is the most outspoken in his criticism of republican government; a number of passages in *The French Revolution* point out its weaknesses, for example:

> Is it the nature of National Assemblies generally to do, with endless labour and clangour, Nothing? Are Representative Governments mostly at bottom Tyrannies too? Shall we say, the *Tyrants*, the ambitious contentious Persons, from all corners of the country do, in this manner, get gathered in one place; and there, with motion and

counter-motion, with jargon and hubbub, *cancel* one another, like the fabulous Kilkenny Cats; and produce, for net-result, *zero* . . . ? (1.2.1)

Twain ignores the Transcendental explanation offered by Carlyle for such weakness and advances another. "Mind," he says, "I believe this: Republican government, with a sharply restricted suffrage, is just as good as a Constitutional monarchy with a virtuous & powerful aristocracy, but with an unrestricted suffrage it ought to perish because it is founded in wrong & is weak & bad & tyrannical." The weakness of such a system and its cause, as Twain sees it, are satirically set forth in Pap Finn's longest speech (chap. 6), wherein he comments upon a Negro's voting:

> "They said he was a p'fessor in a college, and could talk all kinds of languages, and knowed everything. And that ain't the wust. They said he could *vote* when he was at home. Well, that let me out. Thinks I, what is the country a-coming to? It was 'lection day, and I was just about to go and vote myself if I warn't too drunk to get there; but when they told me there was a state in this country where they'd let that nigger vote, I drawed out. I says I'll never vote ag'in . . . and the country may rot for all me."

Pap, portrayed from the start as physically, mentally, and morally despicable, is perfect for satirical utterance and pretty certain, therefore, to voice views completely opposed to those of his creator. Here, for the wrong reason, he attacks a man who is qualified to vote and, for another wrong reason, disqualifies himself as a voter.

But Twain's writers naturally had less to say about common men in republican governments than about them in revolutionary mobs. From the records, he told his friend Fisher, he learned "that men in a crowd do not act as they would as individuals . . . they don't think for themselves, but become impregnated by the mass sentiment uppermost in the minds who happen to be en masse."[40] Compare S. Baring-Gould, *In exitu Israel*, 2:156: "the mob swayed and roared, and cheered, like one living body, not as an assemblage of individuals, each with a will and thoughts of its own." Other writers remark the same phenomenon.

This mass sentiment might be morbid fascination of the sort Carlyle emphasizes as he tells about the execution of Robespierre:

> Never before were the streets of Paris so crowded . . . one dense stirring mass; all windows crammed; the very roofs and ridge-tiles budding forth Curiosity, in strange gladness. . . . All eyes are on Robespierre's tumbril. . . . The Gendarmes point their swords at him, to show the people which is he. . . . Samson's work [with the guillotine] done, there bursts forth shout on shout of applause. (3.6.7)

After Colonel Sherburn shoots down Boggs on the main street of Bricks-ville, the crowd becomes a mob, and when Boggs is carried to the drug-store to die, it manifests "strange gladness." Huck writes (chap. 21):

> Well, pretty soon the whole town was there, squirming and scrouging and pushing and shoving to get at the window and have a look, but people that had the places wouldn't give them up, and folks behind them was saying all the time, "Say, now, you've looked long enough, you fellows, 'tain't right and 'tain't fair for you to stay thar all the time, and never give nobody a chance; other folks has their rights as well as you."

The impression of a surging, packed crowd which Carlyle creates by tell-ing of the jammed streets, the crammed windows, and the stirring mass, Twain achieves by a series of participles, "squirming and scrouging and pushing and shoving."[41] "Scrouging," since it is a word in the vernacular, introduces a comic note not found in Carlyle. The representation of the insatiable curiosity, the refusal to budge, of those by the window initi-ates satire. The satire becomes cutting in the quoted pleas of those be-hind who, ironically, demand in the names of "fairness" and innate human "rights" that they be allowed to sate their inhuman curiosity. The para-graph which follows distils the same commentary into an individual char-acterization:

> The streets was full, and everybody was excited. Everybody that seen the shooting was telling how it happened, and there was a big crowd around each. . . . One long, lanky man, with long hair and a big white fur stove-pipe hat on the back of his head, and a crooked-handled cane, marked out the places on the ground where Boggs stood and where Sherburn stood, and the people following him around . . . watching everything he done . . . and then he stood up straight and stiff where Sherburn had stood, frowning and having his hat-brim down over his eyes, and sung out, "Boggs!" and then fetched his cane down slow to a level, and says "Bang!" staggered backwards, says "Bang!" again, and fell down flat on his back. The people that had seen the thing said he done it perfect; said it was just exactly the way it all happened. Then as much as a dozen people got out their bottles and treated him.

This rivertown Bottom, who grabs both leading roles in his little chronicle play, and his gloating audience are individualized embodiments of the "strange joy" derived from witnessing a gory melodrama. He and the au-dience wallow in morbid memories. And the uptilted bottles at the end, so incongruous with the scene of horror just enacted, climax this bodying-forth of human insensibility.[42]

The crowd next shows the "mob-lawlessness" which Twain equated with "lynch law"—a phenomenon Twain found exemplified in *Le Moniteur*, Carlyle, and Dickens. Dickens' picture in *A Tale of Two Cities* (2.14) of a mob following a funeral procession shows as well as others in the reading how a mercurial group acts in an unreasoning fashion as one man when someone starts it. Somehow, the cry "Spies!" starts, and everyone joins in. "Pull 'em out, there!" shouts someone.

> The idea [says Dickens] was so acceptable in the prevalent absence of any idea, that the crowd caught it up with eagerness, and loudly repeating the suggestion . . . mobbed the two vehicles. . . . The dead man disposed of, and the crowd being under the necessity of providing some other entertainment for itself, another bright genius (or perhaps the same) conceived the humour of impeaching casual passersby, as Old Bailey spies, and wreaking vengeance on them. Chase was given to some scores of inoffensive persons. . . . At last . . . a rumour got about that the Guards were coming. Before this rumour, the crowd gradually melted away . . . and this was the usual progress of a mob.

The Bricksville crowd is similar. Says Huck: "Well, by and by somebody said Sherburn ought to be lynched. In about a minute everybody was saying it; so away they went, mad and yelling, and snatching down every clothes-line they come to to do the hanging with."

What follows resembles many scenes in Twain's reading wherein some forceful figure appears before a raging crowd, speaks to it, and sways or even quells it. Carlyle, as one knowing his theories about heroes might expect, describes several such scenes, picturing, for instance, Mirabeau (2.3.2), Marat and Robespierre (3.2.1), and Danton (3.6.2) as the forceful speakers. Dickens, who acknowledged "Carlyle's wonderful book" as a source in his preface, may have imitated him, as may Baring-Gould in *In exitu Israel*, 2:190, 52–56, and 219–23. Only Carlyle, however, steps into his book to ask, "Is it not miraculous how one man moves hundreds of thousands. . . . Military mobs are mobs with muskets in their hands. . . . To the soldier himself, revolt is frightful, and oftenest perhaps pitiable" (2.2.2).

Sherburn addresses the Bricksville crowd (chap. 22) in circumstances which make his words compel attention. The mob has come to his house "a-whooping and raging" with screaming women and crying children rushing to escape it. It rips and smashes the fence and has "begun to roll in like a wave" when "Sherburn steps out onto his little front porch, with a double-barrel gun in his hand, and takes his stand, perfectly ca'm and deliberate not saying a word." He stares the crowd into silence, then, "slow and scornful," says:

"The idea of *you* lynching anybody! . . . Your mistake is, that
you didn't bring a man with you. . . . You brought *part* of a man —
Buck Harkness, there — and if you hadn't had him to start you, you'd
'a' taken it out in blowing. . . . The pitifulest thing out is a mob; and
that's what an army is — a mob; they don't fight with the courage that's
born in them, but with courage that's borrowed from their mass, and
from their officers. But a mob without any man at the head of it is
beneath pitifulness. . . . Now *leave* — and take your half-a-man with
you."

In addition to the dramatic situation, these words in the speech augment
its significance: "I know you clear through. I was born and raised in the
South, and I've lived in the North; so I know the average all around." Since
fictional probability demands only that Sherburn know Bricksville, these
words suggest that he is Twain's *raisonneur*.[43] The reaction of the crowd
proves Sherburn's claims: "The crowd washed back sudden, and then broke
all apart, and went tearing off. . . ." And Huck's sheepish and comic conclusion makes the speech still more memorable: "I could 'a' stayed if I wanted
to, but I didn't want to."

Twain and his narrator, despite disillusionments about folk along the
river, resemble Carlyle, finally, in being deeply sympathetic toward victims of human cruelty. Whether he admires or despises such victims, Carlyle
shows great compassion when he tells of their suffering — writing of the
dauphin (3.6.3); the queen (3.4.7); Marat and his murderess, Charlotte Cor-
day (3.4.12); particularly of the king, the Girondins, and Robespierre. On
the death of the king (3.2.8) he writes: "For Kings and for Beggars, for
the justly doomed and the unjustly, it is a hard thing to die. Pity them
all: thy utmost pity . . . how far short is it of the thing pitied!" After recounting the executions of the Girondins (3.4.8): "Alas, whatever quarrel
we had with them, has not their cruel fate abolished it? Pity only sur-
vives." And after telling of the death of Robespierre (3.6.7) he says: "His
poor landlord . . . loved him; his Brother died for him. May God be merciful to him, and to us!"

After his account of Boggs's death, Huck similarly centers attention
upon his daughter (chap. 21): "Then they pulled his daughter away from
him, screaming and crying, and took her off. She was about sixteen, and
very sweet and gentle looking, but awful pale and scared." Although Huck
says little here about his own reactions, the details communicate his pity.
When the boy tells about the tarring and feathering of the king and the
duke,[44] he combines a description of the mob's cruel action with an expression of sympathy reminiscent of Carlyle:

Here comes a raging rush of people with torches, and an awful
whooping and yelling, and banging tin pans and blowing horns . . .

and as they went by I see they had the king and the duke a-straddle
of a rail—that is, I knowed it *was* the king and the duke, though they
was all over tar and feathers, and didn't look like nothing in the world
that was human—just looked like a couple of monstrous big soldier-
plumes. Well, it made me sick to see it; and I was sorry for them poor
pitiful rascals, it seemed like I couldn't ever feel any hardness against
them any more in the world. It was a dreadful thing to see. Human
beings *can* be awful cruel to one another. (Chap. 33)

This, like several passages by Carlyle, moves from the mob to its victims
and then to the writer's generalizations, Carlyle's addresses to the reader
are much more obviously literary in tone than Huck's report and brief comment; but, unobtrusive though they are, Huck uses poetic devices which
create an effect. The crowd is figuratively represented as "a raging rush"
moving noisily through torchlit darkness. Then the king and the duke are
shown, first unrecognizable as individuals, then as "nothing in the world
that was human," as if they themselves have become embodiments of the
inhuman abuse of which they are victims. They look like "monstrous big
soldier-plumes," the "monstrous" repeating the unhuman note, and the
soldier-plumes simile doing the same, but adding a grotesque touch. Huck's
report of his reactions, first to the sight of the victims, then to the action
of the crowd, is quite literal except for a phrase which echoes an earlier
one—"in the world"—here connoting death, which is the utmost result of
mob fury. Thus, though it says about the same things Carlyle does, this
passage makes its points in terms more typical of a fictional work.

VI

Twain's reading about the French Revolution seems to have shaped several
passages in *Huckleberry Finn*. Unless (as is possible) I have missed some
specific sources, a minority of these passages derive from individual
works—for instance, the passage burlesquing *Picciola*, Pap's scolding of
Huck, and the duping of the Wilkses. More passages, however—in general, the most interesting ones—are dramatic developments of attitudes
or themes set forth not in one but in several books about the French Revolution. Disregarding the inferior burlesque chapters, I suggest that reflections of his reading on this subject include several short speeches, two long
speeches by Pap, and at least five episodes—a sizable portion of Twain's
book.

    The indication, then, is that Twain's claim that this novel was "taken
straight from life" was inaccurate. Perhaps his notoriously bad memory
misled him, and he would have been more accurate if he had claimed of
this book, as he claimed of *Tom Sawyer* in his preface, only that "most

of the adventures recorded in this book really occurred." Perhaps another statement of his comes closer to indicating what happened:

> If you attempt to create a wholly imagined incident, adventure or situation, you will go astray and the artificiality will be detectable, but if you found on *fact* in your personal experience, it is an acorn, a root, and every created adornment that grows out of it, and spreads its foliage and blossoms to the sun will seem reality, not inventions.[45]

Emphasize the words "wholly" and "found on fact" here, and the implication appears to be that fictional happenings, in Twain's opinion, need only an element of factual foundation to have the quality of reality. In all the passages which have been cited, it is a fact that central characters are based upon people whom Clemens had actually known—Pap, Huck, Tom, Jim, the duke and the dauphin, Boggs and Colonel Sherburn.[46] The characters rather than the happenings, in other words, may have provided the factual foundation which Twain felt was so essential.

But whether or not the inclusion of passages probably reflecting Twain's reading about the French Revolution accords with Twain's theories, several of the passages, in parts of the book not in the mode of burlesque, are of some importance. Pap's long speeches serve to characterize him and to motivate important actions, and one of them gives ironic expression to a belief which is an important part of Twain's vision of mankind. Huck and Jim's argument about the French language reiterates details about their characters, marks a point in the development of a relationship significant throughout the novel, and, because of its humor, contributes to the charming picture of life on the raft—one of the most memorable and significant elements in the book. The impersonation of the dauphin likewise adds touches of comedy, helps Twain enlarge his panorama of life along the river, allows Twain to voice (through Huck) important beliefs of his about hereditary privilege, and makes probable concrete instances of human rapacity. The episode involving the Wilkses, which is made plausible by the dauphin's skill in making outrageous claims, again enlarges Twain's panorama and, in addition, embodies not only human guile but also human gullibility. The two lynching episodes not only picture an important aspect of the life of the time; they also extend and emphasize the commentaries of the book upon "the damned human race." Such thorough integration of seemingly remote material suggests artistry of a high order.

When Was *Huckleberry Finn* Written?

Albert Bigelow Paine, Clemens' first literary executor, believes that Mark Twain composed *Adventures of Huckleberry Finn* in three periods — in 1876, 1880, and 1883. Bernard DeVoto, Paine's successor, holds that he wrote it in two — in 1876 and 1883. Although when DeVoto disagrees with Paine, usually DeVoto is right, in this instance I believe that Paine is nearer the truth. Furthermore, I believe that both, with most other students of Twain, overestimate the influence of Clemens' Mississippi River trip of 1882 on the novel. If my beliefs prove to be well founded, significant revisions of the story of the genesis of the book will be necessary.[1]

Since both Paine's brief account and DeVoto's meticulous and lengthy one of the writing of the book are readily accessible,[2] I shall, for the sake of brevity and clarity, not summarize them, but shall set down my account, presenting whatever evidence for it I can. At appropriate points, I shall offer arguments opposed to those of DeVoto. In conclusion, I shall indicate the implications of my account.

Available evidence includes: (1) letters and recorded conversations relevant to the novel; (2) three groups of Twain's "working notes" — labeled A, B, and C by DeVoto, who first saw their significance; (3) references in Clemens' notebooks; (4) the only MS known to have survived — a partial holograph MS comprising (*a*) an insert of 60 pages (numbered 81-1–81-60) beginning in paragraph ten of chapter 12 and including the rest of that chapter and chapters 13 and 14, and (*b*) chapter 22 to "Chapter the Last" [43], now in the Buffalo Public Library. I shall make use of all this evidence — most of it available to DeVoto, but some not available to him.[3]

American Literature 30 (1958–59): 1–25.

Walterblairy Finn

II

Almost certainly, Twain started his novel early in July 1876, and completed it slightly more than seven years later, as he himself testified shortly after each of these dates. On August 9, 1876, he wrote William Dean Howells that "a month ago" he "began another boys' book—more to be working than anything else. I have written 400 pages on it—therefore it is nearly half done. It is Huck Finn's Autobiography. I like it only tolerably well, as far as I have got, and may possibly pigeonhole or burn the MS when it is done."[4] On August 22, 1883, Twain said that he had almost finished the book—"haven't anything left to do, now, but revise"—and on September 1, 1883, when he wrote his English publisher, he said that he had "just finished" it.[5]

Twain's own statements also indicate that he wrote the novel during more than two periods. These include statements about his customary ways of writing; statements, general and specific, about the writing of *Huck*; and statements about the amount of work which he did during the summer of 1883. Some of this evidence is considered, though not in detail, by Paine; all of it is discounted or ignored by DeVoto.[6]

Clemens—so he claims—habitually returned to work on a book after less than six or seven years. In his autobiography, he tells of finding, at page 400 of *Tom Sawyer*, that he could write no more: "my tank had run dry." Two years later, on picking up the MS, he "made the great discovery that when the tank dries up you have only to leave it alone and it will fill in time." This led, he reports, to his adopting a regular procedure:

> Ever since then, when I have been writing a book I have pigeon-holed it without misgivings when its tank ran dry, well knowing that it would fill up within the next two or three years, and that then the work of completing it would be simple and easy. *The Prince and the Pauper* struck work in the middle . . . and I did not touch it again for two years. A dry interval of two years occurred in *A Connecticut Yankee in King Arthur's Court*. A like interval had occurred in the middle of other books of mine. Two similar intervals have occurred in a story of mine called "Which Was It?" In fact, the second interval has gone considerably overtime, for it is now four years since that second one intruded itself.[7]

If Twain, therefore, left *Huck* untouched for six or seven years, he did something which he regarded as unusual and perhaps as disastrous.

Moreover, several statements of Clemens which possibly or certainly apply to *Huck* indicate that he worked on it during some period or periods between 1876 and 1883. In 1887, Clemens wrote that his habit was "to keep four or five books in process of erection all the time, and every summer to add a few courses of bricks to two or three of them; but I can't forecast which . . . it is going to be. It takes seven years to complete a book by this method."[8] When this was written, Twain's latest full-length book, the only one which had taken seven years to complete, was *Huckleberry Finn*. In 1890, Mark described to Brander Matthews, so Matthews says,

> his method of writing "Tom Sawyer" and "Huckleberry Finn". . . . He began the composition of "Tom Sawyer" with certain boyish recollections in mind, writing on until he had utilized them all, whereupon he put his manuscript aside and ceased to think about it. . . . Sooner or later he would return to his work and make use of memories he had recaptured in the interval. After he had harvested this second crop, he again put the book away, certain that he would be able to call back other scenes and situations. When at last he became convinced that he had made profit out of every available reminiscence, he went over what he had written with great care, adjusting the several instalments to one another.[9]

Although the specific statement here applies to *Tom Sawyer*, and perhaps to that book only, the introductory words suggest that it may apply to *Huck* as well, and even if it does not, at least it does indicate more than two customary stages of writing.

These references alone are not of much value because, in one way or another, all are ambiguous. But in addition, three statements which indubitably refer to *Huck* indicate more than two seasons of work. One introduces the passage removed from the novel and thrown into chapter 3 of *Life on the Mississippi* as "a chapter from a book which I have been working at, by fits and starts, during the past five or six years." Since this was written in 1882, "six years" is accurate; and it is noteworthy that this close to the event the author does not say that he has put the book aside but that he has worked on it intermittently.[10] Another statement in a letter to Howells, July 20, 1883, calls *Huck* "a big one that I half-finished two or three years ago," i.e., not in 1876 but in 1880 or 1881.[11] A third statement, of July 21, 1883, in a letter to Clemens' family, concerns "a book which I have been fooling over for 7 years."[12] *Huckleberry Finn* is not specified; but he had spoken to Howells about working on that book only the day before, and seven years is exactly right for it. And if "fooling over" implies anything, surely it is that he worked on it between 1876 and 1883.

There is also a statement of August 22, 1883, to Howells, about the work done by Clemens in the summer of 1883, which bears on the problem: "I'm done work, for this season . . . two seasons' work in one. . . . I've written eight or nine hundred pages in such a brief time that I mustn't name the number of days. . . ."[13]

Clemens, a man who took great pride in writing rapidly, and who tended to exaggerate, has a habit of overestimating or overstating the amount which he had written. On July 13, 1878, for instance, he estimated that he was writing 112 to 125 words a MS page,[14] when an actual count was to show that the average was 60 to 70 words: the mistake led to his believing that he had half finished *A Tramp Abroad* when the book was only a third completed.[15] Again, upon finishing *The Prince and the Pauper,* he wrote exultantly, "I've got nine hundred pages of manuscript stacked here before me,"[16] though the manuscript in the Huntington Library numbers 866 pages, five of which are end matter. When, therefore, he spoke of writing "eight or nine hundred pages," the likelihood of his having written more than nine hundred pages would have been small. Yet if he wrote all of *Huck* except the initial 400 pages during the summer of 1883, this part of the novel plus the other writings of the summer would have totaled 1054 or more pages.[17] The account which I am presenting subtracts about 200 MS pages from this total, and 854 pages would be much more likely than 1054 MS pages to accord with Twain's generous habit of calculating "eight or nine hundred pages."

III

Clemens' remarks about his working habits, about writing *Huckleberry Finn,* and about the amount of work he did during the summer of 1883, then, indicate that at some time or times between 1876 and 1883 he worked on the book destined to be his masterpiece. I believe that other evidence will support my claim that, specifically, he worked on it between the fall of 1879 and the spring of 1880, while in Hartford, and during some additional period or periods before the final one.[18]

Groups A and B of the working notes, which, as DeVoto saw when he came upon them, are of vital importance as clues, furnish strong evidence of work in 1879–80. The eleven pages of Group A (with some exceptions to be noted) contain suggestions for portions of the novel to be written; and all of page 2 and an interpolated line on page 1 of Group B cite pages in missing portions of the holograph MS of the novel which must have been written before they were made. And there is both external and internal evidence that these notes were written between mid-November 1879 and mid-June 1880.

Believing, as DeVoto did,[19] that a study of the paper and ink used might be helpful in dating these notes, I have compiled information about the nature of the writing materials used in them and in more than 400 letters, 26 MSS, and the notebook entries written by Twain during the years 1876–1884 inclusive.[20]

The study shows that during this period Twain used at least 27 kinds of paper and that he wrote with pencils, typewriters, and at least five kinds of ink. Often his lack of system verged on the sensational: at times, for instance, he used two kinds of paper in two letters written during the same day—or even in one letter; and in a MS of any length, he was fairly sure to use three to six kinds of paper and to change from one kind to another in a seemingly capricious fashion. Nevertheless, there appear to have been some patterns which are relevant in both his use of ink and his use of paper.

Although Clemens might at any time between the beginning of 1876 and the end of 1884 write in pencil, he was often pretty consistent in the type of ink which he used. Group A of the notes is written in violet ink. He used violet ink consistently between these dates: late November 1876 and mid-June 1877; late September 1877 and late March 1878; mid-November 1879 and mid-June 1880. He used it sporadically while in Europe during the winter of 1878–79—for example, in much of the MS of *A Tramp Abroad*. A study of his location during these periods shows that, except during the winter abroad (for reasons which I have not discovered), the ink was used only in Hartford. When he went to Quarry Farm for a stay of some length—in late June 1876, in mid-June 1877, in September 1879, and in late June 1880—he stopped using violet ink and switched to black, blue, bluish-gray, or brown ink (although I suspect that the brown ink was originally another color but underwent chemical changes) or to pencil. Then not until he had returned to Hartford did he resume the use of violet ink.[21] But a very significant fact is this: that when Clemens returned to Hartford in the fall of 1880, he apparently did not, as usual, resume the use of ink of this color. Moreover, I have been unable to find any scrap of writing in letters, datable MSS, or notebooks which he wrote in violet ink from June 15, 1880, to the end of December 1884. The ink used in Group A of the notes therefore seems to indicate that they were written in Hartford (or just possibly in Europe) before the summer of 1880.

The paper used in Group A also is helpful in determining their date. The last page, embossed with a design containing the letters "P & P," is paper of a brand used often, though intermittently, from the early 1870s. It occurs in letters dated 1876–79, in an unfinished novel started not later than the autumn of 1877 and apparently abandoned in January 1879, and in the opening pages of a play about Tom and Huck which may have been written in 1880 and which certainly were not written between 1881 and 1883.[22] It was used in three letters to Howells, dated June 6, 8, and 15, 1880. From the date of the last of these through December 1883, it does not occur in any of the 13 MSS and 226 letters on which I have data.[23] Hence it seems probable that a page of notes made in violet ink on this paper was written before June 15, 1880.

Each of the other ten pages of Group A is paper of a size and texture rather different from most kinds used by Clemens — fairly heavy, white, unlined, torn or cut across the left side, and measuring as a rule 4½ by 7 inches.[24] In the period studied, I have found no letters or manuscripts on this paper datable before his return from Europe in September 1879.[25] The last letter using it which I have seen is one to his brother, Orion, dated June 4, 1881; the last part of a MS (probably) is in a "Burlesque Etiquette" which Paine says was written in 1881[26] — evidence indicates in the spring. During this period, it was used by Twain in at least 19 letters and by his wife in one. In MSS, in addition to the "Etiquette," it occurs in a passage inserted in *Life on the Mississippi* — "The Professor's Yarn" (chapter 36), written in violet ink and therefore before the summer of 1880 — in "A Cat's Tale" of the summer of 1880, and in about 500 pages of *The Prince and the Pauper.*

Since some of the MS of *The Prince and the Pauper* was written during 1879–80 in Hartford, it is mandatory to consider whether this MS conforms with the usages of ink and paper I have described. Paine's claim that Mark wrote 400 pages of this in the summer of 1877 and "did not touch it again for more than two years"[27] is doubtful: pretty clearly he started to write in it Hartford in the fall of 1877 or the winter of 1878;[28] he resumed work on it in Hartford in the fall of 1879 or the winter of 1880, adding 114 pages by March 5,[29] which brought him to p. 326.[30] In Elmira, the following summer, he continued work, finishing the book, so he told T. B. Aldrich, on September 14, 1880.[31] This was apparently a typical overoptimistic estimate, for on January 21, 1881, he was writing his publisher that he had deleted an episode and "added 130 new pages of MS."[32] These well-spaced reports on progress made it possible to tell when and where the various segments of the MS — now in the Henry E. Huntington Library — were written. The pages written in Hartford in 1877–78 and 1879–80 are in violet ink, while those written in Elmira during the summer of 1880 and in Hartford during the following fall and winter are in bluish-grey ink.[33] Moreover, the pages written during 1879 and/or 1880 are on paper of the sort used in pp. 1–10 of Group A.[34] The testimony of the ink and the paper in this MS thus supports other testimony that Group A of the notes was written between mid-November 1879 and mid-June 1880 in Hartford.

Similar evidence indicates that one of the two pages of Group B was written some time during the same period. Both pages of this group are in pencil, a fact which is of no help in dating them. B-2 is Antique Parchment, paper of a sort I have not found elsewhere. But B-1 is Crystal Lake Mills paper: this paper occurs in 36 letters of the period 1876–80, in the play about Simon Wheeler (1877), in study notes for *The Prince and the Pauper* (1877–78), in the novel about Simon Wheeler (1878–79?), in ten pages of an unfinished novel about a village on the Mississippi (1880 or earlier), and in four stretches of the MS of *The Prince and the Pauper* which were written between January and mid-June 1880 (the last of these immediately precedes a 499-page stretch of this MS on the paper of pages 1–10 of Group A). The last letter which I have found in which it is used is one to Howells dated March 11, 1880, four pages of which are Crystal Lake Mills, while the other two are the paper of pages 1–10 of Group A.[35] Thereafter, down through 1884, this paper was not used in any letters or any MSS written by Twain of which I know. B-1, therefore, like the notes in Group A, appears to have been written before the summer of 1880.

IV

Having argued that the violet ink in Group A of the working notes offers proof that they were written in 1882, DeVoto continues, "But the internal evidence proves conclusively that these notes were written after [Mark Twain] came back from his river trip in 1882."[36] As his chief evidence, DeVoto cites three passages in a Secretarial Notebook kept by Roswell Phelps, a stenographer who accompanied Twain on the river trip, which he believes strikingly parallel with lines in A-1. One of these reads: "Negro camp-meeting & sermon—'See dat sinner how he run.' / Swell Sunday costumes of negros." The similar passage in the Secretarial Notebook, however, is about a Negro *church* meeting, the details concerning the sermon are entirely different, and nothing is said in it about the dress of the congregation. Another line reading "Capt. Ed. Montgomery" is offered as a parallel to two entries in the notebook about Montgomery. But, as DeVoto remarks, "Ed. Montgomery had been a companion of Mark's during the period of his piloting": Twain had reminisced about him as far back as January 28, 1866, in the *Golden Era;* so the jotting down of his name does not suggest that Clemens was recalling anything about him which he could not have recollected before the river trip.[37] The third line, "Describe Lara," DeVoto parallels with a passage in the notebook which describes not Lara but a scene "*below* Bayou *Sara*." DeVoto does not notice the discrepancy between the place names, but it may be important: I suggest that in 1879 or 1880 in Hartford, depending solely upon his memory, Clemens got the name wrong, whereas in 1882 at the scene on the river, where his memory would probably be corrected, he was accurate. These are the only parallels pointed out between the Secretarial Notebook and notations in Group A; they are the best ones the notebook provides; and they are not very convincing. The first notation, though the closest parallel, is remote, and like the other two, it could have come from Twain's remembrance in 1879 or 1880. And all the passages in Group A hark back three years or more before the river trip.[38]

These include, in particular, the notations on A-7 concerning the Grangerford-Shepherdson feud of Chapters 17–18 of the novel, which evolved from memories of the Darnell-Watson feud. DeVoto, like others before and after him, assumes that Clemens first heard about the Darnells and the Watsons during the river trip in 1882. But the passage about them in the Stenographic Notebook, dictated by Clemens, disproves this. After giving several details about their Southern vendetta, Clemens says, "I was on a Memphis packet and at a landing we made on the Kentucky side there was a row." The implication is that Clemens, as he himself testifies in an unpublished letter, and as Paine asserts, "himself as a cub pilot, came near witnessing the battle he describes" as part of the feud.[39] Furthermore, before 1879, Twain had made comments on feuds similar to those in *Huck* and had conceived of two of the characters and the chief happening in the Grangerford-Shepherdson episode when writing the fictional version of *Simon Wheeler, Amateur Detective.* The feud in the uncompleted novel started so far back in the past that its very cause has been forgotten, yet it is a matter of honor and glory to continue it. Judge (at one time Colonel) Griswold is described and characterized in terms often identical with those used in representing Col. Grangerford. The daughter of one of the feuding families is the prototype of Sophia Grangerford, and, like the delicate Sophia, she is wooed and won by a member of the clan feuding with hers.[40]

Since Group A refers to no matters not in Twain's thoughts or memories prior to 1879, it provides no internal evidence that it could not have been written during that year or 1880. And two of the pages, A-7 and A-10, seem to indicate that chapters 17–18 of *Huckleberry Finn*, detailing the life of the Grangerfords, Sophia's elopement, and the fight between the clans, probably were written two years before the river trip — during Twain's period in Hartford in 1879 and 1880. A-7 reads as follows:

George Jackson (Huck)		
Shepherdsons		
Bob & Tom Grangerford	28 & 30	*abt. 30*
Old man (Saul) Col. "		60
Betsy (negro) "		
Old lady (Rachel) "		
Buck "		12–14
Emmeline (dead) "		
Charlotte (proud & grand) "		25
Sophia (sweet & gentle) "		20
Harvney Shepherdson[41]		

This page is unique among Group A: (1) It is written with a finer pen and pretty certainly, therefore, at a different time.[42] (2) It is the only page which contains, not a suggestion for an action or an episode, but a list of names of characters in an episode. Among all three groups of working notes, the one most similar to it is C-1, which lists characters in *Huck* almost exactly in the order of their appearance through the first nineteen or twenty chapters. DeVoto soundly deduces that this listing was made when Twain was studying closely what he had written in order to recall characters and facts about them. For instance, "Miss Watson (goggles) sister to Wd Douglas" names that character at the point of her introduction, then records what is said about her. (The parenthesized word "goggles" is inserted. "Her sister, Miss Watson, a tolerable slim old maid, with goggles on," says Huck.) A-7 similarly lists the characters for the most part in the sequence of their presentation and records, usually in their order, the things said about each. A comparison of the notations with the text shows what happened: Huck starts the passage by identifying himself as George Jackson, and shortly the Shepherdsons are mentioned: these details are noted. Meanwhile, Bob and Tom Grangerford are mentioned and described as "thirty or more," Twain writes their names and "abt 30," then proceeds to list other characters and, in the column under "abt 30," their ages. When, however, he comes to "Bob was the oldest and Tom was next," he crosses out "abt 30," and puts into a new column — out of line with earlier notations — "28 and 30." Introducing Colonel Grangerford, Huck initially mentions "the oldest . . . about sixty"; soon after he is addressed as "Saul"; still later, he is called "Col." The entry follows a similar order — "Old man (Saul) Col. Grangerford . . . 60." Mrs. Grangerford is first an "old greyheaded lady"; later she is called "Rachel" — Twain's notation follows the same order. Her age is not given in the story or set down in the note. And so on. This page, I suggest, deals with MS already written — chapter 17 and the first part of chapter 18 (where Harney Shepherdson, misremembered as "Harvey" half way through his name, first appears).

A-10 seems to indicate that by the time it was written, Twain had completed, or nearly completed, writing chapter 18, which ends the Grangerford episode. "Back a little," it reads in full, "CHANGE — raft only *crippled* by steamer." DeVoto assumes that this refers to a passage near the end of chapter 16 which had been written in 1876.[43] But this still reads:

> She aimed right for us. Often they do that and try to see how close they can come without touching; sometimes the wheel bites off a sweep . . . we said she was going to try and shave us; but she didn't seem to be sheering off a bit. She was a big one, and she was coming in a hurry, too. . . . There was a yell at us, and a jingling of bells to

stop the engines, a powwow of cussing, and whistling of steam — and as Jim went overboard on one side and I on the other, she came smashing straight through the raft.

The change so imperatively urged in the note has not been made here: so far as Huck and the reader can know, the raft has been completely destroyed. Not in this passage but in the following one is the fact that the raft has been only crippled revealed:

> "Why [asks Huck] didn't you tell my Jack to fetch me here sooner, Jim?"
>
> "Well, 'twarn't no use to 'sturb you, Huck, tell we could do sumfn — but we's all right now. I ben a-buyin' pots en pans en vittles . . . en a-patchin' up de raf',' nights, when — "
>
> "*What* raft, Jim?"
>
> "Our ole raf'."
>
> "You mean to say our old raft warn't smashed all to flinders?"
>
> "No, she warn't. She was tore up a good deal — one en' of her was; but dey warn't no great harm done. . . ."

This is more than half way through chapter 18 — and it was "back a little" when Twain wrote the note in the ink and on the paper of 1879–80.

Internal evidence in Group B also supports the claim that the feud chapters were written in 1879–80. B-2 was, I suggest, one of a series. It was labeled "2" by Clemens; it shows him going through the MS page by page and jotting down details in the story; but it cites passages only on pages 218–73. A first page of this series (now lost) may well have contained similar jottings down through page 217;[44] subsequent pages (also lost), pages 274–350. B-1, not numbered by Twain, which contains interpolated references to pages 350 and 420, may have finished the survey.[45] The notation concerning the latter pages reads, "Poetry 420," and presumably refers to an obituary ode by Emmeline Grangerford quoted in chapter 17 — evidence that this was set down after the Grangerford episode was written.[46]

V

Pages 1, 2, 5, and 9 of Group A of the working notes look forward to at least the initial chapters in which the king and the duke are involved. Completing *A Tramp Abroad* (which took until January), writing 200 or more MS pages of *The Prince and the Pauper,* and writing chapters 17 and 18 of *Huck* probably kept Twain too busy between the autumn of 1879 and the spring of 1880 to allow him to write the initial chapters about these two con men. But I believe that during the summer of 1880, or during some other period or periods before mid-June 1883, he wrote chapters 19, 20, and 21 for the novel — the first three featuring the king and the duke. My belief is supported by several pieces of evidence, none perhaps conclusive, but all, as a group, rather impressive.

As has been indicated, Twain's estimate of the amount of work he did during the summer of 1883 works out most plausibly when one subtracts at least 200 MS pages from the total suggested by DeVoto — a total including not only the Grangerford chapters but also the three just mentioned which immediately follow them. Again, it is a fact that during three periods — the summer of 1880, the year of 1881, and from mid-January to mid-June of 1883 — he wrote little enough to make possible the writing, in addition, of some or all of these three chapters, for which ideas had already been sketched.[47] Paine, it will be recalled, states unequivocally that during the summer of 1880 Clemens "varied his work . . . , writing alternately on *The Prince and the Pauper* and the story about Huck Finn. . . ."[48] Paine does not state his authority, but it may well have been a statement of Clemens who, in December 1880, spoke in a letter to his sister of a half-finished book which Paine identifies as *Huck* — "two or three months' work on it yet" — then continued, "I shall tackle it on Wednesday or Thursday" under certain conditions.[49] Again, in a letter to Howells, March 1, 1883, Clemens made clear that a period had come during which he had both the time and the urge to write:

> I have been an utterly free person for a month or two; and I do not believe I ever so greatly appreciated and enjoyed and realized the absence of the chains of slavery as I do this time. . . . Of course the highest pleasure to be got out of freedom, and having nothing to do, is labor. But I take my time about it. I work one hour or four as happens to suit my mind, and quit when I please.[50]

If, as scholars have generally believed, the river trip had reawakened the author's interest in *Huck*, it hardly seems likely that, with time available, he postponed work on it from January to June 1883.

During each of these periods, some of the subject matter in chapters 19–21 was fresh in Twain's memory. In the summer of 1880, his recent study of the French Revolution and the distaste for kings and nobles which it inculcated were in his thoughts: these influenced chapters 19 and 20. In 1880, either before, during, or after the summer, while considering selections for a Library of Humor, he reread or recalled in remarkable detail the old humorous sketch about Simon Suggs which was the source of the camp-meeting scene in chapter 20.[51] In the winter of 1883, he had recently completed his river trip and more recently had finished writing *Life on the Mississippi*. During the trip, as he had in the past, he had visited down-at-the-heels towns like the Bricksville described in detail in chapter 21; and in January 1883 he had added a footnote to chapter 40 of *Life on the Mississippi* describing an incident much like the shooting of Boggs in chapter 21.[52]

References to a typescript of part of the novel, some in letters written by Howells and by Twain's business manager, Webster, some in Group C of the working notes, also may indicate a spell of work during one or more of these three periods. DeVoto's brilliant hypothesis that a typescript was made in 1882 or 1883 need be a hypothesis no longer, for newly discovered evidence shows that there was such a typescript.[53] The evidence is in a letter to Webster from Howells dated May 4, 1884, which tells of the latter's getting "the MS of 'Huck' copied here to a certain point where *another duplicate* begins. . . ."[54] An interesting revelation here is that only the first portion had to be recopied for the printer. Whatever the reason for the retyping was,[55] two methods of copying, and therefore two stages, may be indicated.[56] If so, the portion typed in stage one was fairly lengthy, since the copyist probably had to work full time during a week or so to retype it.[57] I suggest that this portion consisted of that part of the book written before the summer, 1883, and that the holograph for this was destroyed. I suggest that the second portion was that part written during the summer, 1883, and that the autograph version of this was preserved, and is the partial MS in the Buffalo Public Library.[58]

Group C of the working notes, assigned to the summer of 1883 by DeVoto, probably correctly,[59] contains nothing to contradict this theory. C-1 shows Mark systematically rereading what he has written and setting down reminders about characters and details—quite an understandable procedure if he had not gone through the MS for some time.[60] Page references are to the typescript. It contains two columns of notations, one citing details in chapters 1–9 of the novel, in order, the other in chapters 16, 17, 19 and (possibly) 20.[61] Although the second of these columns obviously was written later than the first, there is no evidence supporting DeVoto's guess that it was written much later.[62] Undoubtedly, C-1 and C-4 refer retrospectively to passages in the typescript as far along as chapter 19; and none of the notes in the group shows Twain planning incidents which occur earlier than chapter 23, which I believe was the second chapter written during that summer.

Finally, some newly discovered evidence supports my suggestion that chapter 21 was written by the time Twain went to Elmira in mid-June 1883. In the Mark Twain Estate Papers I have found a letter from Charles L. Webster to his aunt, Mrs. Clemens, dated New York, March 19, saying that he has secured three box seats and will be at the Brunswick about 7:30 P.M. The Brunswick was a hotel in which the Clemenses often stopped while in New York; the year was 1883; and evidently during a stay there Clemens persuaded his nephew to take Mrs. Clemens and Mrs. Webster to the opera that night while he enjoyed recreations more congenial to him — as most were.[63] That night or later, Mark wrote, in pencil, on portions of the sheet not used by Webster, a preliminary draft of the mutilated version of Hamlet's soliloquy of chapter 21 — "To be or not to be, that is the bare bodkin," and so on. Quite possibly this was written the very night of the opera, since Clemens considerately wrote in a margin, "Mch 19." Of course, he may have composed the garbled mosaic of quotations with no idea where he would use it, saved it until the following summer, and written a passage around it then. But there is one indication that he wrote it as an insertion: in his Notebook #17, of 1883, among suggested readings from *Huck*, others of which are denoted by typescript page numbers, he has, "—1-2 Hamlet's Soliloquy."[64] As has been indicated, he often numbered interpolations —1,—2,—3, and so forth; so the strong probability is that this was an interpolation. If so, chapter 21 probably was written before March 19, 1883.

Such are my reasons for believing that in 1879–80, Twain wrote chapters 17 and 18 of his novel, and that during some period or periods between then and June 15, 1883, he wrote chapters 19–21. I agree with DeVoto that, after that date, he wrote pages 5–13 of Group C of his working notes and the rest of *Adventures of Huckleberry Finn.*

VI

Dixon Wecter, in one of the best recent brief accounts of Mark Twain's career, admirably summarizes prevalent beliefs about the effect of the river trip of 1882 upon the novel:

> The final draft of *Huckleberry Finn* was intimately bound up with the writing of . . . *Life on the Mississippi.* In working more or less simultaneously on both long-unfinished books, he lifted a scene intended for *Huckleberry Finn* — about Huck and the raftsmen — to flavor the other book; but the great gainer from his trip was not the memoir but the novel. The relative pallor of *Life on the Mississippi*, Part II, is due in a measure to the fact that so much lifeblood of reminiscence is drained off into the veins of *Huckleberry Finn.* The travel notes of 1882 . . . are suffused with some of the finest situations in the novel: the Grangerford-Shepherdson feud, Colonel Sherburn and the mob, and the two seedy vagabonds who come on-stage as the Duke and the King. . . . Mark Twain's renewed contact with life among the river towns quickened his sense of realism. . . . The odyssey of Huck's voy-

age through the South reveals aspects of life darker than the occasional melodrama of *Tom Sawyer.* We are shown the sloth and sadism of poor whites, backwoods loafers with their plug tobacco and Barlow knives, who sic dogs on stray sows and "laugh at the fun and look grateful for the noise," or drench a stray cur with turpentine and set him afire. We remark the cowardice of lynching parties; the chicanery of patent medicine fakirs, revivalists, and exploiters of rustic ribaldry; the senseless feudings of the gentry. . . .[65]

DeVoto voices the additional belief that Group A of the working notes offer "evidence that Mark has found the true purpose of the book. He is going to exhibit the rich variety of life in the great central valley as his trip down the river has recalled it to him and as he remembers it from boyhood to young manhood."[66]

If my account of the writing of Twain's novel is correct, several of these beliefs must be abandoned. Topics which Wecter asserts got into the novel as a result of the river trip, "the senseless feudings of the gentry" in the Grangerford-Shepherdson episode and "the chicanery of patent medicine fakirs, revivalists, and exploiters of rustic ribaldry" in notes and chapters about the king and the duke, did not do so. It is hard to believe, moreover, that the trip of 1882 was needed to recall vividly to Twain's memory "the sloth and sadism of poor whites." He had written descriptions emphasizing these in his representation of Obedstown in chapter 7 of *The Gilded Age* in 1873, in the brief picture of Hannibal "drowsing in the sun" in *Old Times on the Mississippi* in 1874,[67] in an early portion of the *Autobiography* dictated in 1877,[68] and in an unfinished novel about Tupperville or Dobbsville written before 1880. The last of these contains the dilapidated houses on stilts, the fences leaning in every direction, the dust and the mud, the whittlers and spitters who were aroused from somnolence by a dog fight[69] — all details of the masterful description of Bricksville in *Huck*. Aspects of just such descriptions must have been in Twain's mind when he wrote in Group A of the notes: "Poor white family & cabin at Walnut Bend," page 1; "Shabby families," page 3; "Dog-fight — describe in detail," page 3; and "An overflowed Arkansas town," page 6. And if, as DeVoto says, Group A of the notes show that Twain had found the purpose of the book when he wrote them, he had found it in 1879 or 1880.

The influence of the river trip and of the writing of *Life on the Mississippi*, Part II, was, apparently, evident in a number of details in chapters 21–43 of the novel. Chapter 21 of *Huck* starts with rehearsals on the raft of the king and the duke for the presentation of the balcony scene from *Romeo and Juliet*, the sword fight from *Richard III*, and then the "soliloquy" from *Hamlet*. The pair of rogues and Huck then arrive in Bricksville, where they post bills advertising the impending appearance of "David Garrick the younger, of Drury Lane Theatre, London, and Edmund Kean the elder, of the Royal Haymarket Theatre, Whitechapel, Pudding Lane, Piccadilly, London, and the Royal Continental Theatres. . . ." Next, they wander around town, and the dilapidated buildings and sleepy loafers are described. Then Boggs enters, utters his boasts, and is killed by Sherburn. Some of these details were not suggested by the trip or the writing of the book: Group A of the notes had notations on the shabby town and townspeople and also suggested the performance of the scene from *Richard III.* But each is related to the trip or parts of the book about it. On May 2, 1882, while on the trip, Clemens wrote his wife about an evening at Cable's house in New Orleans during which "Guthrie's little boy (aged 6) and little girl (aged 4) performed the balcony scene in Romeo & Juliet in the quaintest and most captivating way. . . ."[70] A passage in chapter 51 of *Life on the Mississippi* tells how, during Twain's boyhood, "a couple of Englishmen came to our town and sojourned for awhile, and one day did the Richard III sword-fight with maniac energy and prodigious powwow. . . ." Another passage, destined to be deleted, remarked that in the early nineteenth century "the stage was almost wholly occupied by English. . . ."[71] And among the footnotes added to chapter 40 of the travel memoir in January 1883 was one of the Mabry-O'Connor fight which bore a striking resemblance to both the Owsley-Smarr shooting of Twain's boyhood and the Sherburn-Boggs encounter. (This noteworthy series of resemblances — and the discovery of the draft of the *Hamlet* "soliloquy" — have led me to suspect that chapter 21 of the novel was written in the spring of 1883.)

Two other episodes related to the trip and the account of it come in later chapters of the novel. Sherburn's contemptuous speech defying the would-be lynchers in chapter 22 is largely a summation of ideas which Twain states as his own in a suppressed chapter in his travel narrative.[72] And chapter 34–40, on Tom's engineering of Jim's escape, modeled on Tom's reading of romantic literature, are foreshadowed by two passages in the travel account — the attack upon the aping in the South of the romances of Walter Scott and the anecdote about the book-muddled carpenter who had "had his poor romantic head turned" by reading *Nick of the Woods.*[73]

Nevertheless, the inference is that, though the Mississippi River trip yielded several incidents in *Huckleberry Finn,* certain of the great episodes formerly thought to have been derived from it and, more important, the panoramic sweep and some of the chief themes of the novel came not from a revisiting of the scenes of the novelist's boyhood and youth, but from another source. In composing his masterpiece, as he had in writing "A Boy's Manuscript," *The Gilded Age, Old Times on the Mississippi,* and *Tom Sawyer,* perhaps Twain showed that he was capable of generating within himself, without external stimuli, the power to summon to his memories vivid recollections of times past and to give them form and meaning.

For the novel as a whole and its ultimate meaning, the chapters for which I have proposed new dates are crucial. The 1879–80 notes and chapters show Twain in the very act of discovering not only ways to get Huck alternately onto the river and ashore, but also, simultaneously, ways to enlarge and develop his theme. Note A-10, "Back a little, CHANGE – raft only *crippled* by steamer," records a momentous decision: instead of leaving the river and striking inland, Huck is to continue to drift downstream. Group A notes looking forward to the boy's adventures during the reign over the raft of the king and the duke show Mark inventing the means to this end. Thus a unifying element which critics often have admired – the continuous river journey[74] – is assured. The chapters of 1879–83, in addition, initiate a vitally important contrast – that between society ashore on the one hand, and the "primitive community . . . of saints"[75] made up of Huck and Jim aboard the raft on the other. Down through chapter 16, once the journey has started, Huck has encountered on the lonely river only individuals or small groups of individuals who happen to be there, and he has shored the raft in sequestered coves. Now he is to meet and, in time, to picture whole families such as the Grangerfords, then whole communities such as Pokeville and Bricksville and, in the end, a whole civilization.

There is evidence that, at some time before the summer of 1883, when he was to finish the book, Twain was thinking in these terms. I have pointed out that, before that summer, he himself had voiced important ideas later to be included in Col. Sherburn's speech in a discarded chapter composed for *Life on the Mississippi*, Part II. What is more, in another chapter deleted from the same MS, Clemens wrote a revealing paragraph about Mrs. Trollope's account of her travels in America:

> Of all these tourists I like Dame Trollope best. She found a "civilization" here which you, reader, could not have endured; and which you would not have regarded as a civilization at all. Mrs. Trollope spoke of this civilization in plain terms – plain and unsugared, but honest and without malice, and without hate. Her voice rose to indignation, sometimes, but the object justifies the attitude – being rowdyism, "chivalrous" assassinations, sham godliness, and several other devilishnesses which would be as hateful to you, now, as they were to her then. She was holily hated for her "prejudices"; but they seem to have been simply the prejudices of a humane spirit against inhumanities; of an honest nature against humbug; of a clean breeding against grossness; of a right heart against unright speech and deed.[76]

Authors have a way of praising other authors for merits which they believe they themselves possess. By the time Clemens wrote this praise of
Mrs. Trollope in 1882 or in January 1883, possibly he himself had had
the vision to portray, similarly but even better than she had, a "civilization" in a book to be published in 1885 which was to have on its title page:
"*Adventures of Huckleberry Finn*/Scene: The Mississippi Valley/Time:
About forty or fifty years ago."

Was *Huckleberry Finn* Written?

Reviewing *Adventures of Huckleberry Finn* a month or so before the American first printing came out, Brander Matthews commended Mark Twain for having readers "see everything through [Huck's] eyes" rather than "a pair of Mark Twain's spectacles," thereby letting "Huck set down, without any comment at all, scenes which would have afforded the ordinary writer matter for endless moral and political and social disquisition." For this and other reasons, scores of later critics also have praised the use of Huck as a fictional voice. Yet a meticulous critic bent on raising questions about Twain's use of his first-person narrator can come up with several. A review of some of these will, I believe, throw light on the book's artistry.

A reading of the very first paragraph will serve as a starter:

> You don't know about me, without you have read a book by the name of "The Adventures of Tom Sawyer". . . . That book was made by Mr. Mark Twain, and he told the truth, mainly. There was things which he stretched, but mainly he told the truth. . . . Tom's Aunt Polly . . . and Mary, and the Widow Douglas, is all told about in that book. . . .

The last page of *Huckleberry Finn* has Huck say that he finished unfolding the story soon after his adventures ended. The title page of the novel tells us: "Time: Forty to Fifty Years Ago." Since the first American edition came out in 1885, that had to be sometime between 1835 and 1845. But "Mr. Mark Twain" never signed his name to any piece of writing until 1863, and *The Adventures of Tom Sawyer,* which Huck is able to summarize, wasn't published until 1876.

There are other puzzlements, for instance: At the start of chapters 4 and 6, the facts about Huck's education are given. During "three or four months" until "it was well into the winter," Huck went to school "most

Mark Twain Journal, 1979.

all the time," or, if some of his statements are correct, he "didn't go to school much," perhaps because "whenever I got uncommon tired I played hookey." The result: he "could spell, and read, and write just a little, and could say the multiplication table up to six times seven is thirty-five, and I don't reckon I could go any further than that if I was to live forever." At this point, Pap began to interfere with Huck's attendance whenever he could. And in April or May, he ended his son's schooling by kidnapping him. Well, how did a boy of "thirteen or fourteen or along there" learn during less than a year of sporadic schooling to write this long novel spelling thousands of words in it correctly except when momentary ignorance or vernacular pronunciation dictated otherwise?

A couple of inconsistencies call attention to other problems. All the words in a 31-word note that Huck writes to Miss Watson (chapter 31) are spelled correctly, and in chapter 17 when Huck quotes himself as telling the Grangerfords his assumed name, he spells it "George Jackson." But a few pages later, when his young friend Buck spells it "G-o-r-g-e J-a-x-o-n," Huck says, "you done it, but I didn't think you could"—and it is obvious that he isn't joking. When Huck quotes Tom Sawyer's writings, Tom, better educated than Huck, is inconsistent at greater length. In chapter 38, when Tom composes graffiti for Jim to copy on his prison walls, he spells 60 words without an error. But at the end of the next chapter, when he writes a 200-word letter to the Phelpses, he misspells 3½ percent of the words.

A pair of Tom's spellings, it may be, represent dialect pronunciations (*northard* for *northward* and *stead* for *instead*); even so, Huck, after less schooling, is more restrained: he holds "dialect spelling," Robert J. Lowenherz calculates, to 1 percent of his total narrative. However, when the boy quotes himself in conversations, he uses twice as many such spellings as he uses in his narrative passages.

"Explanatory," just before the table of contents, leads to another inquiry. The book, it says, uses seven different dialects—that of Missouri blacks; "the extremest form of the backwoods South-Western dialect; the ordinary 'Pike-County' dialect; and four modified varieties of this last." What is more, it uses "shadings" of these, not haphazardly "or by guesswork, but painstakingly." How in the world could an unsophisticated teenage kid manage to notice and to record such distinctions?

One answer that has been given to this question by some commentators is: He didn't. Some claim that "Notice" was just one of Mark Twain's jokes which it is silly to consider at all seriously. Edgar Lee Masters, who spent his youth in Fulton County, Illinois, about 50 miles from Hannibal, among folk whose "lingo" was "just the same" as Huck's, considered it seriously anyhow, and found the dialect "preposterous." The author, he says, "went wrong many times . . . in choosing words for Huck and other characters." Masters gives examples:

> It doesn't sound true for Huck to say, "it don't make any difference." He must have said, "it don't make no difference". . . .
> Would Huck, in speaking of his feelings, say "very well satisfied"? Would he not rather say, "and feelin' all right"? Would he use the word "reticule" instead of saying "one of them things they keep needles in, ratacoul or something"? Would he not say "et" instead of "eat"? Would he not say "the lightning showed her very plain," instead of "the lightning showed her very distinct." Would he say "very gray whiskers" and not "whiskers all white," and "terbacker" instead of "tobacco"? At that Huck sometimes says "tobacker" as well as "tobacco." Would he speak of "astonishing things"? Would he say "gaudiest" and "pat" and "pleasure and astonishment," and "heptarchies" and "Domesday Book," "butt of maumsey" and "histrionic" with the slang word "doxologer" right by its side? Would he say "inscriptions" and "journals" and "responsibility" and "just so" when "that-a-way" was the colloquialism of Missouri and middle Illinois? . . . Huck would say "the other feller," and not "the other fellow." He would likely speak of sheet lightning as "winking and spreading," not as "squirting."

"There are passages, too, in the book," Masters claims, "where Twain is unmistakably talking and not Huck. They are too well expressed and compact for the unlettered brain of Huck to give utterance to." Masters doesn't say what these are; but William Van O'Connor cites examples:

> Huck's parody (Chapter XVII) of the activities of Emmeline Grangerford, poetess, is extremely amusing, but the "voice" is more nearly Twain's than Huck's. Many other things are put into the mouth of the twelve or thirteen year old Huck that, sometimes only weakly humorous themselves, are Twain himself speaking. [An instance is Huck's scrambled history in chapter 23, which O'Connor thinks inappropriate "from a boy with almost no schooling."] There are other witticisms about kings, a theme appropriate enough . . . , but Twain might have found some other way of introducing them. In "An Arkansas Difficulty" [chapter 21] . . . Twain . . . makes Huck relate an observation on "chawing tobacker" that one would expect to find as "filler" in a nineteenth-century newspaper or magazine. Most incongruous of all, perhaps, is Huck's rendition of Hamlet's soliloquy [chapter 21].

The juggled lines of Shakespeare's soliloquies really illustrate, not words "put into the mouth" of Huck, but Huck's quotations of the words of other characters. They therefore illustrate what hostile critics might call another anomaly — Huck's remarkable ability to give us the speeches and writings of some people without injecting grammatical errors or dialect spellings. Some other instances include: the dialogue and the writings of the Grangerfords (except Buck) in chapters 17 and 18, the preacher's exhortation in chapter 22, the playbills composed and displayed by the king in chapter 21, and Col. Sherburn's speeches — the short one to Boggs in chapter 21 and the lengthy one to the mob in chapter 22.

These questionings are of particular passages. Hostile critics may raise a more sweeping one about the composition of the whole novel. For months — up to the very minute his account ends — Huck has been unceasingly busy having adventures — at the Widow Douglas', in Pap's cabin, on Jackson's Island, on the river, in riverside towns, in the homes of the Grangerfords, the Wilkses, and the Phelpses. Whenever and how did he find time to put together this 366-page book?

A literal-minded critic, then, using "commonsense" yardsticks, can make numerous objections to Huck's performance as a narrator. Nevertheless, though commentators have lavished attention on Twain's technical ineptitudes, practically none has complained about any of the anomalies cited above. Instead, the overwhelming majority agree with Lewis Leary that "the honest observations of an attractive boy . . . and his view of the world" are what "secure for this book its high place in American writings." It seems worthwhile to ask why.

We may start with the most sweeping objections — that Huck couldn't possibly have told this lengthy story because he hadn't had enough education and he couldn't ever have found the time. Here a convention centuries old helped acceptance. Beginning in the sixteenth century, in hundreds of picaresque novels and their offspring, rascals, servants, social parasites, shady ladies, and teenage dropouts, many as illiterate and as busy with adventures as Huck, somehow got prose autobiographies assembled and published — the adult Lazo, Gil Blas, Jacke Wilton, Moll Flanders, and Ferdinand, in the past, and in more modern times Holden Caulfield, Jaimie McPheeters, and Addie Pray. Even more improbable autobiographers were accepted without too much trouble by some readers — dogs, cats, and a horse named Black Beauty.

Disparities between the language in the main narrative and in quoted speeches also had long been accepted without hesitation. Henry Nash Smith rightly has said: "As long as Mark Twain uses Huck simply to report dialogue, whether his own or others', he is following a convention which was familiar to Mrs. Stowe, or Cooper, or Scott, or for that matter Richardson. . . ."

Just as most amanuenses ignored awkward questions about such differing styles in dialogue, they usually didn't bother to explain the ways long first-person stories came into being. Mark Twain by contrast took some pains to keep Huck from out-and-out claiming that he wrote his story. In his final paragraph, Huck speaks of himself doing what he reported, in his first paragraph, Mr. Mark Twain had done — "making" a book: ". . . there ain't nothing more to write about, and I am rotten glad of it, because if I'd a knowed what a trouble it was to make a book I wouldn't a tackled it. . . ."

To suggest how the story was told "in the vernacular, through the eyes and sensibility of a river rat," Huck, William M. Gibson imaginatively alleged that something comparable to a modern machine did the job:

> [Huck] addresses the reader orally — for it is a speaking letter, dictated or tape-recorded as it were — and ingratiatingly in the first paragraph; and he confides his plans to the reader in the last paragraph and signs his communication "Yours truly/Huck Finn" to conclude the work. But the absurdity of the form is glimpsed only momentarily as the reader enters into and emerges from the imaginary world of the story, and it vanishes entirely while he is inside that world. The skill, that is, with which Clemens speaks through the double mask of "Mark Twain" and that of the vernacular-voiced adolescent is all but flawless.

Illuminating though it is, Professor Gibson's analogy between the style of the book and that of a tape recording, like most analogies, isn't quite impeccable. As Mark Twain fully realized, the style wasn't exactly that of talk. It was a talklike style, one modified to give the impression of talk — literary dialect. Twain, as he himself said, knew that "the best and most telling speech [in print] is not the actual impromptu one, but the counterfeit of it, [speech that] will seem impromptu." "Written things," he saw, "have to be limbered up, broken up, colloquialized, and turned into the common forms of unpremeditated talk" thanks to "a touch of indifferent grammar flung in here and there, apparently at random." He knew what H. Allen Smith has called "the secret of dialect writing" — "always to stop some distance short of perfection." "Rigid consistency," Smith continues, "is a sin committed by many who try to write in dialect. It's the spacing of the dialect words that is important."

Huck doesn't do what some nineteenth-century humorists, local colorists, and poor spellers did — set up so many dialect roadblocks that would-be readers today are unwilling or unable to track down his meanings. His selective version of vernacular speech is economical and suggestive rather than exhaustive and exhausting. In terms of what it is, Huck's lingo therefore can't legitimately be criticized the way Masters criticizes it. Even granting, for the sake of argument, that every word and phrase which Masters cites isn't one that a Missouri hobbledehoy would know or utter, we can dismiss his gripes as irrelevant, incompetent, and immaterial.

As they justify their all but unanimous liking for the "voice" that tells Huck's story, critics often say why they aren't much bothered by any of the novel's "illogicalities." In addition to Professor Gibson, whom I have quoted, three critics, in fact, offer reasons in passages about the boy's anachronism-filled first paragraph: Carl Van Doren writes that the author, "with the very first sentence . . . fell into an idiom and rhythm flawlessly adapted to the naive, nasal, drawling little vagabond . . . mouthpiece for himself so completely that the whole of his tough, ignorant, generous, loyal, mendacious nature lies revealed." In Huck's brief first sentence, says Pascal Covici, Jr., he "persuades us to take his existence for granted. . . . The illusion that Huck is real is so intense that we never ask ourselves when in the world of time Huck is actually writing his story. He is immediately present as an actor." And Robert J. Lowenherz says of the paragraph: "In 108 words, Mark Twain firmly establishes the vernacular speech of his narrator Huck, characterizes him, enunciates one of the major themes of the story, provides a frame of reference for the action, and even works in some free advertisement for . . . *Tom Sawyer*."

As these commentators argue, two interrelated elements erase most readers' possible worries — the brilliant fleshing out of Huck's rounded character and the highly appropriate style that makes him completely acceptable as a narrator. Frank Baldanza puts it very well:

> Because Huck tells his story himself, the stylistic richness is immeasurably deepened by the rhythms, intonations, and choice of words of this magnificent child. . . . Huck's own vulgar but richly beautiful lingo . . . carries the narration along as smoothly and majestically as the river itself. . . . The highest accolades . . . must be reserved for the complexity of moral awareness on the part of this growing boy.

Bothersome or not (and luckily not) and anachronistic or not, Huck's early mention of "Mr. Mark Twain," preceded as it is in the first edition of the book by Twain's name on the cover, the title page, and (as a signature) under a photograph of a bust of him, stresses an important disparity — between the actual and the fictitious narrators. Unsophisticated, innocent, completely without humor, and sure that his most virtuous acts are wicked enough to damn him to hell, Huck constantly differs from his creator, and time after time the resulting incongruity is essential to the humor of America's funniest classic.

Mark Twain's "High and Delicate Art"

Introduction to *Selected Shorter Writings of Mark Twain*

For nearly two decades before attempting to compose a full-length book from scratch, Samuel Langhorne Clemens wrote only short pieces. Before he was eighteen, in Hannibal in 1852 and 1853, he wrote sketches and skits. Journeying eastward as a tramp printer, he contributed travel letters to his brother's newspaper. Back in the Midwest in 1856 and 1857, he wrote a letter that first mined one of his richest literary veins — that of tall tale fantasy — and three dialect travel letters. Between 1857 and 1861, while a pilot, he published a burlesque prediction of river conditions in the New Orleans *True Delta;* he probably contributed other short pieces, as yet unidentified, to this or other newspapers.[1] Between 1862 and 1868, as a journalist in Virginia City, San Francisco, New York, and Washington, D.C., Mark Twain (as he began to sign himself in 1863) wrote feature stories, political reports, and sketches. *The Innocents Abroad* (1869) was less a unified account than a compilation of travel letters. Not until 1870 did he attempt a full-length book, *Roughing It,* and even here when the going became tough he utilized short pieces. Though he did compose books thereafter, until his last days Twain devoted much time to short works. Between 1894 and his death in 1910 his outstanding achievements were a short story and a novelette.

To trace Twain's development as a writer from its start to its conclusion, therefore, one must study his shorter creations. Any account of Twain's changing philosophy — or, if that seems too pretentious a term, his evolving opinions and prejudices — also depends upon a scrutiny of short works. For his ideas about literary craftsmanship, about the drives determining men's actions, about the damned and doomed human race, often appear first and last and are most clearly set forth in shorter writings.

One who studies such works perceives that, for all his apparent diffusion, Twain works best in small compass. His travel books, autobiographi-

Boston: Houghton Mifflin, 1962.

cal books, and novels are loose or disjointed, varied in tone, wavering in intent. Evidence that they are episodic is the fact that readers recall parts and miss overall patterns and the fact that Twain could use excerpts for platform readings or an anthology without bothering to place them in context. Varied though they are, works which — as wholes — show Twain coming closest to perfection all are short.

I

"Training," wrote the Connecticut Yankee with his creator's concurrence, "is everything." Though the humorist's training was not quite everything shaping his work, it was vastly important. Significantly, it concentrated upon shorter compositions.

During his nine years of schooling the embryonic author probably was escorted through nothing longer than essays, sketches, tales, poems, and brief excerpts in readers (McGuffey's or some less famous rival's), and encouraged to notice little beyond their preachments. Extracurricular reading included Sunday school magazines; *Godey's* and annuals which specialized in the same genres; and of course the Bible, which assembled short units. Longer works included *Pilgrim's Progress*, Ossian, and romantic novels for which, in retrospect at least, Clemens had little liking.

As printer's devil the boy enrolled in what Lincoln called "the poor boy's college." "There is something in the very atmosphere of a printing office," said the Hannibal *Gazette*, April 1, 1847, "calculated to awake the mind and inspire a thirst for knowledge." That year Sam Clemens was apprenticed to a printer — a turning point, he held, in his life: "I became a printer, and began to add one link after another to the chain which was to lead me into the literary profession." "One isn't a printer ten years," he explained, "without setting up acres of good and bad literature, and learning — unconsciously at first, consciously later — to discriminate between the two . . . ; and meantime he is unconsciously acquiring what is called a 'style.'"

Literature young Clemens set up for newspapers could have included anecdotes about authors and brief excerpts and poems. More useful to a budding native humorist were anecdotes, letters, monologues, and tales by Down East and Southwestern humorists also used as fillers. Since even humble newspapers received exchanges free, Sam saw periodicals that were leading purveyors of American humor — the St. Louis *Reveille*, the *Carpet-Bag*, *Yankee Blade*, *Brother Jonathan*, and the *Spirit of the Times*. Some were quoted by newspapers on which he worked.[2] The *Spirit* and *Brother Jonathan* he recalled decades later as publications of those days, and he recalled in detail some humor which he could have seen only in newspapers and magazines.[3]

Particularly revealing are humorists' names which he jotted down at random for possible inclusion in an anthology on which he did a great deal of work between 1879 and 1888. These show that he recalled all the chief pre–Civil War Yankee and Southwestern humorists well enough to specify particular sketches and that he could also name the most popular anonymous hits. He also listed all leading postwar humorists whose rise was contemporaneous with his.[4] *Mark Twain's Library of Humor* (1888) was, as the introduction claims, "representative of every period and section . . . from the days of Irving . . . onward." All the selections are short and for the most part completely self-contained units. If (as much evidence shows) Twain was largely schooled by these native humorists, his training was in writing short pieces.

What he learned can be inferred at the start only from his humorous writings; formulations of theories came later. Apprentice writings show him, under the tutelage of contemporaneous humorists, experimenting with "realistic" fiction, the tall tale, and the burlesque — all important throughout his career.

"The Dandy Frightening the Squatter" (1852), the earliest piece attributed to Clemens,[5] is primitive fiction. Granted that (as I suspect) he wrote it, it shows him using the most common form of humor, the anecdote, portraying ubiquitous type characters and unfolding a story the details and general outlines of which were widespread. In time he would view this genre with contempt and claim that a machine could manufacture such a story; but (just possibly because he wrote it for a Boston magazine or an editor revised it) its telling proves that even an author could not necessarily tell it well. It contains several irrelevancies; an ill-advised transition halts its action half an hour; it orders its happenings anticlimactically. Its diction is stuffy, its choice of details undistinguished. Trite characterizations fail to individualize — "a tall brawny woodsman" and "a spruce young dandy, with a killing moustache, &c." (The "&c." is a giveaway.) The dandy's discomfort and the embarrassing scrutiny of his mishap by the ladies — supposedly high comic points — are so unimaginatively pictured as to have little impact; the squatter's comment — hopefully another high point — is as colorless.

Whether Clemens wrote this or not, its faults point up excellences in his later achievements. So do those of another primordial fiction, the Snodgrass letter of 1856. Like two other travel letters for the Keokuk *Post*, this apes myriads of American skits showing experiences of a bumpkin in a city. The central episode is embarrassingly like one in *Major Jones's Sketches of Travel* (1847), letters by a Georgia hayseed. The Snodgrass letters, like the major's, lean heavily upon dialect, bad grammar, and cacography to render comic misjudgments and mishaps. Most of Snodgrass' phrasings, however, cast no light upon his backgrounds, education, likes and dislikes — his character. The one flash of imagination in the letter is Snodgrass' daydream about the chain of events which may follow his helping the young woman — his courtship, her father's approval, the duel, and a rich marriage;[6] but the depiction of the crass oaf elsewhere makes this flight highly uncharacteristic. Anecdote and letter show that to succeed in fiction the author needed to learn to individualize characters, relate speeches and actions to characterizations, order happenings, embody amusing details, and improve his style.

Between these came the "Bugs" letter, May 25, 1856. When girlfriend Annie Taylor, whose grades in composition at Iowa Wesleyan were "conspicuously low," asked Clemens to ghostwrite an essay, he responded with this fantasy. It was in the mode of the tall tale, which had flourished in every section of America for decades.[7] A masterpiece in the genre, Thorpe's "The Big Bear of Arkansas" (1841), was still being reprinted; another, "Crockett's Morning Hunt," had appeared in 1853 in a *Crockett Almanac* — a publication now ending a twenty-one-year run. Comic magazines were featuring similar yarns. As more immediate models, Clemens may have recalled Negro animal folk tales that as a boy he had heard Uncle Dan'l tell on John Quarles's farm.

Free of any restraints writing for print perhaps inspired, Clemens used a style more authentically colloquial and amusing than one finds elsewhere in his writings of the 1850s. His inventive comic details are impressive. Even more admirable is his narrative ordering, for beginning with insects classifiable scientifically as "all the varieties . . . in natural history," he gives them more and more exclusively human attributes until as a fitting climax they achieve immortal souls capable of "passing away" to heavenly rewards. The twenty-year-old author showed faint but clear signs of genius in a genre which he would bring to perfection. Tradition, chance, or art — or all three — helped him hit upon a climactic arrangement. This procedure of arranging fantasies climactically would become a standby: he would use it in various ways in his best tall tales.

Before returning to this form, Clemens worked in other areas, notably that of burlesque. Throughout his apprentice years, comic magazines and newspapers teemed with short burlesque novels, learned lectures, and travel literature; and popular plays parodied romantic dramas. "River Intelligence" (New Orleans *Daily Crescent*, May 17, 1869), the one newspaper piece certainly ascribable to Clemens in pilothouse days, is in this mode. Inspired by Captain Isaiah Sellers' published prediction of high waters flooding New Orleans streets, this chides the captain for being an over-cautious pilot and in the tradition takes off his faults: It makes even wilder predictions and, in mockery of Sellers' overloaded memory, wallows in distant dates climaxed with a reference to the time "when me and DeSoto discovered the Mississippi." Though obvious, it exploits every possibility.

"A Washoe Joke" (1862) was the most famous of several burlesques produced in Virginia City. On the mining frontier, the first frontier de-veloped chiefly with the aid of science, humorists had given the tall tale a scientific guise, and only recently Clemens had noticed a rush of stories "about petrifactions and other natural marvels."[8] The author was convinced that the piece failed because "I depended on the way the petrified man was *sitting* to explain to the public that he was a swindle" and because details about the creature's thumbing his nose were too obscured by other details for readers to get the point.[9] Luckily the article does not depend upon this trick alone. It combines burlesque of the dispassionate style and the out-landish content of scientific reports, the similarly deadpan and circumstan-tial tone of the tall tale, and caricature. In the manner of Phoenix's earlier Professor Ellenbogen reports, it ponderously records minute details con-cerning an alleged scientific discovery. And incidentally, to pay off a per-sonal grudge, to its "string of roaring absurdities" the author adds another by having Justice Sewell apply irrelevant legalistic and moral formulas in reaching his decision.

II

Apprentice writings, then, prove that Clemens followed trails worn smooth by earlier humorists — unconsciously it may be. But if so far he had learned unconsciously, soon he must have begun to learn consciously, or at least, as he once put it, "half-consciously." In 1863 he adopted a pseudonym iden-tifying a public literary role which he would play throughout the rest of his writing career. In the fall of 1865, praise of his writings by unbiased Eastern editors persuaded him that he had a "call" to write humor and that he should "drop all trifling" and concentrate upon "seriously scribbling to excite . . . *laughter.*"[10]

Not long before voicing this resolution the humorist had written "Jim Smiley and His Jumping Frog," destined to appear in the New York *Satur-day Press*, November 18, 1865, and to be recognized as his earliest master-piece. His numerous revisions of this and his precise discussions of its aims and means show that he gave its writing thoughtful and painstaking con-sideration.

During the following decades, Mark Twain wrote a great many words about the author's craft. Because as a humorist he habitually played the part of an ignoramus, he depreciated his literary achievements even more than Hawthorne had his, and as a result even critics gifted with humor have been misled by his levity. All the same, he was, like Hawthorne, more assured as a craftsman than he consistently admitted. Whether his comments were ironic or not and whether his reasoning was a priori or not, his remarks about writing help a reader see how he went about his work, what he attempted and what he achieved.

In "The Art of Authorship" (1890), he characterizes his training as "unconscious or half-conscious . . . guided and governed and made by-and-by unconsciously systematic, by an automatically-working taste . . . which selects and rejects without asking any help." For various reasons, this statement must be taken with more than the mandatory grain of salt: As the first paragraph of this article indicates, Twain is as usual swathing his serious thought in humor. He admits here that his training and art may be at least "half-conscious," and elsewhere he calls it "conscious." And he characterizes his taste as "systematic," and at least "supposes" that he must have "methods in composition." Sydney J. Krause has good reason to suggest that his probable meaning is "that he had no complete understanding of the underlying methods by which his art was formed and that he felt that the creative faculties were basically unamenable to full analysis. What he did not understand Twain simply transferred to the province of taste. . . . On this basis, creativity may not be strictly *reasoned*, though it does not follow that it must be either unconscious or automatic."[11]

The history of several of Twain's books supports Krause's further claim that, though he often started to write without any formulated plan, Twain's systematic procedure was to discover his plan as he wrote. He might start "a piece of literary work wrong — and again — and again"; but he had faith that "there is a way, if you could only think it out . . . — the one right way, the sole way for *you*." "I've had no end of experience in that," he adds.[12] One who winnows the chaff from his account of the writing of *Pudd'nhead Wilson* sees that upon finding that he has superseded "the original intention (or motif)" with another, he encounters "no further trouble." Writing several versions of "Captain Stormfield's Visit to Heaven," he is troubled until he hits upon "the right plan"; thereafter he is certain that he can finish the story. An indispensable initial step, then, was discovering "a plan" just right for the material and the author.

How inclusive his term "plan" was he nowhere specifies. But creative authors often scold other literary men for committing errors which they believe they themselves avoid and praise their fellows for triumphs which they believe they themselves share. For these reasons, Twain's detailed critiques of fellow craftsmen have value both as evidence about his sophistication concerning techniques and as guides to his own procedures.

"Fenimore Cooper's Literary Offenses" (1895) Twain composed in a typical way, writing out and extensively revising two versions before discovering the scheme for the final one. The published article is admirably organized and inclusive. Rules "governing literary art in the domain of romantic fiction" which begin the essay are systematically ordered to deal in turn with plot, then characters (including necessary relationships between plot and characters), then with style. He turns from these rules, each of which he holds Cooper violated, to the personal shortcomings which caused him to violate them—poverty of invention, "inaccurate observation," and a "word-sense" that is "singularly dull"—noting how each flaw relates to others and to Cooper's works. His summary recapitulates each accusation while particularly stressing Cooper's consequent failure to stir readers.

Twain's discussion of plot, true enough, is laconic, but it is precise: a satisfactory plot must have "order, system, sequence [and] result"; "the episodes of a tale shall be necessary parts of the tale, and shall help develop it." Discussing "the personages of a tale," the author holds that a fictionist should not introduce characters without functions or report dialogues irrelevant to the narrative, and that he should ascribe to characters only consistent actions and speeches. The consistency here is internal; Twain also speaks of external fidelity—lifelikeness—and shows that he is aware of a distinction. So, blind though it is to Cooper's virtues, dogmatic and ebullient though it is, this brief study considers intelligently the chief elements of fiction, the author's relationship to their handling, and the reader's reactions. The almost perfect organization and the inclusiveness of this essay, and the fact that all its main points were repeated seven years later in a critique of Cooper's master, Scott, indicate that the principles set forth were not arrived at without thought.

"How to Tell a Story" (1895), an appreciation of several humorists (modestly including Twain), seems at first glance to champion completely inconsistent beliefs. For instead of neatly plotted narrative it praises a sort which is "rambling and disjointed" and "strings incongruities and absurdities together in a wandering and sometimes purposeless way." Actually, though, what the humorist says applies rule 6 of the Cooper essay—"the conduct and conversation" of a fictional personage should be in character. For Twain conceives of "the American humorous story" as a dramatic monologue. He believes that it must abandon the sparse narrative method of the "comic story" which drives straight to its "nub, point, [or] snapper." "Anybody" can tell such an anecdote but "the humorous story is strictly a work of art—high and delicate art—and only an artist can tell it."

The art here discussed, Twain specifies, is an actor's rather than a writer's. His oral storyteller "does his best to conceal the fact that he even dimly suspects that there is anything funny" in his tale. He throws away his punchline "with the pretense that he does not know that it is a nub." When "after an apparently absent-minded pause," he "adds an incongruous remark in a soliloquizing way," he arouses laughter by pausing precisely long enough, then looks innocently surprised and puzzled to show that the audience's amusement is unexpected. Every detail in Twain's stage directions implies that the superiority of such a performance depends upon its apparently unpremeditated but carefully worked out dramatic creation of a comic character. When Riley tells his wounded soldier story "in the character of a dull-witted old farmer," "The simplicity and innocence and unconsciousness of the old soldier are perfectly simulated, and the result is a performance which is thoroughly charming and delicious"—"about the funniest thing I have ever listened to."

Twain makes clear here and elsewhere that he sees a great difference between the art of this oral performance and that of writing. Yet there is a likeness which he also recognizes. The best oral telling of a tale — or the best speech — "is not the actual impromptu one," says he, "but the counterfeit of it" calculated to make it "seem impromptu." Precisely so, the writer of dialogue may, like Twain, perfect it by "talking and talking and *talking* it till it sounds right." But in the end written speech counterfeits impromptu oral speech: "When one writes for print . . . he follows forms which have little resemblance to conversation, but . . . make the reader understand what the writer is trying to convey." Just as the platform performer becomes the character he portrays, the writer becomes the character he represents: "Experience has taught me long ago that if *I* tell a boy's story, or anybody else's, it is never worth printing; it comes from the head not the heart. . . . To be successful and worth printing, the imagined boy would have to tell his story *himself* and let me merely act as his amanuensis." So in the telling of the written as well as the oral story the choice of a particular kind of a narrator is so fundamental that its every achievement depends upon this choice. To use a modern term, for Twain discovering the proper "point of view" is vital to any successful "plan."

While many critics have managed to miss Twain's demand for an overall plan, few have been able to overlook his many comments upon style. The Cooper essay considers this at length, noticing faults in dialogue and numerous uses of "the approximate word" rather than the precise one. Another version goes into even more detail, analyzing specific passages to show precisely how Cooper violated rules 12–18 and rewriting a 320-word excerpt in 220 words to show how he violated rule 14: "Eschew surplusage." "An author's style," Twain holds here, "is a main part of his business. . . . Style may be likened to an army, the author to its general, the book to the campaign."[13]

In an article about Howells entirely concerned with style, Twain repeats and augments his criteria. The "great qualities" he summarizes as "clearness, compression, verbal exactness, and unforced and seemingly unconscious felicity of phrasing." He reiterates and at one point italicizes the requirement that such qualities must be "sustained," and talks at length about Howells' ability "almost always . . . to find that elusive and shifty grain of gold, the *right word*." His praise of Howells' humor interestingly stresses as a great virtue its look of being impromptu: "I do not think any one else can play with humorous fancies so gracefully and delicately and deliciously as he does, nor has so many to play with, nor can come so near making them look as if they were doing the playing themselves and he was not aware that they were at it." Rhythm he sees as an aid to this: an "easy and effortless flow of his speech," "cadenced and undulating rhythm," and "architectural felicities of construction." Discussing all these qualities (except, unfortunately, humor) Twain shows by citations that he has examined particular passages as he asks his readers to do: "I do not mean examine it in a bird's-eye way; I mean search it, study it. And, of course, read it aloud."[14]

Formally untrained though he was, Twain anticipated modern critics in meticulously studying specific texts. His comments upon larger matters such as plot, characterization, and point of view — "plan" — and upon many aspects of style show that he gave more than casual attention to technique in the works of others and in his own writing.

III

Not all of Twain's short writings after his apprentice period, to be sure, are greatly illuminated by relating them to his theories. His discussions of writing, just considered, for instance, are interesting almost entirely for what they say rather than for any distinction in saying it. His burlesque of Sunday school literature in "Story of the Bad Little Boy" (1865) performs in much the same fashion his apprentice burlesques did: it pillories the authors attacked by reducing their matter and their posturings to absurdities. The piece has particular interest because during its writing and that of a companion piece, "Story of the Good Little Boy" (1870), he uses in burlesque form the essential plan he would eventually use less playfully in *Tom Sawyer*; but it does little that is new.

Most other short pieces, though, gain interest when related to Twain's theories. Least interesting, technically, are those fictions most clearly governed by tenets set forth in the Cooper article, "The Great Revolution in Pitcairn" (1879) and "The Man That Corrupted Hadleyburg" (1899). The "plan" of each probably was determined by its theme: characters and the "order, system, sequence [and] result" of their action develop a moral. In each the chief character invades a community, a tiny island in one, a village in the other. This protagonist is a cynic whose knowledge of human frailties enables him to victimize the natives. In a South Sea paradise, Butterworth Stavely, a Yankee eager for personal power, plays upon the similar ambitions, the dogmatism, the jealousies, and the stupidity of the islanders to become first a magistrate, later an emperor. A bureaucracy and a class system flourish, and the struggle for power intensifies. When conditions become intolerable, the islanders rebel, take over, and return to "the old useful industries and the old healing and solacing pieties." Hadleyburg, as Mary Richards says, "is a mean town, a hard, stingy town, and hasn't a virtue . . . but . . . honesty . . . and if ever the day comes that its honesty falls under great temptation, its grand reputation will go to ruin. . . ." The stranger can bring about such a ruin by tempting the townsfolk with money. They thereupon expose the weakness of their previously untested virtue — expose it, furthermore, in viciously comic protestations and pretensions. The manuscript of this story shows Twain writing away until he discovers his plan, then composing and revising with complete assurance until he reaches his conclusion, an explicit moral stated in the final paragraph and the town's revised motto.[15] Since both these narratives are fables, and the characters are therefore simple, the problem of making speeches and actions correspond to the characterizations is an easy one, and the author handles it easily enough.

These, significantly, are the only noteworthy short works which Twain produced after 1865 written in the third person. The others, in the first person, are the ones to which Twain's theorizings are most relevant, the ones most interesting in technique and style. They represent a continuous preoccupation with the first-person point of view, a series of greatly varied experiments and adaptations.

While it is not a narrative, "The Babies" (1879) illustrates several points made about oral delivery in "How to Tell a Story." The author's most successful after-dinner speech was delivered at a reunion of the Armies of the Tennessee in Chicago, in November 1879. Following fourteen speeches, at two o'clock in the morning, before a well-fortified, stuffed, and dog-tired audience, the humorist responded to a toast which he had worded: "The Babies: As they comfort us in our sorrows, let us not forget them in our festivals." Mounting atop a table, he launched upon a carefully prepared speech — phrasings, climactic conclusion, and of course pauses: "They let my first sentence go in silence, till I paused and added, 'we stand on common ground'— then they burst forth like a hurricane. . . . From that time on, I stopped at the end of each sentence, and let the tornado of applause and laughter sweep around me. . . ." The exact words were taken in shorthand by a reporter for the *Tribune*, and the report interspersed bracketed responses — "Laughter," "Renewed Laughter," "Great shouts," even "Convulsive screams" — which show that not sentences alone but often phrases won riotous responses. For the most part here, though, Twain's role is not that of the humorless innocent he so admired: he is talking as a commonsense humorist and adapting his style to his audience by using military allusions. Only in his last sentence (to the point of the semicolon) does he momentarily assume the guise of an ignoramus. At that instant, while the audience waited in suspense, fearful that he would end with a calamitous descent into bad taste insulting to the guest of honor, he had to make a tricky pause of "exactly the right length — no more and no less." He must have handled it perfectly, for he reported, "when I closed . . . I say it who oughtn't to say it, the house came down with a crash."

The alternation of the direct and the ironic modes briefly exemplified here is managed in various ways in the autobiographical narratives. In the Sandwich Island Letters (1866), Twain uses two characters for this alternation. Strongly influenced, as Franklin R. Rogers has shown, by burlesque travel accounts, "Mark Twain" as first-person narrator provides facts and descriptions, at times rhapsodizing or sentimentalizing in elegant language. For contrast a companion is provided — Mr. Brown, vulgar, unsentimental, and slangy — whose function is to offer homely and cynical addenda. The contrasting pair continue through the *Quaker City* letters, but when the author reworked these into a book he discarded Mr. Brown and made his first-person narrator assume, at intervals, each role.

"In the Station House" (1867), a part of a travel letter reporting experiences in New York in which Mr. Brown does not happen to appear, gives a small foretaste of the method. For the most part the report is straightforward report. "I am not writing a fancy sketch here," avers the author at one point, "but simply jotting down things just as they occurred. . . ." He does pause, though, to sentimentalize about the two streetwalkers after the fashion of "Mark Twain" sentimentalizing about sundry islanders. By contrast, in his best paragraph, that about "a bloated old hag," he is remarkably objective — as Mr. Brown often was — refraining from moral judgments even when the woman offers him a drink. Elsewhere he briefly pretends naïveté when he puts on the same footing "robbing a church, or saying a complimentary word about the police, or doing some other supernaturally mean thing," or when he asserts that he is "glad that I have been in the Station House, because I know all about it now from personal experience," then hastens to add that he is "not anxious to pursue my investigations any further. . . ." At intervals throughout the rest of his career, Twain used such alternating modes. As late as 1901, "To the Person Sitting in Darkness" is by turn directly denunciatory and broadly ironic.

When longer passages in the two manners occur in *The Innocents Abroad* (1869), a problem of consistency in characterization arises. "The Tomb of Adam" shows "Mark Twain" reaching fantastic heights of credulity, illogic, bad taste, and sentimentality. How, one might wonder at least occasionally, can the same "I" also write the jeering attack upon tourists engaging in precisely the same excesses when admiring a battered painting? How can the same "I" write the poetic rhapsody inspired by the Sphinx?

While writing the first half of *Roughing It* (1872) Twain hit upon a procedure which forestalls such awkward questions, and some evidence indicates that he rewrote several chapters so that he might follow it. As Henry Nash Smith suggests, he represents his "I" as an old-timer reminiscing about the Western experiences of himself when young: "The pronoun 'I' here designates two quite different roles or masks adopted by the writer: the mask of innocence, attributed to the protagonist at the beginning . . . ; and the mask of wisdom, attained in the course of [his] experiences, which is worn by the narrator at the moment of writing." (See "A Genuine Mexican Plug" and "Lost in the Snow.")

Twain used this device of the ambivalent "I" in his finest autobiographical narrative, "Old Times on the Mississippi" (1875). The first "I" is a cub fictionized to appear much younger, less experienced, more naïve and romantic than the real Sam Clemens, reared on the river and toughened by travels as a tramp printer, had been when he became an apprentice in his twenty-second year. The character has comic values, especially when portrayed by the second "I," a man who has mastered piloting and some years before has ended his riverboat career. The greenhorn is useful for exposition since he must be told many things the reader must learn. The choice of a narrataor is also related to the sequence and result of the narrative. The ignorant youth is initiated into the mysteries of his trade and his initiation is accompanied by growing disillusionment about the river's glories, the romance of piloting, even his fellows. The choice of narrator, finally, makes possible a pervasive tone which gives the account much of its charm — a mingling of amusement and nostalgia. Twain used a similar dual narrator in another almost equally fine reminiscence, "The Private History of a Campaign That Failed" (1885).

In two other fictional first-person narratives, Twain similarly exaggerates his own traits so that he will have an appropriate narrator. "The Facts Concerning the Recent Carnival of Crime in Connecticut" (1876) is written by a man with flaws which Clemens often reproached himself for having: bad manners, untidy habits, untruthfulness, and crass indifference to the promptings of conscience often followed by excruciating remorse. Indirectly he also pictures the narrator by representing the horrible dwarf who is his Conscience as "a far-fetched, dim suggestion of a burlesque upon me, a caricature of me in little." Twain once wondered if some details were "too personal," but he left them unmodified; and the response of Howells and other friends, as well as the public, showed that his probing of what he called an "exasperating metaphysical question . . . in the disguise of a literary extravaganza" was a comic success.

Twain several times wrote lengthy beginnings for "The Mysterious Stranger" (posthumously published, 1916), and though he once announced that he "was sure it was started right this time," he never finished it. A. B. Paine as literary executor after Twain's death found a final chapter separated from the others and added it. Hence one cannot know how Twain might have managed revisions — always important in his writing. It is likely, however, that any final version would have retained the ambivalent first-person narrator. For such a narrator, Theodor Fischer, an old man looking back upon his boyhood, "with a lifetime stretching back between today and then," gives the novelette its dreamlike atmosphere and makes understandable Fischer's present fatalistic acceptance of the teachings of Philip Traum — teachings which long ago he has found devastating. Using such a narrator also makes possible the portrayal without puzzlement of Traum in diverse roles — attractive youth, godlike creator, deus ex machina, and satirical commentator. In this last guise Traum, like the alternately straightforward and ironic "Mark Twain" of the travel books, in turn denounces and satirizes mankind.

This novelette is distant in time and spirit from the oral tale and the humorous stories written between 1865 and 1883 which seem to me, if one takes the adaptation of means to ends into account, Twain's most perfect achievements. The oral tale concocted for the Whittier's Birthday celebration in 1877 illustrates "How to Tell a Story" by introducing not one but a pair of unsophisticated narrators — "Mark Twain" in the framework, looking back upon himself at a time when, "callow and conceited," he attempted in vain to impress by using his nom de plume, and seriously protested against patent inaccuracy; and the miner, "a jaded, melancholy man of fifty," stupid enough to believe imposters and humorless enough to see nothing funny in their incongruous antics. For this immediate audience the speech was a failure — though less so than Twain believed in retrospect[16] — because he underestimated his audience's veneration for the authors involved. Modern readers, less awed, find the story amusing even without the aid of Twain's voice.[17]

Making the storyteller and his listener also humorless and callow was habitual for Twain. The naïve vernacular storyteller may have been suggested by Thorpe's "Big Bear" and other similar yarnspinners; or more directly by Ben Coon, who told the tale about the frog when Clemens first heard it in Angel's Camp; or by solemn-faced humorous lecturers. Coon,

Twain says, was "a dull person, and ignorant" with "no gift as a story-teller, and no invention, . . . entirely serious . . . he saw no humor in his tale. . . ."[18] Simon Wheeler, in both the Frog and the Jim Wolf stories, stumbles through irrelevancies to his conclusion by good luck. Jim Blaine in 1872 never gets beyond his first sentence without being bogged down in complete irrelevance. Jim Baker in the Jay yarn of 1879 is in the same mold, "middle-aged" and "simple-hearted," though Twain adds a dimension by implying a pathetic reason for his fantasies: for seven years he has lived a solitary life "in a lonely corner of California . . . and has studied the ways of his only neighbors, the beasts and the birds, until he believes he can accurately translate any remark which they make."

Two more serious narratives had prepared for this enriched picturing: In "A True Story" (1874), Twain had realized some of the more tragic possibilities of a vernacular narrator. Here Aunt Rachel gives a completely serious account of her sorrows and her moment of great joy in the old slave days.[19] And in 1876, beginning to delineate the naïve and humorless Huck in *Adventures of Huckleberry Finn* by letting him write in the first person, he had created a character who would deeply touch readers for generations. "Frescoes from the Past" probably was written in 1876: it was inserted in *Life on the Mississippi* (1883) and not returned by Twain to the novel as published. Huck quotes three other vernacular characters, Bob and the Child of Calamity, whose comic boasts carry to pinnacles of invention traditional frontier vauntings, and Ed, who tells a ghost story. Though the ghost story is a serious one, the comments and Huck's deliberately inept lie which follow it end the chapter comically.

The device of representing the listener to such yarns, "Mark Twain," as naïve and humorless the author developed after writing "Jim Smiley and His Jumping Frog" and revising it three times. In the first version the listener is "bored nearly to death" by Wheeler, but he says, "To me, the spectacle of a man drifting along through such a yarn without even smiling was exquisitely absurd"; and at the end when Wheeler wishes to start his cow story, "'O, curse Smiley and his afflicted cow!' I muttered, good-naturedly, and bidding the old gentleman good-day, I departed."

It is in "Jim Wolf and the Tom-Cats" (1867) that listener "Mark Twain" first represents himself without humor, or being subjected to Wheeler's reminiscences. Seeing signs of his reminiscing, "I prepared to leave, because . . . he was going to be delivered of another of his tiresome personal experiences—but I was too slow. . . ." In the framework for Blaine's yarn— probably written in 1871—"Mark Twain" represents himself as so stirred by reports of Blaine's story that he waits impatiently to hear it, belatedly discovering, when Blaine falls asleep after maundering at length, that he has been sold. Only after these uses of the device, when revising "The

Notorious Jumping Frog of Calaveras County" (as he finally called it) for an 1872 English edition did the author claim that Wheeler's story bores him not "nearly to death" but "to death," delete the sentence about finding Wheeler's humorless telling "exquisitely absurd," and substitute for the "good-natured" final sentence a more grumpy conclusion.[20] Twain's enthusiasm about this story varied; but his characterization of it in 1869 as "the best humorous sketch America has produced" and his extensive revisions before he printed it in its final form in 1875 attest to his belief that it merited painstaking care.[21]

In keeping with the noncomic nature of "A True Story," not "Mark Twain" but "Mr. C——" as listener is made only momentarily not naïve but unthinking. "Aunt Rachel," he says to the jolly old servant, "how is it that you've lived sixty years and never had any trouble?" Her immediate serious response "sobers" his manner and speech, and he listens in this mood without comment to her touching account.

"Mark Twain" in "Baker's Blue-Jay Yarn" performs a more complex function. In the opening four paragraphs of the narrative, he is a wanderer in the Neckar forest whose fanciful imaginings provide a transition from reality to the fantasy of Jim's story. All the same, like previous framework figures, he has ridiculous traits which enhance the comedy. Jeered at (as he fancies) by raucous ravens, he suffers humiliation foreshadowing and caricaturing that of the frustrated jay at the end of the enclosed story.

Determining the point of view, or, if ambivalent or dual narrators are used, the points of view, must have been an important part of Twain's discovery of precisely the right plan for any short piece. Intimately associated with this determination was finding an appropriate style, that instrument of which the author was so acutely conscious. In every short piece Twain, as Brander Matthews says (without reference to any of Twain's theorizing), "imparted to the printed page the vivacity of the spoken word, its swiftness and apparently unpremeditated ease." Everywhere at his best Twain achieves the clarity, compression, precision of wording, and rhythm he praises in Howells.

Most critics will agree that these qualities are most often found in vernacular stretches. Robert Frost has said that "nothing American, in prose or verse, is more lyric to my ear than Twain's 'The Jumping Frog of Calaveras County,'" but this is not unique among the author's vernacular passages. Many other passages counterfeiting common speech are as lyric in the subtle "cadenced and undulating rhythm" they employ. They are as lyric also in recreating savored sense impressions. For in addition to being naïve and humorless, Twain's best narrators are gifted with imaginations which vividly evoke details.

To this end, eschewing "the *approximate* word" and using "the *right* word" is particularly necessary in tales that imitate speech by using outright description sparingly and characterize by means of an appropriate vocabulary. Typical are Wheeler's few words about Jim on the roof "cre-e-epin' over that ice, and diggin' his toe nails and finger-nails in to keep from slippin'" or about Smiley's mare on the stretch, "cavorting and straddling up, and scattering her legs around limber." Or Baker's bit about the puzzled jay: "He cocked his head at the hole again, and took a long look; raised up and shook his head; stepped around to the other side of the hole, and took another look from that side; shook his head again."

Figures of speech join verbs in making actions palpable: "quicker'n you could wink [the frog would] spring up and snake a fly off'n the counter there, and flop down on the floor ag'in as solid as a gob of mud. . . ." "Jim . . . was gormed with that bilin' hot molasses candy clean down to his heels, and had more busted sassers hangin' to him than if he was an Injun princess. . . ." "When Sile Hawkins come a browsing around [Sarah], she let him know that for all his tin he couldn't trot in harness alongside of *her*." "They called in more jays; then more and more, till pretty soon the whole region 'peared to have a blue flush about it." "When I' m playful I use the meridians of longitude and parallels of latitude for a seine, and drag the Atlantic Ocean for whales!"

Besides being vivid, such bits are in character; and precisely because they come from the lips of men whose minds naturally associate incongruous ideas, it is appropriate that they be funny in themselves. When, in Twain's best creations, a naïve and humorless narrator, apparently without meaning to, "strings incongruities and absurdities" of this sort "together in a wandering and sometimes purposeless way," the result is "high and delicate art" such as only a master can achieve.

Mark Twain and the Mind's Ear

I start by quoting a paragraph from Mark Twain's first blockbusting book, *The Innocents Abroad*. This book, which established a worldwide reputation for Mark Twain, recounted in a humorous fashion the visit of Clemens and a charter group to Europe and the Holy Land. It made a great deal of fun of credulous and sentimental tourists. The company was an American Victorian crowd which believed that it ought to be terribly impressed by the Holy Land and which understood what it was expected to do when it got to places that the Bible celebrated: everyone should weep copiously. As a result, every time they were informed they had reached one of the proper places, they hauled off and soaked the earth with tears. Mark Twain every now and then in the book impersonated a dribbling pilgrim such as one he spoke of with great admiration. "He never bored but what he struck water." The tomb in which guidebooks authentically informed tourists Adam had been buried naturally called for large expenditures of tears. In his role of a mawkish innocent abroad, "Mark Twain" did what was required:

> The tomb of Adam! How touching it was here, in a land of strangers far from home and friends and all who cared for me, thus to discover the grave of a blood relation. True, a distant one, but still a relation! The unerring instinct of nature thrilled its recognition. The fountain of my filial affection was stirred to its profoundest depths, and I gave way to tumultuous emotion.
>
> I leaned upon a pillar and burst into tears. I deem it no shame to have wept over the grave of my poor dead relative. Let him who would sneer at my emotion close this volume here, for he will find little to his taste in my journeying through Holy Land. Noble old

The American Self: Myth, Ideology, and Popular Culture, ed. Sam B. Girgus. Albuquerque: University of New Mexico Press, 1981.

man — he did not live to see me — he did not live to see his child. And
I — I — alas, I did not live to see *him*. Weighed down by sorrow and
disappointment, he died before I was born — six thousand brief summers before I was born. But let us try to bear it with fortitude. Let
us trust that he is better off where he is. Let us take comfort in the
thought that his loss is our eternal gain.

Read this aloud. I am reasonably sure that Mark Twain would say
that you've just done something that a reader should do to learn or to
demonstrate the qualities of his writings. You have caused it to reverberate
in the mind's ear. I base my belief on things that Twain said about other
writers and about himself over many years of a long career.

Writers have to be egoists. If they weren't, they wouldn't have the nerve
to expect people to spend all the required time reading their books. So
even when they talk about other authors, practically always they are talking about themselves. Do they praise an author for having good qualities?
You can be sure that they think they themselves have those qualities. Do
they condemn an author for having defects? You can be sure that nine times
out of ten they are certain that they don't have those vile faults. So I look
with great interest at what Twain says about one of his very dear friends
and a really great author, William Dean Howells, in one of the few studies
of individual authors that he ever wrote. He said of Howells, "He was in
my belief without a peer in the English-speaking world." (Twain was of
course being modest; he knew of at least one peer that Howells had.) A
thing that strikes you is that he discusses Howells' writings as if they were
talk. He praises not the flow of his writing, but "the easy and effortless
flow of his speech." And his recipe for appreciating a great paragraph by
Howells which he quotes and analyzes in detail is rather interesting. He
says that a reader must examine it. "I do not mean examine it in a bird's-
eye way; I mean search it, study it. And, of course, read it aloud. . . . It
is my conviction that one cannot get out of finely wrought literature all
that is in it by reading it mutely."

One thing that Twain saw as a very fine quality of this same paragraph "after reading it several times aloud" was its wonderful compactness
— "how simple" it is, "how unconfused by cross-currents . . . how compressed." He talks about the impossibility of cutting down the passage in
any way. And I think that when you turn to Mark Twain you'll find many
remarkably compressed passages that read quite beautifully aloud. One
is a passage that occurs in *Huckleberry Finn*, a passage that Bernard De-
Voto called "one of the most blinding flashlights in all fiction." It's a brief
paragraph that introduces a character who thereupon disappears forever.
Like a great many characters in Shakespeare, this one has come alive in

something like a hundred words. Huckleberry Finn has witnessed a brutal killing in a little riverside town. Poor drunken Boggs has been shot by the aristocratic Sherburn. Huck tells about the sequel:

> Everybody that seen the shooting was telling how it happened, and there was a big crowd packed around each one of these fellows, stretching their necks and listening. One long lanky man, with long hair and a big white fur stove-pipe hat on the back of his head, and a crooked-handled cane, marked out the places on the ground where Boggs stood, and where Sherburn stood, and the people following him around from one place to t'other and watching everything he done, and bobbing their heads to show they understood, and stooping a little and resting their hands on their thighs to watch him mark the places on the ground with his cane; and then he stood up straight and stiff where Sherburn had stood, frowning and having his hat-brim down over his eyes, and sung out "Boggs!" and then fetched his cane down slow to a level, and says "Bang!" staggered backwards, says "Bang!" again, and fell down flat on his back. The people that had seen the thing said he done it perfect; said it was just exactly the way it all happened. Then as much as a dozen people got out their bottles and treated him.

In addition to compactness, the passage illustrates another quality that Twain admired in old Howells — concreteness. Reading Howells aloud, he found his friend could "catch that airy thought and . . . reduce it to a concrete condition, visible, substantial . . . like a cabbage . . . translating the visions of the eyes of flesh into words that reproduce their sounds and colors." As I read that statement, I couldn't help but think of what Joseph Conrad said when he defined the task of an author: "By the power of the written word to make you hear, to make you feel . . . before all, to make you see — that and that only is the task of the author."

Twain worked to develop this skill quite early. The first short piece of his that won wide attention was a story that appeared when he was a very young man, "The Notorious Jumping Frog of Calaveras County." A paragraph it contained will show how he made things concrete. Notice how palpable to the sense every sight and movement is made, and how this vividness of detail adds to the fun. The speaker is an old mining rat who's talking about a prodigious gambler, Jim Smiley, who had a whole stable of wonderful animals. They were wonderful, that is, for a gambler because they all looked like Ziggies, as if they were always doomed to fail. Their looks caused people to bet against them, and then when the bets were down, they turned out to be something rather different. Wheeler's talking, for instance, with great admiration about Jim's mare:

Thish-yer Smiley had a mare . . . and he used to win money on that horse, for all she was so slow and always had the asthma, or the distemper, or the consumption, or something of that kind. They used to give her two or three hundred yards' start, and then pass her under way; but always at the fag end of the race she'd get excited and desperate like, and come cavorting and straddling up, and scattering her legs around limber, sometimes in the air, and sometimes out to one side among the fences, and kicking up m-o-r-e dust and raising m-o-r-e racket with her coughing and sneezing and blowing her nose — and *always* fetch up at the stand just about a neck ahead, as near as you could cipher it down.

Reading such a passage aloud made evident not only compactness and concreteness; it also revealed meaning. It was a clarifying device: you could see whether an author wrote lucidly or not.

Something that astonished many of Samuel Clemens' contemporaries happened when he was in his fifties. He became an interpreter of — of all people — Robert Browning. In those innocent days before Ezra Pound and T. S. Eliot, among poets with a reputation of being obscure, Robert Browning was a champion. Ladies who pursued culture — and sometimes caught it — would attend meetings of clubs which would attempt to figure out what Browning was saying, and Mark Twain became a leader of such a group. His recipe for appreciating Browning was one that I think is predictable on the basis of what I've been saying about him. He said, "Put me in the right condition, and give me room according to my strength, and I can read Browning so Browning himself can understand." In other words, read him aloud.

Well, the students in his Browning seminar agreed. One of them testified, "To him there were no obscure passages . . . no guessing at the meaning. His slow deliberate speech and full voice gave each sentence its quota of sound, and sense followed . . . easily."

Anyone who knows Mark Twain's biography and his writings at all well really won't be astonished to find that Browning was a figure he greatly appreciated. For the fact is that at their best Mark Twain and Browning did very much the same thing. They had characters recite dramatic monologues during the course of which they came alive for people who read what they said or heard other people read what they said, aloud. "Experience has taught me long ago," Mark Twain said on one occasion, "that if *I* tell a boy's story . . . it is never worth printing. . . . To be successful and worth printing, the imagined boy would have to tell his story *himself*, and let me merely act as his amanuensis."

I can't say why Browning got into the habit of writing dramatic monologues, but I can guess with some assurance why Mark Twain did. Just before his sixtieth birthday, Mark Twain wrote his chief critical discussion, "How to Tell a Story." In it, he said, "I claim to know how a story ought to be told, for I've been almost daily in the company of the most expert storytellers for many years." And he quickly adds a significant qualification: "Understand, I mean by word of mouth, not print," True enough, as you read the account of Mark Twain's life you find he consorted with, one after another, a parade of tremendous storytellers. His mother, first of all, "that obscure little woman with the enchanted tongue . . . the most eloquent person I met in all my days." Again there was Uncle Dan'l, the slave from whom Jim in *Huckleberry Finn* was copied. Clemens spent all his summers on a farm throughout his formative years. And he said,

> I know the look of Uncle Dan'l's kitchen as it was on privileged nights . . . white and black children grouped on the hearth, with firelight playing on their faces and shadows flickering. . . . And I can hear Uncle Dan'l telling the immortal [Brer Rabbit] tale. . . . And I can feel again the creepy joy which quivered through me when the time for the ghost story was reached — and the sense of regret, for it was always the last story of the evening. . . .

At eleven or twelve, Clemens became a printer's apprentice; for several years he associated with storytelling printers. When he was on the river he heard many stories told by Mississippi pilots. Later miners, prospectors, fellow reporters on newspapers, other comic writers and lecturers, with whom he lived or worked were raconteurs.

I think a very good case can be made for the claim that the crucial turning point in his career came when he was a newspaper reporter out in San Francisco and as a result of certain difficulties with the police department found it necessary to absent himself from San Francisco for a while. He went out to the Gillises in the gold country. He was aged twenty-nine. California was having some of its typical unusual weather, that is, it was raining cats and dogs and houses were sliding down hills. So he and several soggy pocket miners, day after day, night after night, huddled around stoves and fireplaces swapping stories. And one story was the one I mentioned a while back, the Jumping Frog story, which won him his first national fame, "the germ," he said, "of my coming fortune. It gave me a reputation throughout the world and paid me thousands and thousands of dollars."

From that time on, Mark Twain told in print many oral stories he'd heard. For example, at least eight stories, one of them the best short piece he ever wrote (I'll mention that a little later), were stories he heard told around the fires in Angel's Camp or at Jackass Hill. "I amend dialect stuff," he wrote, "by talking and talking it till it sounds right."

Like Browning, he loved to make the storyteller come to life. On occasion, he put the teller above the story he told. "The stories," he once said, "are only alligator pears. One merely eats them for the sake of the salad dressing." The salad dressing was the speaker, the storyteller. What he said and the way he said it made him known to the person who read or heard the story. He gave readers two helpings of humor: one was the enclosed story; the other was the framework. The funny monologue was voiced by a funny monologist. As well as his frog story, the teller, Simon Wheeler, was laughable, Simon was a funny character, typical of Mark Twain's speakers in that he had no sense of humor whatever. One joke in the framework of the jumping frog story was that a man without a sense of humor told a funny story to a listener who had no sense of humor. Twain described Wheeler this way:

> He never smiled. . . . All through the interminable narrative there ran a vein of impressive earnestness and sincerity which showed me plainly that, so far from his imagining that there was anything ridiculous . . . about the story, he regarded it as a really important matter, and admired its two heroes as men of transcendent genius. . . .

Another humorless old coot named Jim Baker told another story (one that I regard as Mark Twain's second masterpiece) that Clemens had heard on that visit to Angel's Camp. Baker had lived alone in the deserted mining camp until he was a mite touched in the head, and as a result he decided that animals were human. He knew they were human because they were so ornery. They could talk and swear and tell lies and cheat. "Why," he said, "a jay hasn't got any more principle than a Congressman!" He told about the prodigious ability of one jay to swear. This jay somehow had got the notion that he'd like to fill up a knothole in a deserted cabin with acorns. I don't know why—he never said. Just because it was there, I suppose. The trouble was that the hole was in the roof of a completely hollow cabin, so as he dropped those acorns in they just disappeared in a vast space. After he had dumped a number of them into that endless pit,

> he begun to get mad. He held in for a spell walking up and down the comb of the roof, and shaking his head and muttering to himself; but his feelings got the upper hand of him presently, and he broke loose and cussed himself black in the face. . . . When he got through he walks to the hole and looks in again . . . then he says, 'Well, you're a long hole, and a deep hole and a mighty singular hole altogether— but I've started to fill you, and I'm damned if I don't fill you if it takes me a hundred years!'
>
> "And with that, away he went. You never see a bird work so. . . . The way he hove acorns into that hole for about two hours . . . was

one of the most exciting and astonishing spectacles I ever struck. . . .
At last he could hardly flop his wings, he was so tuckered out. He
comes a drooping down, . . . sweating like an ice-pitcher, and drops
his acorn in and says, 'Now I guess I've got the bulge on you by this
time!' So he bent down for a look. If you'll believe me, when his head
come up again he was just pale with rage. He says, 'I've shoveled acorns
enough in there to keep the family thirty years, and if I can see a sign
of one of 'em I wish I may land in a museum with a belly full of saw-
dust in two minutes.

"He just had strength enough to crawl up on to the comb and
lean his back agin the chimbly, and then he collected his impressions
and begun to free his mind. I see in a second that what I had mistook
for profanity in the mines was only just the rudiments, as you may say."

Huck Finn, like Simon Wheeler and Jim Baker, had a lousy sense of
humor. In that long book of his, he laughed only twice, I think, and saw
only one joke — and it really wasn't a joke that was there at all. But he
was a keen observer of scenes who set down sensuous descriptions of people and actions. He was interested in relationships, so he was impressed
when one of the townspeople reenacted the death of Boggs, and he appreciated too a theatrical performance that had excellence. A man about whom
he grew ecstatic — I think you'll see for good reason — was an undertaker
who officiated at a funeral in a riverside town. Huck tells about his performance with typical solemnity and appreciation. The mortician is doing
his best act, presiding at a funeral:

When the place was packed full, the undertaker he slid around
. . . with his softy soothering ways . . . getting people and things all
ship shape and comfortable, . . . and making no more sound than
the cat. He never spoke; he moved people around, he squeezed in late
ones, . . . and done it with nods, and signs with his hands. Then he
took his place over against the wall. He was the softest, glidingest,
stealthiest man I ever see; and there warn't no more smile to him than
there is to a ham. . . . Then the Reverend Hobson opened up, slow
and solemn, and begun to talk; and straight off the most outrageous
row busted out in the cellar. . . . only one dog, but he made a most
powerful racket, and he kept it up, right along — the parson, he had
to stand there, over the coffin, and wait. . . . It was right down awkward, and nobody didn't seem to know what to do. But pretty soon
they see that long-legged undertaker make a sign to the preacher as
much as to say, "Don't you worry — just depend on me." Then he
stooped down and begun to glide along the wall, just his shoulders
showing over the people's heads. So he glided along, and the pow-

wow and racket getting more and more outrageous all the time; and at last, when he had gone around two sides of the room, he disappears down cellar. Then, in about two seconds we heard a whack, and the dog he finished up with a most amazing howl or two, and then everything was dead still, and the parson begun his solemn talk where he left off. In a minute or two here comes this undertaker's back and shoulders gliding along the wall again; and so he glided, and glided, around three sides of the room, and then rose up, and shaded his mouth with his hands, and stretched his neck out towards the preacher, over the people's heads, and says, in a kind of a coarse whisper, *"He had a rat!"* Then he drooped down and glided along the wall again to his place. You could see it was a great satisfaction to the people, because naturally they wanted to know. A little thing like that don't cost nothing, and it's just the little things that makes a man to be looked up to and liked. There warn't no more popular man in that town than that undertaker was.

I hope that reading of passages by Twain aloud has shown in addition to other qualities what might be called "poetic techniques." The way he played with that word "glided" was really a poet's trick, you know. Twain praised Howells' style, his prose style mind you, in terms that were applicable to poetry. Not only was it—like the best poetry—concrete and compact, it was also, Twain said, "limpid, fluent, graceful and rhythmical." He talks about Howells' prose as if it were poetry, "unvexed by ruggedness, clumsiness or broken meters." And he's keen on the way emotion permeates the writings of Howells, particularly his humor: "I do not think anyone else can play with humorous fancies so gracefully and delicately and deliciously as he does, nor . . . can come so near making them look as if they were doing the playing themselves. . . . His is a humor which flows softly all around about and over and through the mesh of the page, pervasive, refreshing, health-giving. . . ." To illustrate the fact that as usual when Mark Twain spoke of an achievement of Howells he was praising something he himself did, let me read a paragraph in Huck's book that I guess is my favorite. I find that (again quoting Twain on Howells) it is "full of photographs with feeling in them and sentiment, photographs taken in a dream." What's more, it's got rhythm, no "broken meters" here. It's Huck telling how he and Jim on their raft drifted down the Mississippi River at night:

> Sometimes we'd have the whole river all to ourselves for the longest time. Yonder was the banks and the islands, across the water; and maybe a spark—which was a candle in a cabin window—and sometimes on the water you could see a spark or two—on a raft or a scow,

you know; and maybe you could hear a fiddle or a song coming over from one of them crafts. It's lovely to live on a raft. We had the sky, up there, all speckled with stars, and we used to lay on our backs and look up at them, and discuss about whether they was made, or only just happened — Jim he allowed they was made, but I allowed they happened; I judged it would have took too long to *make* so many. Jim said the moon could a *laid* them; well, that looked kind of reasonable, so I didn't say nothing against it, because I've seen a frog lay most as many, so of course it could be done. We used to watch the stars that fell, too, and see them streak down. Jim allowed they'd got spoiled and was hove out of the nest.

If I have convinced you that reading Twain aloud is the key to appreciating him, I'm very happy. If not, I still have a couple of escape hatches, so I still can recommend this procedure. I have not followed Twain's recipe. He said, "Never *read* a passage. Memorize it." And most of us are too lazy to do that. He had a reason for memorizing: so one can watch that audience and know how long to pause between bits of reading.

There's another error easily made. I recall a story Twain told several times about an event in the early years of his marriage. He won his aristocratic wife, Olivia, by telling her she could reform him. She believed him, and she started to work on a large number of very bad habits he had. One was to carry on the way that bluejay did. Clemens was a superb, a fluent, and an unceasing user of profane language. Almost anything would cause him to soar into eloquent expression. Frequently in the morning, for some reason or other, a calamity occurred — he found a button was off a shirt, or something else, especially at that hour of the day, was very provoking. Livy noticed this tendency — she could hardly manage not to. She asked some kind neighbor what you did about a man who carried on that way. The neighbor said, "Well, the thing to do is listen carefully, then repeat exactly the words that man has used." So, on one occasion, when Clemens, as he described it, was "doing his devotions" because of some horrible calamity, he looked around, and there was a big hunk of silence in the corner of the room, and in it was Livy. Livy believed that if she uttered those awful words, coming from her innocent lips they would so horrify her husband that he would reform. So, to the best of her ability, she repeated verbatim those commentaries of his. To her astonishment and distress, instead of saying, "By God, I'll reform," he lay down on the bed and howled with laughter. She said, "What's the matter?" He said, "Oh, Livy! You got the words, but you ain't got the tune." If I've rendered Twain's words not quite in tune — somewhat off-key — I'm sorry. But I still hope that even an off-key rendition may help you appreciate Mark Twain's writings by storing them in your mind's ear.

Part Four
Practice What You Teach:
A Short Story

The Ugliest Man in the World

That third summer I spent hunting freaks for P. T. Barnum's Moral and Educational Sideshows, Inc., was as fine a one as I ever spent. Looking for freaks, you meet up with the most interesting people there are. Besides, the pay was the highest I ever got except when I was a bank cashier a couple of days back there fifteen — no, sixteen — years ago.

Near the end of that third summer, I'd rounded up a stone-eating guyascutus, two side-hill dodgers, a female gillygaloo and a two-headed man. The gillygaloo I was terribly fond of, since she made possible a nice little sideline for me. That kind of a bird, you may recall, lays square eggs, and I'd hard boil the things and sell them for dice. Not only were they A-1 dice: they likewise were more or less of a curiosity, so they fetched a handsome profit. I was mighty sorry when I had to ship that bird along to old P. T. back in New York.

But the two-headed man, name of Joseph-Horace Smithers-Smithers, was the handsomest freak I ever signed up — that summer or any other. After I'd looked at him a while, you see, and got used to him, I was struck with the idea that there's better *balance* to a two-headed man than there is to an ordinary one. Result was, I never again was quite satisfied with the look of a one-headed man — artistically, I mean. Most people I know, ordinarily, when they've seen a two-headed man or two, tell me they've felt the same way, exactly.

Looking at Joseph-Horace gave me the notion of finding the ugliest man in the world. "I've got the handsomest one," thinks I. "Why not get the ugliest?" So I started to figure where I'd look, and shortly decided on Tennessee. Andy Jackson was from there, I recalled, and they still used his picture to scare bad kids off to bed. Davy Crockett came from there, too — the only man on record that could kill a coon with a grin, or that could smirk the bark plumb off a tree.

The American Mercury 60 (February 1945) 254:166–69.

A few miles into the mountains, a hillbilly opined that the ugliest man he knew of lived nearby in Scratch Shin Thicket. "That man's so ugly," says he, "that every time he looks into a shiny skillet, the reflection busts hit right down the middle."

Well, this Thicket man was in bed when I got there, but I talked to him anyhow, Though the day was as hot as the devil's barbecue pit, he had a big blanket pulled clean up over his head, and just to look at him made me sweat like a water pitcher. Of course, I asked the reason.

"Jist naturally got to," says he. "I'm so downright hideous that unless I hide thisaway, sleep won't come a-near me."

I was ready to sign him up at a huge salary, then and there, and I told him so. "But I won't sign," says he, his voice sort of muffled by the blanket, "account that I'd be cheating you. There's a fellow over to Dry Tripe Creek a mile or so on, that's twict as ugly as I be. He's so ugly that a fly won't light on his face, even when you spread it with the best of clover honey."

So I went over to Dry Tripe Creek. In the pasture, I saw a woman kissing a cow time after time, though she didn't seem to be enjoying it any more than the cow was.

"What's that for?" I wanted to know.

"On account of my Ole Man," says she. "He's so all-fired bad-favored that we've been married up for five years, but I ain't yet managed to kiss the poor cuss. I'm practisin'."

"Whee!" says I. "Lead me to him. I'm looking for the ugliest man in the world for P. T. Barnum, and the work's easy and the salary'll be terrific."

She looked at me cool as the north side of a February tombstone by moonlight. "He wouldn't be interested," she said. "He went into a town a while back where they'd had a horrible train wreck, and everybody figured he was a poor mutulated victim. Took up a collection for him, they did, and gathered him enough money to live the rest of his days in luxury on—thirty-three dollars and seven cents. Besides, he ain't so ugly as that fellow down in Skeleton Hollow, a mile or so northards. That fellow fell in a pond once, and they had to spend the next ten days a-skimmin' off the ugly. Good day to you, stranger!" And she headed back in the direction of the cow, looking fair to middling unhappy but downright determined.

A storm was plopping around big raindrops and darting lightning here and there when I got to the shack in the Hollow. It was the only shack in sight, and I suspicioned that the neighborhood wasn't over-popular. Even the weeds appeared to be more or less blighted, probably, I figured, from this fellow looking at them. The storm turned everything black as the inside of your pocket at the instant when I began to knock.

Just as the door opened, the lightning flashed, and I saw that poor critter's face. He was ugly enough to hire out as a nightmare for a heathen idol with six arms, to scare away the measles, or to give a crocodile the jumping jimjams. I tell you, he was right homely.

"Sign on the dotted line!" I yelled, waving around the contract. "I want you to work for P. T. Barnum at a supercolossal salary. I've been hunting the ugliest man in the world, and my search is ended, sure enough."

"That's a damned lie!" he roared back at me. "Ain't neither ugly!"

Right then, away up in the sky, a whopping bolt of lightning growled, then coiled itself, and set out to strike him. I watched the thing coming closer and closer at a most astonishing clip, and scares pricked me all over, like as if I'd been hugging a porcupine.

When the lightning bolt was about a foot away, it got a look at the ugly man's face—and stopped sharp. Next thing I knew, it had whirled around and was kiting away scared-like twice as fast as it had come. It was whimpering most pitiful, like a hound dog that's seen a ghost.

"If you aren't the ugliest man in the world," says I, "what in Tophet did the lightning go and do that for?"

The fellow shrugged his shoulders.

"Well," he answers me back, "I'm too polite to say. But there's somebody else here besides *me*, ain't there?"

Suggestions for Additional Reading
Notes
Index

Suggestions for Additional Reading

Walter Blair's influence shows as an imprint in the footnotes, tables of contents, and acknowledgments of most books and articles in the field of American humor. His labels of Southwestern, Down East, and Literary Comedian schools of humor have become standard titles. Major surveys of American humor — Jesse Bier's *The Rise and Fall of American Humor* (1968), Richard Boyd Hauck's *A Cheerful Nihilism: Conscience and "The Absurd" in American Humorous Fiction* (1971), and Norris Yates's *The American Humorist: Conscience of the Twentieth Century* (1964) — all begin from premises Blair established. His former students contributed a half dozen essays on topics in American humor in an issue (volume 2, number 1, April 1975) of *Studies in American Humor* dedicated to him.

Blair's abiding interest in the "mock-oral" narrative voice in American humor surfaces with elaborations in both Richard Bridgman's *The Colloquial Style in America* (1966) and David Sewell's *Mark Twain's Languages* (1987). Richard Dorson added to the legends of New England folk humor in *Jonathan Draws the Longbow* (1946), and Cameron Nickels' forthcoming study of New England humor before the Civil War will elaborate Blair's chapter in *Native American Humor,* as David E. E. Sloane's *The Literary Humor of the Urban Northeast* (1983) added a new variant of New England humor.

A much more vigorous exploration of the humor of the Old Southwest followed Blair and Meine's original forays. Kenneth Lynn's *Mark Twain and Southwestern Humor* (1959) and Hennig Cohen and William Dillingham's anthology, *Humor of the Old Southwest* (1964), raised this dubious candidate to the level of gentility, as did Faulkner's (and others') acknowledgment of its significance to their own literary careers.

Among those humorists, George Washington Harris has risen steadily in reputation, as a foreshadower of what seems the very modern school of "black humor." In the four years between 1962 and 1965, the University of Tennessee Press issued four volumes of *The Lovingood Papers,* an annual devoted to rescuing stories of Sut Lovingood's pranks from the files of Tennessee newspapers. Blair was a founding member of the advisory board of that journal, as he was of *Studies in American Humor.*

His pioneering investigation of *Adventures of Huckleberry Finn* anticipated the deluge of scholarship and criticism in the past several decades. His detective work in dating the composition of that novel was one key to its shifting tones, moods, and themes. Dewey Ganzel disputed Blair's chronology in "Twain, Travel Books, and Life on the Mississippi" (*American Literature* 34 [1962]: 40–55), arguing that passages Blair had dated 1880 were actually written in consequence of Mark Twain's 1882 trip down the Mississippi; and in 1989, Sherwood Cummings argued in *Mark Twain and Science* that the Grangerford-Shepherdson feud chapters were written earlier than 1880 (a possibility that Blair had admitted in the original article). And the discovery of the missing first half of the manuscript in 1991 laid hypothesis and conjecture to rest: the 1876 composition stint took Mark Twain about one-third of the way through chapter 18, to Huck's comment about feuds, "Never heard of it before — tell me about it." The 1879–80 productivity carried the humorist through the end of chapter 21, amazingly close to Blair's original chronology.

Blair's interest in the literary sources for episodes and characters in *Huck* — as in "The French Revolution and *Huckleberry Finn*" in 1957 — was an aspect of a general movement toward seeing Twain as a more literate author than he had been credited with being in the early years of the twentieth century. The authoritative outcome of this interest was Alan Gribben's monumental *Mark Twain's Library: A Reconstruction* in two volumes, published in 1980.

Blair played a significant role in the establishment of the canon of "the Matter of Hannibal" with his research into unfinished manuscripts such as "Huck Finn and Tom Sawyer among the Indians," "Tom Sawyer's Conspiracy," and "Villagers, 1840–43," works which he eventually edited for the University of California Press as *Mark Twain's Hannibal, Huck and Tom* in 1969, and revised in paperback in 1989 as *Huck Finn and Tom Sawyer among the Indians and Other Unfinished Stories*. Analyses of those provocative works are now following their availability to scholars and critics in published form.

Notes

Traditions in Southern Humor

1. For details about these writers and for examples of their work, see Franklin J. Meine, *Tall Tales of the Southwest* (New York: Knopf, 1930).

2. John Donald Wade, *Augustus Baldwin Longstreet* (New York: Macmillan, 1924), 148.

3. J. H. McMahon, in *Truth-Teller* (Jackson, Tenn.), quoted by James R. Masterson, *Tall Tales of Arkansaw* (Boston: Chapman & Grimes, 1943), 5.

4. Mody C. Boatright, *Folk Laughter on the American Frontier* (New York: Macmillan, 1949), 9–10.

5. *Narrative of the Life of David Crockett* . . . (Philadelphia, 1834). Crockett had announced to newspapers in 1833 that he would show himself in his autobiography "as I really am, *a plain, blunt, Western man,* relying on honesty and the woods, and not on learning and the law, for a living."

6. Speech in the United States Senate, quoted in Howard W. Odum, *Southern Regions of the United States* (Chapel Hill: University of North Carolina Press, 1936), 531–32.

7. See Walter Blair, *Horse Sense in American Humor* (Chicago: University of Chicago Press, 1942), 24–46.

8. Johnson J. Hooper, *Simon Suggs' Adventures* . . . (Americus, Ga.: Americus Book Co., 1928), 41.

9. Joseph G. Baldwin, *Flush Times in Alabama and Mississippi* (New York, 1853), 84–85.

10. See R. S. Boggs, "North Carolina Folk Tales Current in the 1820's," *Journal of American Folk-Lore,* 47 (Oct.–Dec. 1934), 269–88; Walter Blair, *Native American Humor, 1800–1900* (New York: American Book Co., 1937), 70–75; Richard M. Dorson, "Print and American Folk Tales," *California Folklore Quarterly* (July 1945), 207–15; Richard L. Powers, "The Hoosier as an American Folk-Type," *Indiana Magazine of History,* 38 (June 1942), 107–22.

11. Dorothy Dondore, "Big Talk! The Flyting, the Gabe, and the Frontier Boast," *American Speech,* 6 (Oct. 1930), 45–55.

12. For a brief summary of parallels between "The Big Bear" and the *Beowulf* narrative, see Dorson, "Print and American Folk Tales" 212. For a statement

257

about Scandinavian legendry, see *Westerners Brand Book* (Chicago), 8 (Feb. 1952), 91.

13. See Stuart Tave, "Comic Theory and Criticism from Steele to Hazlitt," doctoral dissertation, Oxford, 1950.

14. Meine first considered this influence in his Introduction, *Tall Tales of the Southwest* xxvii–xxix, and numerous students of humor have since documented his claims.

15. William T. Porter, Preface to *The Big Bear of Arkansas* . . . , ed. Porter (Philadelphia, 1846).

16. Although English sportsmen were acknowledgedly interested in prize-fighting, some Americans — including the editor of the *Spirit* — purported to be repelled by it. The *Spirit* did contain news items about boxers at times, but expressed disapproval of the brutal sport of prizefighting. The delicacy of Porter, however, did not prevent his printing detailed accounts of very ferocious fights by Western-ers or reprinting accounts of prizefights from English magazines.

17. Harold Child, "Caricature and the Literature of Sport," *The Cambridge History of English Literature* (New York: Macmillan, 1917), 14:253.

18. Ibid. 246. Baldwin, *Flush Times*, p. 127, tells of an Alabama saloon that was "the general rendezvous of the fast young gentlemen" where "horse-racing, shooting-matches, quoit-pitching, cock-fighting, and card-playing filled up the va-cant hours between drinks."

19. Statement about the new series of the *Spirit*, published in several issues in 1836. In "To Old Subscribers," issue of March 9, Porter wrote: "It was our re-solve to . . . gratify our own professional pride, by furnishing a journal IDENTI-FIED WITH THE SPORTING INTEREST IN AMERICA" (capitals his).

20. Memorial article by George Wilkes, in *Porter's Spirit of the Times*, a magazine founded by Porter when he left the old *Spirit* in 1858. The article ap-pears in the issue for July 24, 1858.

21. See Francis Brinley's statement in *Life of William T. Porter* (New York, 1869), 34–35, and Porter's statement quoted in same work (45).

22. Porter, "To Old Subscribers," *Spirit*, March 9, 1839; "Profit and Loss Ac-count," *Spirit*, April 1842.

23. Surtees' MSS quoted in *Robert Smith Surtees* . . . , ed. E. D. Cuming (Lon-don: William Blackwood, 1924), 63.

24. Porter, Preface to *The Big Bear of Arkansas*. See also *Spirit*, Jan. 11, 1845, 547.

25. The most detailed study of Noland's career is that in Masterson, *Tall Tales of Arkansaw* 29–54. Masterson says that "nearly the whole substance of Noland's writing included drinking, fighting, horse-racing, gambling, hunting and politics."

26. Donald Day, "The Life and Works of George Washington Harris," disser-tation, University of Chicago, 1942.

27. W. Stanley Hoole, *Alias Simon Suggs: The Life and Times of Johnson Jones Hooper* (University: University of Alabama Press, 1952).

28. *Turf Register*, April 1841, quoted by Brinley, *Life of William T. Porter* 69.

29. For discussions of the realism of the early Southern humorists, see Napier

Wilt, *Some American Humorists* (New York: Nelson, 1929), x–xi; Meine, *Tall Tales of the Southwest* xxix–xxx.

30. Douglas Southall Freeman, Foreword to *A Treasury of Southern Folklore,* ed. B. A. Botkin (New York: Crown, 1949), ix. Compare Mark Twain's talk about "the art of telling a humorous story . . . by word of mouth, not print," in "How to Tell a Story," *Literary Essays* (New York, 1899), 7: "The humorous story may be spun out to great length, and may wander around as much as it pleases. . . ." Compare, too, Twain's best mock oral narratives, such as "The Famous Jumping Frog . . ." and "Jim Baker's Blue-Jay Yarn."

The Popularity of Nineteenth-Century American Humorists

1. For details concerning the success of the play, see G. O. Seilhamer, *History of the American Theatre* (New York, 1888–91), 2:275–85.

2. A history of such characters is given in Perley Isaac Reed's "The Realistic Presentation of American Characters in Native American Plays Prior to Eighteen Seventy," *Ohio State University Bulletin,* 22, no. 26 (May 1918).

3. Eli Perkins, *Thirty Years of Wit* (New York: Cassell, 1891), 295–96.

4. Archer B. Hulbert, *The Paths of Inland Commerce* (New Haven: Yale University Press, 1921), 62–63.

5. For a brief account of these actors, see Arthur Hornblow, *A History of the Theatre in America* (Philadelphia: J. B. Lippincott, 1919), 2:64–65, 68–69.

6. Burdette may have prepared some monologues for Sol Smith Russell. See Clara B. Burdette, *Robert J. Burdette: His Message* (Philadelphia: John C. Winston, 1922), 126.

7. Valentine, Smith, and Hill published volumes of anecdotes.

8. Joel Chandler Harris, *The World's Wit and Humor: American* (New York: Review of Reviews, 1906), 1:xx.

9. See V. L. Parrington, *The Romantic Revolution in America* (New York: Harcourt, Brace, 1927), 172–79.

10. W. P. Trent, "Retrospect of American Humor," *Century,* 63 (Nov. 1901), 54–55.

11. F. L. Pattee, *A History of American Literature since 1870* (New York: Century 1915), 27–28.

12. "Witty Paragraphs," *Yankee Doodle,* June 19, 1847.

13. Review of Artemus Ward's *Travels* in *North American Review,* 102 (April 1866), 589.

14. Frederick Hudson, *Journalism in the United States from 1690–1872* (New York: Harper, 1873), 695–96.

15. Edmund Clarence Stedman to Bayard Taylor, Sept. 16, 1873, in Laura Stedman and G. M. Gould, *Life and Letters of Edmund Clarence Stedman* (New York: Moffatt, Yard, 1910), 1:447. The italics are Stedman's.

16. A list including only the most popular would name, in addition to the above, *Atlanta Constitution, Baltimore Every Saturday, Baltimore Sun, Bloomington Eve, Boston Commercial-Bulletin, Boston Evening Star, Boston Transcript, Boston Traveler, Bridgeport Standard, Brooklyn Eagle, Buffalo News, Buffalo Our*

Record, Buffalo Times, Burlington Hawkeye, Cambridge Tribune, Carson Appeal, Chicago Commercial Advertiser, Chicago National Weekly, Chicago Tribune, Cincinnati Star, Danbury News, Denver Tribune, Detroit Free Press, Elmira Free Press, Erie Herald, Fairfield Times, Galveston News, Huntsville Item, Kansas City Times, Kokomo Tribune, La Crosse Democrat, Laramie Sentinel, Lowell Courier, Marathon Independent, Marlborough Times, Meriden Recorder, New Haven Register, New Orleans Picayune, New Orleans Times-Democrat, New York Commercial Advertiser, New York Express, New York Graphic, New York Herald, Owego Recorder, Peoria Transcript, Philadelphia Bulletin, Philadelphia Kronicle Herald, Pittsburgh Leader, Portland Courier, Providence Star, Quincy Modern Argus, Richmond State, Rochester Democrat, Rochester Express, Rome Sentinel, St. Louis Spirit, San Francisco Chronicle, San Francisco News Letter, Somerville Journal, Southport Times, Steubenville Herald, Syracuse Times, Toledo Blade, Towanda Enterprise, Troy Press, Turners' Falls Reporter, Virginia City Enterprise, Waterloo Observer, Wheeling Leader, Whitehall Times, and *Yonkers Statesman.*

17. *Boneville Trumpet* (Bridgeport, Conn.), March 13, 1861, 1, 6.

18. *Yankee Doodle, Spirit of the Times,* and *Puck* carried on vehement campaigns against the failure of papers to give credit to exchanges from which they pilfered material.

19. All of the publications mentioned in note 16 and in the paragraph to which it refers furnished exchange material to two or more humorous columns.

20. M. A. Wyman, *Two American Pioneers* (New York: Columbia University Press, 1927), 235–36.

21. Perkins, *Thirty Years of Wit* 132.

22. George H. Derby, *Fifty Years among Authors, Books and Publishers* (New York, 1886), 419–20.

23. *National Cyclopedia of American Biography* (New York: James T. White, 1929), 6:27.

24. C. B. Burdette, *Robert J. Burdette* 127.

25. Ibid. 114.

26. *National Cyclopedia of American Biography* 6:28. For additional testimony, see J. L. Ford's article in *Munsey's Magazine,* 25 (July 1901), 488, and Slason Thompson's *Life of Eugene Field* (New York: Appleton, 1927), 60–61.

27. H. C. Lukens, "American Literary Comedians," *Harper's Magazine,* 80, (April 1890), 791–92. Only a portion of the list given by Lukens is reproduced.

28. Frank Luther Mott, *A History of American Magazines, 1741–1850* (New York: Appleton, 1930), 424.

29. Ibid. 609–10.

30. Franklin J. Meine and the writer are attempting to compile a complete list. The most helpful sources have been J. Brander Matthews, "The Comic Periodical Literature of the United States," *American Bibliopolist,* 7 (August 1875), 199–201; L. W. Kingman, "The Comic Periodicals of America," *American Bibliopolist,* 7 (December 1875), 262–65; Mott, *History of American Magazines;* and Ernest L. Hancock, "The Passing of the American Comic," *Bookman,* 22 (September 1905), 78–84. The lists given in these works, however, are quite incomplete, and *Union*

List offers little help. It has been necessary to look for a large share of material in articles and books about the humorists and in comic journals which mentioned exchanges or gloated over rival publications that passed away.

31. *Yankee Doodle*, Preface to Vol. 2 (1847).

32. Advertisements in *Yankee Doodle* in most of the issues of 1847.

33. Albert H. Smyth, *Philadelphia Magazines and Their Contributors* (Philadelphia, 1892), 235.

34. Mott, *History of American Magazines*.

35. *Pick*, March 12, 1853.

36. Ibid., Feb. 5, 1853.

37. Ibid., Dec. 11, 1852.

38. Ibid., Jan. 1, 1853.

39. Ibid.

40. Will M. Clemens, *Famous Funny Fellows* (New York, 1883), 134.

41. W. C. Vischer, "Opie Read," in *Library of Southern Literature* (New Orleans: Martin and Hoyt, 1909), 10:4358.

42. *The Journalist, a Pictorial Souvenir* (New York: Allan Forman, 1887), 101.

43. "Century of American Humor," *Munsey's Magazine*, 25, (July 1901), 490.

44. Maximilian La Borde, *History of South Carolina College* (Charleston, 1874), 462.

45. Derby, *Fifty Years among Authors* 407–11.

46. Ibid. 413–16.

47. *Eclectic Magazine*, 35 (June 1855), 269.

48. Don C. Seitz, *Artemus Ward* (New York: Harper, 1919), 119. See also Derby, *Fifty Years among Authors* 242.

49. Will M. Clemens, *Famous Funny Fellows* 201.

50. Kingman, "Comic Periodicals of America" 262.

51. Francis S. Smith, *Life and Adventures of Josh Billings* (New York: G. W. Carleton, 1883), 41–44. For additional testimony, see *National Cyclopedia of American Biography* 6:29, and Derby, *Fifty Years among Authors* 243. Though the figures are not precisely the same, there is essential agreement to the effect that early issues sold more than 100,000.

52. Will M. Clemens, *Famous Funny Fellows* 162–63.

53. *National Cyclopedia of American Biography* 6:28.

54. *The American Catalogue, 1884–1890* (New York: Publishers' Weekly, 1891).

55. *The American Catalogue, 1890–1894* (New York: Publishers' Weekly, 1895).

56. For details on the early history of the lyceum, consult G. W. Cooke's *Introduction to The Dial* (Cleveland, 1902), 1:42–43, and *Ralph Waldo Emerson* (Boston: James R. Osgood, 1881), 256–57. For the later growth of the lyceum system, see John S. Noffsinger, *Correspondence Schools, Lyceums, Chautauquas* (New York: Macmillan, 1926), 99–105.

57. E. P. Hingston, *The Genial Showman* (New York: Harper, 1870), 42.

58. Ibid. 43.

59. Seitz, *Artemus Ward* 101–222. This is the source for all the material on Ward the lecturer given here.

60. Smith, *Life and Adventures of Josh Billings* 48–55. See also C. B. Burdette, *Robert J. Burdette* 134, and *National Cyclopedia of American Biography* 6:29.

61. Interview in *Newark Courier,* Nov. 19, 1871.

62. *National Cyclopedia of American Biography* 6:29.

63. W. L. Visscher, *Ten Wise Men and Some More* (Chicago, 1908), 54.

64. *National Cyclopedia of American Biography* 6:32.

65. *Kings of the Platform and Pulpit,* ed. Eli Perkins (Chicago: Bedford-Clarke, 1890), 275, 239, 194, 437, 425.

66. Visscher, *Ten Wise Men and Some More* 100.

67. James Barr, *The Humour of America* (New York: Scribners, 1893), 441.

68. J. L. King, *Dr. George William Bagby* (New York: Columbia University Press, 1927), 172–75.

69. *American Punch,* I (July 1879), 80.

70. Will M. Clemens, *Famous Funny Fellows* 114.

71. C. H. Dennis, *Eugene Field's Creative Years* (Garden City: Doubleday, Doran, 1924), 241.

72. For details, see C. B. Burdette, *Robert J. Burdette* 121–32.

73. F. W. Nye, *Bill Nye: His Own Life Story* (New York: Century, 1926), 98–108. The letters were reprinted in *Remarks.*

74. *National Cyclopedia of American Biography* 6:25.

75. F. W. Nye, *Bill Nye* 45–95.

76. W. M. Clemens, *Famous Funny Fellows* 117.

77. Melville Landon, in *Kings of the Platform and Pulpit* 306.

78. *Mark Twain's Library of Humor* (New York: Charles L. Webster, 1888), 383.

79. F. W. Nye to the writer, Feb. 19, 1930.

80. Ibid.

81. F. W. Nye, *Bill Nye* 128–397, to which I am chiefly indebted, gives a detailed account of Nye as a lecturer.

82. Visscher, *Ten Wise Men* 96.

83. Marcus Dickey, *The Maturity of James Whitcomb Riley* (Indianapolis: Bobbs Merrill, 1922), 182–84. For details concerning the lecture trips of the pair, see 234–56. Landon has preserved a record of an entire Nye-Riley appearance in *Kings of the Platforms and Pulpit* 315–25.

84. Will M. Clemens, *Famous Funny Fellows* 117.

85. Letter to the writer, February 19, 1930.

86. Ibid.

87. Ibid. My estimate on the history would be 200,000 higher. It went through eight large editions in 1894 alone.

"A Man's Voice, Speaking": A Continuum in American Humor

1. Frances Trollope, *Domestic Manners of the Americans,* ed. Donald Smalley (New York: Alfred A. Knopf, 1949), 209–210, 305, 324.

2. *Life and Letters of Edmund Clarence Stedman,* ed. L. Stedman, G. M.

Gould (New York, 1910), 1:447; James T. Thurber, "The Future, If Any, of Comedy," *Harper's Magazine*, 223 (December 1961), 40–45; Melvin Maddocks, "We Are Not Amused—and Why," *Time*, July 20, 1970, 30–31.

3. Norris W. Yates, *William T. Porter and "The Spirit of the Times"* (Baton Rouge: Louisiana State University Press, 1957); Richard M. Dorson, *American Folklore* (Chicago: University of Chicago Press, 1959), 39–73.

4. It is incorrect to claim, as some scholars have, that "most" antebellum stories took this form. Actually, even in the Southwest, most did not. Nevertheless many did, including some of the best ones. See Walter Blair, *Native American Humor* (New York, 1937; rev. ed. San Francisco, 1960), 79–101, which dealt with oral influences and initiated discussions of framework stories and mock oral tales in Southwestern humor.

5. Wilson M. Hudson, *Andy Adams: His Life and Writings* (Dallas: Southern Methodist University Press, 1964), 71 and *passim*.

6. O. Henry's own favorite, "The Atavism of John Tom Little Bear," first published in 1903, is in *Rolling Stones* (New York, 1912), 34–52.

7. Henry Watterson, Preface to *Oddities in Southern Life and Character* (Boston, 1883), vii–viii.

8. Andrew Lang, "Western Drolls," in *Lost Leaders* (London, 1889), 186–87.

9. John Kronenberger, "Jean Shepherd Tells It Like It Was, Maybe," *New York Times*, June 6, 1971.

10. Joel Chandler Harris "Humor in America," in *American Wit and Humor*, 5 vols. (New York, 1909), 1:xxi–xxii.

11. J. Frank Dobie, "Storytellers I Have Known," in *Singers and Storytellers* (Dallas: Southern Methodist University Press, 1961), 61; Dunlap, *History of the Rise and Progress of the Arts of Design in the United States* (New York, 1834), 2:90; Richard M. Dorson, "Oral Styles of American Folk Narrative," in *Folklore in Action*, ed. H. P. Beck (Philadelphia: University of Pennsylvania Press, 1962), 93–98; *Mark Twain in Eruption*, ed. B. DeVoto (New York: Harper, 1940), 358–366; Fred A. Lorch, *The Trouble Begins at Eight* (Ames: Iowa State University Press, 1968), 236.

12. G. Legman has started a classification which includes a number in *Rationale of the Dirty Joke* (New York: Grove Press, 1968), Vol. 1. A second volume is planned. As the title indicates, the book omits cleanly jokes—and the author has not classified a great number of less antiseptic anecdotes which have been included in other compilations.

13. Twain discusses this fact in *Eruption* 216–24, and sets down a platform version of "His Grandfather's Old Ram" that differs greatly from the version printed in *Roughing It*, chapter 53.

14. James H. Delargy, *The Gaelic Story-Teller* (London: British Academy, 1945), 16; Mercier, "The Irish Short Story and Oral Tradition," in *The Celtic Cross* (Lafayette: Purdue University Press, 1964), 113. Mercier suggests that "attitudes and techniques based on oral literature can revivify written literature in a period of sterility" and that this happened at the beginning of the Romantic movement.

15. Ball's article appeared in *Folk-Lore*, 56 (December 1954), 170; Dorson's is "Esthetic Form in British and American Folk Narrative," in *Medieval Literature*

and Folk Studies, ed. J. Mandel and B. A. Rosenberg (New Brunswick: Rutgers University Press, 1970), 308. Dorson has described the varying dramatic performances of a number of storytellers in "Oral Styles" 79–92.

16. Frank O'Connor, *Stories* (New York: Vintage Books, 1956), vii.

17. The quoted phrases are from "William Dean Howells," *Works,* 37-vol. definitive ed. (New York, 1922–25), 26:228–38; and "On Speech-Making Reform," *Mark Twain's Speeches,* ed. A. B. Paine (New York, 1923), 2–3. Mark Twain praised novelist E. W. Howe for writing "as a man talks" in a letter of 1883 — "Mark Twain's Criticism of *The Story of a Country Town,*" ed. C. E. Schorer, *American Literature,* 27 (March 1955), 110. A perceptive summary is that by Sydney J. Krause, "Twain's Method and Theory of Composition," *Modern Philology,* 56 (February 1959), 166–77.

18. George Washington Harris, "The Widow McCloud's Mare," *Sut Lovingood's Yarns,* ed. M. Thomas Inge (New Haven, 1966), 46; Mark Twain, "The Notorious Jumping Frog of Calaveras County," in *Selected Shorter Writings of Mark Twain,* ed. Walter Blair (Boston, 1962), 15; William Faulkner, "Spotted Horses," *Scribner's Magazine,* 89 (June 1931), 587–88. A third-person version in *The Hamlet* (1940), pt. 4 offers an illuminating contrast.

19. Max Eastman, *The Enjoyment of Laughter* (New York: Simon & Schuster, 1936) cites Leacock's statement and comments upon it (305–6). One of the most popular antebellum stories was Hamilton C. Jones's "Cousin Sally Dilliard," which continually digressed; beginning in the 1830s, it was reprinted often. "Colonel Wanderwell," by *Delta,* published in the *Spirit of the Times* in 1833, utilized the same pattern; so did Frances Whitcher's "Hezekiah Bedott," in *Widow Bedott Papers* (1855), frequently reprinted in newspapers and periodicals.

20. Dorson, "Esthetic Form" 321.

21. Yates, *William T. Porter* 161–63. For an analysis of Thorpe's story, see Walter Blair, "The Technique of 'The Big Bear of Arkansas,'" in this volume.

22. *Eruption* 224, 243; "How to Tell a Story," *The Complete Works of James Whitcomb Riley* (New York, 1916), 10:2670–73. In the same volume, p. 2662, Riley has a vernacular character discuss the reading of monologues.

23. Albert Bigelow Paine, *Mark Twain: A Biography,* 4 vols. (New York: Harper, 1912), 3:846–47; *Mark Twain to Mrs. Fairbanks,* ed. Dixon Wecter (San Marino: Huntington Library, 1949), 260–61; DeLancey Ferguson, *Mark Twain: Man and Legend* (Indianapolis: Bobbs-Merrill, 1943), 207.

24. H. L. Davis, *Honey in the Horn,* (New York: Avon Books 1935), 143.

25. Richard Boyd Hauck, *A Cheerful Nihilism* (Bloomington: University of Indiana Press, 1971), 51–63.

26. Interview with Jean Stein, *Paris Review,* 1956, in *William Faulkner: Three Decades of Criticism,* ed. F. J. Hoffman and O. Vickery (Lansing: Michigan State University Press, 1960), 79.

27. *Lion in the Garden: Interviews with William Faulkner, 1926–1962,* ed. J. F. Meriwether and M. Millgate (New York, 1968), 11, 38–39; H. M. Campbell and R. E. Foster, *William Faulkner: A Critical Appraisal* (Norman, 1951), 99, 102–7; M. Thomas Inge, "William Faulkner and G. W. Harris," *Tennessee Studies in Literature,* 7 (1962), 47–59.

28. The community attributes each of Joe's actions to either his black or his white blood. Lawrance Thompson, *William Faulkner* (New York, 1963), 79, notices that, ironically, highly educated Gavin Stevens reveals precisely the same prejudices.

A German Connection: Raspe's Baron Munchausen

1. Clarence Gohdes, *American Literature in Nineteenth-Century England* (New York: Columbia University Press, 1944), 57; Bret Harte, "The Rise of the 'Short Story,'" *Cornhill Magazine*, n.s. 7 (July 1899), 3; Will D. Howe, "Early Humorists," *Cambridge History of American Literature* (New York: Macmillan, 1918, 1938), 2:158; Max Eastman, *The Enjoyment of Laughter* (New York: Simon and Schuster, 1936), 90.

2. *A Dictionary of Americanisms*, ed. Mitford M. Mathews (Chicago: University of Chicago Press, 1951), 1701.

3. Ernest W. Baughman, *Type and Motif-Index of the Folktales of England and North America* (The Hague: Mouton & Co., 1966), xvii. References to "Munchausen Tales" cited hereafter are on 51–57, 407–9.

4. Gershon Legman, *The Horn Book* (New Hyde Park, N.Y.: University Books, 1966), 462.

5. Details concerning Raspe's biography here and throughout the present essay come from John Carswell, *The Prospector: Being the Life and Times of Rudolf Erich Raspe* (London: Cresset Press, 1950), as do the critical comments of Carswell cited. Bibliographical data concerning early editions of the *Narrative* and sequels are in *Singular Travels, Campaigns and Adventures of Baron Munchausen by Rudolf Erich Raspe and Others* (New York: Dover Publications, 1961); so are quoted passages from these eighteenth-century books. Two volumes containing extensive lists of editions and adaptations in several languages, and accounts of sources and of the baron's growing fame, frequently drawn upon, are *Münchhaussen und Münchhausiaden*, ed. Werner R. Schweizer (Munich: Francke, 1969) and *Münchhausiana*, ed. Erwin Wackermann (Stuttgart: Eggert, 1969), the latter augmented by a *Supplement 1969–1978*, ed. Wackermann (Stuttgard: Eggert, 1978).

6. Edwin G. Gudde, "An American Version of Munchausen," *American Literature*, 13 (Jan. 1942), 372–90; Henry A. Pochman, *German Culture in America* (Madison: University of Wisconsin Press, 1957, 1961), 327, 346, 677, and Wackermann's bibliography.

7. Otto Weinreich, *Antiphanes und Münchhausen* (Vienna and Leipzig: Holder-Pichler-Tempsky, 1942).

8. Stith Thompson, *Motif-Index of Folk-Literature* (Bloomington: Indiana University Press, 1955–58), 5:404–8.

9. Harold Thompson, "Humor," in *Literary History of the United States* (New York: Macmillan, 1948, 1953), 728.

10. Leonard Roberts, *Old Greasybeard: Tales from the Cumberland Gap* (Detroit: Folklore Associates, 1969), 165–66, 207. The same scholar's *South from Hell-fer Sartin: Kentucky Mountain Folk Tales* (Lexington: University of Kentucky Press, 1955) contains (144–47) versions of three other Munchausen tales, with commentaries on other occurrences (162–63). Other variants, with valuable comments, will

be found in the books of Ozark tales by Vance Randolph published between 1955 and 1976.

11. Letter received from Ernest Baughman, October 14, 1981. My thanks to Professor Baughman for many helpful suggestions.

12. Richard M. Dorson, *American Folklore* (Chicago: University of Chicago Press, 1959), 14, 44, 57, 200–01, 227. Professor Dorson notices that many American exaggerations "depend upon stock fictions current throughout the country, which they adopt as authentic experiences [in] the manner of the most redoubtable truth twister, Baron Munchausen . . . whose solemn faced *Narrative* . . . made his name synonymous for gorgeous fabrications."

13. Baughman, *Type and Motif Index* 54.

14. Norris Wilson Yates, *William T. Porter and "The Spirit of the Times"* (Baton Rouge: Louisiana State University Press, 1957), 173.

15. Ibid. 174.

16. Here I can make a modest footnote contribution. In 1911, aged eleven, I first heard a tall tale told. My uncle John W. Merritt told it beside a campfire on the shore of Lake Coeur d'Alene, Idaho — the first one in Raspe's *Narrative*, about the man halted by a bad snowstorm who tied his horse to a "pointed stump," lay down in the snow and slept through a thaw. When he awoke, he saw his horse tied to a weathercock on a steeple, and had to shoot him down. My uncle had heard it told without any recognition of a printed source. Oral tellings, one as recently as 1965, have been recorded by folklorists. In some, sand which has replaced the snow was blown away during the night.

17. Carswell, *The Prospector* 189.

18. A slight possibility is that the artist who drew the frontispiece portrait of the baron for the 1792 edition of the sequel had seen Raspe and pictured him, and that Doré saw this likeness.

19. Most of these are discussed in Walter Blair, "A Man's Voice, Speaking: A Continuum in American Humor," in this volume, and Walter Blair and Hamlin Hill, *America's Humor: From Poor Richard to Doonesbury* (New York: Oxford University Press, 1978). These treat ways storytellers emphasize relationships with listeners.

20. Bret Harte, "The Rise of the 'Short Story'"; George Washington Harris, "Sut Lovingood Sets Up with a Gal," *Knoxville Press and Messenger*, Sept. 29 1869; T. B. Thorpe, "The Big Bear of Arkansas" [1841] in *Native American Humor*, ed. Walter Blair (San Francisco: Chandler Publishing Co., 1960), 348. The last of these cites other instances (90–92). Professor Baughman summarized in a letter of May 31, 1983: "Because the Munchausen tales must have served as sources for many tellers in this country, their style probably had its effects also: what I call the yarning style–first person narrator, deliberate manner of telling (poker-face), digression, insistence on veracity, etc."

Mike Fink in Legend and Story

1. Here and in Cadot's account there is the possibility that an old man is, humanly enough, showing wisdom superior to that of people who have actually known the boatman by attacking stories that he has heard or read.

2. In 1829, an anonymous author, probably the Rev. Timothy Flint, had mentioned a rifle shot test but had felt impelled to omit the anecdote and in 1839, a *Crockett Almanac* had presented a censored version.

3. One may wonder whether the story in all its horrors ever appeared in print. Is it possible that Mike was so beyond the pale of decency that on occasion he had his woman hold the cup between her thighs while he shot at it?

4. It should be noted that Chunk erroneously placed Mike's death "at Smithland, behind the Cumberland bar."

5. One very recent story tells about Mike's winning a seven-mile keelboat race. This is the only reference to keelboat races that we have encountered prior to 1955, when Walt Disney produced a movie in which Mike raced Davy Crockett. Disney stated that his story was based upon a legend, but we have not had the pleasure of seeing his source.

6. A. B. Hulbert, *The Paths of Inland Commerce* (New Haven, 1921), 64. A similar comment is made by Dale L. Morgan, *Jedidiah Smith and the Opening of the West* (Indianapolis, 1953) 47.

7. See Constance Rourke, *American Humor: A Study of the National Character* (New York, 1931), 33–55; Walter Blair ed., *Native American Humor, 1800–1900* (New York: American Book Co., 1937), 27–37; Mody C. Boatright, *Folk Laughter on the American Frontier* (New York: Macmillan, 1949), 1–33.

8. Mathew Carey, *Miscellaneous Essays* (Philadelphia, 1830), 396.

9. James H. Perkins," The Pioneers of Kentucky," *North American Review*, 62 (Jan. 1846), 87.

10. Leland D. Baldwin, *Western Pennsylvania Historical Review*, 16 (May 1933), 146.

11. A letter from Professor Gilbert H. Barnes of Ohio Wesleyan, Aug. 11, 1930, mentioned his seeing the account in a Pittsburgh newspaper.

12. William E. Connelly, Secretary of the Kansas State Historical Society, said in a letter of May 10, 1930: "In some of my manuscript writings I have an account of a fight between three Big Sandy backwoodsmen who had taken some produce to Louisville in canoes, for sale. Mike Fink and his crew came along and attacked these . . . pioneers who lived in what is now Johnson county, Kentucky. They were powerful men and they completely defeated Mike Fink and all his keelboatmen. One . . . was Henderson Milum, who was six feet, six, and supposed to be the strongest man in the Big Sandy Valley in his day. I knew his discendents [sic] very well. Another was a man named Hanna who had killed a bear on the Big Sandy River without weapons. . . . Another . . . was Peter Mankins, who lived many years on the . . . River but finally moved to Washington county, Arkansas, where he died at the age of 111 years. . . . This fight was on a wharf boat." A keelboat crew usually totaled at least six men.

13. Daniel C. Hoffman, *Paul Bunyan: Last of the Frontier Demigods* (Philadelphia, 1952), 19.

14. Rourke, *American Humor* 54.

15. *Times Literary Supplement* (London), Nov. 16, 1933, 794.

16. Bernard DeVoto, *Mark Twain's America* (Boston, 1932), 60.

17. *Times Literary Supplement* (London), Nov. 16, 1933, 794.

18. Neihardt's *Song of Three Friends* (1919) is based upon only three of the stories.

19. Richard M. Dorson, *Southern Folklore Quarterly*, 6 (June 1942), 95–102. Dorson cites as authorities consulted on heroic literature H. M. and N. K. Chadwick, *The Growth of Literature*, 3 vols. (Cambridge, 1932–40); W. P. Ker, *The Heroic Age* (Cambridge, 1912); W. P. Ker, *Epic and Romance* (London, 1922), chap. 1; and N. K. Sidhanta, *The Heroic Age of India* (London, 1929). A book published since Dorson's article was written and which extends these studies in C. M. Bowra, *Heroic Poetry* (London, 1952), 91–131. Constance Rourke (*American Humor* 55) was, we believe, the first student to point out that "Mike Fink embodied the traditional history of the hero. . . ." She did not, however, elaborate upon this claim. In 1844, J. M. Field had seen the "gathering of the mythic haze . . . which . . . invests distinguished mortality with the sublimer attributes of the hero and the demigod."

20. See Dorothy Dondore, "Big Talk! The Flyting, the Gabe, and the Frontier Boast," *American Speech*, 6 (Oct. 1930), 45–55.

21. In chap. 82 of *Moby Dick* he reverses the procedure of writers about Mike Fink who compare the keeler with Hercules when he characterizes Hercules as "that antique Crockett and Kit Carson." Elsewhere in the book he talks of the legendary White Steed of the Prairies.

22. For a brief consideration of the problem and its initial solution see Blair, *Native American Humor* 17–37.

23. W. H. Gardiner, *North American Review*, 15 (1822), 251–52. Compare George F. Ruxton's characterization of western trappers, *Adventures in Mexico and the Rocky Mountains* (1847), 13.

24. See Arvid Shulenberger, *Cooper's Theory of Fiction* (Lawrence, Kan., 1955), 11–37; Nathaniel Hawthorne, Prefaces to *Blithedale Romance* (1852) and *The Marble Faun* (1860).

25. Leland D. Baldwin, *The Keelboat Age on Western Waters* (Pittsburgh, 1941), 194.

26. *Rienzi, the Last of the Tribunes* (1835), *The Last of the Barons* (1843), and *Harold, the Last of the Saxon Kings* (1848).

27. T. B. Thorpe, "The Disgraced Scalp-Lock" (1842). For a discussion of the elegiac motif in frontier literature see Henry Nash Smith, *Virgin Land: The American West as Symbol and Myth* (Cambridge, 1950), 51–89.

28. Ruth Benedict, "Folklore," *Encyclopaedia of the Social Sciences*, 6 (New York, 1931), 291.

29. Bernard DeVoto, "Bully Boy," *Saturday Review of Literature*, April 8, 1933, 523.

30. V. L. Parrington, *The Romantic Revolution in America* (New York, 1927), 138.

31. *Times Literary Supplement* (London), Nov. 16, 1933, 794.

32. Jared Sparks, "Recent American Novels," *North American Review*, 21 (July 1825), 82–83.

33. *Southern Literary Messenger*, 3 (Nov. 1837), 692.

34. Constance Rourke, *New York Herald Tribune*, April 2, 1933, 4.

35. Mark Van Doren, *Nation*, May 3, 1933, 507.

The Technique of "The Big Bear of Arkansas"

1. The story, first published in the *Spirit of the Times*, 40, 37 (March 27, 1841), has been reprinted in *Tall Tales of the Southwest*, ed. Franklin J. Meine (New York, 1930); *Native American Humor, 1800–1900*, ed. Walter Blair (New York: American Book Co., 1937), and *Ring-Tailed Roarers*, ed. V. L. O. Chittick (Caldwell, Id., 1941).

2. Introducing the story to his subscribers in 1841, William T. Porter, the editor of the *Spirit* and a great connoisseur of current humor, told his readers "on no account" to miss it, since it was "the best sketch of backwoods life, that we have seen in a long time." In a short time the tale was widely known, and when Porter published an anthology in 1845 he called it *The Big Bear of Arkansas and Other Sketches*. . . . In his introduction to this volume, the editor mentioned that Thorpe's "sketches of the men and manners of the valley of the Mississippi . . . have been read and admired wherever our language is spoken." Thereafter the story was frequently anthologized during the nineteenth century, and it was known, by name at least, to many down to the present day. Scholars of American humor such as Miss Constance Rourke and Messrs. Franklin J. Meine, V. L. O. Chittick, and Bernard DeVoto have recognized the yarn as one of the best and most influential of its time.

3. It seems to me rather typical of American humor thus to anchor the soaringly imaginative to earth with vulgar, realistic, homely details. Thus Crockett, after telling how he liberated the sun, frozen at daybreak, gave mundane details about the bear steaks he ate for breakfast. Thus Snow White, in the Disney picture, ended a poetic day in the forest by meeting the sweaty Seven Dwarfs, the most ingratiating of whom was named Dopey.

The Funny Fondled Fairytale Frog

1. Wolfgang Mieder, "Modern Anglo-American Variants of 'The Frog Prince,'" a typescript of which the author made available before its publication in *New York Folklore*. The article cites spinoffs in addition to those that I mention, as do Lutz Röhrich, *Der Witz: Figuren, Formen, Funktionen* (Stuttgart and Tubingen) 1977); Lutz Röhrich, "Der Froschkönig und seine Wadlungen," *Fabula*, 20 (1979), 170–92, and Professor Mieder, *Grimms Märchen-modern: Lyrik, Prosa, Karikaturin* (Stuttgart, 1979).

2. Antti Aarne and Stith Thompson, *The Types of the Folk Tale*, 2d rev. ed. (Helsinki and Bloomington, 1955–58), not only assigns this classification but also cites widespread appearances of the type. Additional citations are provided by Emlyn Elizabeth Gardner, *Folklore from the Schoharie Hills* (Ann Arbor, 1937); Vance Randolph, *The Devil's Pretty Daughter and Other Ozark Folk Tales* (New York, 1955), and Ernest Baughman, *Type and Motif-Index of the Folktales of England and North America* (The Hague, 1966).

3. Randolph, *Devil's Pretty Daughter* 92.

4. Christina Stead, *Letty Fox* (New York, 1946), 296. Stead cites oral sources.

5. Quoted by Polly C. Williams, "Sexton in the Classroom," in *Anne Sexton: The Artist and Her Critics*, ed. J. D. McLatchy (Bloomington, 1974), 99.

6. For Miss Welty's testimony, see Merrill Maguire Skaggs, "The Uses of Enchantment in Frontier Humor and *The Robber Bridegroom*," *Studies in American Humor*, 3 (Oct. 1976), 96–102, and Welty, *Fairy Tale of the Natchez Trace* (Jackson, 1975), 11–18, 21, 26. For Randall Jarrell's comments, see Suzanne Ferguson, *The Poetry of Randall Jarrell* (Baton Rouge, 1971), 64, 103, 158–59. The other authors are cited in Roger Sale, *Fairy Tales and After: From Snow White to E. B. White* (Cambridge, 1978), passim.

7. Quoted by Jack Zipes, *Breaking the Magic Spell: Radical Theories of Folk and Fairy Tales* (Austin, 1979), 1.

8. Michael C. Kotzin, *Dickens and the Fairy Tale* (Bowling Green, 1972), 26.

9. Sale, *Fairy Tales and After* 24.

10. Max Lüthi, "Zum Schutz von Dornröschen," *Neue Zürcher Zeitung*, Dec. 1977, 31.

11. Quoted by Röhrich, *Der Witz* 127. Röhrich adds, "In past epochs, the supernatural was not available for fun making. Märchen, fables and sagas represented supernatural happenings, but as yet jokes did not. Comic perspectives were prerequisites for complete rationality. This, in fact, is the basic reason why the surrealistic joke is not a folk product: more or less, it is a joke for intellectuals."

12. Quoted by Hugh Sidey in "Today Is No Time for Gags," *Chicago Sun-Times*, Feb. 24, 1980.

13. Bruno Bettelheim, *The Uses of Enchantment* (New York, 1974), 289–90.

14. Anne Sexton, *Transformations* (Boston, 1971), 99.

15. Letter to the author, Jan. 9, 1980, quoted with Professor Stone's kind permission.

Mark Twain, New York Correspondent

1. The most detailed account is found in Paine's *Mark Twain: A Biography* (New York, 1912), 1:308–23.

2. The series started with seven articles written during the trip to New York, which appeared Jan. 18, Feb. 22, 24, March 15, 16, 17, 23. The letters from New York, seventeen in number, appeared March 28 (dated Feb. 2), March 30 (Feb. 18), April 5 (Feb. 23), April 9 (March 2), May 26 (April 16), June 2 (April 19), June 10 (April 30), June 16 (May 17), June 23 (May 18), June 30 (May 19), July 7 (May 20), July 14 (May 23), July 21 (May 26), July 28 (May 28), Aug. 4 (June 2), Aug. 11 (June 5), Aug. 18 (June 6). Letters from St. Louis appeared in issues of May 13 (March 15) and May 19 (March 25). I am indebted to the Mark Twain Society of Chicago for permission to use photostats of these accounts.

3. Some notion of the variety of his activity is suggested by his partial summary: "I have seen the horse 'Dexter' trot a race. . . . I went to a billiard tournament. . . . I have heard all the great guns of the New York pulpit preach. . . . I have been through the dens of poverty, crime and degradation . . . in the Five Points; I have been in the Bible House, and also in the Station House. . . . I have gone the rounds of the newspaper offices and the theatres. . . . I have seen Brooklyn,

and the ferry-boats and the *Dunderberg*, and the boot-blacks, and Staten Island, and Peter Cooper, and the Fifth Avenue, and the Academy of Design, and Rosa Bonheur's Horse Fair . . . and behold I have tried the Russian bath, and skated while the winter was here . . ." (*Alta California*, Aug. 18, 1867).

4. Paine did not recount the experience in the *Biography*. Bernard DeVoto, in *Mark Twain's America* (Boston, 1932), 202, credits his mention of Clemens' "being jailed for drunkenness" to "private but unimpeachable information."

5. *Alta California*, March 28. Hereinafter dates will refer to issues of this paper.

6. April 5. In spite of his dislike for various tradesmen, Clemens had a good word to say for New Yorkers in general.

7. Aug. 4. The fortunes of the Pig in the Clover puzzle in *The American Claimant* (Hartford, 1892), chap. 24, are very similar. This newsletter also mentions a puzzle mania.

8. March 28.

9. March 30. The description of Southgate's church contains humorous diction much like that employed in the description of the Greek chapel in *Innocents Abroad*.

10. For example, March 28, June 2 and 16.

11. A number of dispatches ended with reports headed "Gossip" or "Personal," chiefly about Westerners.

12. June 16. In the issue of June 23, Clemens reported that nobody had appeared against Fall, and he had been released.

13. June 30.

14. March 28.

15. April 9.

16. June 23.

17. June 30.

18. March 30.

19. March 30.

20. April 15.

21. July 28.

22. July 28. The passage about the old master was, of course, a preliminary exercise for the famous chapter in *Innocents Abroad*. The painting he admired is notable for the humor of "humanized" animals, as are "The Famous Jumping Frog," "Dick Baker's Blue-Jay Yarn," and several of Clemens' choicest tall tales.

23. April 9.

24. July 14.

25. June 16.

26. March 28.

27. March 28.

28. March 28. Clemens evidently ferreted out the most iniquitous displays shortly after arriving in New York, since he was able to write shocked reports in his first newsletter. About a year later (issue of March 3, 1868), after his trip abroad, Clemens reported on the even more shocking *White Fawn*. "The best thing New York can do now, and the other cities and towns of America as well," he suggested,

"will be to build — not warehouses and buildings, but houses of ill-fame — let them build thousands and tens of thousands of them, and the Black Crook, the White Fawn and the infernal literature they have bred will stock them all."

29. Aug. 18.

30. The whole story about the visit to the Station House appeared June 23. The letter was dated May 18.

31. Howells' story is quoted by Paine in *Mark Twain's Notebook* (New York, 1935), 400. "He did not make any excuse," said Howells, "he did not say that it had been a mistake and that he had made it warm for the authorities afterwards."

On the Structure of *Tom Sawyer*

1. Critics who have noted the departure of the novel from conventional literature about children include Carl Van Doren, *The American Novel* (New York, 1921), 168; Stuart P. Sherman, "Mark Twain," in *The Cambridge History of American Literature* (New York, 1921), 3:15; and Percy H. Boynton, in his Introduction to the Harper's Modern Classics ed., xx–xxii.

2. A typical comment is that of F. L. Pattee who, in his *A History of American Literature since 1870* (New York, 1915), 59–60, says of Twain's writings (including *Tom Sawyer*): "They are not artistic books. The author had little skill in construction. He excelled in brilliant dashes, not in long continued effort." Compare Carl Van Doren (*American Novel* 169), speaking of *Tom Sawyer*: "To a delicate taste, indeed, the book seems occasionally overloaded with matters brought in at moments when no necessity in the narrative calls for them. . . . Nor can the murder about which the story is built up be said to dominate it very thoroughly. The story moves forward in something the same manner as did the plays of the seventies, with entrances and exits not always motivated." More recently A. H. Quinn, in *American Fiction: An Historical and Critical Survey* (New York, 1936), 256, has asserted that Clemens' "definition of the humorous story as one that 'may be spun out at great length and wander about as much as it pleases, and arrive nowhere in particular' is illuminating in its explanation of his strength and weakness as a writer of fiction. Like Bret Harte he is best in his episodes, and it is through them that he built up the characters . . . by which he will be remembered," including Tom Sawyer.

3. Exceptions, in some ways, to these generalizations had been some characters in novels by Louisa M. Alcott, Elijah J. Kellogg, and J. T. Trowbridge. These exceptions, however, do not, I think, invalidate the generalizations.

4. Little Rollo, created by Jacob Abbott in 1834 to survive at least twenty-four volumes of boyhood, was surrounded by wise instructors who quickly reasoned him out of impulses toward sin. The same careful nurture kept upright his brothers and sisters in four series of books. Goodrich's Peter Parley narratives, in much the same tradition, were roughly contemporaneous.

5. Horatio Alger, *Ragged Dick* (Philadelphia, n.d.), 15–18. During the course of the book, however, Dick reformed, and his evil habits were replaced with good ones. It is notable that Alger indicated his departure from the tradition of the completely virtuous hero when he said, "I have mentioned Dick's faults and defects because I want it understood, to begin with, that I don't consider him a model boy."

6. Frederick Lewis Allen, "Horatio Alger, Jr.," *Saturday Review of Literature*, Sept. 17, 1938, 4.

7. Some exceptions included, in addition to some Alger boys, the heroes of Oliver Optic's *In School and Out* (1863) and of Francis Forrester's *Dick Duncan* (1864), who, after sinning divertingly for several chapters, were allowed to reform. See Richard Allen Foster, *The School in American Literature* (Baltimore, 1930), 134–35.

8. E. K. Maxfield, "'Goody-goody' Literature and Mrs. Stowe," *American Speech*, Feb. 1920, 201.

9. The story of the truant, which appeared in a reader, and the poem about the idle boy, from *Youth's Casket* (1857), are reprinted in E. Douglas Branch, *The Sentimental Years, 1836–1860* (New York, 1934), 312–13. For details concerning the preachments in the McGuffey readers, see Mark Sullivan, *Our Times* (New York, 1927), 2:23–45.

10. He had so far observed the amenities as to grow up to be a rascal, but since his creator obviously delighted in his rascality, Hooper was considered a most immoral person by contemporaries.

11. B. P. Shillaber, *Life and Sayings of Mrs. Partington* (New York, 1854). Ike, for all his resemblance to the later Tom Sawyer, was a rather sketchy character because, as a rule, he committed his crimes in the final lines of a narrative chiefly devoted to his aunt.

12. Henry Ward Beecher, *Eyes and Ears* (Boston, 1862), 73–74.

13. Thomas Bailey Aldrich *The Story of a Bad Boy* (Boston, 1869), 8–9.

14. Ferris Greenslet, *The Life of Thomas Bailey Aldrich* (Boston, 1908), 92.

15. James M. Bailey, *Life in Danbury* (Boston, 1873), 72–73. A section on 275–83 called "The Danbury youth" burlesques the old rewards-and-punishment fiction by remarking that "boys who put stones in snow balls grow up to be bad men, and finally die a miserable death in a New York custom house," and foreshadows passages in *Tom Sawyer* by recounting how a boy "whose imagination had become diseased by too much close devotion to dime novels started off yesterday to seek fame as a slayer of bears and Indians. He . . . was gone nearly two hours."

16. M. Quad [C. B. Lewis], *Quad's Odds* (Detroit, 1875), 379–87. The Bad Boy, like Tom Sawyer after him, had "an ambition which nothing could check. He wanted to be a bold pirate and sail on the raging main. . . ." "Jeems," on 354–55 of the same volume, tolerantly told of the difficulty a mother had getting her son started to Sunday school.

17. Robert Burdette, *The Rise and Fall of the Mustache and Other Hawk-Eyetems* (Burlington, 1877), 165.

18. The former first appeared in *The Celebrated Jumping Frog of Calaveras County and Other Sketches* (New York, 1867), the latter in *The Galaxy* for May 1870. Both were frequently reprinted before their inclusion in *Sketches New and Old* (Hartford, 1875). Both therefore appeared early enough to merit consideration as germinal for Clemens' famous story of boyhood.

19. Quoted in Will M. Clemens, *Mark Twain: His Life and Work* (Chicago, 1894), 126. The writer is identified as "a well-known literary critic," and the pas-

sage is drawn from a review. I have been unable, however, to find the original review.

20. Chap. 5. See also chap. 1, in which the author says, approvingly, of Tom: "He was not the Model Boy of the village. He knew the model boy very well though — and loathed him."

21. A feminine critic so strongly conditioned by preachy literature that she managed to find a moral, of all places, in *Huckleberry Finn*, in 1887 called attention to outstanding examples of Tom's nobility. "Only a noble and tender heart," she said admiringly, "could have taken the blame upon itself when Becky accidentally tore the teacher's book, and received 'without an outcry the most merciless flogging that even Mr. Dobbins had ever administered,' and 'when he stepped forward to go to his punishment the surprise, the gratitude, the adoration that shone upon him out of poor Becky's eyes seemed pay enough for a hundred floggings.' The scene in the cave, of the rough boy folding in his arms the lost and weeping little girl, is a beautiful one." Sarah K. Bolton, *Famous American Authors* (New York, 1887), 369.

22. "My story," said the author in his preface, "is intended mainly for boys and girls." He made changes in his manuscript with his childish audience in view. See *Mark Twain's Letters* (New York, 1917), 1:272, 273. However, he was not always sure that the book was not for adults.

23. Booth Tarkington's shrewd suggestion is that Clemens gave his youthful character "adventures that all boys, in their longing dreams, make believe they have. He made extravagant, dramatic things happen to them; they were pitted against murderers, won their ladyloves, and discovered hidden gold. He made them so real that their very reality is the stimulus of the adult reader's laughter, but he embedded this reality in the romance of a plot as true to the conventional mid-nineteenth century romantic novel-writing as it was to the day-dreams the boy Mark Twain himself had been." Introduction to Cyril Clemens, *My Cousin Mark Twain* (Emmaus, Pa., 1939).

24. Clemens at least wanted to do this. "Part of my plan," he said in his preface, "has been to try to pleasantly remind adults of how they thought and talked, and what queer enterprises they sometimes engaged in."

25. The famous whitewashing scene, to cite one example, played upon some of these discrepancies: Tom, vainly trying to escape his chore, was the mischievous and ignorant boy. When, later, he got other boys, less canny than he, to do the job for him, he displayed the sort of wisdom — perhaps even of morality — becoming to an adult. "He," said his approving historian, "had discovered a great law of human action, without knowing it — namely, that in order to make a man or boy covet a thing, it is only necessary to make the thing difficult to attain."

26. Chaps. 1 (which is expository), 5, 8, and 21. Chap. 22, however, contains only one sentence concerning the Becky Thatcher story. This narrative occurs in twelve chapters, the Injun Joe story twelve, the Jackson's Island episode seven, and the Muff Potter subplot five. Eight chapters contain elements of two lines of action.

27. *Letters* 1:258.

28. Two kinds of probability are, I believe, theoretically involved here — one

that which represents the intelligent person's general conception of the way a boy matures, the other that which derives from a study of the character of Tom as it is displayed in the book. In this instance, I think, the two kinds of probability coincide.

29. Edgar Lee Masters, *Mark Twain: A Portrait* (New York, 1938), 125. Tom's age is not specified in the book, except by his actions. The fact that the action and the book requires only a few months seems irrelevant, since fictional rather than actual time is involved.

30. It is not incongruous, for example, with the list of Tom's treasures in chap. 2.

31. If Clemens' book was to be on a level above that of travesty, such potentialities had to be indicated. A rule of literary art which Twain himself formulated in "Fenimore Cooper's Literary Offenses," in *Literary Essays* (New York, 1899), 81, was "that the characters in a tale shall be so clearly defined that the reader can tell beforehand what each will do in a given emergency." Thus his very divergence from the simple motivation of earlier fictional works necessitated more complex characterization than they contained.

32. Kindhearted Muff Potter, the grave-robbing Dr. Robinson, and the Temperance Tavern keeper who bootlegs are the nearest approach to native sin. Injun Joe and his vague companion from somewhere "up the river" are not of the community. The chief hints of vice Tom picks up anywhere are in the novels he reads.

33. The Becky Thatcher story, the exception, is, as has been suggested, also a natural expression of Tom's character.

34. *Letters* 1:259.

35. Clemens wrote: "As to that last chapter, I think of just leaving it off and adding nothing in its place. Something told me the book was done when I got to that point—and so the temptation to put Huck's life into detail, instead of generalizing it in a paragraph was resisted" (*Letters* 1:267).

Mark Twain's Other Masterpiece: "Jim Baker's Blue-Jay Yarn"

1. Mark Twain, *A Tramp Abroad* (Hartford: American Publishing Co., 1880), 36–37. Later quotations also are from 31–42 of this edition.

2. Bernard DeVoto, *Mark Twain's America* (Boston: Little, Brown, 1932), 251.

3. W. E. Henley, *Athenaeum*, April 24, 1880, 529.

4. DeLancey Ferguson, *Mark Twain: Man and Legend* (Indianapolis: Bobbs, Merrill, 1943), 200. Social satire, realistic low life characterization, and highly imaginative fantasy in combinations occur in much American humor.

5. Fred W. Lorch, *The Trouble Begins at Eight* (Ames: Iowa State University Press, 1968), 10–12, gives a good summary.

6. Walter Blair, Introduction, *Native American Humor* (San Francisco: Chandler, 1960), 38–124.

7. Ibid. 147–50; Edgar Branch, *The Literary Apprenticeship of Mark Twain* (Urbana: University of Illinois Press, 1950).

8. Most accounts of the stay are gathered in *Mark Twain's Frontier*, ed. James E. Camp and X. J. Kennedy (New York: Holt, Rinehart and Winston, 1963), 89–136. The notebook jottings are in *Mark Twain's Notebook*, ed. Albert B. Paine

(New York: Harper, 1935), 6–8, and Mark Twain, *The Great Landslide Case*, ed. Frederick Anderson and Edgar M. Branch (Berkeley: Friends of the Bancroft Library, 1972), 3–4. Twain assesses the power of Angel's Camp whiskey in "An Unbiased Criticism," *Californian*, March 18, 1865.

9. *Mark Twain in Eruption*, ed. Bernard DeVoto (New York: Harper, 1940), 360; *Mark Twain's Letters*, ed. A B. Paine (New York: Harper, 1917), 1:170.

10. "An Unbiased Criticism."

11. *My Dear Bro*, ed. Frederick Anderson (Berkeley: Berkeley Albion, 1961). Clemens said that the "high praise" of his writings by Eastern editors brought his decision.

12. *Letters* 1:170.

13. "An Unbiased Criticism" appeared in March 1865. "Jim Smiley and His Jumping Frog," later "The Celebrated [or Notorious] Jumping Frog of Calaveras County," first appeared Nov. 18, 1865, and was frequently reprinted; it was revised in 1867, 1872, and 1875. Versions of "The Great Landslide Case," which the humorist evidently heard told orally for a second time during his pocket mining days, appeared in the Buffalo *Express*, April 2, 1870, and as chapter 34 of *Roughing It* (1872). "Jim Blaine and His Grandfather's Old Ram," chapter 53, and "Dick Baker's Cat," chapter 61, of *Roughing It* were other mining camp tales. The year 1880 brought the blue-jay yarn; 1884 "The Royal Nonesuch," a story originally told, apparently, by Stoker but attributed by Clemens much later to Gillis, in *Adventures of Huckleberry Finn*, Chapter 23; 1893 brought "A Californian's Tale" and 1907 the lecture circuit version of the old ram story. The frog story, the ram story, and the blue-jay yarn were included in *Mark Twain's Library of Humor* (1888), an anthology he helped compile.

14. *Eruption* 283–84, 358–66.

15. "How to Tell a Story," *Youth's Companion*, Oct. 3, 1895, rpt in *Literary Essays* (New York, 1899), 7–15; Ernest J. Moyne, "Mark Twain and the Baroness Alexandra Gripenberg," *American Literature*, 45 (Nov. 1973), 376. Two discussions of the humorist's theories about writing and speaking are Sydney J. Krause, "Mark Twain's Method and Theory of Composition," *Modern Philology*, 56 (Feb. 1959), 171–72, and Introduction to *Selected Shorter Writings of Mark Twain*, ed. Walter Blair (Boston: Houghton Mifflin, 1962).

16. *Letters* 2:504.

17. *Mark Twain-Howells Letters*, ed. H. N. Smith and W. M. Gibson (Cambridge: Harvard University Press, 1960), 1:26.

18. "On Speech-Making Reform," *Mark Twain's Speeches* (New York: Harper, 1923), 2–3.

19. Again and again, Twain praised the rambling storyteller and imitated him. The frog story was an example, the ram story a more extreme one. In *Life on the Mississippi* (1883), chapter 13, he gave a sample of the art of Brown, who "could *not* forget anything." Huck tells a rambling history of English royalty in *Adventures of Huckleberry Finn*, chapter 23, In "How to Tell a Story," Twain nominates as "about the funniest thing I ever listened to" James Whitcomb Riley's impersonation of an old farmer "who gets all mixed up and wanders hopelessly round and round" as he tries to tell an ancient joke.

20. "William Dean Howells," *Works* Definitive Edition (New York: 1922–25), 26:228–38.

21. *Tramp Abroad*, 35. The humorist liked these birds so well that, carrying them to India and calling them *Indian* crows, he put them into *Following the Equator* (1897): "If I sat on one end of the balcony, the crows would gather on the railing at the other end and talk about me; . . . they would sit there, in the most unabashed way, and talk about my clothes, and my hair, and my complexion, and probable character and vocation and politics, and how I came to be in India . . . and how I had happened to go unhanged so long . . . and so on, until I could no longer endure the embarrassment of it. . . ."

22. Notebook 14 (1879), Mark Twain Papers, Bancroft Library, University of California, Berkeley.

23. *Eruption* 202.

24. William Dean Howells, "Mark Twain: An Inquiry" (1901), in *My Mark Twain* (New York: Harper, 1910), 182.

25. *Eruption* 361 — autobiographical dictation of 1907.

26. *Joel Chandler Harris, Editor and Essayist*, ed. Julia Collier Harris (Chapel Hill: University of North Carolina Press, 1931), 148–49.

27. Cf. Sut Lovingood telling in an 1867 book that Twain reviewed how it was when a rampaging bull smashed into a little bald-headed man: "he jis' disappear'd frum mortul vishun sumhow, sorter like breff frum a lookin-glass." George Washington Harris, *Sut Lovingood's Yarns*, ed. M. Thomas Inge (New Haven: College and University Press, 1966), 110. Twain listed George W. Harris, the author of this book, and its publishers in his notes on American humorists in 1880, and he included one of Sut's stories in his anthology.

28. Max Eastman, *The Enjoyment of Laughter* (New York: Simon and Schuster, 1948), 76–80. Eastman cites as an example a memorable Arizona colloquialism: "He's so stingy he wouldn't pay ten cents to see Christ wrastle a bear."

29. Howells, "Mark Twain: An Inquiry" 179. Twain in turn praised Howells for "translating . . . the vision of the eyes of flesh into words that reproduced their forms and colors."

30. Julia C. Harris, *The Life and Letters of Joel Chandler Harris* (Boston, 1918), 168; *Letters* 2:401–2.

31. *Letters* 2:504–5.

32. The first "Mark Twain" is cornered by Simon Wheeler in the frog story; the second is inveigled into hearing the drunken Jim Blaine tell about his grandfather's ram and many unrelated matters.

33. DeVoto, *Mark Twain's America*, 251. Another "Mark Twain" listens with pleasure to a long story and appreciates its mining camp teller — clearly Jim Baker although here he is called Dick Baker: "Whenever he was out of luck and a little down-hearted, he would fall to mourning over the loss of a wonderful cat he used to own (for where women and children are not, men of kindly impulses take up with pets, for they must love something). And he always spoke of the strange sagacity of that cat with the air of a man who believed in his secret heart that there was something human about it — maybe even supernatural." *Roughing It*, chapter 61.

34. Walter Blair, *Mark Twain and Huck Finn* (Berkeley: University of California Press, 1960), 235–328, passim, treats numerous instances.

35. Brander Mathews, writing about "the immense variety" of Twain's style, writes: "Consider the tale of the Blue Jay . . . wherein the humor is sustained by unstated pathos: what could be better told than this, with every word the right word and in the right place?" "An Appreciation," in Mark Twain, *Europe and Else-where* (New York: Harper, 1923), xxviii. In *Mark Twain & "Huck Finn"* 172–78, I have discussed various factors in the humorist's personal situation that caused him to write sympathetically about the misanthropic Jim Baker and the frustrated blue jay.

The French Revolution and *Huckleberry Finn*

1. Bernard DeVoto, "Mark Twain and the Limits of Criticism," in his *Forays and Rebuttals* (Boston, 1936), 377.

2. Personal letter to the writer dated Oct. 2, 1939.

3. Brander Matthews, "Memories of Mark Twain," in his *The Tocsin of Revolt and Other Essays* (New York, 1922), 268–69.

4. Bernard DeVoto, *Mark Twain's America* (Boston, 1932), 253–55.

5. Walter Blair, *Native American Humor, 1800–1900* (New York, 1937), 150–54.

6. *Mark Twain's Speeches*, ed. Albert Bigelow Paine (New York, 1910), 56–58.

7. *Mark Twain's Letters*, ed. Albert Bigelow Paine (New York, 1917), 1:267.

8. The original letter, dated Sept. 14, 1876, in the Berg Collection, is cited with the permission of the New York Public Library; part of it was published in *Letters* 1:285–86.

9. Bernard DeVoto, *Mark Twain at Work* (Cambridge, 1942), 50, 62, 81.

10. Albert Bigelow Paine, *Mark Twain: A Biography* (New York, 1912), 512; see also Matthews, "Memories" 267.

11. *Letters* 2:490. The interest may have developed as early as the 1860s, when, says Paine, Clemens at night "as ever, would prop himself up in bed, light his pipe, and lose himself in French or English history until sleep conquered" (*Mark Twain* 254).

12. Letter to Mollie Fairbanks, *Mark Twain to Mrs. Fairbanks*, ed. Dixon Wecter (San Marino, 1949), 207–9). Twain evaluates the books mentioned.

13. Paine, *Mark Twain* 643–44; Henry W. Fisher, *Abroad with Mark Twain and Eugene Field* (New York, 1922), 59. Fisher is not completely dependable, although he says that he bases some reminiscences on "notebooks, diaries and such," because admittedly some reports were not set down until 1921. His assertions on this point, however, are supported elsewhere.

14. *Letters*, 2:489; Paine, *Mark Twain* 643–44. In the letter following Paine's editorial note in the former, Twain indicates frequent readings between 1871 and 1887.

15. *Mark Twain to Mrs. Fairbanks* 207.

16. Fisher, *Abroad* 60. There is much evidence that, from the 1860s on, Twain knew various writings of Dickens quite well.

17. Notebook No. 19, quoted through the courtesy of the Mark Twain Estate. This and several other notebook passages comment upon Twain's inability to be amused by the *Pickwick Papers*.

18. O. H. Moore, "Mark Twain and *Don Quixote*," *PMLA*, 37 (1922), 325. Experience had reinforced Twain's reading: his *Innocents Abroad* (1869), Vol. 1, chaps. 11 and 22, told of his seeing verses, prayers, and complaints scratched by prisoners on the walls of their cells. Baring-Gould's *In exitu Israel* (London, 1870), 1:235–36, which Clemens called "a very able novel" in his letter of 1877, contained a passage which must have amused Twain, about Latude's recreations in the Bastille: "He wrote his appeals for mercy, and pardon for crimes he had never committed, on rags, in his own blood; then they buried him in holes underground without light, where he spent long years in domesticating rats." Another tenant of the Bastille (2:39) talks affectionately about a pet toad.

19. Twain mentioned reading this in the letter of 1877. The book also contains most of the commonplaces of prison literature mentioned by Professor Moore.

20. *The French Revolution* appeared in 1837, *A Tale of Two Cities* in 1859. A prefatory note tells us that the time of *Huckleberry Finn* was between 1834 and 1844. However, the first sentence in Twain's novel contains an anachronism.

21. A conscious source probably was Robert Montgomery Bird's *Nick of the Woods* (1837), since the hacking of a cross on victims in that book is specifically cited by Clemens in a passage written in 1883 (*Life on the Mississippi*, chap. 54).

22. Tom expresses a preference (chap. 35) for Dickens' recipe for ink: "The best authorities uses their own blood." Baring-Gould, as the quotation in n. 18 has indicated, was another authority preferring blood.

23. This is mentioned by most historians of the French Revolution, since the king, the queen, and the princess donned nonroyal garb and the dauphin dressed as a girl for the flight which ended at Varennes.

24. Carlyle 2.4.1–8; J. Michelet, *Historical View of the French Revolution* (London, 1888), 591–606. Yonge, *The Life of Marie Antoinette, Queen of France* (London, 1888), 2:171–83, gives a very different account, which minimizes mistakes in the planning and the execution of the escape.

25. Twain may also have noticed in Carlyle a word which that author uses in talking of the king's escape: Tom justifies his own use of it when he says: "When a prisoner of style escapes, it's called an evasion. It's always called so when a king escapes, f'rinstance" (chap. 39). The word occurs, however, in translations into English of various French authors, Dumas and Michelet, for example. What probably is involved is a failure to translate the French word *évasion*.

26. In the Buffalo manuscript of *Huckleberry Finn* Twain has written a passage wherein Tom tells Jim he wants "to get up just at early daylight, every morning," to care for the plant. Although this is based upon a detail of Saintine's novel, Twain apparently decided that it was one touch too many, for he deleted it.

27. The former of these resembles a statement that Dantès, disguised as an abbé, makes about himself in *The Count of Monte Cristo*, Vol. 1, chap 26. "Edmond Dantès died in prison of sorrow and a broken heart."

28. DeVoto, *Mark Twain at Work* 92.

29. The reference to royalty on the police force, Henry Nash Smith suggests, recalls Twain's remark that Napoleon III "kept his faithful watch and walked his weary beat a common policeman in London" (*Innocents Abroad*, Vol. 1, chap. 13).

30. Folklore of the pre-Revolutionary period may have been drawn from one or both of two works of Dumas, the novel *The Man in the Iron Mask* and a section on this legendary figure in Dumas's compilation, *Celebrated Crimes*. Both refer to the use of plates with messages scratched on them to communicate with the outside world, and when Jim is told to scratch messages on tin plates, Tom cites his authority (chap. 36): "The Iron Mask always done that, and it's a blame' good way, too." The former (chap. 1) refers to a note smuggled to the famous prisoner in a loaf of bread—a possible source of Tom's witch pie. The latter tells of a prisoner writing on his shirt and contains a version of the story which may have inspired in part an inscription which Tom wrote for Jim to scribble on the wall (chap. 38): "Here, homeless and friendless, after thirty-seven years of bitter captivity, perished a noble stranger, natural son of Louis XIV." In *Innocents Abroad* (1869), Vol. 1, chap. 11, Twain had referred to the cell of "the celebrated 'Iron Mask,'" but the reference does not prove that he was familiar with the book. In the same chapter, he speaks of a passage in *Monte Cristo* which tells of the abbé's book being written in blood with a pen made from an iron hoop; but he misremembers the abbé's recipe for ink. The details are also used in *Huckleberry Finn*.

31. He wrote in a note to himself: "Back yonder, Huck reads & tells about monarchies & kings &c. So Jim stares when he learns the rank of these 2" (DeVoto, *Mark Twain at Work* 75). The number of ms pages indicates that the episode was inserted.

32. The copy, certified as from the library by Albert Bigelow Paine, is owned by Franklin J. Meine of Chicago, who has kindly let me consult it.

33. Fuller emphasizes these qualities of rascals and their gulls in his accounts not only of the dauphins but also of the other imposters about whom he writes.

34. In Dumas, *The Countess de Charney*, chap. 83, upon hearing that the king has left Paris under the name of "M. Capet, the Austrian," Desmoulins says, "Ah ha! The name is good, and henceforth I will call Louis XVI. Capet." "And," says another character, "there is but one thing with which you can be reproached for doing so; his name is not Capet, but Bourbon." "Bah!" replies Desmoulins. "Who knows that? Only some half dozen pedants like yourself. Is not Capet a good name . . . ?"

35. Paine, *Mark Twain* 644.

36. *Letters* 2:490. This was written in 1887 after *Huckleberry Finn* had been published; but, as has been indicated, he read Taine before 1877, and he may also have read Saint-Simon while the book was in progress.

37. Edmund Wilson, *To the Finland Station* (New York, 1940), 53.

38. Typical diatribes written later include *Letters* 2:514, 519–20; *Mark Twain's Notebook*, ed. Albert Bigelow Paine (New York, 1935), 197–200, 509; Paine, *Mark Twain* 874, 890.

39. Michelet, *Historical View* 10.

40. Fisher, *Abroad* 59.

41. The passage by Twain which is closest to that by Carlyle in detail occurs in the first paragraph of chap. 22: "every window along the road was full of women's heads, and there was nigger boys in every tree, and bucks and wenches looking over every fence." This is not close enough to suggest specific and conscious influence; its chief value is for purposes of comparison.

42. Dickens also shows a character smacking his lips over his memories of violent deaths — the little wood-sawyer, *Tale of Two Cities* (3.15), but I doubt that Twain had this scene specifically in mind. However, the contrast in methods is of interest. Dickens' character is ironically humorous in his talk; Twain's lanky ham actor, as well as the crowd watching him, is completely humorless.

43. Several points which Sherburn makes were made by Twain as his own in a chapter discarded from *Life on the Mississippi* (see the Heritage Press edition [New York, 1940], 412–16).

44. The incident recalls Fuller's surprise that the false dauphins were not "dragged to horse-ponds." Twain's emphasis upon human cruelty is aided by his giving his imposters the exit described.

45. Notebook entry, 1887 or 1888, *Mark Twain's Notebook* 193.

46. *Mark Twain's Travels with Mr. Brown*, ed. Franklin Walker and G. Ezra Dane (New York, 1940), 144; Preface to *The Adventures of Tom Sawyer*; Paine, *Mark Twain* 26, 32–33, 798; Dixon Wecter, *Sam Clemens of Hannibal* (Boston, 1952), 100, 106–7, 150–51.

When Was *Huckleberry Finn* Written?

1. For a number of years this topic has been a favorite one for discussion and research in my courses dealing with Mark Twain. I thank collectively the many students who have helped answer this question. In particular, I am grateful to George E. Schindler, Jr., who in 1952 suggested doubts about DeVoto's description of the hypothetical typescript of the novel, and to Dewey Ganzel, who in 1955 first pointed out what I think must be the true functions of pp. 7 and 10 of Group A of the working notes.

2. Albert Bigelow Paine, *Mark Twain: A Biography* (New York, 1912), 578, 683–84, 754; Bernard DeVoto, Introduction to *Adventures of Huckleberry Finn* (New York: Limited Editions Club, 1942); "Noon and Dark," in *Mark Twain at Work*, ed. Bernard DeVoto (Cambridge, 1942), 45–82 (hereinafter cited as *MTAW*).

3. Most of the new material is in the correspondence of Clemens' business manager, Charles L. Webster, published in *Mark Twain, Business Man*, ed. Samuel Charles Webster (Boston, 1946), or available in transcripts in the Mark Twain Estate Papers, University of California, Berkeley. All citations and quotations from the Mark Twain Estate Papers are published with the consent of the Mark Twain Estate, and are copyright by Mark Twain Company, 1958.

4. *Mark Twain's Letters*, ed. Albert Bigelow Paine (New York, 1917), 1:282–83.

5. *Letters* 1:436, and "Mark Twain to His English Publishers," ed. W. B. Gates, *American Literature*, 11 (March 1939), 79.

6. *MTAW* 57.

7. *Mark Twain in Eruption,* ed. Bernard DeVoto (New York, 1940), 197–98. Although this was dictated in 1906, there is fairly good evidence that Twain was correct in remembering a two-year gap in the work on each of the three novels mentioned.

8. Unposted letter to Jeannette Gilder, May 14, 1887 (*Letters* 2:486).

9. Brander Matthews, "Memories of Mark Twain," *The Tocsin of Revolt and Other Essays* (New York, 1922), 265.

10. In the MS, after "working," Twain originally wrote "lazily," and then crossed it out. This suggests that he was making some effort to be precise.

11. *Letters* 1:434. In *MTAW* 57, DeVoto says that there is "no need to take 'two or three years' literally, since we know that he had half-finished the book in 1876." But the portion which DeVoto believes was finished in 1876 is much closer to a fourth than it is to a half of the novel; and a literal reading is most consistent with other statements.

12. *Letters* 1:434.

13. *Letters* 1:436. During the rest of August he was very busy working out his history game in detail (*Business Man* 218–19) and, as has been indicated, on September 1 he told his English publisher that the had recently finished *Huck.* The total number of pages to which he refers, therefore, probably was very close to that for the summer.

14. Typescript of letter to Frank Bliss, Mark Twain Estate Papers, University of California, Berkeley.

15. *Mark Twain to Mrs. Fairbanks,* ed. Dixon Wecter (San Marino, 1949), 226.

16. *Mark Twain the Letter Writer,* ed. Cyril Clemens (Boston, 1932), 37.

17. DeVoto, in *MTAW* 81, calculates that Clemens' figure applied to the summer's total output rather than the portions of the novel written. This, according to DeVoto, included at least 200 MS pages for chaps. 17–21, which have disappeared, plus the 627 pages of the Buffalo MS, plus the 167 pages of the MS of "1002." It is possible that Twain worked on other MSS and included their pages in his total.

18. Paine does not say that he composed any of the book in the 1879–80 period; he does say that he alternated work on the book with work on *The Prince and the Pauper* during the summer of 1880 in Elmira (*Mark Twain* 683–84). As will be indicated, I list this period with others as one during which Twain might have worked on *Huck.*

19. Of Group A, he writes: "This group consists of eleven pages, the last one larger than the rest, all written in violet ink. (Mark used such ink frequently during the 1870s, used less often during the early 1880's, and not at all thereafter . . .)" (*MTAW* 63).

20. I examined most of these in the Mark Twain Estate Papers, University of California; the Buffalo Public Library; the Houghton Library, Harvard University; the Morse Collection, Yale University; the Henry W. and Albert A. Berg Collection of the New York Public Library; the Pierpont Morgan Library, New York; the Boston Public Library; and the private collections of C. Waller Barrett, New York, and Franklin J. Meine, Chicago. The following people supplied information that has been useful: Frederick Anderson and Henry Nash Smith, the University

of California; William B. Todd, the Houghton Library, Harvard University; Tyrus G. Harmsen, Henry E. Huntington Library, San Marino, Cal.; William S. Dix, Princeton University Library; Mrs. Connie Griffith, Tulane University Library; Prentice Miller, Emory University; and Gwin J. Kolb of the University of Chicago, who examined letters in the British Museum. To these institutions and these helpful scholars, I am very grateful for assistance.

21. In 1879, he continued to use black ink in Hartford from his return in mid-October through November 17, but the next day he switched to violet ink. He used it until June 15, 1880, except in one letter of January 24, 1880, written from Elmira during a brief visit. One letter bearing the same date is in violet ink, but since it was sent from Hartford, I believe that it was misdated. These are the only possible exceptions to the pattern that I have found, and both are easily explained.

22. The novel was a rewriting in fictional form of a play, *Simon Wheeler, Amateur Detective*, written in the summer of 1877. A letter of Jan. 21, 1879, indicates that he had abandoned it by that date (*Letters* 1:346). Two plays about Tom and Huck were written, the first before 1880, the second in the winter of 1883–84. Even if the surviving version is that of the latter date, quite possibly the pages were transferred from the earlier version. Regardless, *Huck* was completed by the time it was written.

23. In a letter of Feb. 12, 1882, to James R. Osgood (original at Harvard) Clemens enclosed a copy of "that rhuematic preventive from Clara Spaulding" (a close friend of Mrs. Clemens) written on paper of this sort. When this enclosure was written cannot be determined.

24. Some sheets, probably discolored by exposure, are creamy in color, though most are a colder white. All are 7 inches long, but some are 1/16 of an inch narrower or wider than 4½ inches—probably the result of his cutting or tearing sheets 9 by 7 inches in two.

25. I have not seen all of the widely scattered sheets of the MS of *A Tramp Abroad*, started in Europe in the spring of 1878 and finished in Hartford in January 1880. The paper does not occur in parts of the MS that I have seen, but I should not be surprised to learn that some of it was used in the writing of this book, e.g., an insert in *Life on the Mississippi*, chap. 36, on this paper, may have been written initially for *A Tramp Abroad*.

26. Paine, *Mark Twain* 1679.

27. Ibid. 598.

28. *Mark Twain to Mrs. Fairbanks* 218.

29. *Business Man* 143, 145.

30. Letter to W. D. Howells, Berg Collection, cited with the permission of the New York Public Library.

31. *Letters* 1:386.

32. Quoted in Park-Bernet Galleries *Catalogue* for Sale No. 325, Dec. 10, 11, 1941.

33. Page 8 of Group A contains an interpolated line in blue ink. Ink of this color was also used during this summer, e.g., in the MS of "A Cat's Tale," which is on paper such as that in pp. 1–10 of Group A.

34. I am grateful to Frederick Anderson for information about a discarded page of this MS in the Mark Twain Estate Papers, and to Tyrus G. Harmsen of the Henry E. Huntington Library for a detailed description of the MS which made possible this account.

35. It is a temptation to guess that Clemens ran out of his stock of Crystal Lake Mills paper on March 11, 1880, and that therefore partway through a letter switched to another kind. But one who has noticed how unsystematic he was in alternating kinds of paper will find this temptation easy to resist. Of some interest is the fact that April 11, 1880, John Lewis, a workman at Quarry Farm in Elmira, wrote Clemens a letter on Crystal Lake Mills paper, using violet ink of the sort Clemens seems to have used only in Hartford. In Hartford, Clemens made a notation on it in violet ink. The letter is in the Mark Twain Estate Papers.

36. *MTAW* 63.

37. Of the two notebook entries about Montgomery the only one which would have been suitable for the novel is a reminiscence dating back to Clemens' days as a pilot. The notebook is in the Mark Twain Estate Papers.

38. Working note A-4, to cite an instance which may need documentation, contains the cryptic line "Mrs. Halliday." Clemens had suggested to himself that he might use this character in working notes for "Autobiography of a Damned Fool" (1876, in the Mark Twain Estate Papers, and in working notes for the novel about Simon Wheeler in the Berg Collection, cited with the permission of the New York Public Library). Again, notes A-1, A-2, A-5, and A-9 concern "the two printers" who become the king and the duke in the novel; they are to perform *Richard III* and a hoax called "The Burning Shame" in the holograph MS but changed to "The Royal Nonesuch" in the printed novel. "The Burning Shame," as DeVoto remarks (*MTAW* 67–68), was a story Clemens heard during his fateful visit to Gillis' cabin in Jackass Gulch in 1865. An entry made at the time in a notebook (in the Mark Twain Estate) reads, "The 'Tragedian' and the Burning Shame. No Women Admitted." The notes for "Autobiography of a Damned Fool" include "Listens to the printer-tramp and is charmed. Goes on month's expedition with him, delivering temperance lectures and sermons and spreeing on proceeds," and immediately after, "Burning Shame." The "mesmeric foolishness" mentioned as a possible adventure for Huck and the king on A-9 is, as DeVoto notices, a reminiscence from Twain's boyhood.

39. The Secretarial Notebook is in the Mark Twain Estate Papers. Also in the Estate Papers is a letter to Reginald Cholmondely dated March 28, 1885, in which Clemens says, "I came very near being an eye-witness of the general engagement detailed in the book. The details are historical and correct." Paine's statement is in *Mark Twain* 796.

40. The MS is in the Berg Collection (details cited with the permission of the New York Public Library).

41. *MTAW* 66. Italicized letters and numerals have been crossed out. The columns are spaced as in the note.

42. DeVoto, noting this, says it "may possibly be later" than the other pages in Group A: also, it may be earlier. Only A-1 and A-2 have been numbered by

Clemens, and DeVoto is quite correct in saying that there is no way of being sure about the right sequence of the pages. Those he has numbered A-1–A-7, though, at some time were folded lengthwise; the others were not.

43. "When Mark Twain returned to the manuscript in 1882 (to consult it for *Life on the Mississippi* — he did not begin writing again until 1883), it ended with, or shortly after, the wreck of the raft. (See the note [numbered 10] in Group A. . . .) That was where the book had got tired in 1876. The destruction of the raft had stopped him short; he had not known what to do with the story" (*MTAW* 62).

44. The first line on B-2, eventually crossed out, may refer back to the real B-1: "Widow Douglas — then who is 'Miss Watson?'"

45. The references in both notes in Group B to pages in the holograph MS raise questions about DeVoto's account. According to him, a working typescript was "made absolutely necessary by the involved state of the [holograph] manuscript of 1876" (*MTAW* 62). Why and how, then, did Clemens use this chaotic MS when reviewing what he had written? The typescript, DeVoto believes, was made in 1882; the interpolation on B-1 was made after "he had begun writing again," probably in the summer of 1883 (*MTAW* 71). Why, many months after the portion written in 1876 had been typed, did he refer in the interpolated line to p. 350, written in holograph in 1876?

46. The unfinished novel about Simon Wheeler contains (p. 6) a passage in which a character unfolds what is, except for its happy ending, the tragic story told in Emily's poem: "Why once when Hank Miller got the cramp in the river — . . . they pumped & pumped — well, they pumped about a barrel of water out of him, & by & by, sure enough, he came to" (quoted with the permission of the New York Public Library). On April 25, 1880, Howells acknowledged receipt of an attack on obituary poetry written for the *Atlantic* "Contributor's Club" and later published there. (The letter is in the Mark Twain Estate Papers.)

47. See "A Chronological List of Mark Twain's Work — Published and Otherwise . . ." (Paine, *Mark Twain* 1678–79). This is not complete, but it contains practically all important items for 1880–83.

48. Paine, *Mark Twain* 683.

49. Ibid. 696. The conditions were not fulfilled; but the sentence indicates that Twain had time and inclination to work on *Huck,* and he may have done so.

50. *Letters* 1:430.

51. In an unpublished portion of Notebook No. 15, used during 1880, he wrote, at one point, "Simon Suggs," and at another, "The man who 'went in on nary a pair' (at camp meeting)." The phrase quoted is a relatively insignificant one in a chapter from a book by Johnson J. Hooper which had been popular during Clemens' youth. This chapter, as DeVoto notes, is clearly the analogue of the king's *coup* at a similar gathering (*Mark Twain's America* [Boston, 1932], 255). The notebook is in the Mark Twain Estate Papers.

52. A letter of Osgood dated Jan. 15, 1883, in the Morse Collection (quoted with the permission of the Yale University Library) notifies the publisher that Twain "put in some Southern assassinations there." The shooting described is so much like the shooting in Hannibal during Clemens' boyhood of old Smarr by Owsley

that one wonders whether the "newspaper story" purportedly quoted was authentic or was concocted. See Dixon Wecter, *Sam Clemens of Hannibal* (Boston, 1952), 106–8. A few parallels to be found in the Hannibal episode and the novel, but not in the "newspaper item": The man who committed the murder was a leading merchant of the town; he called out his victim's name before shooting; only two shots were fired; only one man was killed; the victim was carried to a nearby store to die; some fool tortured the dying man by placing a Bible on his chest. In the typescript (in the Mark Twain Estate Papers) of the passage in *Mark Twain's Autobiography* (New York, 1924), 1:131, Clemens has annotated his mention of "the shooting down of poor old Smarr in the main street" in his own handwriting thus: "See 'Adventures of Huckleberry Finn.'"

53. DeVoto, I believe, made an error of minor importance concerning the nature of this typescript, which can, of course, be described only by comparing page references to it by Twain with passages in the surviving handwritten manuscript or the novel as printed. Like Mark Twain in this period, DeVoto seems to have overestimated the number of words per average handwritten page. This led him to believe that the typescript must have averaged 520 words per page and hence must have been written, single-spaced, on legal paper 14 inches long, although a check of page references to a typescrpt of 520 words per page against passages in the novel which they designate will show great disparities. My calculations indicate a typescript averaging 336 words per page, which could have been written, double-spaced, on paper of the sort used in the typescript of *Life on the Mississippi* with small margins, or on legal paper with generous margins. (Some of the typescript of *Life on the Mississippi* is in the Henry Munroe Rogers Collection in the Houghton Library; a typescript of "1002" on legal paper is in the Mark Twain Estate files.)

54. Italics mine. Copy of the letter in Mark Twain Estate Papers, University of California, Berkeley. Howells substituted "MS" for the word "copy," which was crossed out. Probably the earlier word was the more precise one but Howells changed it to avoid repetition. Osgood had arranged for the typing of *The Prince and the Pauper*, Twain for that of the 1882 portion of *Life on the Mississippi*. Howells probably was commissioned to arrange for this typescript because he was going through the novel for Clemens at this time, and because Howells was always extraordinarily ready to do miscellaneous chores for his friend.

55. It hardly seems likely that the interpolation of pp. 81-1–81-60 necessitated retyping, since Clemens had a way of handling such insertions. There is another possibility: that Twain was hurrying the process of preparing the book. On April 28, 1884, he wrote Webster, "*Remind me to give you all of Huck Finn that Howells has revised for the artist & printer*" (*Business Man* 251). In order that the artist and the printer might work simultaneously, he may have wanted two copies, one for each. But this seems doubtful, since Kemble seems to have finished the illustrations (some without the related parts of the MS at hand) before the MS went to the printer. However, two copies were sent to Webster: Howells, in his letter of May 4, told Webster that "to-morrow I will send you one copy of that part—and Tuesday another copy. You can work from either, for both are ready to go into

the printer's hands." Possibly the second part of the book was copied with a carbon duplicate, as was "1002" during the summer of 1883.

56. DeVoto believes — on the basis of "a study of page numbers and renumbered passages" — that "a secretary typed the new manuscript . . . as [Twain] completed it, up through chapter XXI, but in irregular 'takes'" (*MTAW* 63). I have been unable to reconstruct his reasoning. Twain, however, had recently voiced strong dissatisfaction with a similar procedure used in typing *Life on the Mississippi* (*Letters* 1:425). And DeVoto's account raises a difficult problem concerning the relationships between notes and typescript: C-1, he believes, "was written before Mark resumed writing," and B-1 "after Mark resumed writing." But if this is so, the earlier of the entries refers to the typescript and the later, inexplicably, to the holograph.

57. A letter, Webster to Clemens, Sept. 2, 1884, lists as paid to Howells May 9 "for typing 'Huck Finn' — $15.00" (Mark Twain Estate Papers). At this time, copyists were paid between $7 and $20 — an average of $10 a week (Bruce Bliven, *The Wonderful Writing Machine* [New York, 1954], 67, 71, 78).

58. The holograph manuscript may have been used by Kemble, and this may account for its being saved; it also would have made a carbon copy of the part of the book written later unnecessary. Another possibility is that Twain did not learn until 1881 or 1882 that collectors were interested in his holograph MSS. A letter from Benjamin H. Ticknor to Twain dated Nov. 16, 1885, in the Mark Twain Estate Papers, indicates that Ticknor asked for the MS of *The Prince and the Pauper* after it had been returned to Twain, probably in 1881 or 1882. See also, concerning the MS of *Life on the Mississippi*, Caroline Ticknor, "Mark Twain's Missing Chapter," *Bookman*, 39 (May 1914), 298–309.

59. The paper is that of the *Huckleberry Finn* MS; C-1 contains on its verso some working notes for "1002," which Twain was writing that summer.

60. It would be a puzzling procedure, though, if — as DeVoto holds — he had engaged in a very similar rereading and had set down very similar reminders on B-2 only a short time before.

61. C-1 contains two references to the appearances of the king and the duke in the typescript — on pp. 136 and 147; C-4 a reference to their appearance on p. 143. A check of successive references to them in the novel as printed indicates that the last reference may be to chap. 20.

62. *MTAW* 73.

63. See *Twins of Genius*, ed. Guy Cardwell (East Lansing, 1953), 92; *Business Man* 212.

64. Mark Twain Estate Papers.

65. Dixon Wecter, *Literary History of the United States*, rev. ed. (New York, 1953), 932–33.

66. *MTAW* 69.

67. This became paragraph 2 of chap. 4 of *Life on the Mississippi* (New York: Heritage Press, 1944), 28 (hereafter cited as *LOM*). *Old Times* contained a number of scenes germinal to *Huck*. The steamboat pilots' hatred for raftsmen (*LOM* 69–70) and the avoidance by Tom, the apprentice pilot, of annihilation by diving under the paddle wheel of a steamboat (*LOM* 81) are combined in the collision

of the raft and Huck and Jim's similar escape in chap. 16. The seedy night watchman who lies to young Mark about his picturesque past as "the son of an English nobleman — either an earl or an alderman, he could not remember which" (*LOM* 37) is a preliminary sketch for the duke and the king and their similar lies in chap. 19.

68. *Mark Twain's Autobiography* 1:7–10.

69. Mark Twain Estate Papers. This is written in violet ink on Crystal Lake Mills paper.

70. *The Love Letters of Mark Twain*, ed. Dixon Wecter (New York, 1949), 212.

71. *LOM* 406.

72. *LOM* 412–16.

73. *LOM* 271–73, 321–23.

74. For instance: "The River gives the book its form. But for the River, the book might be only a sequence of adventures with a happy ending" (T. S. Eliot, Introduction, *The Adventures of Huckleberry Finn* [New York, 1950], xii).

75. The phrase is that of Lionel Trilling in his Introduction, p. x, to an edition published in New York in 1948. Trilling also notes (viii) that "after each sally into the social life of the shore [Huck] returns to the river with relief and thanksgiving," and praises the "noble grandeur" of the river "in contrast with the pettiness of men."

76. *LOM* 392.

Mark Twain's High and Delicate Art:
Introduction to *Selected Shorter Writings of Mark Twain*

1. Ernest E. Leisy has nominated a series in the New Orleans *Crescent*, Jan. 21–March 30, 1861. The style and content and recent discoveries of Allan Bates have convinced me that Clemens did not write these.

2. Minnie M. Brashear, *Mark Twain, Son of Missouri* (Chapel Hill, 1934), 142–43; E. M. Branch, *The Literary Apprenticeship of Mark Twain* (Urbana, 1950), 3–7.

3. See notes for an unfinished novel of 1898–99 about David Gridley, DV 302h, Mark Twain Papers, University of California, Berkeley. See also Twain's mention in *Alta California*, July 14, 1867, of yarns by G. W. Harris published in the 1850s in humorous magazines and not collected until 1867.

4. Notebooks 14–23, Mark Twain Papers.

5. Discovered by Franklin J. Meine, this anecdote in the *Carpet-Bag*, May 1, 1852, has been assigned to Clemens because: (1) the *Carpet-Bag* was frequently quoted in the Hannibal *Journal* for which Sam worked; (2) its setting is "the now flourishing city of Hannibal"; (3) it is signed "S.L.C."; (4) it has the look of a composition by a beginner.

6. This may well have been based upon an anecdote which was circulating orally. See "Why the Old Farmer Wouldn't Tell the Drummer the Time of Day," *A Treasury of American Anecdotes*, ed. B. A. Botkin (New York, 1957), 238–39, for a similar imaginative extrapolation.

7. The author, considering it an essay, may have recalled, as he wrote, Franklin's eighteenth-century humanization of insects, "The Ephemera."

8. One may have been Jim Bridger's widely quoted yarn about the "peetrified" laws of gravitation in the petrified forest, of which Twain reminded himself in a notebook entry of 1889.

9. Mark Twain, *Sketches New and Old* (New York, 1875), 241. Twain himself here inaccurately remembers his petrified man's posture.

10. *My Dear Bro A Letter from Samuel Clemens to His Brother Orion* (Berkeley, 1961), 6. Interestingly, in this letter (Oct. 10) Clemens laments his lack of education.

11. Sydney J. Krause, "Twain's Method and Theory of Composition," *Modern Philology*, 56 (Feb. 1959), 171–72.

12. *Mark Twain-Howells Letters*, ed. Henry Nash Smith and William M. Gibson (Cambridge, 1960), 2:675. See also *Mark Twain in Eruption*, ed. Bernard DeVoto (New York, 1940), 190.

13. "Fenimore Cooper's Further Literary Offenses," ed. Bernard DeVoto, *New England Quarterly*, 19 (Sept. 1946), 291–301.

14. Mark Twain, *Works* (Definitive Edition) 26:228–38.

15. See D. M. McKeithan, "The Morgan Manuscript of *The Man That Corrupted Hadleyburg*," University of Texas Studies in Literature and Language, 11 (Winter 1961), 476–80.

16. See Henry Nash Smith, "That Hideous Mistake of Poor Clemens's," *Harvard Library Bulletin*, 9 (Spring 1955), 145–80.

17. Readers of the time who read the version in the Boston *Transcript*, Dec. 18, 1877, had in many instances heard Twain lecture. Even those who had not, benefitted from a better familiarity with oral tales, well told, than modern readers have.

18. *Literary Essays* (Definitive Edition) 22:101.

19. Twain claimed that this story, told by Auntie Cord in Elmira, he did not alter "except to begin it at the beginning, instead of the middle, as she did. . . ." Howells thought it one of Twain's masterpieces.

20. Nevertheless, if Twain remembered correctly in 1894, the humorless listener may have been suggested by the audience's reaction to Coon's original telling: "he saw no humor in his tale, neither did his listeners; neither he nor they ever smiled or laughed; in my time I have not attended a more solemn conference . . . none of the party was aware that a first-rate story had been told in a first-rate way, and that it was brimful of a quality whose presence they never suspected — humor."

21. Revisions of punctuation — 40, italicization — 8; words deleted — 6, substituted — 29, added — 2; phrases deleted — 3, added — 2; sentences deleted — 3, added — 1.

Index